CCNA Security Cram Sheet

This Cram Sheet contains key facts about the CCNA Security exam. Review this information as the last thing you do before you enter the testing center, paying special attention to those areas in which you feel that you need the most review. **Strategy note:** Plan to transfer memorized facts onto a blank sheet of paper immediately before you begin the exam.

Categories of Security Controls

(Remember "PAT"):

➤ **Physical:** Mostly mechanical.

➤ **Administrative:** Mostly policies and procedures.

➤ **Technical:** Network elements, hardware, software, and devices.

Types of Security Controls

(Hierarchy = Category -> Type):

➤ **Preventative:** Controls that prevent access.

➤ **Deterrent:** Controls that deter access.

➤ **Detective:** Controls that detect access.

Types of Laws

➤ **Criminal:** Concerned with crimes. Penalties involve fines and/or imprisonment.

➤ **Civil:** Concerned with righting non-criminal wrongs. Penalties may include monetary awards paid to winner of lawsuit.

➤ **Administrative:** Typically government agencies enforcing regulations. Monetary penalties divided between government and victim (if any).

Due Care vs. Due Diligence

➤ **Due Diligence:** Concerns itself with the implementation of adequate security controls and establishing best practices for ongoing risk assessment and vulnerability testing (static, planning).

➤ **Due Care:** Operating and maintaining security controls that have been implemented through due diligence (dynamic, day-to-day).

Seven Steps for Compromising Targets and Applications

1. Perform footprint analysis (reconnaissance).
2. Enumerate applications and operating systems.
3. Manipulate users to gain access.
4. Escalate privileges.
5. Gather additional passwords and secrets.
6. Install back doors.
7. Leverage the compromised system.

Types of Testing Techniques

➤ Network scanning

➤ Vulnerability detection

➤ Password cracking

➤ Log analysis

➤ Integrity checkers

➤ Virus detection

➤ War dialing

➤ War driving (802.11 or wireless LAN testing)

➤ Penetration testing

D0733632

Signature Micro-Engines in IOS 12.4(6)T

Signature Micro-Engines	Signature Categories
Atomic	Signatures that examine simple packets; for example: IP, ICMP, and UDP (see the following note).
Service	Signatures that examine attacks on "services," such as application layer protocols like HTTP, FTP, and SMTP.
String	Signatures that use REGEX-based patterns to detect intrusive activity.
Multi-String	Supports flexible packet matching (FPM) and supports signatures by Trend Labs.
Other	Internal engine dedicated to miscellaneous signatures.

Common VoIP Threats
➤ Reconnaissance
➤ SPAM over IP Telephony (SPIT)
➤ DoS Attacks
➤ Eavesdropping
➤ Man-in-the-Middle Attacks

SIP Vulnerabilities
➤ Registration Hacking
➤ Message Tampering
➤ Session Tear-Down

VLAN Hopping by Double-Tagging Attack Mitigation:
Ensure that the native VLAN of the trunked ports is different than any of the users' ports—VLAN 10, for example:

```
Catalyst1(config-if)switchport trunk native vlan 10
```

Port Security Commands:

```
Catalyst1(config-if)#switchport port-security maximum 32
Catalyst1(config-if)#switchport port-security violation shutdown
Catalyst1(config-if)#switchport port-security mac-address 0013.b638.8567
Catalyst1(config-if)#switchport port-security mac-address sticky
Catalyst1(config-if)#switchport port-security aging time 100
Catalyst1(config-if)#switchport port-security aging type inactivity
```

Configuring SPAN (Switch Port Analyzer):

```
Catalyst1(config)# monitor session 1 source interface gigabitEthernet0/1
Catalyst1(config)# monitor session 1 destination interface gigabitEthernet0/2
encapsulation replicate
```

Storm Control:

```
Catalyst1# show running-config interface GigabitEthernet0/1
interface GigabitEthernet0/1
 storm-control broadcast level 62.50
 storm-control multicast level pps 3k 2k
 storm-control unicast level bps 50m 25m
 storm-control action shutdown
```

CCNA Security

Eric L. Stewart

CCNA Security Exam Cram

Copyright © 2009 by Pearson Education, Inc.
All rights reserved. No part of this book shall be reproduced, stored in a retrieval system, or transmitted by any means, electronic, mechanical, photocopying, recording, or otherwise, without written permission from the publisher. No patent liability is assumed with respect to the use of the information contained herein. Although every precaution has been taken in the preparation of this book, the publisher and author assume no responsibility for errors or omissions. Nor is any liability assumed for damages resulting from the use of the information contained herein.

ISBN-13: 978-0-7897-3800-4
ISBN-10: 0-7897-3800-7

Library of Congress Cataloging-in-Publication Data

Stewart, Eric L.
  CCNA security exam cram / Eric L. Stewart.
     p. cm.
  Includes bibliographical references and index.
  ISBN-13: 978-0-7897-3800-4 (pbk. w/cd)
  ISBN-10: 0-7897-3800-7 (pbk. w/cd)
  1. Computer networks--Security measures--Examinations--Study guides.
  2. Cisco Systems, Inc. I. Title.
  TK5105.59.S758 2009
  005.8076--dc22
                                    2008038852

Printed in the United States of America
First Printing: October 2008

Trademarks

All terms mentioned in this book that are known to be trademarks or service marks have been appropriately capitalized. Que Publishing cannot attest to the accuracy of this information. Use of a term in this book should not be regarded as affecting the validity of any trademark or service mark.

Cisco, Cisco Systems, and CCNA are registered trademarks of Cisco Systems, Inc. or its affiliates in the U.S. and certain other countries. All other trademarks mentioned in this book are the property of their respective owners.

Warning and Disclaimer

Every effort has been made to make this book as complete and as accurate as possible, but no warranty or fitness is implied. The information provided is on an "as is" basis. The author and the publisher shall have neither liability nor responsibility to any person or entity with respect to any loss or damages arising from the information contained in this book or from the use of the CD or programs accompanying it.

Bulk Sales

Que Publishing offers excellent discounts on this book when ordered in quantity for bulk purchases or special sales. For more information, please contact

U.S. Corporate and Government Sales
1-800-382-3419
corpsales@pearsontechgroup.com

For sales outside the United States, please contact

International Sales
international@pearson.com

Associate Publisher
David Dusthimer

Executive Editor
Brett Bartow

Development Editor
Andrew Cupp

Managing Editor
Patrick Kanouse

Project Editor
Mandie Frank

Copy Editor
Water Crest Publishing

Indexer
Ken Johnson

Proofreader
Leslie Joseph

Technical Editors
William G. Huisman
Ryan Lindfield

Publishing Coordinator
Vanessa Evans

Multimedia Developer
Dan Scherf

Book Designer
Gary Adair

Composition
TnT Design, Inc.

Contents at a Glance

Table of Contents

Part VI: Appendixes

About the Author

Eric Stewart is a self-employed network security contractor who finds his home in Ottawa, Canada. Trained as a computer engineer at the Royal Military College, and later in computer science and economics at Carleton University, Eric has over 20 years of experience in the information technology field—the last 12 years focusing primarily on Cisco Systems routers, switches, VPN concentrators, and security appliances. He likes to divide his time evenly between his two great loves in the field: teaching and doing! The majority of Eric's consulting work has been in the implementation of major security infrastructure initiatives and architectural reviews with the Canadian Federal Government, working at such departments as Foreign Affairs and International Trade (DFAIT) and the Canadian Air Transport Security Authority (CATSA). A Cisco Certified Systems Instructor (CCSI), he especially enjoys imparting the joy that he takes in his work to his students, as he will often be found enthusiastically teaching Cisco CCNA, CCNP, and CCSP curriculum to students throughout North America and the world.

His previous work with Cisco Press has been as the development editor for two titles, *Authorized CCDA Self-Study Guide: Designing for Cisco Internetwork Solutions (DESGN) (Exam 640-863)* and *Router Security Strategies: Securing IP Network Traffic Planes*.

Eric has a lovely wife, Carol Ann, who is an accomplished music teacher, as well as two teenage children, Scott and Meaghan.

Dedication

I would like to dedicate this book to my wife and best friend, Carol Ann.

Acknowledgments

Projects like this don't happen without the hard work and dedication of a supporting cast. I would like to thank the wonderful people at Pearson for asking me to write this book in the first place. Opportunities like this don't happen often, and I am extremely grateful for the chance to write my very own book. Drew Cupp deserves special acknowledgment because his patience and attention to detail are particularly infectious and much appreciated. The technical editors, Bill Huisman and Ryan Lindfield, kept me honest. This is very important because in attempting to distill technical ideas for the purpose of an Exam Cram, sometimes the explanations of these ideas become at best oversimplified, and at worst inaccurate. Last, but certainly not least, I would like to thank my family, wife Carol Ann and children Scott and Meaghan. Without their support and encouragement, I could not have maintained the enthusiasm and creativity that is necessary to do a good job.

We Want to Hear from You!

As the reader of this book, *you* are our most important critic and commentator. We value your opinion and want to know what we're doing right, what we could do better, what areas you'd like to see us publish in, and any other words of wisdom you're willing to pass our way.

As an associate publisher for Que Publishing, I welcome your comments. You can email or write me directly to let me know what you did or didn't like about this book—as well as what we can do to make our books better.

Please note that I cannot help you with technical problems related to the topic of this book. We do have a User Services group, however, where I will forward specific technical questions related to the book.

When you write, please be sure to include this book's title and author, as well as your name, email address, and phone number. I will carefully review your comments and share them with the author and editors who worked on the book.

Email: feedback@quepublishing.com

Mail: David Dusthimer
            Que Publishing
            800 East 96th Street
            Indianapolis, IN 46240 USA

Reader Services

Visit our website and register this book at www.informit.com/title/9780789738004 for convenient access to any updates, downloads, or errata that might be available for this book.

Introduction

Welcome to *CCNA Security Exam Cram*! The fact that you are reading this means that you are interested in the CCNA Security certification that Cisco announced in July of 2008. Cisco has done a thorough job of revamping the certification path for the Cisco Certified Security Professional (CCSP), with the CCNA Security certification being the cornerstone upon which the CCSP certification depends. Implementing Cisco IOS Network Security (IINS) is the recommended training course for CCNA Security certification. If you already hold the prerequisite valid CCNA certification, passing the 640-553 IINS exam enables you to obtain the CCNA Security certification—likely to become one of the hottest certifications in IT. This book helps prepare you for that exam. The book assumes that you already have your CCNA certification or an equivalent level of knowledge. If you do not have a CCNA level of knowledge, you should consider putting down this book and first pursuing more robust fundamental training, such as a full CCNA course book or a recommended CCNA course. And remember that CCNA is a prerequisite to CCNA Security certification.

This book is a synthesized, distilled, and pared-down effort, with only enough information as is necessary to provide context for the information you need to pass the exam. This is not to say that this book is not a good read, but it is a fair reflection of the type of material that you will need to master in order to be successful with the exam. Read this book, understand the material, and drill yourself with the practice exams, and you stand a very good chance of passing the exam. That said, it's possible that in the course of working through this book, depending on your prior CCNA Security training or on-the-job experience, you might identify topics you are struggling with and might require you to look up more fundamental resources to deal with. This book discusses all the topics on the exam and tests you on all of them, but it does not always provide detailed coverage of all those topics.

Organization and Elements of This Book

When designing a secure network infrastructure, the workflow moves from the perimeter of the network to the inside of the network. After the perimeter is properly secured, the security architect can turn his or her attention to securing devices on the inside of the network perimeter where the endpoints reside. This structured approach is mimicked in the basic organization of this book.

The chapters of this book are organized into four major parts, with each part encapsulating a major idea in the field of network security:

► Part I: Network Security Architecture

► Part II: Perimeter Security

► Part III: Augmenting Depth of Defense

► Part IV: Security Inside the Perimeter

You can use this book's organization to your advantage while studying for the CCNA Security 640-553 IINS exam because each part of the book is selfcontained. Although it is recommended that you follow the parts sequentially, there are frequent cross-references to content contained in other chapters if you choose to follow your own path through this book.

Each chapter follows a uniform structure, with graphical cues about especially important or useful material. The structure of a typical chapter is as follows:

► **Terms You'll Need to Understand:** Each chapter begins with a list of the terms you'll need to understand, which define the concepts that you'll need to master before you can be fully conversant with the chapter's subject matter.

► **Exam Topics Covered in This Chapter:** Cisco publishes a list of exam topics for the 640-553 IINS exam. Each chapter of this book begins by listing the exam topics covered in that chapter. See the following "Self Assessment" element for a complete list of the topics and the chapters where they are covered.

► **Exam Alerts:** Throughout the topical coverage, Exam Alerts highlight material most likely to appear on the exam by using a special layout that looks like this:

EXAM ALERT

This is what an Exam Alert looks like. An Exam Alert stresses concepts, terms, or activities that will most likely appear in one or more certification exam questions. For that reason, any information found offset in Exam Alert format is worthy of unusual attentiveness on your part.

Even if material isn't flagged as an Exam Alert, *all* content in this book is associated in some way with test-related material. What appears in the chapter content is critical knowledge.

Self Assessment

This section helps you to determine your readiness for the CCNA Security certification exam. You will be invited to assess your own skills, motivations, education, and experience and see how these match up against thousands of CCNA Security candidates.

NOTE

You can also pre-assess your CCNA Security readiness by using the exams on the accompanying CD.

Who Is a CCNA Security?

Throughout my years of teaching Cisco CCNA, CCSP, and CCNP courses, I am often asked about the application of a concept in the "real world"…as if there is doubt that material presented might not speak to the same world that the students work in. The same question might be asked about being a CCNA Security-certified IT professional. Does the certification hold any real-world value in itself, or is it simply a rung in the long ladder of certifications that one must climb before you can say that you've finally "arrived?" In my own career, I can safely say that this climb never ends. In reality, any knowledge gained, if properly applied, has real-world application. This is true of the CCNA Security. It is a very useful and practical certification, one that attests to the person's ability to absorb and also apply basic principles of network security—principles that bear greatly against the fundamentals of networking.

And that's when we can start feeling that we're close to arriving at our destination; when we can start applying the fundamentals that we've previously learned in new and artful ways. Network security is like that. It is an applied science, though hardly rocket science. The very best network security practitioners are those who have not forgotten the fundamentals on which this science is founded: routing, switching, and network protocols. This information will have been learned and reinforced in the prerequisites for the CCNA Security, namely the CCNA certification itself.

So, what are the tangible takeaways from the CCNA Security? What are some of the attributes of this certification that you can proudly trumpet on your resume after you have passed the exam? Here are a few:

▶ **You possess the ability to put network security concepts in proper context:** The strangest phenomenon that I have witnessed in my decade of teaching and consulting in the area of network security is how few network security professionals understand the basics of networking. The CCNA Security proves the ability to absorb and apply network security concepts in the complete confidence that only comes through understanding these concepts' network underpinnings.

▶ **You can confidently take on new challenges:** While saying that network security is not rocket science, it is still science. You now possess the ability to offer advice and guidance using Cisco's Self-Defending Network as a blueprint. You know how network security can be implemented using Cisco's Security System Development Lifecycle, and you can use it as an implementation framework for your own IT projects.

▶ **You will be the go-to person for network security:** Cisco's certifications are recognized as the gold standard certification in the networking industry. Passing this certification demonstrates that you have the right stuff and that you are technically quite competent. Applying the lessons learned will prove to be rewarding.

The successful CCNA Security candidates have distinguished themselves as being top-drawer practitioners of network security concepts. Ultimately how this translates to the real world is that when a prospective employer is weighing candidates' qualifications for a job, everything else being equal, the CCNA Security certification will stand head and shoulders above the crowd.

The Ideal CCNA Security Candidate

We have all heard of people who can pass Cisco certification exams based on studying the prerequisite materials and using just book knowledge, without real-world experience. Well, that is the exception and certainly not the rule—especially when considering intermediate-level certifications such as the CCNA Security. The key to passing this exam is practice, practice, and more practice. Certainly this is something that you will have learned through passing the CCNA certification, the prerequisite certification for the CCNA Security. Here are some of the attributes of the ideal CCNA Security candidate:

▶ **The ability to learn:** As any teacher will attest, "We can teach you but we can't learn you!" If you have had trouble quickly absorbing information in the past and recalling this information in the pressure of an exam, you need to have realistic expectations for yourself. Everyone learns differently, and you might need more time to absorb the same amount of information as someone else. So, give yourself time, and do not make unrealistic demands of yourself.

▶ **The willingness to ask questions:** If something isn't clear to you, ask a question. This can be to your instructor if you are taking an instructor-led course, a work colleague, a peer, or any number of online discussion forums. Don't use asking questions as a substitute for good study habits, but if you're truly stumped about something, or something isn't being properly explained in a context that you understand, don't be afraid to ask a question. The only stupid question is the one that you don't ask. This includes asking yourself questions in the process of self examination as you are studying for the certification.

▶ **The ability to put things in context:** This seems to be an overarching theme. Ultimately, the test of technical knowledge's usefulness is whether it can be applied in some way. Adult learners need context. The ideal CCNA Security candidate possesses the ability to see the application of a concept and use the resulting context as a type of memory aid or mnemonic. Rote memorization only works so far. If you want things to truly stick in your brain, the ultimate glue for this knowledge to stick to your synapses is to organize it and index it in the brain's database using the concept as the key.

▶ **The ability to use prior experience:** This attribute bears against all the others mentioned. Without experience, you might have problems seeing the applicability of the great volume of new concepts, which are taught in IINS. Whether this experience is in the real world or whether it is obtained in the closed world of a lab environment, it is experience.

A good attitude on your own part and the ability to leverage on whatever prior experience you may have—however that might have been obtained—are keys to success. Network security is seeing its own renaissance from a dark age, where the principles involved were seen as dark arts and magic tricks passed on by masters and gurus to their apprentices and acolytes. Today, network security is seen for what it is: a discipline and an applied science. The ideal CCNA Security candidate can see this and reach past the fluff and grasp the firm, structured knowledge therein.

Put Yourself to the Test

You are the best judge as to whether you are ready to attempt the exam. Here are some questions that will help you decide. Score how many you answer "yes" to:

1. Do you already possess your CCNA certification?

   The CCNA certification is the prerequisite for attempting the exam.

2. Do you have an educational background in computer science?

   An educational background in computer science would be very helpful. It means that you can put the knowledge necessary for the CCNA Security in context.

3. Do you work in the network industry?

   If you are already working in the industry, you are likely regularly exposed to the technology and terminology.

4. Do you work in the network security industry?

   Ideally you work in the industry, which means that you are exposed to its technology and terminology. Hopefully, you haven't learned any bad habits!

5. Have you worked long with Cisco equipment?

   As much of this course centers around the CLI, regular exposure to Cisco IOS devices equipment would be very useful in comprehending the new information.

6. Do you have any other network security certifications?

   Possessing other network security certifications, even in competing vendors' equipment, will make the Cisco security learning curve no less steep, but certainly shorter.

7. Do you have experience with Cisco exams?

   It is likely that you have already taken some Cisco exams if you are attempting the CCNA Security certification. (In fact, CCNA certification is a prerequisite.) Experience can't be learned. Cisco exams, while straightforward, have a particular look and feel.

8. Can you absorb new ideas?

   The ability to absorb new ideas (not necessarily quickly) is crucial.

9. Are you a disciplined student?

Organized, disciplined study habits go a long way to ensuring adequate preparation for a stress-free exam.

10. Have you done much self-study in network security?

If you are a student of network security—someone who enjoys the ideas and is engaged by the concepts—this will go a long way toward making you an enthusiastic and motivated learner.

How do you measure up? The following scores are guidelines only. If your score indicates that you are probably not ready for the exam, treat this information not as a discourager, but as motivation to close the gap on the areas in which you are lacking. Rome wasn't built in a day!

Number of "yes" answers:

▶ **8 to 10:** You're ready to start, and you can hardly wait to get busy studying and pass the exam. Use this book to master the exam topics and for the practice questions.

▶ **6 or 7:** You're almost there. Perhaps with a bit more experience or self-study, and maybe an instructor-led course, you can consider studying in preparation for the exam.

▶ **4 or 5:** There is a significant, but not insurmountable, gap between where you are and where you need to be. With significantly more experience and/or self-study and formal instruction, you should be able to close the gap in a reasonable period of time. You need confidence, but this confidence will only come with knowledge.

▶ **Less than 4:** You're not there yet, but you have a good idea as to where you need to improve to close the gap. Give yourself some time and gain some confidence-boosting knowledge that you can leverage on to get where you need to be in as short a period as possible.

Of course, you need to be CCNA certified before you can become CCNA Security certified, so CCNA training is the logical first step if you are starting at square one. If you have that, then you have some experience with Cisco equipment and exams, but you'll need to make the next step by mastering the specific CCNA Security topics. If you have prior security on-the-job experience or have taken an official CCNA Security course, you are ideally prepared to use this book for final exam preparation.

Exam Topics for 640-553 IINS (Implementing Cisco IOS Network Security)

Cisco publishes the topics for this exam on cisco.com. The exam topics provide an excellent place to start assessing yourself about the specific material on the exam. Go through these topics methodically. Take the time to determine where you might be strong and where you might be weak. The exam topics Cisco provides can be somewhat vague and general, but this Exam Cram should fill in the specific blanks. Through the explanations and practice questions in this book and on the CD, be sure to continually identify topic areas you consistently struggle with so you can address your weaknesses.

Table 1 lists the 640-553 IINS exam topics and identifies the chapter of this book where they are covered. Cisco divides these into topic areas, and those are also listed in the table. The material in Table 1 comes from the IINS 640-553 exam information at cisco.com. Check cisco.com periodically for any updates to this list of exam topics.

TABLE 1   IINS 640-553 Exam Topics

Topic	Chapter
Describe the security threats facing modern network infrastructures	
Describe and list mitigation methods for common network attacks	1, 9
Describe and list mitigation methods for Worm, Virus, and Trojan Horse attacks	1, 9
Describe the Cisco Self-Defending Network architecture	2
Secure Cisco routers	
Secure Cisco routers using the SDM Security Audit feature	4
Use the One-Step Lockdown feature in SDM to secure a Cisco router	4
Secure administrative access to Cisco routers by setting strong encrypted passwords, exec timeout, login failure rate and using IOS login enhancements	3
Secure administrative access to Cisco routers by configuring multiple privilege levels	3
Secure administrative access to Cisco routers by configuring role based CLI	3
Secure the Cisco IOS image and configuration file	4
Implement AAA on Cisco routers using local router database and external ACS	
Explain the functions and importance of AAA	2, 3
Describe the features of TACACS+ and RADIUS AAA protocols	3

TABLE 1   *Continued*

Topic	Chapter
Configure AAA authentication	3
Configure AAA authorization	3
Configure AAA accounting	3
Mitigate threats to Cisco routers and networks using ACLs	
Explain the functionality of standard, extended, and named IP ACLs used by routers to filter packets	5
Configure and verify IP ACLs to mitigate given threats (filter IP traffic destined for Telnet, SNMP, and DDoS attacks) in a network using CLI	5
Configure IP ACLs to prevent IP address spoofing using CLI	5
Discuss the caveats to be considered when building ACLs	5
Implement secure network management and reporting	
Use CLI and SDM to configure SSH on Cisco routers to enable secured management access	4
Use CLI and SDM to configure Cisco routers to send Syslog messages to a Syslog server	4
Mitigate common Layer 2 attacks	
Describe how to prevent layer 2 attacks by configuring basic Catalyst switch security features	10
Implement the Cisco IOS firewall feature set using SDM	
Describe the operational strengths and weaknesses of the different firewall technologies	5
Explain stateful firewall operations and the function of the state table	5
Implement Zone Based Firewall using SDM	5
Implement the Cisco IOS IPS feature set using SDM	
Define network based vs. host based intrusion detection and prevention	8
Explain IPS technologies, attack responses, and monitoring options	8
Enable and verify Cisco IOS IPS operations using SDM	8
Implement site-to-site VPNs on Cisco Routers using SDM	
Explain the different methods used in cryptography	6
Explain IKE protocol functionality and phases	6, 7
Describe the building blocks of IPSec and the security functions it provides	6, 7
Configure and verify an IPSec site-to-site VPN with pre-shared key authentication using SDM	7

Strategy for Using This Exam Cram

In the end, reading this book is an important part of the exam preparation process. The fact that you are reading this means that you are serious about passing the exam. You can read it cover to cover (it is a good read), but probably the best strategy is to go through the sample exam questions at the end of each chapter first. If you aren't scoring 90% or higher on the first attempt, you owe it to yourself to read through that chapter in detail, taking brief notes as you go in the areas you were having issues.

After you have gone through the 10 chapters, then you are ready to attempt the two practice exams using either the accompanying CD or the book. These practice exams contain an additional 100 questions not found in the chapter-ending questions. Do one exam first. At the end of each sample exam, there is a summary (just like the live Cisco exams) that gives you a score by subject area. Use this as a guide for the areas where you need to drill down. Study these areas hard, looking at the sample exam questions at the end of the chapter again. When you feel confident that you have closed your knowledge gap, attempt the second practice exam.

When you are adequately prepared, you can look forward to the exam. It can be eagerly anticipated as an interesting measure of not only your aptitude but your attitude. The most closely-guarded secret about the field of network security is that it's like Legos for adults—it's not about the knowledge, but what you can build with the knowledge. It can be fun, too!

Good luck!

PART I
Network Security Architecture

1

Network Insecurity

Terms You'll Need to Understand:

✓ The CIA triad (Confidentiality, Integrity, Availability)

✓ Threat categories

✓ Security controls

✓ Denial of Service (DoS) attacks

✓ Spoofing (blind and nonblind)

✓ Man-in-the-Middle attacks

✓ Phishing

✓ Pharming

Exam Topics Covered in This Chapter:

✓ Describe and list mitigation methods for common network attacks

✓ Describe and list mitigation methods for Worm, Virus, and Trojan Horse attacks

NOTE

These exam topics are from cisco.com. Check there periodically for the latest exam topics and info.

To be CCNA Security certified, you need to leverage your grasp of basic network fundamentals to achieve a broad-based understanding of network security concepts and ideas. This chapter introduces some of these concepts and points out key areas that will be tested on the CCNA Security exam. These concepts are crucial because they form a solid foundation for understanding the rest of this book. We explore network security basics and the need for network security, while also getting to know our adversaries and exploring the taxonomy of network attacks. This should definitely make you feel a bit of healthy network insecurity. Thankfully, there are ways to mitigate the effectiveness of attacks against our network's confidentiality, integrity, and availability (CIA); thus, we finish off the chapter with Cisco's recommendations for best practices for defense against the identified network attacks.

Exploring Network Security Basics and the Need for Network Security

In this section, we examine some of the key principles involved in creating a secure network. We establish building blocks that will be used in formulating an effective security policy. The principles are as follows:

▶ Open networks and knowledgeable attackers with sophisticated attack methods create the requirement for flexible, dynamic network security policies.

▶ Examine the CIA triad: confidentiality, integrity, and availability.

▶ Define data classification categories in the public and private sectors.

▶ Examine the three top-level types of security controls: administrative, technical, and physical.

▶ Explore some of the incident response methods when a security breach has occurred.

▶ List key laws and ethical codes by which INFOSEC professionals are bound.

The following section illustrates how the advent of sophisticated attack methods combined with open networks has resulted in a growing need for network security and flexible security policies, which can be dynamically adjusted to meet this threat.

The Threats

According to Cisco, there are two major categories of threats to network security:

▶ **Internal threats.** Examples are network misuse and unauthorized access.

▶ **External threats.** Examples are viruses and social engineering.

The most foolproof way of protecting a network against external threats would be to sever its connections completely to public networks. In theory, this is OK; in practice, however, it is not practical because many businesses require connectivity to public networks, such as the Internet, in order to perform E-commerce in today's connected world. The challenge, therefore, is to strike a balance between three often-competing needs:

► Evolving business requirements

► Freedom of information initiatives

► Protection of data: private, personal, and intellectual property

It is axiomatic in the field of network security that the tradeoff is largely between the first two items, which are necessary for a business or government organization to reach the public, and the last item. Essentially, the battle is fought between these opposing camps—openness vs. security. Often, more security means less openness, and vice versa.

Internal Threats

According to Cisco, internal threats are the most serious, because insiders often have the most intimate knowledge of the network. They leverage on their knowledge of the internal network to achieve security breaches. They often don't need to crack passwords because they already have sufficient access.

Insider attacks often render technical security solutions ineffective. This problem is exacerbated because human nature dictates that often the last place we look for security breaches is within the fortification! We are so busy looking for the enemy climbing the outside walls that we don't look behind us.

A best practice for hardening systems from internal (as well as external) threats includes following the systems' vendor recommendations.

External Threats

External attackers lack the insider's knowledge and often rely on technical tools to breach your network's security. Technical tools such as Intrusion Prevention Systems (IPSs), firewalls, and routers with access control lists (ACLs) are usually effective in mitigating an organization's vulnerability to this type of attack.

NOTE

Firewalls and ACLs are discussed in Chapter 5, "Using Cisco IOS Firewalls to Implement a Network Security Policy."

IPSs are discussed in Chapter 8, "Network Security Using Cisco IOS IPS."

EXAM ALERT

Know the difference between internal and external threats and how they may be mitigated.

Other Reasons for Network Insecurity

An alarming trend is that as the sophistication of hacker tools has been on the increase, the technical knowledge required to use them has been on the decrease.

According to the 2007 CSI/FBI Computer Crime and Security Survey, organizations are suffering a two-fold increase in financial losses but on slightly fewer reported attacks in the report's four-year period. Financial frauds have overtaken viruses as the greatest cause of loss.

> **NOTE**
>
> The 2007 CSI/FBI Computer Crime and Security Survey can be downloaded from this site, http://i.cmpnet.com/v2.gocsi.com/pdf/CSISurvey2007.pdf.

In the past, hackers have been motivated as much by notoriety and intellectual challenge as for profit. A disturbing recent trend has been what Cisco calls "custom" threats, which focus on the application layer of the OSI model. These attacks may be written to breach a known vulnerability in an organization's own customized application. Traditional signature-based intrusion detection systems (IDSs) and IPS products will not detect this type of attack because the products' signatures match against a database of *known* vulnerabilities. Even following best practices in ensuring that vendor patches are tested and applied regularly to application servers may prove to be ineffective. Compounding the issue is that the applications themselves may have been written by programmers who have little or no formal training in network security, let alone an appreciation for the subject. According to Theresa Lanowitz of Gartner Inc., 75 percent of all attacks today are application layer attacks with three out of four businesses being vulnerable to this type of attack.

> **NOTE**
>
> You can read more about the emergence of custom threats and their ability to go undetected by traditional signature-based intrusion detection systems (IDSs) and IPS products at this site: http://www.eweek.com/c/a/Security/App-Developers-Need-to-Redouble-Security-Efforts/.

The CIA Triad

This section describes the three primary purposes of network security, which are to secure an organization's data *confidentiality*, *integrity*, and *availability*—the C-I-A triad. Here are some basic definitions:

▶ **Confidentiality.** Ensuring that only authorized users have access to sensitive data

▶ **Integrity.** Ensuring that only authorized entities can change sensitive data. May also guarantee *origin authentication* (see the following note), meaning an assurance that the data originated from an authorized entity (like an individual).

▶ **Availability.** Ensuring that systems and the data that they provide access to remain available for authorized users.

> **NOTE**
>
> Origin authentication is often overlooked in designing network security architecture. In some texts, this is the "A" in CIA.

A security professional must constantly weigh the tradeoffs between threats, their likelihood, the costs to implement security countermeasures, and cost versus benefit. In the end, someone has to pay for security (more on this later in the chapter), and there must be a solid business case and return on investment (ROI) for the measures implemented.

Let's look at confidentiality, integrity, and availability separately.

Confidentiality

Confidentiality is often discussed in the context of hiding an organization's data with encryption technologies—using a Virtual Private Network (VPN), for example. In a broader context, assuring confidentiality involves any method of separating an organization's data from its adversaries. Here are some other thoughts about confidentiality:

▶ Confidentiality means that only authorized users can *read* sensitive data.

▶ Confidentiality countermeasures provide separation of data from users through the use of:

 ▶ Physical separation

 ▶ Logical separation

Thus, the risk of confidentiality breaches can be minimized by effective enforcement of access control, thereby limiting access to the following:

▶ **Network resources** through use of VLANs, firewall policies, and physical network separation.

▶ **Files and objects** through use of operating system-based controls, such as Microsoft™ Active Directory™ and domain controls and Unix host security.

▶ **Data** through use of authentication, authorization, and accounting (AAA) at the application level.

When attackers successfully read sensitive data that they are not authorized to view, a breach has occurred. This is almost impossible to detect because the attacker may have breached the confidentiality of the data by making a copy of the data from the network and using tools offline, leaving no trace. This is why much of the focus of network security in the context of confidentiality is for preventing the breach in the first place. Technologies such as Virtual Private Networks (VPNs) would be an example. This is discussed in Chapter 7, "Virtual Private Networks with IPsec."

Integrity

Data integrity guarantees that only authorized entities can *change* sensitive data. It can also provide for optional authentication in proving that only authorized entities created the sensitive data. This provides for *data authenticity*. There are a number of methods to ensure data integrity and authenticity including the use of hashing functions and digital signatures. Some of these methods are described in Chapter 6, "Introducing Cryptographic Services," and will not be discussed here.

Integrity services provide for some guarantee that:

▶ Data cannot be changed except by authorized users.

▶ Changes made by unauthorized users can be detected.

Availability

Availability refers to the safeguards that provide for *uninterrupted access* to data and other computing resources on a network during either accidental or deliberate network or computer disruptions.

Given the complexity of systems and the variety of current attack methods, this is one of the most difficult security services to guarantee. Attacks that prevent legitimate users access to system or network resources are called Denial of Service (DoS) attacks.

DoS attacks are usually caused by one of two things:

▶ A device or an application becomes unresponsive because it is unable to handle an unexpected condition.

▶ An attack (remember, this can be accidental!) creates a large amount of data causing a device or application to fail.

DoS attacks are relatively easy to launch, often with tools downloadable offline such as vulnerability assessment tools. There is a fine line between a network probe designed to determine a network's resiliency against various types of attack, and an actual DoS attack. Some vulnerability assessment tools even give the user the choice as to whether to enable probes that are known to be dangerous when leveraged against vulnerable networks.

EXAM ALERT

Know the difference between (C)onfidentiality, (I)ntegrity, and (A)vailability.
Understand that confidentiality is proof against reading data. Understand that integrity
is proof against changing data, as well as providing for data authenticity. Understand
that availability countermeasures provide for uninterrupted access to data.

Data Classification

Proper data classification will indicate what level of confidentiality, integrity, and availability services will be required to safeguard the organization's data. It recognizes that not all data has the same inherent value, but that the divulgence of some data may even cause embarrassment to an organization. It also helps focus the development of the security policy so that more attention can be given to data that needs the most protection. As well, some laws require that information be classified for an organization to be compliant.

Classification Levels

Classification levels are typically different for private (non-government) and public (government) sectors.

The following are the levels of classification for data in the public sector:

- **Unclassified.** Data with minimum confidentiality, integrity, or availability requirements; thus, little effort is made to secure it.

- **Sensitive but Unclassified (SBU).** Data that would cause some embarrassment if revealed, but not enough to constitute a security breach.

- **Confidential.** First level of classified data. This data must comply with confidentiality requirements.

- **Secret.** Data that requires concerted effort to keep secure. Typically, only a limited number of people are authorized to access this data—certainly fewer than those who are authorized to access confidential data.

- **Top Secret.** The greatest effort is used to secure this data and to ensure its secrecy. Only those people with a "need to know" typically have access to data classified at this level.

There are no specific industry standards or definitions for data classification in the private sector. Standards, where they exist, will vary from country to country. That aside, Cisco makes these specific recommendations for data classification in the private sector:

- ▶ **Public.** Data that is often displayed for public consumption such as that found on public websites and in marketing literature.

- ▶ **Sensitive.** Similar to SBU data in the public-sector model.

- ▶ **Private.** Data that is important to the organization and whose safeguarding is required for legal compliance. Some effort is exerted to maintain both the secrecy (confidentiality) and accuracy (integrity) of the data.

- ▶ **Confidential.** The greatest effort is taken to safeguard this data. Trade secrets, intellectual property, and personnel files are examples of data commonly classified as confidential.

Classification Criteria

There are four basic metrics that determine at what level data should be classified and consequently what level of protection is required to safeguard that data:

- ▶ **Value.** Most important and perhaps the most obvious.

- ▶ **Age.** Data's sensitivity typically decreases over time.

- ▶ **Useful Life.** Data can be made obsolete by newer inventions.

- ▶ **Personal Association.** Some data is particularly sensitive because of its association with an individual. Compromise of this data can lead to guilt by association.

Information Classification Roles

Another advantage of properly classifying data is that it helps define the roles of the personnel that will be working with and safeguarding the data:

- ▶ **Owner.** Ultimate responsibility for the data, usually management, and different than the custodian.

- ▶ **Custodian.** Responsible for the routine safeguarding of classified data. Usually an IT resource.

- ▶ **User.** These persons use the data according to the organization's established operational procedures.

Security Controls

Now that the information classification roles have been established, the types of security controls over an organization's data can be defined. Controls are the engine of a security policy. They define the levels of passive and active tools necessary for a custodian to enact a security policy and to meet the three objectives (remember those?!) of confidentiality, integrity, and availability. This is essential in order to provide defense in depth. Subcategories or "types" of controls are investigated a little later on in this section.

Controls can be divided into three broad categories, as follows:

- **Administrative.** Mostly policies and procedures.

- **Technical.** Involving network elements, hardware, software, other electronic devices, and so on.

- **Physical.** Mostly mechanical.

> **EXAM ALERT**
>
> Here's a useful way to remember these categories of controls. If they are in place, you can "stand pat." PAT = Physical, Administrative, Technical.

Here are some of the attributes of administrative, technical, and physical controls.

Administrative Controls

The following are attributes of administrative controls:

- Security awareness training

- Security policies and standards

- Security audits and tests

- Good hiring practices

- Background checks of employees and contractors

Technical Controls

IT staffs usually think of network security as a technical solution because it is in their nature. That said, implementation of devices and systems in this category, while important, should not be the sole part of an effective Information Security (INFOSEC) program. Here is a list of some common technologies and examples of those technologies that fit in the category of technical controls.

- **Network devices.** Firewalls, IPSs, VPNs, Routers with ACLs.

- **Authentication systems.** TACACS+, RADIUS, OTP.

- **Security devices.** Smart cards, Biometrics, NAC systems.

- **Logical access control mechanisms.** Virtual LANs (VLANs), Virtual Storage Area Networks (VSANs).

> **NOTE**
>
> The focus of this Exam Cram is largely a technical one because this is the primary focus of the Cisco course material and therefore also the exam. It is important, however, to note that technical controls should only be implemented as part of a broader security policy.

Physical Controls

If the purpose of your security policy is to build a castle around your data with technical controls and manage it with administrative controls, how effective do you think it will be if you leave the drawbridge down or forget to lock or at least post sentinels at the front gate? This is where physical controls come in. Physical controls consist of the following:

- ▶ **Monitoring Equipment.** Intruder detection systems.

- ▶ **Physical Security Devices.** Locks, safes, equipment racks.

- ▶ **Environmental Controls.** Uninterruptible Power Supplies (UPSs), fire suppression systems, positive air flow systems.

- ▶ **Security Guards.** Human, canine.

Types of Controls

A control "type" is a further subdivision of a control "category" (refer to the next Exam Alert):

- ▶ **Preventative.** Controls that prevent access.

- ▶ **Deterrent.** Controls that deter access.

- ▶ **Detective.** Controls that detect access.

> **EXAM ALERT**
>
> It is important to note that although the three broadest categories are administrative, technical, and physical, these can be further subdivided by type. The hierarchy is Category of Control -> Type of Control. For example, an IPS would be an example of a Technical -> Preventative system, whereas an IDS would be an example of a Technical -> Detective system.
>
> Remember this definition: A security control is any mechanism that you put in place to reduce the risk of compromise of any of the three objectives: confidentiality, integrity, and availability.

Some controls can take from more than one type. For example, a security camera in the lobby of a high-security government office building could be both a deterrent and detective control.

Now that you have built comprehensive security controls into our network design, what do you do when a security breach occurs? What internal procedures do you follow? Who do you notify? How do you contain the damage? What steps do you take to document the breach? How do you recover compromised data? So many questions! Adding to this complexity is the whole quagmire of the law, law enforcement agencies, and the question of legal and ethical responsibilities in both reporting a breach, as well as whether we may be somehow responsible for the breach because of bad network design and a lack of due diligence. Let's look at answering these questions in two different contexts:

► Incident response

► Laws and ethics

Incident Response

So it's happened. Someone has hacked into your network and either accessed your confidential data or denied access to your network by authorized users. Assuming that you have implemented Technical -> Detective controls, and you have evidence that a breach has, in fact, occurred, you must decide how to move forward and use the evidence gathered to improve your existing network and/or prosecute the hacker. Let's look at some of the complex issues involved in prosecuting computer crimes.

> **NOTE**
>
> You shouldn't decide what response you will take at the moment that the breach has been detected. You should plan an incident response as part of a comprehensive Network Security Policy. This is discussed a little later in this chapter.

Computer Crime Investigations

For successful prosecution of computer crimes, law enforcement investigators must prove three things: motive, opportunity, and means (MOM). Anyone who enjoys watching crime shows on television will recognize these:

► **Motive.** Did the individuals have something to gain from committing the crime?

► **Opportunity.** Were the individuals available to commit the crime?

► **Means.** Did the individuals have the ability to commit the crime?

Computer Crime Complications

Then there's the complication of dealing with both gathering evidence and maintaining its integrity. This is not an easy chore, particularly with computers and leads to certain complications:

- ▶ **A virtual world.** The virtual nature of computers means evidence is not physical—it cannot be held and touched.

- ▶ **Data integrity.** Evidence can be easily tainted if not handled properly. A single flipped bit can totally change the data and render it useless.

- ▶ **Chain of custody.** The chain of custody of data that is used as part of a forensic case is crucial and not easy to prove or to maintain.

NOTE

You will often see the term "chain of custody" in discussions about incident response. Chain of custody means that you can prove that from the time that the incident occurred, the copies you made of your system (see below) never left your control and were never changed while under your control and before they were presented as evidence to the investigating agency. Lawyers might question the completeness of this definition, but it is sufficient for this discussion.

Although it is advisable to immediately quarantine a breached system from the network, basic rules must be followed in order to collect evidence and to preserve its integrity:

- ▶ **Make a copy of the system.** A complete copy of the system, both persistent and non-persistent storage, should be made. This means that the contents of RAM should be dumped to a file and multiple images should be made of the hard drive(s), flash drive(s), and so on.

- ▶ **Photograph the system.** Photograph the system before it is moved or disconnected.

- ▶ **Handle evidence carefully.** The chain of custody must be preserved.

Laws and Ethics

As if computer crime isn't complicated enough, a security expert also needs to deal with the jurisdictional, procedural, and legal issues within the framework of the law of the land.

Types of Laws

There are three types of law found in most countries:

- ▶ **Criminal.** Concerned with crimes. Penalties usually involve possible fines (paid to the court) and/or imprisonment of the offender.

- ▶ **Civil (also called "tort").** Concerned with righting wrongs that do not involve crimes or criminal intent. Penalties are typically monetary and paid to the party who wins the lawsuit.

- ▶ **Administrative.** Typically, government agencies in the course of enforcing regulations. Monetary awards are divided between the government agency and the victim (if any) of the contravened regulation.

Although these categories are common for most countries, some governments do not follow or even recognize them. Further complicating this is that computer crimes often cross international boundaries, meaning that jurisdiction must be established before the crime can be prosecuted.

Ethics

Sometimes we are motivated to do something, not because we will be punished if we don't do it, but because we know it's the right thing to do. This is why ethics are considered to be moral principles and a higher standard than the law. These codes of ethics are as follows:

- ▶ Moral principles that constitute a higher standard (or "code") than the law.

- ▶ Guides for the conduct of individuals or groups.

- ▶ Supported by a number of organizations in the INFOSEC field:

  - ▶ ISC^2 (International Information Systems Security Certification Consortium, Inc.) Code of Ethics

  - ▶ Computer Ethics Institute

  - ▶ IAB (Internet Activities Board)

  - ▶ GASSP (Generally Accepted System Security Principles)

A good example of why codes of ethics are an important INFOSEC principle would be the subject of entrapment. *Entrapment* is the process of luring someone to commit an illegal act that they might not otherwise commit were the opportunity not there. They might have motive. They might have means. You have provided them opportunity. An example of this might be a "Honey Pot" consisting of a deliberately easy-to-compromise system. You may have deployed this system to see what bees are interested in your honey and as an early warning system for penetration of your network. In this manner, private use of the data so collected may be legitimate from a security control (Technical -> Detective) perspective, but it may contravene legal, regulatory, and ethical standards if it was used for prosecution. Seek legal and ethical advice before deploying such a system as part of your network security architecture.

Liability

Organizations are responsible for the proper protection of their systems against compromise. If a loss of service occurs due to a security breach, and if it is discovered that the organization did not have adequate security controls in place, that organization might be held liable for damages. Organizations are required to practice the following:

▶ **Due Diligence.** Concerns itself with the implementation of adequate security controls (administrative, technical, and physical) and establishing best practices for ongoing risk assessment and vulnerability testing.

▶ **Due Care.** Operating and maintaining security controls that have been implemented through due diligence.

EXAM ALERT

Security practitioners are very fond of using the terms "due care" and "due diligence" when describing exposure to liability. Cisco's definitions are listed previously, and you need to know them for the exam, but they still look very similar, don't they? Think of due diligence as being exercised in the planning and overall design of a network security architecture. This includes all the security controls (discussed in a previous section) put in place to meet expected threats. It is relatively static. Due care, on the other hand, is more dynamic and involves the day-to-day operating, maintaining, and tweaking of the security architecture. Remember the old axiom, "Security is a process, not a product." Due care is that process.

Legal and Government Policy Issues

Here are some examples of U.S. government regulations that have been introduced to enforce network and system security and to raise awareness of privacy and (more recently) INFOSEC issues:

▶ **Gramm-Leach-Bliley Act (GLBA) of 1999.** Enacted to allow banks, securities firms, and insurance companies to merge and share information with one another.

▶ **Health Insurance Portability and Accountability Act (HIPAA) of 2000.** Requires national standards for the confidentiality of electronic patient records.

▶ **Sarbanes-Oxley (SOX) Act of 2002.** Law to ensure transparency of corporations' accounting and reporting practices.

▶ **Security and Freedom Through Encryption Act (SAFE) of 1997.** Entrenches the rights of U.S. citizens to any kind of encryption of data without the requirement of a key escrow.

▶ **Computer Fraud and Abuse Act.** Last amended in 2001 by the **USA PATRIOT Act** (Uniting and Strengthening America by Providing Appropriate Tools Required to Intercept and Obstruct Terrorism). Intention of this act is to reduce hacking by defining specific penalties when damages result from a compromised system.

▶ **Privacy Act of 1974.** Privacy of individuals is to be respected unless a written release is obtained.

▶ **Federal Information Security Management Act (FISMA) of 2002.** Intended to strengthen IT security in the U.S. federal government by requiring yearly audits.

▶ **Economic Espionage Act of 1996.** Enacted to criminalize the misuse of trade secrets.

EXAM ALERT

Be able to recognize these pieces of legislation on the exam.

Exploring the Taxonomy of Network Attacks

In this section, we conduct a quick survey of the methodologies of attacks against our network infrastructure and the resulting threats against confidentiality, integrity, and availability. It won't be all bad news, however, because we'll summarize some of the best practices used to mitigate the effect of these attacks. We will:

▶ Define adversaries, their motives, and types of attacks.

▶ Summarize the concept of defense in depth.

▶ Examine the threat of IP spoofing.

▶ List and briefly summarize attack methods used to compromise confidentiality, integrity, and availability.

▶ Summarize some best practices for defense.

According to Cisco:

▶ A *vulnerability* is a weakness that can be exploited by an attacker.

▶ *Risk* is the likelihood that a vulnerability might be exploited by a specific attack.

▶ An *exploit* is an attack that takes advantage of a vulnerability.

EXAM ALERT

Know the difference between vulnerability, risk, and exploit.

Categories of vulnerabilities are as follows:

▶ Poor design

▶ Weaknesses in protocols

▶ Software

▶ Misconfiguration

▶ Hostile code

▶ Human factor

Adversaries

So, who wants our stuff or wants to make our stuff unusable by us? Sounds simplistic, but answering this question and thus knowing your enemy (and their motivations) will go a long way toward acquiring the right mindset for designing network security controls. Remember, we are not at *risk* with all of these adversaries, so we should focus on only those where there is likelihood that they may *exploit* our *vulnerabilities*. Some examples are as follows:

▶ Nations or states

▶ Government agencies

▶ Hackers (we'll examine these further)

▶ Terrorists

▶ Competitors

▶ Disgruntled employees

▶ Organized crime

Hackers

Hackers are the most obvious external threat to network security. There are several different species of hackers according to Cisco:

- **Hacker.** A computer enthusiast. They can also be grouped by their motivations:

    - **White hat.** Ethical hacker.

    - **Black hat.** Unethical hacker.

    - **Gray hat.** We're not sure! (This is a hacker who has a real job and sometimes plays both sides of the law, often motivated by intellectual challenge and notoriety but usually not monetary gain.)

    - **Blue Hat.** Bug testers (from "blue collar").

- **Cracker.** Hacker with criminal intent, motivated by economic gain.

- **Phreakers (or Phone Phreaks).** Hackers of telephone systems.

- **Script Kiddies.** Wannabe hackers with little or no skill.

- **Hacktivist.** Hacker with a political agenda.

Hacker Specializations

Whether a hacker wears a white, black, gray, or blue hat, they can be further defined by the type of hacking they perform:

- **Computer Security Hackers.** Usually secretive and specialize in computers and computer networks.

- **Academic Hackers.** Not usually secretive. Specialize in designing elegant software and gravitate toward Unix and the open source movement.

- **Hobby Hackers.** Usually hack code related to video games and gaming hardware and other home computing.

Motivations

As we've seen, in a broad sense, hackers can be categorized by their motivations but so too can the other adversaries. What makes them do it? Here are some motivations:

- Intelligence gathering

- Theft of intellectual property

- DoS

- ▶ Embarrassment of the target
- ▶ Intellectual challenge

> **NOTE**
>
> From this point forward, the term "hacker" will be used as a general term for any of the adversaries previously listed and who attacks an organization's network and other systems.

How Do Hackers Think?

Hackers are said to think "outside the box." Imagine that the hacker is a very clever lab animal that, when presented with a maze to run through as part of an experiment, chooses to run outside the maze to the prize. In so doing, the animal bypasses all the clever little turns in the maze that are supposed to make it difficult to get to the other side. The inference is clear. If our network is a maze, and the hacker is that clever animal, we will be in big trouble if we don't start to think like him! This is not to say that all hackers take shortcuts, either. Nor do all hackers use the same methods, but here is an example of a typical structured attack.

Seven Steps for Compromising Targets and Applications

According to Cisco, the seven steps for compromising targets and applications are as follows:

1. Perform footprint analysis (reconnaissance).
2. Enumerate applications and operating systems.
3. Manipulate users to gain access.
4. Escalate privileges.
5. Gather additional passwords and secrets.
6. Install back doors.
7. Leverage the compromised system.

> **EXAM ALERT**
>
> Memorize these steps. They are sure to be on the exam. To make it easier to remember, note that, generally, network attacks follow two broad steps: Explore, then exploit!

Concepts of Defense in Depth

Security is only as strong as its weakest link. Although this is a commonly held belief, it is not as commonly followed in practice. Defending a network with only one type of security control (administrative, technical, or physical) is bad enough, but many networks are only protected by one control. For example, protecting a home broadband connection with a single technical control such as an integrated firewall/router/wireless access point may be sufficient. It would certainly not be sufficient for a large e-commerce site that sells books online and keeps credit card information and other personal information about their customers. Clearly, the solution needs to be scaled to need and single points of failure should be avoided wherever possible.

To summarize, the Defense in Depth philosophy entails the following:

- **Diversity and Redundancy.** Use multiple security mechanisms to back up each other.

- **Independence.** Security mechanisms are self-sufficient and do not rely on one another.

- **Augment Weakest Links.** Single points of failure can be avoided.

Defense in Depth recommendations are as follows:

- Build a multi-layered defense.

- Place controls in multiple places.

- Use hardened, quality components.

- Use IDS or IPS (consider also Host IPS (HIPS)).

- Employ effective credential and key management.

Figure 1.1 shows an example with no depth of defense. A single Cisco IOS firewall establishes a perimeter between an outside, hostile network and an e-commerce site's inside network, where the employees' computers and the book-selling server all reside. The firewall is configured to open up access from the outside to allow Internet users to connect to the server. This is an example of a single technical security control. The single technical control might be sufficient for a home network, but note that the file server coexists on the inside network with the employees' computers. If hackers compromised the server, they could leverage the compromised server to attack other inside hosts including the switch, PC, and laptop. Without the use of an IDS or IPS, we might not even know that the attack had taken place. If this was a company's e-commerce site, it doesn't make sense to deploy a server in the same part of the network as knowledge workers' computers. This is clearly a security incident waiting for a place to happen.

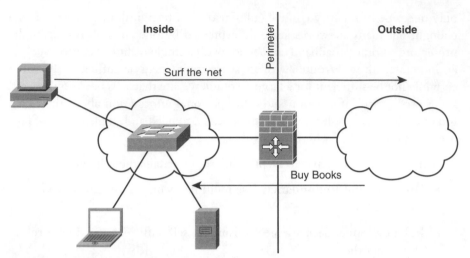

FIGURE 1.1 Single IOS firewall and no defense in depth.

Some simple modifications to the security architecture illustrate the principle of depth of defense, as illustrated in Figure 1.2. The IOS router is configured as an IPS (see Chapter 8, "Network Security Using Cisco IOS IPS") and can now detect and prevent intrusion attempts into and out of the inside network. The e-commerce server is deployed into a separate demilitarized zone (DMZ). Access Control Lists (ACLs) are configured on the IOS router to ensure that the e-commerce server cannot initiate a connection to an inside host, neutralizing the threat of its compromise leading to a compromise of our inside network. ACLs are covered in Chapter 5, "Using Cisco IOS Firewalls to Implement a Network Security Policy." The IOS router is hardened against attack using principles discussed in Chapter 3, "Security at the Network Perimeter." This also separates data planes, making it harder for an attacker to gain access to an inside host.

IP Spoofing Attacks

IP spoofing is the networking equivalent of identity theft. If you fake some other device's IP address, you can pretend to be that other device in order to:

- ▶ Gain root access.

- ▶ Inject erroneous data into an existing conversation.

- ▶ Fool other devices in order to divert packets to the hacker.

- ▶ Overload resources on servers (DoS).

- ▶ Accomplish a task as part of a larger attack.

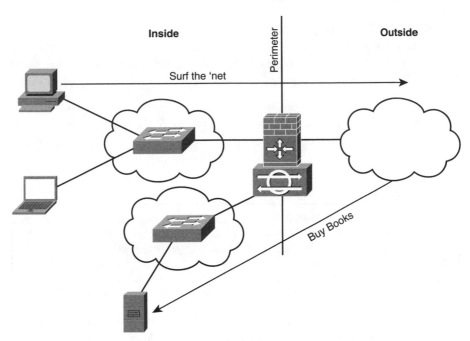

FIGURE 1.2 Single IOS firewall with defense in depth.

One of the things that makes IP spoofing so effective is that the process of routing is destination based, meaning that routers make their best path determination based on the destination IP address in an IP packet, often ignoring completely the source address. For example, if an attacker on the outside guesses correctly source addresses of devices internal to your network, they can inject packets into your network that appear to be coming from trusted hosts on the inside.

NOTE

The Open Systems Interconnect (OSI) model defines a packet as a network layer (layer 3) protocol data unit (PDU). An IP datagram is an example of a packet. Try to avoid using the term "packet" for PDUs at other layers of the OSI model. This will become very important in later chapters, where we will discuss TCP segments (layer 4) and Ethernet frames (layer 2) in the context of network security. This is terminology that you will have learned in your CCNA studies. If you don't know them, now is the time to go back over your ICND1 and ICND2 notes to review them.

Recall that logical communication between TCP/IP hosts occurs at the transport layer of the OSI model. This is where dialog occurs between end systems. The Transmission Control Protocol (TCP) keeps track of the sequence number of segments both sent and received. Among other things, this allows an end system to put segments received in the right order, as well as retransmit segments from its transmit queue where the other device indicates that it has not received them.

Types of IP Spoofing

If an attacker were able to actually see these sequence numbers, maybe through the use of a packet capture tool, the IP spoofing attack would be called *nonblind spoofing*. They would need physical access to your network to accomplish this.

If an attacker were simply guessing at sequence numbers—essentially using tools to calculate them—then the attack would be called *blind spoofing*. Physical access to your network is not required. Furthermore, with blind spoofing, the guesswork involved means that there is no verification of a successful attack.

> **NOTE**
>
> Another thing that aids the attacker is that although it is completely up to the end systems what initial sequence numbers they use to build a TCP session, some vendors' TCP/IP implementations always use the same one. If an attacker were to know what type of system they were dealing with through footprinting (recall "Seven Steps for Compromising Targets and Applications" in a previous section), the guessing would be much easier.

In any case, the information learned through IP spoofing in the course of network reconnaissance may lead to several types of attacks, including:

- ▶ **Man-in-the-middle attacks (MiM).** The attacker assumes the identity of a trusted host on the network and steals information. An example of this is session hijacking.

- ▶ **DoS Attacks.** The information gained leads to a flooding of resources on a targeted system. An example would be excessive hard drive thrash of an unpatched web server.

- ▶ **Distributed DoS Attacks (DDoS).** The information learned during the reconnaissance leads to a flooding of resources on a targeted system from multiple hosts and simultaneously. An example would be an attack on a core network device that consumes all the bandwidth into and out of a network.

> **NOTE**
>
> MiM attacks attack the network's confidentiality. They also attack the network's integrity because invalid data can be replayed into the network by a spoofed system. DoS and DDoS attacks attack the network's availability.

Attacks Against Confidentiality

If effective administrative, technical, and physical security controls are in place, the risk of the following attacks would be minimal.

EXAM ALERT

According to Cisco, attacks against confidentiality are successful if you have been lax with access control (network, OS, application) or protection of data moving over hostile, untrusted networks.

Examples of attacks that may lead to confidentiality (and other) breaches include the following:

▶ **Protocol Analysis (Packet Sniffing).** As indicated previously, this is very effective if the attacker has physical access to your network. Packets can be captured and often analyzed offline for cleartext, confidential information.

▶ **Port Scanning.** This is very common during the reconnaissance phase of an attack, using tools like *nmap* or *Nessus* to scan a network to find out what TCP ports are open.

▶ **Ping Sweeps.** Often used in the initial phases of reconnaissance. First find out what hosts are answering to the ping (ICMP echo packet); then drill down on them with a port scan (see previous).

▶ **Dumpster Diving.** Organizations often accidentally throw out sensitive information that would be of use to an attacker.

▶ **Social Engineering.** Subverting an individual through social skills within a targeted organization to provide information that is either confidential by itself or that can lead to the breach of a network's security controls.

▶ **Overt Channels.** Hiding something out in the open sounds like an oxymoron. An attacker can craft an attack that tunnels one protocol inside another protocol. If the security appliance or IDS/IPS is not configured to check protocol compliance at the application layer, it will be successful. An example might be a Peer-to-Peer (P2P) file transfer of malicious code using Kazaa inside an HTTP session. Another example might be the process of *steganography*. This is typically executed through the secretion of hidden messages into image files, themselves embedded in overt objects such as HTML for transport.

▶ **Covert Channels.** Hiding information (perhaps by encryption) within a network session. An example might be injecting some malicious code within a legitimate client-server session. This is sometimes called a back channel attack.

▶ **Emanations Capturing.** Capturing electrical and radio frequency emissions (from wireless networking gear, for example) using passive means and decoding their meaning. Can be countered with TEMPEST standard equipment.

> **NOTE**
>
> TEMPEST is a U.S. government standard. Equipment or rooms that are certified as TEMPEST standard are leakage-free but it is an expensive standard. Other nations have similar standards. Interestingly, TEMPEST is actually not an acronym, though many have tried to make it into one. One of the most common examples of this "bacronym" is "Transient Electromagnetic Pulse Emanation Surveillance Technology." It sounds cool, but it's incorrect. Why not "Tiny ElectroMagnetic Particles Emitting Secret Things?" TEMPEST is an unclassified U.S. government code word coined by the National Security Agency (NSA) in the late 60's and early 70's for an operation for compromising emanations. The general term for preventing unwanted electromagnetic emissions is now more properly called Emissions Security (EMSEC).

Phishing, Pharming, and Identity Theft

Two very real exploits that are commonly in the news are phishing and pharming. Both these exploits are threats against a user or site's identity.

▶ **Phishing.** This is a social engineering attack. By posing as a legitimate, trusted third party, an attacker attempts to acquire confidential or sensitive information from the victim. The most common vehicles for phishing are email messages that entice victims to visit a legitimate-looking website where their credit card information, PINs, and so on, are stolen.

▶ **Pharming.** This is the process of farming (get it?) or harvesting traffic from one website by redirecting it to another. A common method is commandeering vulnerable Domain Name System (DNS) servers and altering their records so that users are redirected to a site not operated by the real owner of the domain name.

Antivirus, antispyware, and anti-spam software are somewhat effective against phishing attacks. Nevertheless, this type of technical control is not a replacement for the administrative control of educating users.

There is no specific technical control to thwart pharming, however. The best defense is to make sure that vulnerable servers are properly patched (problematic across the whole Internet!) and to regularly test DNS resolution against root servers in the Internet to ensure that an organization's fully-qualified domain name (FQDN) resolves properly to the correct IP address.

Attacks Against Integrity

> **EXAM ALERT**
>
> Like attacks against confidentiality, attacks against integrity are successful if you have been lax with access control (network, OS, application) or protection of data that moves over hostile, untrusted networks.

We've done a good job at defining integrity previously, so let's look at a list of common attacks against a system or a network's integrity. These attacks might also be used to breach availability and confidentiality:

- **Salami Attacks.** Salami, like sausage, is made up of a variety of ingredients. It's not a single meat. This is true with a salami attack. It is a larger attack that is comprised of a series of smaller attacks. An example would be an attacker launching an attack that makes small compromises of the integrity of several different systems' databases simultaneously. This type of granular, spread-out attack is difficult to detect.

- **Data Diddling.** Interfering with data before it is stored on a computer, prior to or during data input. This may be the result of a virus or even malicious code designed into the program.

- **Trust Exploits.** An attacker leverages on a trust relationship between devices on a network. Port redirection is an example of this type of attack. A walk-through of a port redirection is found in Figure 1.3.

- **Password Attacks.** This is any attack that is geared toward making a system divulge its password database. Viruses, trojans, keyloggers, protocol analyzers (sniffers), and brute force attacks are common vectors. Application protocols such as Telnet and FTP that use cleartext passwords are the most vulnerable to the use of protocol analyzers. Even protocols like NTLM (Windows NT LAN Manager) and Active Directory, which exchange hashes of passwords vs. cleartext passwords, are vulnerable to offline, brute force tools such as John the Ripper.

> **NOTE**
>
> Hashing is explained in Chapter 6, "Introducing Cryptographic Services." Although theoretically a hash cannot be cracked, there are cracking programs such as RainbowCrack, which can match a hash against a database of known hashes captured with protocol analyzers.

- **Session Hijacking.** This is the most common Man-in-the-Middle (MiM) attack. It's not so much an attack in itself, as it is a *result* of a successful attack.

EXAM ALERT

Memorize the names and port numbers of several popular protocols that use authentication, as shown in Table 1.1.

TABLE 1.1 Some Applications That Require Authentication

Application	Port Number	Use
FTP	TCP 21	Bulk file transfers
Telnet	TCP 23	Remote administration
Simple Network Management Protocol (SNMP)	UDP 161	Managing and gathering information from network hosts
Point-to-Point Tunneling Protocol	TCP 1723	Microsoft™ Remote Access VPN protocol
Direct Host	TCP 445	Network File and Print Sharing
NetBIOS over TCP (NBT)	TCP 139	Network File and Print Sharing (largely superseded by TCP port 445)
Terminal Services	TCP 3389	Microsoft™ Remote Desktop Protocol (RDP)

Attack Against Integrity Example: Port Redirection Attack

This example should help bring together some concepts about attacks against integrity. Revisit the simple network from a previous example now in Figure 1.3. Figure 1.3 shows an IOS router with three interfaces: one facing the Internet, another one facing the inside, and a third that establishes a DMZ where the e-commerce server is deployed.

Figure 1.3 shows a port redirection attack in which "Z" trusts "Y" and "Y" trusts "X." The attacker is trying to trick "Z" into trusting "X" too. Arrow "A" illustrates that the router is configured to allow connections from the outside to the web server in the DMZ on TCP port 80 (or else, how could we sell books?).

The router will *not* allow connections to be initiated from the outside to the inside.

However, the router is configured to allow the DMZ server to initiate connections to the inside (arrow "B") perhaps to synchronize its clock on a time server or to authenticate users on a AAA server. Here's how an attack might unfold:

1. A hacker "X" conducts a port scan of the network and discovers that there is a web server "Y." The hacker footprints the network using a tool such as nmap and learns that the web server software used may have some vulnerabilities that could be exploited. This peaks his interest!

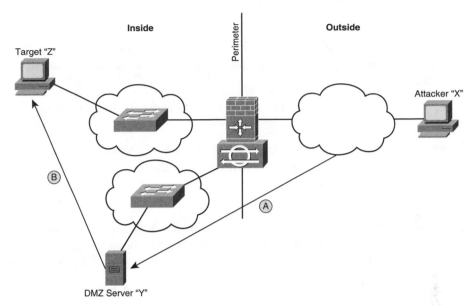

FIGURE 1.3   Port redirection attack.

2. The attacker uses a hacking tool such as *netcat* to compromise the web server and installs a port forwarding tool, such that when inbound WWW traffic from the attacker's workstation is sent to the compromised web server, it will redirect it to a different port entirely (TCP port 3389 = Terminal Services, for example).

3. Now the attacker can essentially tunnel the desired protocol inside HTTP to the DMZ server and then use the DMZ server to attempt to establish a connection to an inside host "Z."

4. Because the attacker has control over the DMZ server, he can complete a remote reconnaissance of the internal network from the DMZ server using a ping sweep to find out what IP addresses are active.

5. The attacker conducts a port sweep to see what services are available on the active IP addresses.

6. The attacker then attempts to exploit vulnerabilities on inside hosts, perhaps also installing keylogger software, and so on.

The attacker has now successfully leveraged the trust relationships. "Z" trusts "Y." "Y" trusts "X." Now "Z" trusts "X," too. Ouch! This is what makes port redirection an example of a trust exploit.

The risk of this exploit happening can be mitigated by:

- Installing a firewall or IPS, which can examine inbound HTTP traffic to ensure that it is protocol compliant, block traffic that isn't, and also alert a custodian.

- Installing Host Intrusion Protection System (HIPS) software on inside hosts.

- Using ACLs on the IOS firewall to tighten the rules as to which IP addresses and applications the DMZ server is allowed to initiate connections to on the inside.

NOTE

ACLs, firewalls, IPS, and HIPS will be discussed in later chapters, although hopefully you are getting a feel for their respective roles in the context of this discussion at this point in the Exam Cram.

Attacks Against Availability

Now we move on to the last letter of our C-I-A triad and more reasons for network insecurity! We look at what constitutes an availability attack and how to mitigate their effects.

EXAM ALERT

Availability attacks are DoS attacks. If these attacks are successful, it is because the system fails to either handle:

- Unanticipated, exceptional conditions (such as malicious code, buffer overflows, and so on).
- Enormous floods of data, crashing a system or bringing it to a halt.

...leading to a compromise of availability.

Also know that many availability attacks can be used to attack confidentiality and integrity too.

NOTE

Heads up! Strictly speaking, any type of attack that seriously impedes the availability of a network or system is a DoS attack. By that definition, availability attacks *are* DoS attacks. Nevertheless (and confusingly) DoS is often also identified as a category of availability attack, typically a network-borne attack. Don't be confused by this inconsistency. Just know that the term DoS can be used correctly in those two contexts.

Aiding an attacker is the relative simplicity of the attack methods. Even a script kiddy would have no problem executing some of these attacks.

Some common types of availability attack include the following:

▶ Botnets

▶ ICMP floods

▶ DoS

▶ DDoS

▶ SYN floods

▶ Electrical power

▶ Computer environment

▶ MAC flooding

The following sections go over each type of availability attack in more detail.

Botnets

A botnet is a collection of infected computers or "robots" that can be controlled by crackers. The location of infected computers is shared by circles of crackers who can then seize control of these machines, typically on Internet Relay Chat (IRC), and use them in the commission of larger attacks such as a DDoS. For crackers, locating these computers' IP addresses can be done fairly easily if they register their domain names dynamically with a Dynamic DNS provider. Whole communities of infected computers might resolve to the same domain suffix, such as "ivebeenhacked.net."

ICMP Floods

ICMP floods work like they sound. A constant stream of ICMP messages is sent against a system. No response is necessary; the ICMP message just has to be received by the host being attacked. Conducting a constant ping from one host is unlikely to completely consume bandwidth and/or CPU cycles on an attacked host. However, when used as part of a DDoS attack (maybe combined with spoofed source IP addresses!), it can be quite effective.

DoS

In general terms, DoS attacks occur when an attack is leveraged against a system that slows its response to legitimate requests. The affected server will eventually drop requests from legitimate clients when there are too many unanswered requests for resources in its receive queue.

DDoS

A DDoS attack is a DoS attack from many sources simultaneously, perhaps from hosts enlisted from a botnet. This remains a common attack due to both its efficacy and its relative simplicity to execute.

SYN Floods

This is a type of DoS attack. This attack leverages on the requirement within the Transmission Control Protocol (TCP) that a server answer a synchronization attempt from a client (SYN) when a connection is being established to his well-known port number. Think of the SYN, which is carried inside a TCP segment, as pushing a doorbell. A web server has a doorbell with the number "80" on it. The server, if it is polite (or at least protocol compliant!) is required to answer the SYN with a SYN, ACK. Of course, in between the time that the attacker has pressed the server's doorbell and the time the server has gotten out of his comfortable chair to answer the door, perhaps thousands of other doorbell presses to port 80 have happened ... some of them even from legitimate clients of the server. The attacker won't even wait around to see if the server has come to the door because unlike a legitimate client, his goal is not to actually create a connection with the server but to frustrate him. Meanwhile the server has to allocate memory and other resources for each connection attempt. Eventually, the server is going to get so tired of coming to the door only to find that there is no one there, that he will no longer answer the door for anybody, attacker and legitimate user alike.

Electrical Power

Any attack against an organization's electrical power is an availability attack. There are three categories, as follows:

▶ Excess power (spikes and surges)

▶ Complete power outage (brief faults and blackouts)

▶ Reduced power levels (sag and brownouts)

Computer Environment

One of the most neglected parts of network security. This falls under the broad category of physical controls (remember "PAT"?). Ensure that the physical environment is regulated for the following:

▶ Temperature

▶ Ventilation

▶ Humidity

MAC Flooding

This kind of attack will be examined in more detail in Chapter 10, "Protecting Switch Infrastructure." This is an OSI layer 2 (data link layer) attack. Essentially, an attacker can use some commonly available tools (such as the macof utility) to inject a switch with vast quantities of Ethernet frames with fictitious source addresses. The normal behavior of the switch is cache these addresses in its MAC address table. The MAC address table can contain a finite number of entries. For example, a Cisco Catalyst 2924-XL-EN can contain 4096 entries in its MAC address table. Eventually, the switch will become so full of bogus MAC addresses that when it receives a frame, it will flood it out all its ports, effectively acting like a hub. If an attacker is connected to one of the switch's ports, they will potentially see all the traffic served by that switch, compromising confidentiality as well as availability.

> **NOTE**
>
> Do you know how on some vacuum cleaners, you can reverse their operation so they will blow air rather than suck particles? Some protocol analyzers can be configured to not only suck traffic off a wire, but to blow engineered traffic back (for example, Ethernet frames) into a network. Instant attack tool!

Best Practices to Thwart Network Attacks

If common sense were so common, we wouldn't have to call it common. Cisco makes specific recommendations as to some best practices for ensuring that you reduce the risk footprint of your network through three categories of controls: administrative, technical, and physical security controls.

Administrative Controls

Administrative controls include the following:

- ▶ **Written Security Policy.** Put your security policy in writing! Make sure all the stakeholders: owners, custodians, and users understand and respect their responsibilities. (This will be discussed in Chapter 2, "Building a Secure Network Using Security Controls.")

- ▶ **Education.** Ensure all stakeholders are aware of the dangers of social engineering.

- ▶ **Patches.** Keep up-to-date with firmware, hardware, and software patches, particularly those that address security vulnerabilities.

Technical Controls

Technical controls include the following:

- ▶ **Unnecessary Services and TCP/UDP Ports.** Configure the network such that only necessary services are exposed. Don't forget to configure servers so they only have the necessary services active.

- ▶ **Encryption.** Encrypt all sensitive data, especially if it passes over hostile networks.

- ▶ **Passwords.** Rotate passwords often and make them complex (strong).

- ▶ **Hardware and Software.** Use hardware and software that can mitigate risk to an appropriate level.

Physical Controls

Physical controls include the following:

- ▶ **Physical Access.** Limit physical access to systems to a select few and only those who need it.

- ▶ **Environmental.** Equipment should be in a controlled environment with regulated temperature, power, and ventilation.

Exam Prep Questions

1. Which of the following constitutes the elements in the C-I-A triad?

   ○ **A.** Consolidation, Integration, Authentication

   ○ **B.** Confidentiality, Integrity, Availability

   ○ **C.** Confusion, Impact, Animosity

   ○ **D.** Central, Intelligence, Agency

   ○ **E.** None of the above.

2. Cisco says that there are two major categories of threats to network security. Pick them from the following list:

   ○ **A.** External threats

   ○ **B.** Viruses

   ○ **C.** Social engineering

   ○ **D.** Internal threats

   ○ **E.** Unauthorized access

   ○ **F.** Network misuse

3. Which of the following is the best definition for integrity safeguards? (Choose one):

   ○ **A.** Ensuring that only authorized users have access to sensitive data.

   ○ **B.** Ensuring that only authorized entities can change sensitive data.

   ○ **C.** Ensuring that systems and the data that they provide access to remain available for authorized users.

   ○ **D.** Ensuring that only legitimate users can access the network subject to time of day (ToD) controls.

   ○ **E.** Configuring access control lists (ACLs), such that only specified protocols are allowed through the perimeter.

4. Match the following data classification levels for the *public* sector with their definitions:

   ▶ Unclassified: _____

   ▶ Secret: _____

   ▶ Confidential: _____

   ▶ Sensitive but Unclassified (SBU): _____

   ▶ Top Secret: _____

Definitions:

    A. Data with minimum confidentiality, integrity, or availability requirements; thus, little effort is made to secure it.

    B. Data that would cause some embarrassment if revealed, but not enough to constitute a security breach.

    C. First level of classified data. This data must comply with confidentiality requirements.

    D. Data that requires concerted effort to keep secure. Typically, only a limited number of people are authorized to access this data, certainly fewer than those who are authorized to access confidential data.

    E. The greatest effort is used to secure this data and to ensure its secrecy. Only those people with a "need to know" typically have access to data classified at this level.

5. Which of the following are *not* considered categories of security controls? (Choose all that apply.)

    ○ **A.** Preventative control

    ○ **B.** Physical control

    ○ **C.** Deterrent control

    ○ **D.** Administrative control

    ○ **E.** Technical control

    ○ **F.** Detective control

6. Match the three types of laws found in most countries with their definitions:

Types of Law:

    ► Civil: _____

    ► Criminal: _____

    ► Administrative: _____

Definitions:

    A. Concerned with crimes. Penalties usually involve possible fines (paid to the court) and/or imprisonment of the offender.

    B. Concerned with righting wrongs that do not involve crimes or criminal intent. Penalties are typically monetary and paid to the party who wins the lawsuit.

    C. Typically government agencies in the course of enforcing regulations. Monetary awards are divided between the government agency and the victim (if any) of the contravened regulation.

7. True or false: An exploit is the likelihood that a vulnerability might be exploited by a specific attack.

8. Put the following seven steps for compromising targets and applications in the correct order:

- ○ **A.** Install back doors.
- ○ **B.** Escalate privileges.
- ○ **C.** Perform footprint analysis.
- ○ **D.** Manipulate users to gain access.
- ○ **E.** Enumerate applications and operating systems.
- ○ **F.** Gather additional passwords and secrets.
- ○ **G.** Leverage the compromised system.

9. Fill in the blank for the following definition with the letter corresponding to the correct answer below:

If an attacker were simply guessing at sequence numbers—essentially using tools to calculate them—then the attack would be called _____ spoofing. Physical access to your network is not required.

Choices:

- ○ **A.** Statistical
- ○ **B.** Invasive
- ○ **C.** Blind
- ○ **D.** Nonblind
- ○ **E.** Stochastic

10. True or false: Man-in-the-Middle (MiM) attacks attack a network or system's availability.

11. Which of the following strategies help mitigate against trust exploits?

- ○ **A.** Installing a firewall or IPS that can examine inbound traffic to ensure that it is protocol compliant, block traffic that isn't, and also alert a custodian.
- ○ **B.** Installing Host Intrusion Protection System (HIPS) software on inside hosts.
- ○ **C.** Using ACLs on an IOS firewall.
- ○ **D.** All of the above.

Answers to Exam Prep Questions

1. Answer B is the correct answer. This is pretty much industry-wide.

2. Answers A and D are correct. This is a trick question because the other answers are sub-categories of external and internal threats. Viruses and social engineering are examples of external threats and unauthorized access and network misuse are examples of internal threats.

3. Answer B is the correct answer. Answer A is a definition for confidentiality. Answer C is a definition of availability. Answers D and E are trick answers.

4. The answers are:

   ▶ Unclassified: A

   ▶ Secret: D

   ▶ Confidential: C

   ▶ Sensitive but Unclassified (SBU): B

   ▶ Top Secret: E

5. Answers A, C, and F are not categories of controls. Controls can be divided into three broad categories: physical, administrative, and technical. Remember the acronym PAT! Also recall that they can be further subdivided by type. Preventative, deterrent, and detective are examples of types of controls and not categories of controls.

6. The correct answers are:

   ▶ Civil: B

   ▶ Criminal (also called "tort"): A

   ▶ Administrative: C

7. False. An exploit is an attack that takes advantage of a vulnerability. The definition given is that for a "risk."

8. The correct order is C, E, D, B, F, A, G. In other words:

   1. Perform footprint analysis (reconnaissance).

   2. Enumerate applications and operating systems.

   3. Manipulate users to gain access.

   4. Escalate privileges.

   5. Gather additional passwords and secrets.

   6. Install back doors.

   7. Leverage the compromised system.

9. The answer is C. Blind spoofing is often done at a distance from your network and does not require physical network access.

10. False. DoS and DDoS attacks attack the network's availability. MiM attacks attack a network's confidentiality and integrity.

11. The correct answer is D. Cisco recommends all strategies in mitigating against the possibility of a trust exploit.

CHAPTER TWO

Building a Secure Network Using Security Controls

Terms You'll Need to Understand:

✓ Cisco's Secure System Development Life Cycle (SDLC)
✓ Separation of Duties (SoD)
✓ Scanner
✓ Sensor
✓ Disaster recovery plan (DRP)
✓ Business continuity planning (BCP)
✓ Risk management
✓ Quantitative Risk Analysis Formula
✓ Least privilege
✓ Self-Defending Network
✓ Cisco Security Monitoring Analysis and Reporting System (MARS)
✓ Cisco Access Control Server (ACS)
✓ Cisco Application Control Engine (ACE)
✓ Cisco Application Velocity System (AVS)

Exam Topics Covered in This Chapter:

✓ Describe the Cisco Self-Defending Network architecture
✓ Explain the functions and importance of AAA

NOTE

These exam topics are from cisco.com. Check there periodically for the latest exam topics and info.

Hopefully, the preceding chapter has given you a feeling of network insecurity. Now it is time to leverage on some of the best practices that the last chapter left us and incorporate them in a practical way into the day-to-day operations of an organization. This is documented in a comprehensive security policy. Finally, we examine Cisco's model of the Self-Defending Network.

Defining Operations Security Needs

As with any IT project, there must be a demonstrable need for the technology before its acquisition and implementation. Unfortunately, many organizations succumb to the temptation of caving in to the wish list of their IT staff and purchasing equipment without performing the required needs analysis. Many IT professionals can speak to the experience of being asked to architect a need to fit the technology rather than the other way around—architecting the technology to fit the need … the preferred approach. There is a basic lesson to be learned here for both IT staff and their management. Without a needs analysis, followed by a gap analysis and finally a proper methodology in place for the implementation of the technology, a network security project is doomed to fail. Vendors such as Cisco usually have their own methodology for these facets of a secure network project. Because Cisco's customers often look to Cisco sales engineers for direction in their technology projects, it makes good business sense that Cisco should have their own system development life cycle for secure networks. This approach is certain to help sell equipment and also (but less cynically) to ensure that the customer is satisfied with the solution. We examine this cycle in the context of both operational security principles and disaster recovery planning and business continuity planning.

Cisco System Development Life Cycle for Secure Networks

Cisco System Development Life Cycle (SDLC) for secure networks recommends a five-phase approach for security projects. When performed in order, these five steps help organize the workflows that need to coincide throughout the life cycle of a network. Figure 2.1 illustrates these phases.

Table 2.1 contains the steps defined in Figure 2.1, as well as a breakdown of the separate elements within each step.

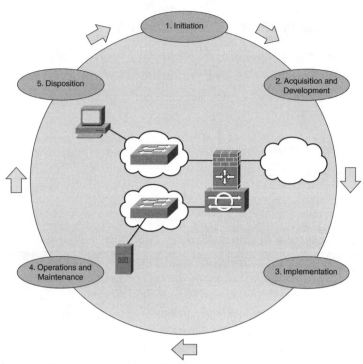

FIGURE 2.1 Cisco Recommended Secure Network Life Cycle

TABLE 2.1   Secure Network Life Cycle Matrix

Step	Elements
1. Initiation	Security Categorization Preliminary Risk Assessment
2. Acquisition and Development	Risk Assessment Security Functional Requirements Analysis Security Assurance Requirements Analysis Cost Considerations and Reporting Security Planning Security Control Development Developmental Security Test and Evaluation Other Planning Components
3. Implementation	Inspection and Acceptance System Integration Security Certification Security Accreditation
4. Operations and Maintenance	Configuration Management and Control Continuous Monitoring
5. Disposition	Information Preservation Media Sanitization Hardware and Software Disposal

Operations Security Principles

INFOSEC professionals need to be aware of a few overarching principles to ensure secure operations. Some of the principles are as follows:

- ▶ Separation of Duties (sometimes Segregation of Duties)
- ▶ Rotation of Duties
- ▶ Trusted Recovery
- ▶ Change and Configuration Controls

Table 2.2 summarizes the elements within each principle.

TABLE 2.2   Elements of Operations Security Principles

Principle	Elements
Separation of Duties (SoD)	Ensures that no one person can compromise the whole system. Includes two-man and dual operator (see the following note).
Rotation of Duties	Individuals rotate security-related duties so that no one person is permanently responsible for a sensitive function. Involves continuous retraining of personnel. Easier to implement in large companies where duties can be separated (see SoD).
Trusted Recovery	Both expect and prepare for the unexpected! Prepare for the following: **Failure:** ▶ System data is continuously backed up. ▶ The backup process is secure, using encrypted databases, for example. ▶ Backup media is physically secured, including preserving chain of custody for possible forensic purposes. **Recovery:** ▶ You have a plan for recovering the data. This data should include: ▶ Files that were open/active at the time of the failure. ▶ Security parameters, including encryption keys necessary to recover the data. ▶ Critical system files. ▶ Consider the principles of SoD and Rotation of Duties in developing a Trusted Recovery strategy.
Change and Configuration Controls	The primary purpose of Change and Configuration Controls is to guarantee that proposed changes do not increase the risk footprint of a system by introducing unintentional vulnerabilities to exploits. There are three main goals: ▶ Minimize network and system disruption ▶ Prepare to reverse changes ▶ Efficiently utilize resources

NOTE

Here are the separate controls that comprise SoD:

▸ **Two-Man Control.** Multiple individuals audit and approve each other's work. This is an example of an administrative control.

▸ **Dual Operator Control.** Two individuals are required to complete a single task. An example might be a safe deposit box that requires the use of both the customer's and the bank's keys to open. This is an example of a technical control.

EXAM ALERT

Know the difference between "two-man control" and "dual operator control." They sound the same, but have entirely different meanings.

Network Security Testing

There are a number of utilities and other tools that you can use to assess your network's security from the perspective of a potential attacker. Don't forget that networks should be resilient against attack both from internal and external threats. Also, the vulnerabilities discovered must be measured against their relative likelihood (that is, risk) and, in a practical sense, whether the cost of the corrective controls employed might outweigh the benefit of their implementation. According to Cisco, this is why we implement security controls:

▸ Create a baseline for corrective action.

▸ Define ways to mitigate discovered vulnerabilities.

▸ Create a baseline of an organization's current security measures.

▸ Measure an organization's progress in fulfilling security policy.

▸ Analyze the relative cost vs. benefit of security improvements.

▸ Support the steps of the Security SDLC.

Types of Testing Techniques

Network security testing tools can be grouped into different types. See if you can determine whether the following test the network's or system's confidentiality, integrity, or availability? (The answers appear in the note at the end of this section.)

▸ Network scanning

▸ Vulnerability detection

- ▶ Password cracking
- ▶ Log analysis
- ▶ Integrity checkers
- ▶ Virus detection
- ▶ War dialing
- ▶ War driving (802.11 or wireless LAN testing)
- ▶ Penetration testing

Common Security Testing Tools

Here is a list of some common security testing tools, along with the organization behind them:

- ▶ **Network Mapper (Nmap).** Open Source from Insecure.org.
- ▶ **Nessus.** Tenable Network Security Inc.
- ▶ **GFI LANGuard.** GFI Software Inc.
- ▶ **SuperScan.** Foundstone (division of McAfee Inc.).
- ▶ **Metasploit.** Metasploit LLC.
- ▶ **Tripwire.** Tripwire Inc.

The following is a more detailed explanation of some of the more important testing tools from this list.

EXAM ALERT

Scanners are testing utilities that probe a network for specific vulnerabilities. There is a fine line between scanning a network and hacking a network because often the same tools are used; the difference is the degree to which they are employed. For example, Tenable Security Corporation's Nessus product is a scanner that, when carelessly employed, can create a denial of service (DoS) on a vulnerable network or end system if dangerous plug-ins are enabled. In Chapter 8, "Network Security Using Cisco IOS IPS," we examine the role of intrusion detection systems (IDS) and intrusion protection systems (IPS). These are also known as sensors. Scanners probe networks, and carefully tuned sensors can detect such probes.

In short:

- ▶ *Scanners* (like Nessus, Nmap, and SuperScan) probe a network for vulnerabilities and can even simulate an attack when certain plug-ins are enabled.
- ▶ *Sensors* monitor a network for signs of probes and attacks. IDSs and IPSs are sensors.

Nmap is a popular scanner, running on Windows, Unix, and Linux systems, and an example of an excellent Open Source tool.

Some features of Nmap include the following:

▶ Low-level scanner, because it will probe for vulnerabilities in layer 3 and 4 of the OSI model but no higher.

▶ Often employed as a general-purpose scanning tool, often by hackers, to perform the initial reconnaissance of a network.

▶ Both ping sweeping and stealth port scanning functionality to make it difficult for IPSs to detect.

▶ OS footprinting (explained in Chapter 1, "Network Insecurity").

Figure 2.2 shows an example of Nmap using its new GUI, Zenmap.

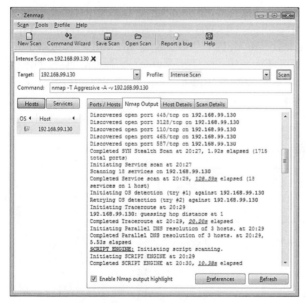

FIGURE 2.2 Zenmap screen-shot.

SuperScan is another example of a scanner. Here are some of SuperScan's features according to Foundstone:

▶ Superior scanning speed

▶ Support for unlimited IP ranges

▶ Improved host detection using multiple ICMP methods

▶ TCP SYN scanning

- ▶ UDP scanning (two methods)

- ▶ IP address import supporting ranges and CIDR formats

- ▶ Simple HTML report generation

- ▶ Source port scanning

- ▶ Fast hostname resolving

- ▶ Extensive banner grabbing

- ▶ Massive built-in port list description database

- ▶ IP and port scan order randomization

- ▶ A selection of useful tools (ping, traceroute, Whois, and so on)

- ▶ Extensive Windows host enumeration capability

Figure 2.3 illustrates the main screen of SuperScan. Interestingly, the scan against the network node at IP address 192.168.99.130 returned no results. This could indicate that an intermediate device such as a firewall (discussed in Chapter 5, "Using Cisco IOS Firewalls to Implement a Network Security Policy") has detected the scan as an attack and has employed countermeasures to hide the scanned host, at least temporarily.

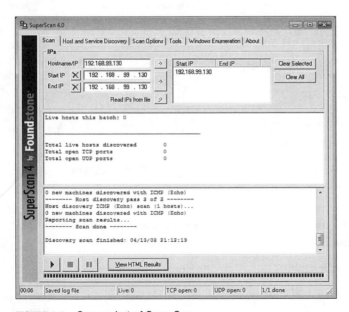

FIGURE 2.3   Screenshot of SuperScan.

Disaster Recovery and Business Continuity Planning

As indicated previously in the discussion of the Trusted Recovery as a principle of Operations Security, you must both expect and plan for a disaster. Although it is impossible and also impractical to plan for every eventuality and contingency, plans must be put into place for the events that are the most likely to occur. For example, it makes no sense to have a recovery procedure in place in case of an earthquake disaster in an area where the risk is minimal, but where risk of loss due to military action or civil unrest is the most likely.

The Three Phases of DRP and BCP

In chronological order, the three phases that disaster recovery procedures (DRP) and business continuity planning (BCP) cover are as follows:

1. Emergency response

2. Recovery

3. Return to normal operation

Let's look at the differences between disaster recovery and business continuity planning separately in the context of these three phases.

Business Continuity Planning

Business continuity planning focuses on the short- to medium-term requirements essential to continuing an organization's operations with the following objectives:

- ▶ **Relocation.** Relocation of elements critical to an organization's operations to a remote or mirror site, while faults at the original site are remedied. An example of this might be a federal government department relocating operations temporarily to a mirror site and using data recovered from backup at the moment of the disaster (emergency response and recovery).

- ▶ **Alternate Communication Channels.** Use of alternate communication channels with suppliers, customers, shareholders, knowledge workers, and so on, until primary channels can be phased back in when the disaster is remedied (recovery).

Disaster Recovery Procedures

Disaster recovery procedures are concerned with the actions that are taken to deal with the disaster immediately after it has occurred. In this sense, they are a subset of business continuity planning. It is the *process* of restoring access to systems, data, software, and hardware critical to business operations. It deals with the second phase in the three phases of DRP and BCP.

> **EXAM ALERT**
>
> Disaster recovery procedures are part of business continuity planning.

Here are some key objectives of disaster recovery procedures:

- ▸ Minimize the requirement for on-scene decision-making during the emergency by setting out specific procedures.

- ▸ Ensure the safety of workers as well as their ability to return to work quickly.

- ▸ Ensure that data integrity is not compromised during the emergency.

- ▸ Ensure that key business functions are not impaired and can return to normal as quickly as possible.

Categories of Disruption

As we saw in the section "Cisco System Development Life Cycle for Secure Networks," the initiation phase is used to categorize the risks and to do an initial risk assessment. Not all disruptions are the same magnitude. Here's a list of disruption categories:

- ▸ **Nondisaster.** A business process is disrupted for a finite period of time.

- ▸ **Disaster.** A facility is unusable for an entire day or more.

- ▸ **Catastrophe.** The entire facility is destroyed.

Backups

Redundancy is the key to dealing with destruction. There are three types of backup, as follows:

- ▸ **Replacement with a redundant component.** A failed or destroyed component is replaced with an equivalent component.

- ▸ **Service-Level Agreements (SLAs) with vendors.** When a service is disrupted, it is replaced with another service and/or restitution is made to an insured value stipulated in the agreement.

► **Complete off-site backup facilities.** Production can be moved to the following:

  ► **Hot sites (or mirror sites).** Redundant site with real-time copies of data from the primary site. The site is maintained in operational readiness with data synchronized from the primary site. When a disaster occurs, only the very last, incremental changes in data need to be restored for the site to be fully operational.

  ► **Warm sites.** Redundant sites without real-time copies of data and software. The disaster recovery team needs to pay a physical site visit to restore data to the site for it to become fully operational.

  ► **Cold sites.** Redundant sites that have the minimum power, environmental controls, and network links but no equipment. During disaster recovery, equipment would have to be sourced and installed and backups restored before full functionality can be recovered.

NOTE

Here are the answers to the exercise from the "Types of Testing Techniques" section. You were asked to determine whether the following test confidentiality, integrity, or availability. The suggested answers appear in parentheses beside the item: C = confidentiality; I = integrity; A = availability.

► Network scanning (A)
► Vulnerability detection (C, I, A)
► Password cracking (C, I)
► Log analysis (I, A)
► Integrity checkers (I)
► Virus detection (I)
► War dialing (C, I)
► War driving (802.11 or wireless LAN testing) (C, I)
► Penetration testing (C, I)

Establishing a Comprehensive Network Security Policy

A comprehensive network security policy is a contract amongst all the stakeholders in an organization. It spells out clear rules for how to protect an organization's people, information systems, and network devices both from external and internal threats. According to Request for Comment (RFC) 2196, "The Site Security Handbook," a security policy is:

"... a formal statement of the rules by which people who are given access to an organization's technology and information assets must abide."

Also, according to the same RFC:

"The main purpose of a security policy is to inform users, staff, and managers of their obligatory requirements for protecting technology and information assets. The policy should specify the mechanisms through which these requirements can be met. Another purpose is to provide a baseline from which to acquire, configure, and audit computer systems and networks for compliance with the policy.

Therefore, an attempt to use a set of security tools in the absence of at least an implied security policy is meaningless."

According to Cisco's Security SDLC, we must first determine whether we have anything of value to protect. Whether our assets are intellectual property, an inventory of items, people, or precious commodities, the assets must be defined and valuated at the outset of the *Initiation* phase. This demonstrates the need for a network security policy, risk assessment, and the ongoing maintenance of the secure network. These are detailed in this section. Understanding these principles teach you valuable context in which to remember the details. This is important for the exam and also for that real world that we work in!

> **NOTE**
>
> RFC 2196, "The Site Security Handbook," is referenced in Appendix B, "Need to Know More?" It is an excellent, plainly written, and common-sense approach that can be used as a template to network security policy planning and implementation.

Defining Assets

We've seen the attackers in Chapter 1, "Network Insecurity." We know their motivations. We can infer from this that whatever the type of organization, there is something there that an attacker wants. It might not have any monetary value to the attacker, but an organization always has assets that it needs to protect from access and DoS attacks. Figure out what you are protecting. The first step in developing a comprehensive security policy is to define an organization's assets. What constitutes an asset?

▶ Anything that others might want.

▶ Processes, systems, and data that is critical to an organization's operations.

▶ Anything that, if compromised, would stop an organization from conducting its affairs.

Placing value on these assets is a separate exercise, as we see in the "Risk Management" subsection later.

The Need for a Security Policy

Remember the axiom, "Security is a process, not a product"? No surprise then, that a security policy, which defines the objectives and rules for that process, is never finished. It is a living document, a contract between all the stakeholders in an organization to constantly revisit and evolve an organization's security posture in the face of new threats and technology.

Three Reasons for Having a Security Policy

Why do we need a security policy? Here are three reasons. Security policies serve to do the following:

▶ Inform stakeholders (users, staff, and managers) of their respective responsibilities.

▶ Specify security controls/mechanisms (administrative, technical, and physical).

▶ Create a baseline from which to improve security.

> **EXAM ALERT**
>
> Know these three reasons for security policies. They're sure to be on the exam!

Three Things That Security Policies Do

What do security policies *do*? Comprehensive security policies contain high-level statements that set out and outline management's position with respect to protecting an organization's people and data and how these goals might be accomplished. Specifically, the security policy defines rules for the following:

▶ **Protection.** Provides confidentiality, integrity, and availability protection for people and information.

▶ **Expected Behavior.** Defines the rules for expected behavior (see the Exam Alert).

▶ **Consequences.** Specifies the consequence of security violations.

▶ **Investigation.** Authorizes staff to investigate security violations.

▶ **Monitoring.** Authorizes and designates staff to monitor and log system activity.

EXAM ALERT

The Acceptable Use Policy (AUP) is the component of the security policy most visible to users and the most common. The AUP sets out very specific rules as to what constitutes allowed versus not allowed behavior to prevent misinterpretation. For example, an AUP might list the specific websites and types of websites that users are prohibited from visiting. Not coincidentally, an effective AUP can help promote productive Internet use.

Policies

Groan … not policies, standards, guidelines, and procedures! This sounds like a lot of writing, meetings with people who love legalese, and people with big sticks making sure that the policies are enforced. Many texts do not do a good job on differentiating this important terminology. Essentially, there is a hierarchy here:

▶ Policies *do* specify overall statements of direction, management position on security issues, organization goals in the context of security, definitions of roles, and so on.

▶ Policies *do not* stipulate the details of day-to-day implementation.

Standards, guidelines, and procedures are derived from policies. These stipulate the details of day-to-day implementation per the last bulleted point. Policies do not answer "how," but they do variously answer "who, what, when, where, and why." See if you can determine in the following list which of "who, what, when, where, and why" the policy type answers.

There are three types of policies, as follows:

▶ Governing policy

▶ Technical policies

▶ End-user policies

Figure 2.4 shows how these policies relate, and the following section describes them in more detail.

Governing Policy

Note that there is only one governing policy because it is the over-arching, high-level policy that describes security concepts that are important to the organization as a whole. The audience is management and technical custodians.

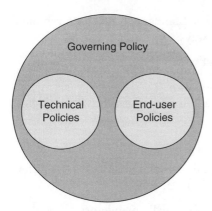

FIGURE 2.4   Security policy framework.

Technical Policies

These policies are more detailed than the governing policy. The audience is technical custodians. They detail the security responsibilities required to address specific systems or issues. For example, a technical policy might specify the policies for site-to-site confidentiality of data and physical access controls, but not how it might be accomplished. Examples of technical policies include the following:

- ▶ General policies
- ▶ Email policies
- ▶ Remote-access policies
- ▶ Telephony policies
- ▶ Application policies
- ▶ Network policies
- ▶ Wireless communication policies

End-User Policies

These documents specify the details of all security topics that are important to an end user. An example of an end-user policy is the AUP.

Standards, Guidelines, and Procedures

Now that the policies are in place, let's develop a plan for their actual implementation and enforcement. Policies are too general. Standards, guidelines, and procedures detail the specific "how" the policies are implemented. While agreeing that they are related, what is the difference between standards, guidelines, and procedures? Here are some definitions.

A security policy is compared against standards. Standards can be differentiated from other security policy elements in these ways:

▶ They define the measuring stick against which the efficacy of security controls is judged.

▶ Standards result in consistent, uniform application of specific technologies.

▶ Standards are usually mandatory.

Security policies also include a number of guidelines. Guidelines can be differentiated from other security policy elements in these ways:

▶ Guidelines are similar to standards but not usually mandatory.

▶ Guidelines create a general envelope of rule application that remains more flexible than standards.

▶ Guidelines can aid in standards development. Guidelines can be tightened up to standards if they prove effective.

▶ Guidelines are used to ensure adherence to more general security policies.

▶ Some widely-accepted guidelines include the following:

    ▶ NIST Computer Security Resource Center

    ▶ NSA Security Configuration Guides

    ▶ The Common Criteria "standard"

    ▶ Rainbow Series

The arms and legs of a security policy are found in its procedures, as follows:

▶ Procedures are usually required.

▶ Procedures are the most granular—the lowest level of all.

▶ Procedures contain detailed steps to accomplish certain tasks.

▶ Procedures contain step-by-step tasks to implement policies, standards, and guidelines.

▶ Procedures are sometimes known as practices.

Who Is Responsible for the Security Policy?

Generally speaking, there are three main groups of stakeholders responsible for the security policy: senior management (or owners), security staff, and users.

- ▶ **Senior Management.** Ultimately responsible for the whole security policy, its operation, and implementation.

- ▶ **Security Staff:**

  - ▶ **Senior Security/IT management (CSO, CIO, CISO).** Responsible for the security policy.

  - ▶ **Senior Security/IT Staff.** Have input on the security policy, possibly drafting parts of it.

  - ▶ **Security / IT Staff.** Responsible for implementing the security policy. These are the "foot soldiers."

- ▶ **End Users.** Responsible for complying to the security policy.

Risk Management

As was seen in the section "Defining Operations Security Needs," the first part of the "Cisco System Development Life Cycle for Secure Networks" was the Initiation Phase, where security categorization and a preliminary risk assessment occurred. Refer to Figure 2.1.

Risk management has two components, as follows:

- ▶ **Threat Identification.** This is the process of identifying the threats faced by a system or network. This is sometimes called threat modeling.

- ▶ **Risk Analysis.** This is the process of estimating the probability and threats that a system faces. Two principles are adhered to:

  - ▶ An estimate of potential loss can be calculated for each risk.

  - ▶ Strive for worst- and best-case estimates.

Risk Analysis

The main purpose of risk analysis is to try to quantify the possible impact or loss of a threat. There are two categories of risk analysis:

- ▶ **Quantitative.** Using asset value as a starting point, develop a *mathematical model* to come up with a monetary figure of expected losses.

- ▶ **Qualitative.** This is a *scenario-based* model. This is particularly useful for countries, large cities, and states where it is impractical to list all assets (the starting point for quantitative risk analysis).

Because quantitative risk analysis assumes that risk can be determined mathematically, it stands to reason that there should be a *Quantitative Risk Analysis Formula*. Figure 2.5 illustrates the formula and the variables that can be plugged into the formula.

EXAM ALERT

Memorize the formula in Figure 2.5 and the meanings of the variables.

$$\overbrace{ALE = (AV * EF)}^{SLE} * ARO$$

Variable	Meaning
AV	**Asset Value:** The cost of an individual asset
EF	**Exposure Factor:** Loss, represented as a percentage, that a realized threat is expected to occur.
ARO	**Annualized Rate of Occurrence:** Estimated frequency that a threat is expected to occur.
SLE	**Single Loss Expectancy:** The result of AV * AF, or the cost of a single instance of a threat.
ALE	**Annualized Loss Expectancy:** The "answer" to the equation. The expected financial loss that an individual threat will cause an organization.

FIGURE 2.5   The Quantitative Risk Analysis Formula.

It's fun to plug numbers into the formula and see what pops out, but in the end, it's only a bit better than guessing. In most organizations, the risk assessment teams use a combination of quantitative and qualitative methods to determine the risk factor of a specific threat. For example, who determines whether the exposure factor (EF) of a tornado is 75% destruction of a place of business for any single occurrence? It might be easier to estimate the annualized rate of occurrence (ARO) based on weather data, but what value is an annualized loss expectancy (ALE), which is itself a product (literally) of three estimates? The best that can be hoped for is to provide some measure of the relative risks of specific threats. The numbers generated also help justify the expense of implementing a comprehensive security policy and focusing costs where they can be of the most benefit.

Here is an example of applying the Quantitative Risk Analysis Formula. What is the Annualized Loss Expectancy (ALE) of a knowledge worker carrying a new laptop through airports in a given year?

AV of a laptop = $1,500

EF of carrying the laptop through airports is estimated at .25% based on industry data.

ARO of carrying the laptop is estimated at 48 occurrences because the knowledge worker will take 24 trips abroad in a year, and each visit will require the worker to go through an airport twice.

Answer: ALE = $1,500 * .25 * 48 = 18,000

This number means nothing by itself, but when comparing relative risks of other threats, it can help an organization prioritize risks and develop a more effective implementation strategy for its security policy.

Risk Management Versus Risk Avoidance

Why do we have to manage risk in the first place? Can't we eliminate it entirely? There are two, complimentary schools of thought about risk. These are outlined below. You can either manage risk or run away from it:

▶ **Risk Management.** Reduces risks to levels deemed acceptable by the system's stakeholders.

▶ **Risk Avoidance.** Eliminates risk by avoiding threats entirely. This is not a practical option in the business world where some risk = profits. Even in the public sector this makes no sense. For example, cutting access to an important website such as a weather information portal may in itself increase the risk to the very stakeholders the site is meant to serve.

Risk Management Countermeasures

What are some ways to reduce risk to acceptable levels? Table 2.3 covers some sample threats and possible procedures (remember them?) to counter their risk.

TABLE 2.3   Threat Scenarios and Safeguards

Threat Scenario	Safeguard
Internal system breach	Implement the policy of least privileges, giving users only the access that they need to perform their job function.
Stolen customer data on an e-commerce website	Customers' data should only be warehoused in internal network segments.
DoS attack on hosted email server interrupts service to customers	Consider redundant, high-speed links for hosted services, as well as high availability and integral host protection for the email server.
Customer's authentication tokens are lost or stolen	Employ quick revocation of customer credentials and frequent refresh of revocation lists.

Principles of Secure Network Design

The first principle of secure network design is to understand that the finished product, a secure system, is never truly finished.

The traditional approach is to develop a security policy, taking into account business needs and risk analysis, as well as industry best practices, as depicted in Figure 2.6. This security policy is implemented, leading to a secure system. Ongoing security operations are carried out by security staff (see "Who is Responsible for the Security Policy?" in an earlier section). Then we stop, right? Of course not! Unless we are lazy or lax, we use what we learn during the operation of the secure system to improve the secure system (arrow "A" in Figure 2.6), as well as the overarching security policy. Similarly, organizations should constantly educate themselves using industry best practices to improve the secure system in real-time, as well as to incorporate this knowledge in the security policy (arrow "B" in Figure 2.6). This requires some flexibility in the security guidelines. As long as the standards dictated by the security policy are met or exceeded, this shouldn't present a problem.

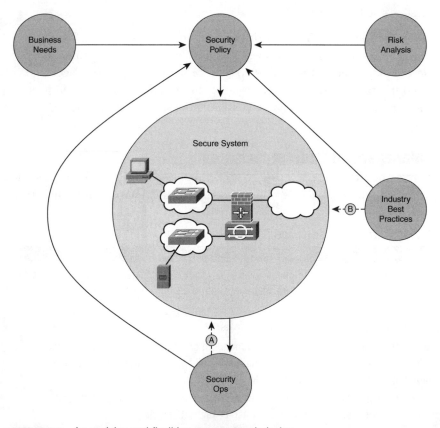

FIGURE 2.6   An evolving and flexible secure network design.

NOTE

Referring to Figure 2.6, *Security Ops* include incident response, monitoring, maintenance, and auditing the system for compliance on an ongoing basis.

Realistic Assumptions

History has proved that many security controls are breached simply because the secure network design was based on incorrect assumptions about the vulnerabilities, risks, and threats that might target the system. Unfortunately, one key wrong assumption may have a ripple effect in impacting other related systems. A good secure system design will have built-in resilience against its own design flaws and will be modular enough in design that when flaws are discovered, they can be corrected without rethinking the whole architecture. Designing a system without single points of failure would be one principle to achieve this goal. You have heard Murphy's Law before: "Anything that can go wrong, will." A good network design assumes that it is impossible to anticipate everything that can go wrong, but nevertheless we should be prepared for everything that can go wrong to key systems.

Here is a summary of design factors that follow the realistic assumptions principle:

▶ **Failure Scenarios.** What if an element fails? Is the security impact isolated? Does it affect other systems?

▶ **When an Element Fails.** Adopt a fail-open or fail-closed approach for the failure of key components of your network, subject to the security policy.

▶ **Attack Possibility.** Identify vulnerabilities and try to identify possible attacks that can be leveraged against them.

▶ **Attack Probability.** Evaluate a realistic probability that the system might be compromised. Don't assume that because a technology is new and that an attack has not yet been invented to compromise it, that it won't happen.

▶ **Evolving Technology.** Keep up to date on the latest technological advances and factor them both into your security policy, the secure network, and operations.

▶ **Human Element.** Assume people will make mistakes leading to an unintentional system compromise.

▶ **Review.** Subject your assumptions to peer review.

Concept of Least Privilege

The concept of least privilege is no element (users, programs, hosts, and so on) should have more than the minimum privileges necessary to perform a task. Because not every repercussion of a compromise can be planned for or even seen, following the concept of least privilege minimizes the possibility that an unanticipated compromise may have system-wide consequences. This might be the single most important principle of secure network design. Here are two examples of the concept of least privilege:

▶ **Example 1.** If a user has no system administrative level of authority, it is much less likely that a compromise of this account will lead to a privilege escalation.

▶ **Example 2.** A compromised web server in a DMZ is less likely to be used to attack an internal network if the router that establishes the DMZ is configured to allow only Network Time Protocol (NTP) to be initiated to an inside network from the DMZ.

Design and Implementation Simplicity

It has often been said that, "Complexity is the worst enemy of security." A military corollary is, "No plan survives first contact with the enemy." So, these sayings mean that designing a network security architecture is doomed to failure? Not at all! Simply put, complexity can lead to unintended interactions with other systems when a network is under attack. The simpler a design and implementation is, the easier it will be to 1) anticipate; and 2) deal with feature interaction. The not-inconsequential side benefit to a simple system is that it is more likely to be embraced by the users as it is likely also simple to understand. Users not only need to be educated in the system; they have to believe in the system as well. How can they embrace the security goals of a security policy and its procedures if they don't understand the system that implements them?

Security Awareness

All the stakeholders (senior management, security staff, and users) require awareness, education, and training. Keeping up on industry best practices, technological innovations, and the operation of your own secure network are essential to maintaining the living security policy and the resultant secure system.

Examining Cisco's Model of the Self-Defending Network

Several trends in network security point out the need for a flexible, resilient, and fast-acting defensive strategy. Both evolving threats and the blurring of the network perimeter serve to underline this need. In Cisco's model of the Self-Defending Network, every network device has a part to play in a cooperative, homogeneous network security strategy. It is still useful to know the answers to questions such as these:

- Where the threats are coming from (both internal and external to an organization)?

- Across what parts of the network are these threats traveling?

- In which direction are these threats flowing?

Although these questions are open-ended and can only be answered in the course of an organization's risk assessment, one central question needs to be answered, and that is, "where is the network perimeter?" This will be examined (if not totally answered!) in the next subsection.

Where Is the Network Perimeter?

Before examining which devices to deploy in a secure network architecture, it would be useful to determine where the trusted network boundaries or perimeters are. Here is a simple definition of a network perimeter:

Network perimeters are established by firewalls. A network perimeter is a logical boundary between parts of the network with differing levels of trust.

For now, per the (unfair?) stereotype of a politician, we will evade directly answering the question of where the perimeter is. Instead, the next few thoughts and examples aid you in determining where *your* network perimeters are in *your* network. Once you have established a definition of a perimeter that works for your network, stick with it, as your network security philosophy will be built around it.

Some network security experts have opined that the network perimeter is extinct. Most would disagree, at least in part, while agreeing that determining where the perimeter is has become somewhat blurred. For example, firewalls have traditionally established the perimeter by establishing security zones of various levels of trust and using technical controls such as ACLs to control traffic across it. This also made it fairly simple to define ingress and egress flows of traffic because ingress (or inbound) would be defined as traffic that flows from a less-trusted to a more-trusted security zone. Egress (or outbound) traffic would be the opposite direction. Although the definition of ingress versus egress has not changed, what has changed is the location of the perimeter itself in some cases. Here are two examples of cases where the location of the perimeter is somewhat blurred:

▶ **Example 1: Perimeter on an application server.** If TCP port 80 (HTTP) traffic is allowed in through a firewall, and that firewall is only analyzing traffic to OSI layer 4 (the transport layer), it can be argued that the firewall is no longer creating perimeter security for that protocol. The perimeter might actually be established on the web server itself, using whatever application layer firewall capabilities that may or may not be deployed on that device. The security of the entire network may hinge on the razor edge of patch management and proper configuration of the web server. Clearly, an application layer firewall will be needed in order to inspect the traffic for protocol compliance, as well as for malicious intent such as Instant Messaging (IM), Peer-to-Peer (P2P), file sharing, embedded code, and so on. A good security policy defines protocols that are absolutely not allowed on a network, but how is this policy enforced?

▶ **Example 2: Moving Perimeter.** At one of your training facilities, one of the employee-students brings in a wireless access point and connects it to a wired Ethernet jack in the classroom, creating a wireless network without encryption in the classroom. On the face of this, it seems OK—if the individual connects to the data jack, they are inside the perimeter, and this is allowed by your security policy; then you realize that one of your competitors, who has offices in the floor above you, has access to your corporate network. Where is your perimeter now? Has it moved? Are internal systems at risk?

NOTE

Security practitioners are often heard saying things like, "After we establish the perimeter…" or "That attack is trying to breach our perimeter…" or such. The word "perimeter" will always remain a source of disagreement and anxiety unless the network security policy defines it in a consistent way. Cisco used to offer a simple definition (simple is good, right?) that went something like this, "A firewall is a device that establishes a trusted network boundary (perimeter) and then manages traffic across that boundary." We examine firewalls in detail in Chapter 5.

Building a Cisco Self-Defending Network

The Cisco Self-Defending Network recognizes that all network elements— whether switch, router, security appliance, firewall, or application server—have a role to play in creating a secure networking environment.

The Three Key Principles of the Cisco Self-Defending Network

The Cisco Self-Defending Network is a unified approach to identify, prevent, and adapt to threats. There are three key principles in Cisco's Self-Defending Network. A network should be the following:

- **Integrated.** Every network element is part of both defense and policy enforcement.

- **Collaborative.** Devices and services collaborate to prevent attacks.

- **Adaptive.** Threats are automatically prevented through proactive security technologies.

Four Collaborative Systems

Cisco specifies four systems that leverage on the three just-defined principles of the Cisco Self-Defending Network (integration, collaboration, and adaptation) to prevent attacks. The word "system" in this context defines a logical grouping or type of Cisco network device or software. The following are these four systems:

- **Policy Management.** Cisco Security Management.

- **Threat Management.** Cisco Security MARS.

- **Endpoint Security.** Cisco NAC Appliance and Cisco Security Agent.

- **Network Infrastructure.** Cisco IPS Sensor Software, Cisco IOS Software, and Cisco ASA Adaptive Security Appliances.

There are more details on some of these Cisco Self-Defending Network solutions in the following section.

EXAM ALERT

Be able to list these systems and match them to the appropriate Cisco solution. Remember that Cisco's use of the word "system" here defines a logical grouping or type of Cisco network device or software.

Components of the Cisco Self-Defending Network

The components of a Cisco Self-Defending Network are three technical controls and one administrative control. This ties in with the terms physical, administrative, and technical controls found in Chapter 1. Here are the terms:

- ▸ **Secure Network Platform.** Use devices where security is an integral, fundamental network feature. This is a technical control.

- ▸ **Threat Control and Containment.** Employ advanced technologies that mitigate the effects of outbreaks and ensure employee productivity in a constantly-evolving threat environment. This is a technical control.

- ▸ **Secure Communications.** Configure devices to ensure the confidentiality and integrity of data, voice, and wireless communication. This is a technical control.

- ▸ **Operational Control and Policy Management.** Deploy a suite of controls that creates a framework for operational control and policy management to ensure end-to-end security. This is an administrative control.

A secure network platform will be the subject of discussion in subsequent chapters including Chapter 3, "Security at the Network Perimeter." Let's examine the last three of the four elements in Cisco's Self-Defending Network separately: threat control and containment, secure communications, and operational control and policy management.

Threat Control and Containment

The Cisco solution for threat control and containment contains three elements: threat control for endpoints, infrastructure, and email. Table 2.4 summarizes these threat control and containment elements and lists the Cisco products used.

TABLE 2.4   Threat Control Product Matrix

Threat Control

Element	Description	Cisco Product
Threat control for endpoints	Defends against threats typically as a result of Internet use, including spyware, viruses, trojans, and general malicious content.	Cisco Security Agent for Desktops
		Cisco ASA 5500 Series Adaptive Security Appliances (Content Security Edition)
		Cisco Integrated Services Routers
		Cisco IPS
		Cisco NAC Appliances

TABLE 2.4   Threat Control Product Matrix   *Continued*
Threat Control

Element	Description	Cisco Product
Threat control for infrastructure	Defends servers, application servers, and network devices against attacks and intrusions through OS and application vulnerabilities.	Cisco Security Agent for Servers Cisco IPS Cisco firewall solutions including ASA 5500 Series and Cisco Catalyst 6500 Series Firewall Services Module Cisco ACE Application Control Engine Module Cisco AVS Application Velocity System XML Security Cisco Security MARS Cisco Security Manager
Threat or email	Protects against email-borne threats.	IronPort

Secure Communications

Secure communications leverages on advanced technologies such as VPN services (both IPsec and SSL), as well as secure voice and wireless, to maintain confidentiality while increasing flexibility and in a cost-effective manner.

> **NOTE**
>
> Cisco really emphasizes secure communications in not only the traditional "triple play" of data, voice, and video, but also in wireless. This is also a constant thread in this Exam Cram.
> Cisco's secure communications solutions use encryption to ensure confidentiality.

For example, Cisco's IPsec VPN portfolio can be relied on to provide secure communications for both remote access and site-to-site connections. This would be very useful, for example, if an organization wanted to protect the communication path between a sales executive sipping coffee at a local designer coffee shop and the head office, while simultaneously wirelessly connected to the Internet.

Operational Control and Policy Management

Employs network management solutions that aid in the speed and accuracy of policy deployment and provides visibility throughout the network to monitor end-to-end. The controls also help in enforcement of the security policy and manage workflows.

Let's briefly look at two products in the Cisco Self-Defending Network product portfolio: Cisco Security Manager and Cisco Security MARS.

Cisco Security Manager

Cisco Security Manager is a solution that provides for the central provisioning of all aspects of device configuration for the Cisco family of security products. It scales from networks with fewer than 10 devices to truly enormous networks with thousands of devices. Here are some of Cisco Security Manager's benefits:

- ▶ Provisions IOS router platforms, which use the Cisco IOS Security image, as well as ASA 5500 Series Adaptive Security Appliances, Cisco PIX 500 series Security Appliances, Cisco 4200 Series Sensors, and the Advanced and Prevention Security Services Module (AIP-SSM) on the Catalyst 6500 Series and ASA 5500 Series Security Appliances.

- ▶ Centrally managed policies with multiple views, including the ability to graphically represent the entire network.

- ▶ Graphical user interface.

- ▶ Integrates with Cisco Security MARS (see the next section) for event correlation with firewall rules.

- ▶ Integrates with Cisco Secure Access Control Server (ACS) to create detailed role-based access control (RBAC) to multiple devices and management functions.

- ▶ Integrates into change management and change control by assigning tasks for deploying policies.

Cisco Security MARS

The Cisco Security Monitoring and Reporting System monitors network security devices made not only by Cisco, but also by other companies. It has the following benefits:

- ▶ False positives are reduced by an end-to-end network view.

- ▶ Its understanding of the network topology and configuration promotes effective attack mitigation.

- ▶ NetFlow network behavior analysis helps detect environmental anomalies.

▶ MARS has over 150 built-in (but customizable) reports, which aid in audit compliance.

▶ Visual tools, such as detailed topological graphs, aid in identifying threat sources, and making specific recommendations for threat remediation through layer 2 to 7 of the OSI model.

Cisco Integrated Security Portfolio

Cisco offers a portfolio of products, both hardware and software, to implement the Self-Defending Network. Its modular nature enables you to progressively layer on security features to an existing core IP network.

Figure 2.7 illustrates the following:

1. An organization starts with an existing core IP network (depicted as a star).

2. The core IP network can be enhanced with Cisco's portfolio of Security Point Services (depicted as a circle wrapping the core IP network's star).

3. The network can further evolve as Advanced Technologies and Services are integrated into the solution.

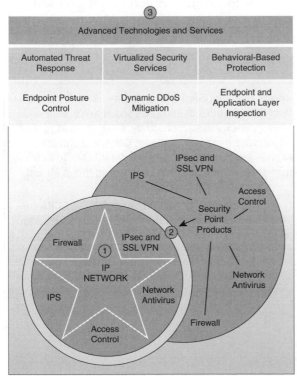

FIGURE 2.7 Secure network platform security services progressively integrated into the network.

Because no one product can offer all the security services required to secure network infrastructure, Cisco has a broad portfolio of integrated security products. Here is a sampling of some of those products:

▶ Cisco IOS platforms with integrated IPS, VPN, and stateful firewall technologies.

▶ Cisco ASA 5500 Series Adaptive Security Appliances with integrated VPN services to enforce perimeter security and access control and IPS (with the AIP-SSM card).

▶ Cisco PIX 500 Series Security Appliances with integrated VPN services to enforce perimeter security and access control.

▶ IDS and IPS appliances (blade servers) and integrated IDS and IPS for Cisco IOS routers, Cisco PIX Security Appliances, and Cisco ASA Adaptive Security Appliances.

▶ Cisco Security Agent endpoint protection software, which protects servers and workstations from known and also unknown threats.

▶ Security modules (VPN, firewall services) for Cisco Catalyst 6500 Series Switches and Cisco 7600 Series Routers.

▶ Security Management products for single devices (Cisco Router and Security Device Manager, Cisco Adaptive Security Device Manager) and multiple devices (Cisco Security Manager, Cisco Security MARS).

NOTE

Arguably, the Cisco Integrated Services Routers (ISRs) with a security IOS is the single device that integrates the majority of these features. It integrates secure voice, data, and video services. Some ISRs also offer secure wireless connectivity, either as an integrated feature or with add-on modules. If you have picked up this Exam Cram, you probably already possess the necessary skills, as stated in the course goals for ICND2, "to install, operate, and troubleshoot a medium-sized network, including connecting to a WAN and implementing network security."

ICND2 is the second of the two courses that comprise the CCNA material. The CCNA curriculum is based on IOS routers; therefore, it's no mystery that the IOS router is used to demonstrate these technologies in subsequent chapters.

Exam Prep Questions

1. Put the following steps in the Cisco Secure Network Life Cycle in the right order:

   ○ **A.** Acquisition and Development

   ○ **B.** Disposition

   ○ **C.** Operations and Maintenance

   ○ **D.** Initiation

   ○ **E.** Implementation

2. Which of the following are elements of the Separation of Duties (SoD) principle of Operations Security? (Choose all that apply.)

   ○ **A.** Individuals rotate security-related duties so that no one person is permanently responsible for a sensitive function.

   ○ **B.** Continuous retraining of personnel.

   ○ **C.** Includes two-man and dual operator controls.

   ○ **D.** Ensures that no one person can compromise the whole system.

   ○ **E.** Operators maintain an arms-length relationship with security controls.

3. Which of the following is not considered a type of testing technique? (Choose all that apply.)

   ○ **A.** Network scanning

   ○ **B.** War driving

   ○ **C.** Penetration testing

   ○ **D.** Log analysis

   ○ **E.** Password cracking

   ○ **F.** None of the above.

4. Fill in the blanks in the following definition with a letter corresponding to the correct technology from the list below.

   _____ probe a network for vulnerabilities and can even simulate an attack, whereas _____ monitor a network for signs of probes and attacks.

   Technologies:

   ○ **A.** Firewalls

   ○ **B.** Syslog servers

   ○ **C.** Sensors

   ○ **D.** Scanners

   ○ **E.** Monitoring and reporting systems

5. In the context of the Initiation Phase of the Cisco System Development Cycle for Secure Networks, we have seen that the Initiation Phase is used to categorize risks. Which of the following are considered disruption categories? (Choose all that apply.)

   ○ **A.** Catastrophe

   ○ **B.** Act of God

   ○ **C.** Man-made calamity

   ○ **D.** Nondisaster

   ○ **E.** Disaster

6. True or false: Warm sites are redundant sites without real-time copies of data and software. The disaster recovery team needs to pay a physical site visit to restore data to the site for it to become fully operational.

7. Match the following words with their definitions:

   1. Policies: ___

   2. Standards: ___

   3. Guidelines: ___

   4. Procedures: ___

   Definitions:

   ○ **A.** Contain detailed steps to accomplish certain tasks.

   ○ **B.** Define the measuring stick against which the efficacy of security controls is judged, resulting in the consistent, uniform application of specific technologies. Usually mandatory.

   ○ **C.** Used to ensure adherence to more general security policies. Usually not mandatory.

   ○ **D.** Specify overall statements of direction, management position on security issues, organization goals in the context of security, definitions of roles, and so on.

8. Choose the one answer that correctly fills in the blanks. There are two categories of risk analysis, _____ and _____.

Choices:

- ○ **A.** Mathematical, statistical
- ○ **B.** Predictive, scenario-based
- ○ **C.** Qualitative, quantitative
- ○ **D.** Idiomatic, stochastic
- ○ **E.** General, specific

9. A company is having a difficult time with compromises that have resulted with several internal systems being compromised with viruses, worms, trojans, and corrupt data. Although the company has a reasonable disaster recovery plan in place and regular backups are being made, they can't understand why this is necessary in the first place; the only traffic they are allowing inbound through their old reliable firewall product is HTTP to a server in the DMZ. This is an example of the _____ of the perimeter.

- ○ **A.** Evolution
- ○ **B.** Strengthening
- ○ **C.** Devolution
- ○ **D.** Blurring
- ○ **E.** Targeting

10. Match the following Cisco devices with the type of threat control they provide. (Hint: Some devices provide more than one type of threat control.)

- **1.** Cisco Security Agent for Desktops _____
- **2.** Cisco Security Agent for Servers _____
- **3.** Cisco Integrated Services Routers _____
- **4.** Cisco IPS _____
- **5.** Cisco NAC Appliances _____
- **6.** Cisco ASA 5500 Series Security Appliances _____
- **7.** Cisco AVS _____
- **8.** Cisco Security MARS _____

Threat Control:

- ○ **A.** Threat control for infrastructure
- ○ **B.** Threat control for endpoints

Answers to Exam Prep Questions

1. The correct order is D, A, E, C, and B: Initiation -> Acquisition and Development -> Implementation -> Operations and Maintenance -> Disposition.

2. Answers C and D are correct. Answers A and B are elements of the principle of Rotation of Duties. Answer E is a trick answer.

3. The correct answer is F. Every other choice in the list is considered to be a network security testing tool. Remember that you use these tools to test the network's or system's confidentiality, integrity, or availability.

4. The correct choices are D and C, respectively. Choices A and E are not correct because firewalls and security appliances are devices that secure the network perimeter. Choice B is incorrect because syslog servers have not yet been covered in this Exam Cram, but even if they were, they are simply repositories of logged events and do not, as a rule, analyze the logs for signs of attack.

5. Choices A, D, and E are correct.

6. True. One of the characteristics of a warm site is that, unlike a hot site, the data isn't continuously synchronized with production systems, and some physical intervention is required to bring the site to an operational state.

7. The answers are: 1—D; 2—B; 3—C; 4—A.

8. The correct answer is C. The other answers are decoys that sound like they might be right, but are largely nonsensical.

9. Answer D is correct. Firewalls have historically been devices that establish a clear perimeter between zones of trust. This clear perimeter is getting blurred with the advent of tunneled services as a common vector of attack.

10. The correct answers are as follows:

    1. Cisco Security Agent for Desktops   (B)

    2. Cisco Security Agent for Servers   (B)

    3. Cisco Integrated Services Routers   (A, B)

    4. Cisco IPS   (A, B)

    5. Cisco NAC Appliances   (A)

    6. Cisco ASA 5500 Series Security Appliances (A, B)

    7. Cisco AVS   (B)

    8. Cisco Security MARS   (B)

PART II

Perimeter Security

CHAPTER THREE

Security at the Network Perimeter

Terms You'll Need to Understand:

✓ Cisco Security Device Manager (SDM)

✓ Cisco Security Device Manager (SDM) Express

✓ Local access

✓ Remote access

✓ Console

✓ Privilege levels

✓ Views

✓ Quiet mode

✓ Banners

✓ Authentication, Authorization, and Accounting (AAA)

✓ Terminal Access Control Access Control System Plus (TACACS+)

✓ Remote Access Dial-in User Service (RADIUS)

✓ Cisco Secure Access Control Server (ACS)

✓ Cisco Secure Access Control Server (ACS) Solution Engine

✓ Cisco Secure Access Control Server (ACS) Express

Exam Topics Covered in This Chapter:

✓ Secure administrative access to Cisco routers by setting strong encrypted passwords, exec time-out, login failure rate, and using IOS login enhancements

✓ Secure administrative access to Cisco routers by configuring multiple privilege levels

✓ Secure administrative access to Cisco routers by configuring role based CLI

✓ Explain the functions and importance of AAA

✓ Describe the features of TACACS+ and RADIUS AAA protocols

✓ Configure AAA authentication

✓ Configure AAA authorization

✓ Configure AAA accounting

> **NOTE**
>
> These exam topics are from cisco.com. Check there periodically for the latest exam topics and info.

It could be argued that before we consider how the router can protect the network, we must first look at hardening the router itself from attack. That will come later, in Chapter 4, "Implementing Secure Management and Hardening the Router." When you're reading through this chapter, keep in the back of your mind that the theme of this chapter is how to make sure that only authorized personnel have access to the router in the first place. We'll need to introduce Cisco's line of Integrated Services Routers (ISRs) first and get some sense of where they might be deployed to provide security at the network perimeter.

Cisco IOS Security Features

Although the primary purpose of an IOS router is to be a router, there are a number of built-in security features that can be leveraged such that the router takes its proper place in the Cisco Self-Defending Network. In this section, we look at typical deployment scenarios for an IOS router and examine some of the features of Cisco Integrated Services Routers (ISRs) at a high level.

Where Do You Deploy an IOS Router?

Before we get into the features of Cisco's product portfolio, we should probably cover the question of where a router is deployed as part of the implementation of a comprehensive security policy. We discussed the "blurring of the perimeter" in Chapter 2, "Building a Secure Network Using Security Controls," but it is typically at the perimeter, or edge, of a network where we deploy routers. They are often the first bastion of defense against attack because many enterprises, both large and small, use routers as their first connection to an Internet Service Provider's IP cloud. The router might be a customer-managed solution, in which case the customer has at least partial control of the configuration and management of the router, or the equipment could be wholly owned, configured, and managed by the ISP. Of course, the size of the network, the customer, the assets they are trying to protect, and so on, will determine both the type and depth of defense implemented. A small office/home office (SOHO) user or a teleworker probably doesn't need multiple layers of defenses and different zones of security that a large e-commerce site requires. Common sense dictates that all of these considerations will bear on both the scope of the solution as well as the capabilities of the router that will be required.

Refer to Figure 3.1 for three common examples of where a router might be deployed. Keep in mind that the firewall in Figure 3.1 is assumed to be a stateful firewall. The reason it is deployed instead of another router is that the firewall will be able to keep track of the state of connections that are built across it (both ingress and egress) and thereby afford an extra level of protection to the network. The firewall could very well be an IOS router firewall. IOS firewalls and types of firewalls in general are examined in Chapter 5, "Using Cisco IOS Firewalls to Implement a Network Security Policy."

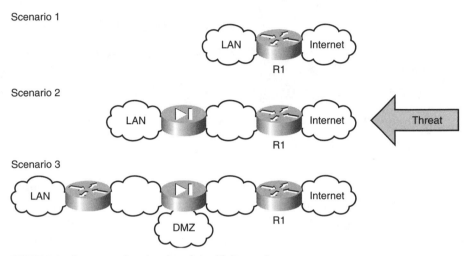

FIGURE 3.1 A company's network grows with its needs.

The following is a detailed explanation to the three deployment scenarios in Figure 3.1:

> ▶ **Scenario 1—Single Perimeter.** The router establishes the trusted network boundary at the Internet and protects a single LAN. This is a small business (but with growth aspirations!), and they need a solution that will grow with them.

> ▶ **Scenario 2—Two Perimeters.** Business is improving and the company has more need for protection of its assets, including intellectual property. The security policy grows with the business and dictates that a firewall is purchased to establish a second perimeter behind the router, thus providing an extra level of protection for the single LAN.

> ▶ **Scenario 3—Screened Subnet.** The company's business needs dictate that an e-commerce site be implemented. Recalling that business needs are a big driver for security policies, the company uses industry best practices to change. A DMZ is established on the firewall where the

organization's e-commerce servers are deployed. The security policy dictates that another router be deployed inside the firewall to maintain two perimeters between the Internet and the LAN.

Cisco ISR Family and Features

According to Cisco, what makes an Integrated Services Router integrated are the following features:

▶ **Integrated Security.** 3DES and AES encryption; NAC.

▶ **Unified Network Services.** PVDM modules; media authentication and encryption with SRST.

▶ **Mobility.** 3G wireless WAN; wireless LAN services.

▶ **Application Intelligence.** Performance routing; Cisco WAAS.

▶ **USB Port.** USB eToken; USB flash support.

Figure 3.2 illustrates the Cisco ISR product spectrum. The Cisco ISR routers range from SOHO devices with the 800 series ISR, all the way up to a large branch office where the 3800 series ISR would be an appropriate solution. One of the main advantages of Cisco's router solution is that they all share common configuration interfaces in the form of the Cisco command-line interface (CLI) for character-based terminal configuration and the Cisco Security Device Manager (SDM) as a web-based GUI. The user interface's look and feel is close to identical from one device to another.

> **EXAM ALERT**
>
> A good way to remember the model number nomenclature is to realize that all these models have the number 800 in their series designation: 800, 1800, 2800, and 3800. Also, the larger the number, the more capable the ISR.

> **NOTE**
>
> For more information on the Integrated Services Routers, browse to this link: http://www.cisco.com/en/US/prod/routers/networking_solutions_products_ genericcontent0900aecd806cab99.html.
>
> Cisco also introduced a new series of high-performance routers, the 1000-series Aggregation Services Routers (ASRs), in Q2 of 2008. Here's a link to those devices: http://www.cisco.com/en/US/prod/routers/networking_solutions_products_ genericcontent0900aecd806cab99.html.

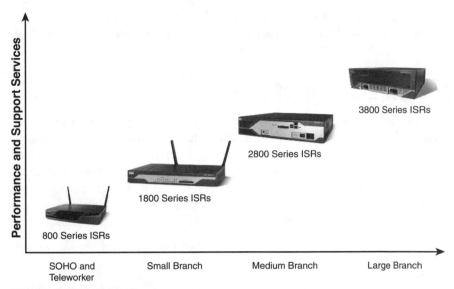

FIGURE 3.2 ISR product spectrum.

Securing Administrative Access to Cisco Routers

In this section, we examine some best practices for setting passwords on network devices (not just routers), as well as selected topics where we examine and configure other administrative security features, such as role-based access control to the command-line interface and basic operating system and configuration security practices.

Let's focus on some of the technical controls needed to secure both local and remote administrative access to Cisco routers. As was discussed in Chapter 2, "Building a Secure Network Using Security Controls," security controls are either physical, administrative, or technical (PAT).

Before we look at specific technical security controls, we must define the types of access that might be made to the router platform itself for the purpose of configuring the device. There are two categories of router configuration access: local access and remote access:

- ▶ **Local Access.** Direct, physical access to the device through its integral console port. Often referred to as *out-of-band* access.

- ▶ **Remote Access.** Indirect access to the device through a TCP/IP network. Often referred to as *in-band* access. Encryption of management traffic is recommended if it will be on the same links as other traffic. A dedicated management network, perhaps a separate VLAN, should be considered too.

Review Line Interfaces

Line interfaces differ from other interfaces (such as GigabitEthernet, Serial, ATM, and so on) in that they are interfaces that terminate or accept *configuration* traffic only. They are not traffic-passing interfaces in the sense that they route traffic. Line interfaces are a critical interface from a security standpoint because they are the interfaces that all configuration traffic terminates on. Curiously, many organizations overlook setting up even the simplest security on these interfaces. There are two broad types of line interfaces:

▶ **Those that you can touch (physical line interfaces).** Console port and auxiliary ports.

▶ **Those that you can't touch (virtual terminal line interfaces).** vtys.

To configure a line interface, you use the **line** global configuration command, as illustrated with the following command sequence:

```
CiscoISR(config)#line ?
  <0-6>     First Line number
  aux       Auxiliary line
  console   Primary terminal line
  vty       Virtual terminal
CiscoISR(config)#line console 0
CiscoISR(config-line)#
```

As you can see, when you select a line interface with the **line** command (for example, **line console 0**), the prompt changes and indicates that you are now in line configuration mode.

The following CLI output shows the section of a typical router's configuration where the different line interfaces are configured:

```
line con 0
  transport input all
  login
  password N3v3rGu355M3!
line aux 0
  transport input all
  password N3v3rGu355M3!
line vty 0 4
  transport input telnet ssh
   login local
```

Let's briefly review the console, auxiliary, and vty line interfaces:

Console Line Interface

The console line interface is a serial DCE RJ45 port on the router. It provides a clock, and you have to match its settings. You can connect a dumb terminal or a computer running a terminal emulation program to it with a Cisco rollover cable and access the various command prompts on the router. The default settings for the console port are 9600 bps, no parity, 8 data bits, and 1 stop bit—or 9600-N-8-1 for short. The terminal settings can be changed by modifying the configuration register using the **config-register** global configuration mode CLI command. Of course, router security starts with physical security controls, so make sure that only a privileged few have physical access to your router, or you might see it for sale on an online auction site! This is an out-of-band line interface.

Auxiliary Line Interface

All routers also have another physical line interface called the auxiliary port. You can attach an external modem to this interface so that you can dial in to the device's auxiliary port over the plain old telephone system (POTS) to perform out-of-band configuration.

> **NOTE**
>
> Cisco 800-series ISRs have a virtual auxiliary port because the console port and auxiliary port share the same physical RJ45 jack on the router. All other ISRs have separate RJ45 jacks for the console and auxiliary port and are clearly labeled.

Virtual Line Interfaces

Finally, let's review the virtual terminal line interfaces or *vtys*. By default, all Cisco routers (and many other Cisco devices) come with five virtual terminal line interfaces: vty 0, 1, 2, 3, and 4. These virtual line interfaces are pseudo or dummy interfaces that terminate configuration traffic that arrives on the router *in-band*.

> **NOTE**
>
> *Out-of-band* versus in-band have a special meaning in the context of these configuration interfaces. *In-band* means that a user must use a TCP/IP network and application protocols such as Telnet and Secure Shell (SSH) to configure the device. The virtual terminal line interfaces are thus *in-band*. *Out-of-band* means that a user does not depend on a TCP/IP network to configure the device and therefore must physically connect to the device in order to configure it. The console port and auxiliary port are thus *out-of-band*.

Password Best Practices

You knew it was coming! We have to configure passwords to protect the router from unauthorized access, but what constitutes a good password according to Cisco? Cisco makes specific recommendations about this. The following is not an exhaustive list. You may want to add your own rules for password complexity, for example, but here are the Cisco recommendations for creating strong passwords:

- ▶ Passwords should have at least 10 characters.

- ▶ Passwords must begin with an alphabetic character.

- ▶ Passwords can include the following:

  - ▶ Alphanumeric characters

  - ▶ Symbols and spaces

- ▶ Do not use dictionary words, even as part of a password.

- ▶ Leading spaces in passwords are ignored. All other spaces after the first character are not ignored.

- ▶ Change the password often.

Configuring Passwords

When you put passwords on the console, auxiliary, and virtual terminal line interfaces, you are protecting user-level access only. Cisco makes specific recommendations for security best practices for passwords and other login settings on these line interfaces. We examine basic security of the user and enable modes (essentially review from CCNA) and then look at some more advanced security features, including how to secure the ROM Monitor (ROMMON) mode on the router.

Console Password

The console password protects the first configuration mode that a user sees when connected to the console line interface: user mode. The following commands illustrate how to set a password on the console:

```
CiscoISR(config)#line console 0
CiscoISR(config-line)#login
% Login disabled on line 0, until 'password' is set
CiscoISR(config-line)#password cisco
```

Virtual Terminal Password

The console password protects the first configuration mode that a user sees when connected to the virtual terminal line interface, the user mode. The following commands illustrate how to set a password on the vtys:

```
CiscoISR(config)#line vty 0 4
CiscoISR(config-line)#login
% Login disabled on line 2, until 'password' is set
% Login disabled on line 3, until 'password' is set
% Login disabled on line 4, until 'password' is set
% Login disabled on line 5, until 'password' is set
% Login disabled on line 6, until 'password' is set
CiscoISR(config-line)#password sanjose
```

Enable Password

Setting an enable password or, better yet, an enable secret password, protects the enable (super user) mode of the router:

```
CiscoISR(config)#enable password cisco
```

Secret Password

The following command creates an encrypted secret password for the enable mode using an MD5 hash. When the enable secret password is set, it supersedes the enable password that is subsequently ignored:

```
CiscoISR(config)#enable secret sanfran
```

Service Password Encryption

For even better security, you can encrypt all the passwords on the device (with the exception of the hashed enable secret). This is not as strong encryption as the MD5 hash on the enable secret, but it will prevent accidental discovery of the router's passwords.

```
CiscoISR(config)#service password encryption
```

> **NOTE**
>
> If you are using the auxiliary port, aux 0, for access, don't forget to password protect its access too! The 800 Series ISR has a single console port that can be configured as a virtual auxiliary port if you want to connect a modem to it for example. Other ISRs (1800, 2800, and 3800 Series) have a separate auxiliary port.

Setting Timeouts for Router Lines

Common sense (and hopefully your security policy, too!) dictates that no one should be able to remain forever on an inactive line interface (console, auxiliary, vty). The **exec-timeout** *minutes seconds* command terminates an inactive connection. For example, if you wanted to terminate an inactive console connection after 2 minutes and 15 seconds, you would type the following two commands.:

```
CiscoISR(config)#line console 0
CiscoISR(config-line)#exec-timeout 2 15
```

Configuring Minimum Password Length

While Cisco recommends a minimum password length for all passwords there is no enforcement by default. The **security passwords min-length** command enforces a minimum password length. For example, if you wanted the minimum password length to be 16 characters, you would type in the following command:

```
CiscoISR(config)#security passwords min-length 16
```

Username Password Security

Usernames and passwords are often stored in a local database on the router to enhance Authentication, Authorization, and Accounting (AAA) configurations. The passwords are not encrypted by default. Although these passwords would be encrypted with the **service password encryption** command, this level of encryption is not as good as a Message Digest 5 (MD5) hash. The following command will encrypt the password of a user called *rtradmin* with an MD5 hash. Note that a **0** denotes that what follows is a cleartext (unencrypted) password. When viewing the configuration, a **5** denotes that what follows is a hidden password. We can use context-sensitive help to demonstrate in the following sequence of commands. The password before (cleartext) and after (encrypted) is highlighted in the output:

```
CiscoISR(config)#username rtradmin secret 5 ?
  WORD  The HIDDEN user secret string
CiscoISR(config)#username rtradmin secret 0 ?
  LINE  The UNENCRYPTED (cleartext) user secret
CiscoISR(config)#username rtradmin secret 0 Can'tGue55M3
```

> **NOTE**
>
> Hashing functions, including Message Digest 5 (MD5), are discussed in Chapter 6, "Introducing Cryptographic Services."

Verify that the user's password is encrypted:

```
CiscoISR(config)#do show running-config ¦ include username rtradmin
username rtradmin secret 5 $1$C0GC$mSvkJRen9Qf4UjfnQ4tPH/
```

Securing ROMMON Mode

The ROM Monitor (ROMMON) mode is most often used while performing password recovery. To recover passwords, you must have physical access to the device with a terminal connected to the console port. If your security policy dictates that no one can recover passwords in this fashion, you need to disable the ability to break out of the router's boot-up process in order to enter ROMMON mode with the **no service password-recovery** command. This is very dangerous, to say the least, because executing this command will disable the password recovery mechanism on the router. If you lose the enable password, your only remedy is to send the router back to Cisco for replacement!

```
CiscoISR(config)#no service password-recovery
WARNING:
Executing this command will disable password recovery mechanism.
Do not execute this command without another plan for
password recovery.

Are you sure you want to continue? [yes/no]: yes
CiscoISR(config)#
```

Setting Multiple Privilege Levels

So far, we've treated user privilege as binary. They either have next-to-none (level 0) or they have super-user privilege when they're in enable mode (level 15). There might be a number of people who need access to the router. The ISP might need access; the ACL administrator might need access; the Change Control and Configuration Management Policy might dictate that only one person is privileged enough to save the router's configuration; and so on. To account for the need for these various privilege levels of access, the interim privilege levels (1–14) can be customized in a very granular fashion. You can assign what configuration mode(s) a user who has a defined privilege level is allowed to use. Optionally, you can set what commands they are allowed to execute. Let's look at a simple example.

If you wanted to allow users at privilege level 3 to enter the **configure** command (something that they're not normally allowed to do), you could type in these commands:

```
CiscoISR(config)#privilege exec level 3 configure
CiscoISR(config)#enable secret level 3 sanjose
```

Now, when a user logs in, either in-band or out-of-band to the user mode, they can enable privilege level 3. The **show privilege** command indicates the current privilege level:

```
CiscoISR>enable 3
Password: sanjose
CiscoISR#show privilege
Current privilege level is 3
```

Configuring Role-Based Access to the CLI

With the parser view feature, you can create a "view" that is a collection of all the commands that someone who has the password to that view is allowed to execute. A view is a contained shell environment that limits their view of the router. Unlike access granted via privilege levels where someone with level 10 access also has access to commands authorized at levels 1–9, role-based CLI is more modular. Access that is granted within one view is separate from other views. We'll go through it step-by-step in a moment, but sometimes it's better to take a look at an example first and use intuition.

Here's an example of how views may be used in real life. Let's say our router is managed by an ISP.

The following bullets list the items we want the ISP user to be able to accomplish while logged into the view, followed by the command keywords to enable this command in the view. These keywords are highlighted in the subsequent command output so you can pair them up with their descriptions below. Note that the parser view defines separately which *exec* commands and which *configuration* mode commands you are authorized to execute in the view. This follows the general hierarchy of CLI commands:

- **Exec Commands:**
  - Ping IP hosts: **ping**
  - Use all show commands: all **show**
- **Configuration Modes:**
  - Enter global configuration mode: **configure**
  - Create ACLs: **access-list**
  - Enter interface configuration mode: all **interface**
  - Use all IP configuration commands: all **ip**

> **NOTE**
>
> If it's not in the view, they can't do it! For example, we don't want our ISP to be able to write the configuration to the router's NVRAM. If we don't authorize them to use the **copy** command or the **write** command, then it's not going to happen. Once *authenticated* to the view, the view will determine what they are *authorized* to do. No surprise, then, that we have to first enable AAA on the router. This is done using the **aaa new-model** command before we can proceed.

First, we enable the AAA system on the router:

```
CiscoISR(config)#aaa new-model
```

Then we enable the view context and supply the enable secret password. The view hasn't been created yet. The view context tells the router that subsequent commands are executed within the context of creating a view.

```
CiscoISR#enable view
Password: enablesecretpassword
```

Now we enter global configuration mode and create the view by giving it a name, specify a password, and then we specify which exec mode commands can be executed in the view.

```
CiscoISR#config terminal
Enter configuration commands, one per line.  End with CNTL/Z.
CiscoISR(config)#parser view ISP
CiscoISR(config-view)#secret 0 hardtoguess
CiscoISR(config-view)#commands exec include ping
CiscoISR(config-view)#commands exec include all show
```

Here we specify that the user can configure from all sources (for example: terminal, memory, terminal):

```
CiscoISR(config-view)#commands exec include all configure
```

Now we specify which global configuration commands the user can execute. He can use the **access-list** command, and all forms of the **interface** command and **ip** command:

```
CiscoISR(config-view)#commands configure include access-list
CiscoISR(config-view)#commands configure include all interface
CiscoISR(config-view)#commands configure include all ip
```

Once you've configured this view for the ISP, here's what it looks like from the ISP's perspective. Should he be able to execute the **write mem** command? The answer is no, because we have not given the ISP view access to that command. Let's enable the view and try out all the commands that the ISP user is authorized to execute, as well as the **write mem** command, which he is not authorized to execute:

```
CiscoISR>enable view ISP
Password: hardtoguess
Apr 19 13:19:03.892: %PARSER-6-VIEW_SWITCH: successfully set to view 'ISP'
CiscoISR#configure terminal
Enter configuration commands, one per line.  End with CNTL/Z.
CiscoISR(config)#exit
CiscoISR#ping www.ciscopress.com
Translating "www.ciscopress.com"...domain server (206.248.154.22) [OK]
Type escape sequence to abort.
Sending 5, 100-byte ICMP Echos to 209.202.161.68, timeout is 2 seconds:
!!!!!
Success rate is 100 percent (5/5), round-trip min/avg/max = 52/52/56 ms
```

Everything works great up to now, but then the ISP user tries to execute a command that he is not authorized to execute:

```
CiscoISR#write mem
         ^
% Invalid input detected at '^' marker.
CiscoISR#
```

The **show parser view** command can be used to verify the views configured on the system:

```
CiscoISR#show parser view all
Views/SuperViews Present in System:
 ISP
— — —·(*) represent superview— — —·
CiscoISR#
```

In summary, here are the steps to create a view:

1. Enable AAA on the router (if it hasn't already been enabled):

   aaa new-model

2. Enable the router's view context:

   enable view

3. Enter global configuration mode:

   configure terminal

4. Create a new view or enter an existing view:

   parser view *view-name*

5. Assign a password for logging into the view:

   secret 5 *encrypted-passwd* (or **secret 0** *cleartext passwd*)

6. Specify the commands that can be executed in exec and configure modes:

   commands (see the examples for syntax of two parser modes)

7. Exit from view configuration mode:

   exit

EXAM ALERT

You should know the following about the enable view command and setting up parser views in general:

1. The enable view command is not entered in global configuration mode. This is easy to remember if you recall that all enable commands are entered in an exec mode. This sounds like it might be a great trick question.

2. Know at least two of the parser modes for the views, exec and configure, as these are the ones in Cisco's course material and therefore likely to be on the exam.

Configuring the Cisco IOS Resilient Configuration Feature

The Cisco IOS resilient configuration feature enables the router to take secure snapshots of the router's running configuration file and image. This protects the router against attempts by an attacker to erase the contents of NVRAM and flash (persistent storage). These secured files are hidden from standard commands that view the contents of persistent storage. For example, the **show flash** command will not show the secure image file. If a router has been compromised, the resulting down time is reduced because the router maintains secure archives of the required files and there is no need to search for backups of these files elsewhere.

The first command creates a secure copy of the IOS image. It also indicates what happens if you don't have an ATA disk (required):

```
CiscoISR(config)#secure boot-image
CiscoISR(config)#
032787: Apr 18 14:08:30.989 NewYork: %IOS_RESILIENCE-5-IMAGE_NOTFOUND:
Running image not found on removable disk
```

That didn't work too well. Let's try to make a secure copy of the running configuration file:

```
CiscoISR(config)#secure boot-config
CiscoISR(config)#
032788: Apr 18 14:09:36.099 NewYork: %IOS_RESILIENCE-5-
NO_SUPPORTED_DEVICE: No ATA disk found for storing archives
ios resilience:failed to remove chkpt file
```

NOTE

The **secure boot-config** command functions properly only when the system is configured to run an image from a disk with an Advanced Technology Attachment (ATA) interface. The commands captured above were from a Cisco 871 ISR that does not support ATA; thus, we observe the notification "...No ATA disk found for storing archives."

Now, we'll execute the command that verifies the bootset:

```
CiscoISR#show secure bootset
%IOS image and configuration resilience is not active
```

EXAM ALERT

Remember that the only way you can view the secured copies of the configuration and IOS image is to execute the **show secure bootset** command.

Protecting Virtual Logins from Attack

Recall from Chapter 1, "Network Insecurity," that there are two broad categories of attacks: access attacks and DoS attacks. We will examine three methods to mitigate the successfulness of these attacks against SSH, Telnet, and HTTP login to the IOS router:

▸ Shutting down or "blocking" the login system if DoS attacks are suspected.

▸ Enforcing a delay between successive login attempts.

▸ Generating syslog messages for login detection.

Blocking the Login System

When a DoS attack on the login system is detected, subsequent login *attempts* can be blocked for a specified time [in seconds]. You must set the threshold of number of *tries* within a specified period [in seconds]. Here is the format of the command:

```
login block-for seconds attempts tries within seconds
```

For example, if your security policy stipulates that five login attempts within 60 seconds constitutes a possible DoS attack, you might want to block subsequent logins for 120 seconds:

```
CiscoISR(config)#login block-for 120 attempts 5 within 60
```

This enforced blocking period (120 seconds in the preceding example) is known as a *quiet period*. During that quiet period, no login attempts will be accepted by the router. If you want to specify a policy as to who would be allowed to attempt a login during this quiet period, you can use an ACL to describe the IP addresses that can. Perhaps this is a management VLAN or IPsec VPN user. Recall from your CCNA studies that the way to limit access to the virtual terminal lines is to use the **access-class** command to apply an ACL to the vtys. In this example, packets that match the named IP ACL "RA-VPN-Users" will be allowed to login during the quiet period. Note the use of the *access-class* parameter in the command syntax:

```
CiscoISR(config)#access-list RA-VPN-Users permit 10.1.1.0 0.0.255
CiscoISR(config)#login quiet-mode access-class RA-VPN-Users
```

Enforcing a Delay Between Logins

To protect the IOS router against possible dictionary attacks, you can enforce a delay between successive login attempts. This will help frustrate an attacker and will also protect the login system such that legitimate users will get an opportunity to login to the device. For example, if you want to enforce a login delay of one second between attempts, issue this command:

```
CiscoISR(config)#login delay ?
  <1-10>  Time period in seconds
CiscoISR(config)#login delay 1
```

> **NOTE**
>
> If you use the **auto secure** command, a login delay of one second is automatically configured. The **auto secure** command is discussed in Chapter 4.

Generating Syslog Messages for Login Detection

The following two commands generate logging messages for successful and failed login attempts respectively:

```
CiscoISR(config)#login on-success log
CiscoISR(config)#login on-failure log
```

Verifying the Login Configuration

The **show login** command verifies that the modifications that we have made to the login subsystem of the router will be enforced. The shaded parts of the following output indicate these changes:

```
CiscoISR#show login
     A login delay of 1 seconds is applied.
     Quiet-Mode access list RA-VPN-Users is applied.
     All successful login is logged.
     All failed login is logged.

     Router enabled to watch for login Attacks.
     If more than 5 login failures occur in 60 seconds or less,
     logins will be disabled for 120 seconds.

     Router presently in Normal-Mode.
     Current Watch Window
         Time remaining: 57 seconds.
         Login failures for current window: 0.
     Total login failures: 0.
CiscoISR(config)#
```

Configuring Banner Messages

Five different banners can be configured on the IOS router:

> ▶ **Exec.** This banner is displayed when an exec mode (user or enable) is entered on the router.

> ▶ **Incoming.** This banner is displayed when there is an incoming connection to a terminal line from a network host.

> ▶ **Login.** This banner is displayed before the username/password prompt.

> ▶ **MOTD.** The message-of-the-day banner.

> ▶ **SLIP-PPP.** This banner is displayed for dial-in users on a Serial Line Internet Protocol (SLIP) or Point-to-Point Protocol (PPP) connection.

Remember that the router, in its role as a perimeter device, is often the first device an attacker is likely to see as he probes the network. The banners are the first thing that users see when they login to the routers. This would be an appropriate place to put warning messages and legal statements, such as the repercussions of unauthorized access to the system. Don't give away any information in your banner message that might be useful to an attacker. Above all, don't tell anyone that they're "Welcome." If they're an attacker, they certainly aren't, and the router's login banners should not be the equivalent of a welcome mat in any case. Here's a partial configuration showing an example of a MOTD banner:

```
banner motd ^C
  WARNING:  You are connected to $(hostname) $(domain)
  This system is the property of ABC LLC.
  UNAUTHORIZED ACCESS TO THIS DEVICE IS PROHIBITED.
  You must have explicit permission to access this
  device. All activities performed on this device
  are logged. Any violations of access policy will result
  in disciplinary action.
^C
```

NOTE

You can use replaceable parameters in the banner message. For example, the parameters $(hostname) and $(domain) will be replaced with the system's hostname and domain name suffix respectively when the banner is displayed upon login.

Introducing Cisco SDM

Cisco Security Device Manager (SDM) is a web-based tool that can be used to manage Cisco IOS routers. It can be used as an alternative to the CLI because the majority of tasks that can be performed with the CLI can also be completed with the SDM. As the Security Device Manager evolves, Cisco is putting heavier emphasis on its use in their courses. Time mastering the SDM here will be time well spent.

> **NOTE**
>
> In Q2 of 2008, Cisco announced a new web-based GUI tool called the Cisco Configuration Professional (CCP). It is expected that CCP will eventually replace SDM. Not all ISRs are supported by CCP, however, though this support is coming. For more information on CCP, navigate to http://www.cisco.com/go/ccp.

There are five basic services that SDM manages:

- Routing
- Switching
- Security (including VPN, firewall, and IOS)
- Wireless
- QoS

It also contains a knowledge base of Cisco IOS configurations. Its built-in tutorials, context-sensitive help, and smart wizards supplement its ease of use.

Figure 3.3 is a screenshot of the opening Cisco SDM screen on a Cisco 871 ISR.

Not all ISRs have enough flash to run the full SDM out of flash. If this is the case, you can either:

- Install Cisco SDM locally on a Windows PC.
- Run the Cisco SDM Express.

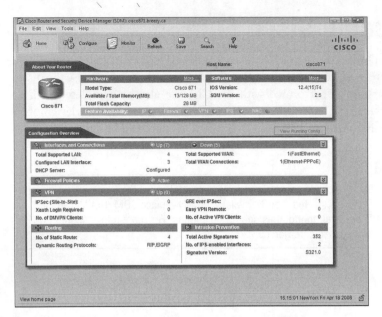

FIGURE 3.3   Cisco router and Security Device Manager (SDM).

Files Required to Run Cisco SDM from the Router

There are certain files that are required to run the Cisco SDM from the router's flash file system. If these files don't exist, they will need to be downloaded from Cisco. They come as part of a comprehensive download that also includes the files required to run the SDM applet from a PC workstation. Factory fresh routers from Cisco will have these files in flash. If they are not there, it means that someone has deleted them, perhaps because the organization's security policy specifies that only the CLI can be used to configure the router.

> **NOTE**
>
> For more information about Cisco SDM and to download a package that contains the files necessary to run SDM from flash as well as the standalone SDM applet for use on a PC, navigate to http://www.cisco.com/go/sdm.

These files are needed to run Cisco SDM 2.2a and later from the router:

- sdmconfig-*modelxxx*.cfg: The default configuration for the model of ISR (for example: sdmconfig-2811.cfg)
- sdm.tar

- ▶ es.tar (for SDM Express; can be deleted if only the SDM is being used)

- ▶ common.tar

- ▶ home.shtml

- ▶ home.tar

- ▶ wlanui.tar (if ISR has wireless interfaces)

This router does not have all the files necessary to run SDM:

```
cisco871#show flash
28672K bytes of processor board System flash (Intel Strataflash)

Directory of flash:/
    1  -rwx    18924888  Mar 15 2008 16:51:09 -05:00  c870-
advipservicesk9-mz.124-15.T4.bin
    2  -rwx        3179  Feb 14 2008 19:21:31 -05:00  sdmconfig-8xx.cfg
    3  -rwx        1038  Feb 14 2008 19:21:10 -05:00  home.shtml
    4  -rwx      112640  Feb 14 2008 19:21:46 -05:00  home.tar
    5  -rwx      931840  Feb 14 2008 19:23:48 -05:00  es.tar
    6  -rwx     1505280  Feb 14 2008 19:28:44 -05:00  common.tar
… output omitted …
27611136 bytes total (4065280 bytes free)
```

Using Cisco SDM Express

Because the router in the previous example doesn't have enough flash memory, not all the files necessary to run the Cisco SDM are present. If you browse to **https://**router-ip-address, the Cisco SDM Express will launch instead.

On a new router, you browse to **http://10.10.10.1** that is the default IP address of a new router. The initial configuration is completed by using the Cisco SDM Express Wizard. After the initial configuration of the router is complete, the Cisco SDM Express is no longer offered. Subsequent changes to the configuration use the full Cisco SDM.

Figure 3.4 illustrates the Cisco SDM Express.

FIGURE 3.4 Cisco SDM Express.

Launching Cisco SDM

After you have completed the router's initial configuration with the SDM Express, you can now launch the SDM for more advanced configuration chores. There are two ways to launch the SDM, as follows:

> ▶ **Cisco SDM on a PC.** Use the Cisco SDM Launcher. The default location is **Start->Programs->All Programs->Cisco Systems->Cisco SDM->Cisco SDM**.

> ▶ **Cisco SDM in Router Flash Memory.** Open up a web browser and browse using either HTTP or HTTPS to the IP address that has been configured on the router.

Figure 3.5 shows both the SDM Launcher and using a web browser to access the Cisco SDM.

If you choose to use a web browser to launch SDM, it must meet the requirements in Table 3.1.

SDM Launcher

Check this box to use HTTPS

Web browser

FIGURE 3.5 Two methods to launch the SDM.

TABLE 3.1   Browser Software Requirements

Software	Requirements
Browser	Microsoft Internet Explorer 5.5 or later.
	Netscape Navigator 7.1 or 7.2.
	Mozilla Firefox 1.0.5.
Java Software	Java Virtual Machine–enabled browsers are required.
	Java plug-in: Java 2 Standard Edition (J2SE); Java Runtime Environment (JRE) Version 1.4.2_05 or later.

NOTE

Other java-enabled web browsers are likely to work, but Cisco TAC will support those listed in Table 3.1.

Accomplishing tasks on the Cisco SDM is done through buttons along the top of the SDM home page corresponding to different modes. Figure 3.6 illustrates these buttons.

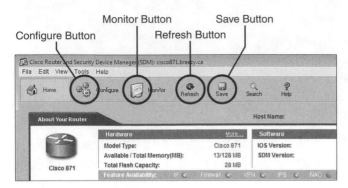

FIGURE 3.6 SDM modes.

In summary, these modes are as follows:

▶ **Configure Mode.** Provides its own task panel with buttons that represent the different configuration tasks and wizards for the novice.

▶ **Monitor Mode.** Provides its own task panel with views to the current status of the router.

▶ **Refresh.** Updates the current running configuration on the router with the Cisco SDM.

▶ **Save.** Saves the running configuration to the startup configuration on the router (CLI: **copy running-config startup-config**).

Cisco SDM Smart Wizards

When you press the **Configure** mode button, a task panel appears. Pressing some of the buttons in this task panel will launch a smart wizard. Figure 3.7 shows some of the tasks that come up when you press the **Configure** mode button.

The following smart wizards are available from the tasks shown in Figure 3.7. Note that there is more than one wizard for each task. For example, in the Virtual Private Network (VPN) Wizards, you can configure site-to-site IPsec VPNs, remote-access Ipsec and Secure Sockets Layer (SSL) VPNs, Dynamic Multipoint VPNs (DMVPNs), and others. VPNs are discussed in Chapter 7, "Virtual Private Networks with Ipsec."

▶ **Interfaces and Connections Wizards.** Configure serial and LAN interfaces.

▶ **Firewall and ACL Wizards.** Configure basic or advanced firewall.

▶ **VPN Wizards.** Configure different types of VPNs.

FIGURE 3.7 Configuration task panel.

▶ **Security Audit Wizards.** Perform a router security audit.

▶ **Routing Wizards.** Configure static routes and dynamic routing protocols.

▶ **NAT Wizards.** Configure basic and advanced NAT.

▶ **Intrusion Prevention Wizards.** Configure the IOS IPS.

▶ **Quality of Service Wizards.** Configure QoS to prioritize traffic as it flows through the router.

▶ **NAC Wizards.** Configure Network Admission Control policies.

Advanced Configuration with SDM

If you scroll down one more button in the Configuration Task Panel (shown in Figure 3.7), you see a button marked **Additional Tasks**. Figure 3.8 shows the advanced configuration tasks that come up when you click the **Additional Tasks** button.

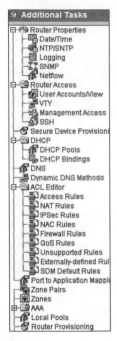

FIGURE 3.8 Additional configuration tasks.

Here are the tasks that can be completed in the Additional Tasks menu illustrated in Figure 3.8:

▶ **Router Properties.** Some of the tasks that you can complete include configuring the router hostname, domain, password, date, and time.

▶ **Router Access.** Some of the tasks that you can complete include role-based user access, management, and SSH.

▶ **DNS and DDNS.** Some of the tasks that you can complete include configuring Domain Name Service (DNS) and Dynamic DNS.

▶ **ACLs.** You can create and edit standard, extended, and named ACLs here.

▶ **AAA.** The major tasks that you can accomplish include configuring local and external authentication and authorization.

▶ **Router Provisioning.** The USB port can be configured here for secure device provisioning.

▶ **802.1X.** Port-based authentication through IEEE standard Extensible Authentication Protocol (EAP) using IEEE 802.1X can be configured here.

Cisco SDM Monitor Mode

In monitor mode, you can view important information about your router, including the firewall status, interface status, and active VPN connections. You can also view the router event log. This is illustrated in Figure 3.9.

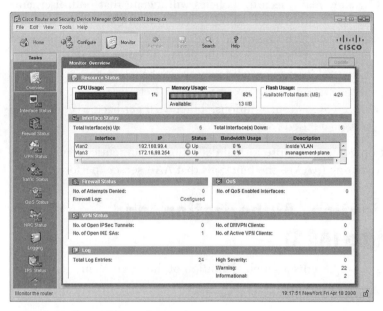

FIGURE 3.9 Cisco SDM monitor mode.

Here is a summary of the information that can be viewed in monitor mode:

- ▶ **Monitor Overview Window.** Shows router status (CPU usage, flash memory usage, and flash usage) and a list of the error log entries.

- ▶ **Interface Status.** Shows whether interfaces are up or down, bandwidth utilization, and so on.

- ▶ **Firewall Status.** Shows a log with the number of access attempts that the router's firewall has denied.

- ▶ **VPN Status.** Statistics about active VPN connections.

- ▶ **QoS Status.** Shows policy information on the interfaces.

- ▶ **NAC Status.** Shows the number of NAC sessions on the router.

- ▶ **Logging.** Contains the router event log grouped by severity level.

Configuring Local Database AAA on a Cisco Router

There are many instances where simple password-based authentication will not be adequate. Certainly many security policies will dictate that both username and password will be required if for no other reason than that the person who logs in to the router needs to be identified (authenticated) and his activities need to be tracked (accounted). What users are allowed to do (authorization) is something else we can control if we know who they are in the first place. You can't do all these things if the system simply uses passwords. Let's first define AAA, and then quickly itemize Cisco's four solutions. Then we'll get back to configuring local database AAA on a Cisco router.

The next section contains a more formal definition of authentication, authorization, and accounting (AAA)—the functions that AAA servers perform.

Authentication, Authorization, and Accounting (AAA)

The following list represents a simple definition of the three A's in AAA.

- **Authentication.** Establishes who *you* are.
- **Authorization.** Now that we know who *you* are, we can establish what *you* can do and what *you* can access.
- **Accounting.** Also, now that we know who *you* are, we can establish what *you* did, how long *you* did it, and how often *you* did it.

Note the heavy emphasis on *you*. (This isn't a comment on society, by the way!) Clearly it all starts with authentication, because authorization and accounting would not be possible without establishing an individual's identity first.

> **EXAM ALERT**
>
> Memorize the meaning of the three A's in AAA.

Two Reasons for Implementing AAA on Cisco Routers

Cisco specifies two main reasons for implementing AAA on Cisco routers. These are outlined in the following list:

▶ **Remote User Network Access.** AAA is performed in support of IPsec and SSL VPN users and dial-up users before they are permitted access to an organization's network.

▶ **Administrative Access.** AAA is performed before a user is permitted administrative access to a router (console, Telnet/SSH/HTTP, auxiliary).

Cisco's Implementation of AAA for Cisco Routers

Let's now look at how Cisco implements AAA for Cisco routers. There are two main categories of AAA implementations: local AAA (or "self-contained" AAA) and external AAA. These are outlined next:

▶ **Self-Contained AAA.** Local authentication on the router or other network access server (NAS) using a local username/password database. Essentially, the device is acting both as AAA client and server.

EXAM ALERT

The terms "Network Access Server (NAS)" and "AAA client" mean the same thing. Cisco favors the term "AAA client" mostly, but you will still see the term NAS here and there in Cisco literature.

▶ **External Authentication.** Authentication using an external Cisco Secure Access Control Server (ACS). There are three separate Cisco Secure ACS external AAA solutions:

   ▶ Cisco Secure Access Control Server for Microsoft Windows Server.

   ▶ Cisco Secure ACS Express: An entry-level RADIUS and TACACS+ AAA 1U server appliance. Supports up to 50 AAA clients, as well as 350 unique user logons in a 24-hour period.

   ▶ Cisco Secure ACS Solution Engine: An appliance that supports many more AAA clients and unique user logons than Cisco Secure ACS Express.

NOTE

Readers who are familiar with AAA will note the heavy emphasis on Cisco solutions for external AAA. In reality, Cisco is one of many vendors of external AAA solutions. The market abounds with choices, including Microsoft IAS (Internet Authentication Service), FreeRadius (Open Source), and Livingston's Steel-Belted Radius.

Recall from the "Two Reasons for Implementing AAA on Cisco Routers" section in this chapter that there are two types of access. Access *to* the *router* is called "remote administrative access". Access *through* the *router* to networks beyond the router is called "remote network access." Figure 3.10 illustrates this difference, as does Table 3.2, which defines how Cisco further categorizes these two main types of access.

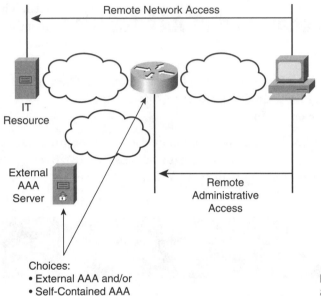

FIGURE 3.10 Types of access and AAA placement.

TABLE 3.2   Types for Router Access

Type of Access	Modes	NAS (AAA Client) Ports	Common AAA Command Elements
Remote Administrative Access	Character mode (line or EXEC mode)	tty, vty, auxiliary, and console	login, exec, and enable
Remote Network Access	Packet mode (interface mode)	async, group-async, BRI, and PRI	ppp and network

Tasks to Configure Local Database AAA on a Cisco Router

There are four basic tasks to configuring local AAA (whether character or packet mode) on a router:

> **Task 1:** Configure user accounts by creating a username/password database on the router.

Task 2: Enable AAA on the router.

Task 3: Configure AAA on the router, defining what type of remote access (administrative or network) AAA is to be performed and tying it to the username/password database.

Task 4: Verify and possibly troubleshoot the AAA configuration.

These tasks are the same whether you are using the Cisco SDM or the CLI. The following sections show the detailed steps in each task. Let's perform the first three tasks using the SDM. The equivalent CLI command appears as a separate note with each task. Judge for yourself whether you prefer to use the GUI or the CLI.

Task 1: Configuring User Accounts

Figure 3.11 illustrates the Add an Account dialog that you use to add a local user account on the router.

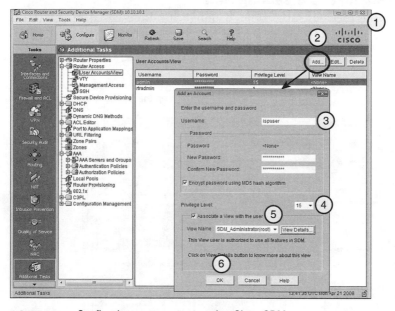

FIGURE 3.11 Configuring user accounts using Cisco SDM.

The separate steps to add a user per the dialog illustrated in Figure 3.11 are detailed next. The labels on Figure 3.11 correspond to the steps in the list:

1. Choose **Configure->Additional Tasks->Router Access->User Accounts/View** in the SDM.

2. Click **Add** to create a new user.

3. In the resulting window, enter the username and password.

4. If you haven't created views or lesser privilege levels, change this user's **Privilege Level** to **15**.

5. (Optional) If views have been defined, you can check the **Associate a View with the user** check box and select a view from the drop-down list.

6. Click **OK** and you're done.

NOTE

The SDM generates the **username ispuser privilege 15 view root secret 5 1Q0Kr$YNRAK9n/9Y1SqprgqpmYC/** CLI command.

Task 2: Enabling and Disabling AAA

As we saw in the previous subsection, "Configuring Role-Based Access to the CLI," we must enable AAA even for local AAA on the router. Figure 3.12 illustrates the SDM dialog that is used to enable or disable AAA.

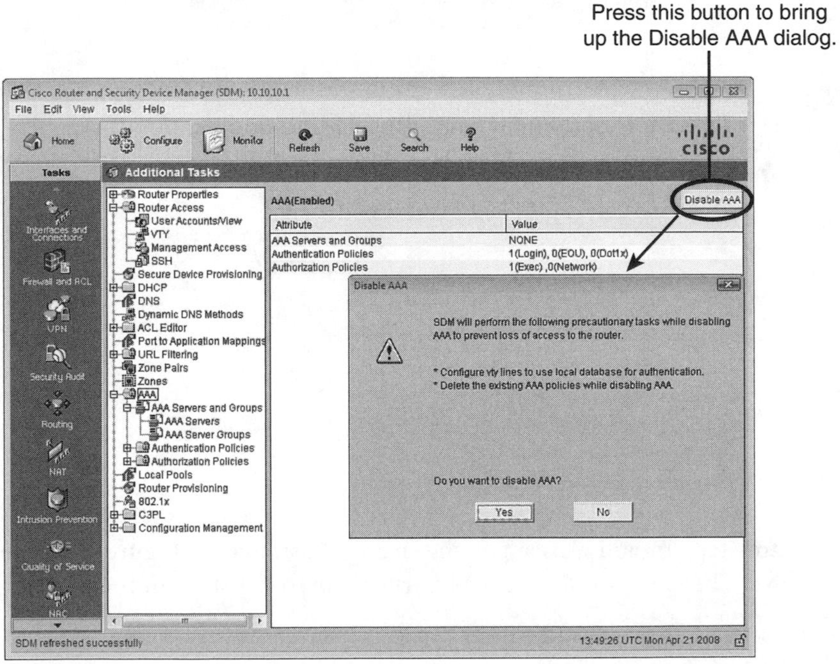

Press this button to bring up the Disable AAA dialog.

FIGURE 3.12 Enabling and disabling AAA using Cisco SDM.

Choose **Configure->Additional Tasks->AAA-> Enable** (or **Disable**). Note the status of AAA. The GUI will tell you if it is enabled or disabled. If it is enabled, the button will be labeled **Disable**. If it is disabled, the button will be labeled **Enable**. If you click the **Disable** button, you will be warned that all AAA will be disabled. Recall that enabling AAA was a prerequisite for creating privilege levels and for views.

NOTE

The SDM generates the **aaa new-model** CLI command when you click **Enable**. The CLI command **no aaa new-model** disables AAA.

Task 3: Configuring AAA on the Router

Figure 3.13 illustrates the basic steps required to configure AAA on the router.

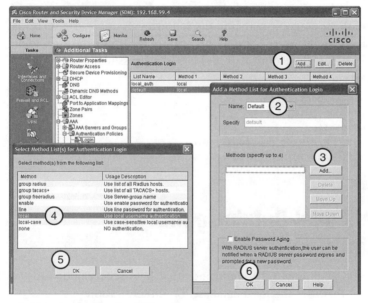

FIGURE 3.13 Configuring AAA on the router.

What follows are the basic steps required to configure AAA on the router. The labels on Figure 3.13 correspond with the numbers of the following steps:

1. Choose **Configure->Additional Tasks->AAA->Authentication Policies->Login** and click **Add**.

2. In the resulting "Add a Method List for Authentication Login" window, verify that **Default** is selected in the **Name** drop-down list.

3. Click **Add**.

4. From the "Select Method Lists(s) for Authentication Login" window, choose **local**.

5. Click the **OK** button on the **Select Method List(s) for Authentication Login** window.

6. Click the **OK** button on the **Add a Method List for Authentication Login** window to complete the task.

> **NOTE**
>
> The SDM generates the **aaa authentication login default local** CLI command.

Task 4: Verifying the AAA Configuration

The **debug aaa authentication** CLI command helps you verify that AAA authentication is functioning. Note that in the following example, the **terminal monitor** command was necessary because this capture was made during a telnet session with the router. The output represents a successful login using the "default" AAA method:

```
CiscoISR#debug aaa authentication
AAA Authentication debugging is on
CiscoISR#terminal monitor
Apr 21 14:24:56.511: AAA/BIND(00000032): Bind i/f
Apr 21 14:24:56.511: AAA/AUTHEN/LOGIN (00000032): Pick method list
'default'
```

Additional Local Database AAA CLI Commands

Let's examine some additional CLI commands that help secure and verify an AAA configuration that uses the local database for authentication.

If you want to lock out any user after 10 failed login attempts for local AAA, you can issue this command:

```
aaa local authentication attempts max-fail 10
```

To identify local AAA users whose accounts have been locked out, you type in this command:

```
show aaa local user lockout
```

Here's an example. It appears that the ISP user has been locked out. What were they doing working on the weekend anyway?

```
CiscoISR#show aaa local user lockout

    Local-user                  Lock time
    ispuser                         14:28:49 UTC Sun Apr 20 2008
```

To clear (re-instate) all local AAA users who have been locked out, type in this command:

```
clear aaa local user lockout
```

If you want to clear a single local AAA user, you can use this form of the command, where *ispuser* is the locked-out user:

```
clear aaa local user lockout ispuser
```

To display detailed statistics of all logged-in users, you type in this command:

```
show aaa user all
```

The following command displays current sessions of users who have been authenticated, authorized, or accounted by the AAA module. It shows AAA sessions with their unique IDs:

```
show aaa sessions
```

Here's an example of its output:

```
CiscoISR#show aaa sessions
Total sessions since last reload: 48
Session Id: 45
   Unique Id: 50
   User Name: admin
   IP Address: 192.168.0.114
   Idle Time: 0
   CT Call Handle: 0
CiscoISR#
```

Configuring External AAA on a Cisco Router Using Cisco Secure ACS

Recall that we have two choices for authentication in AAA:

- ▶ Self-contained AAA (local authentication)
- ▶ External authentication

This section covers authentication in the contexts of both self-contained AAA and external authentication. Authorization and accounting will not be covered. We modularize the basic tasks required to set up authentication in both self-contained AAA and external authentication, and along the way examine the strengths and weaknesses of the protocols RADIUS and TACACS+ and see how these protocols might be implemented for external authentication. Cisco strategic product for external AAA is Cisco Secure Access Control Server (ACS). We introduce Cisco Secure ACS, and leverage on its ease of use in describing and implementing an example external AAA solution for external authentication. We will also examine some CLI commands useful in verifying the configuration.

> **NOTE**
>
> There is a complete module on configuring AAA, including authentication authorization and accounting configuration in Cisco's "Securing Networks with Routers and Switches" course. Because we focus on authentication and (later) authorization and accounting in this book, there is a danger that you may equate AAA with authentication. Remember that authentication is only the first A of three A's in AAA!

There are two important differences or "deltas" in configuring external authentication as compared to local authentication:

> **Delta 1: The username/password database is on the AAA server.**
>
> In the section titled "Tasks to Configure Local Database AAA on a Cisco Router," we configured a local username/password database. With external AAA using Cisco Secure ACS, the database will be on the AAA server instead. (Although we might use the local database as a fallback should the AAA server fail or otherwise be unreachable.)

> **Delta 2: You must set up communication between the AAA client and the AAA server.**
>
> When defining the authentication method (see "Task 3: Configuring AAA on the Router"), we won't be using local AAA. This implies that we will have to set up a relationship between the AAA client (our router) and the AAA server (Cisco Secure ACS). As we will see, this involves the following AAA policy elements, as well as a way to group them:
>
> > ▸ Choosing the AAA protocol, TACACS+, or RADIUS, to communicate between the client and server.
> >
> > ▸ Configuring the IP addresses and pre-shared key of the client and the server.

Clearly Cisco Secure ACS is a deep topic all by itself. In this section, we will just scratch the surface of its features in the context of external AAA. We will also quickly compare RADIUS and TACACS+ protocols.

Why Use Cisco Secure ACS?

Cisco Secure ACS is most often used in networks where there are a large number of devices that need to be configured for AAA, and configuring local AAA on each device is thus made impractical and cumbersome. Here are some main reasons for implementing Cisco Secure ACS:

▶ Local authentication on a Cisco router does not scale well.

▶ Cisco Secure ACS can create a central user and administrative access database for an entire network (see the following note).

▶ Cisco Secure ACS works with many external databases, such as existing Active Directory, LDAP, and others.

> **NOTE**
>
> Perhaps the principle of "Separation of Services" is a guideline that your organization has formulated based on the material in Chapter 2, "Building a Secure Network Using Security Controls."
>
> Also, if your organization already has database repositories such as Active Directory, LDAP, or NDS, for example, Cisco Secure ACS can work with them. Why reinvent the wheel?

Cisco Secure ACS Features

These are the features shared by all versions of Cisco Secure ACS:

▶ Web-based GUI

▶ Supports LDAP, Active Directory, Novell Directory Services (NDS), and ODBC databases

▶ Rich accounting and user reporting features

▶ Supports TACACS+ and RADIUS

▶ Tightly integrated with Cisco IOS router and Cisco VPN solutions

▶ Supports third-party OTPs

▶ Access restrictions through dynamic quotas

Figure 3.14 illustrates the home page for Cisco Secure ACS.

FIGURE 3.14 Cisco Secure ACS home page.

Cisco Secure ACS for Windows Installation Requirements

Unlike the Cisco Secure ACS Solution Engine and the Cisco Secure ACS Express, which are appliances, Cisco Secure ACS for Windows must be installed as an application on top of an existing Windows server.

The Cisco Secure ACS for Windows software requirements are as follows:

▶ Windows 2000 Server with Service Pack 4

▶ Windows 2000 Advanced Servers with Service Pack 4

▶ Windows Server 2003 Standard Edition

▶ Windows Server 2003 Enterprise Edition

The Cisco Secure ACS for Windows hardware requirements are as follows:

▶ Pentium IV processor 1.8GHz or faster

▶ 1GB of RAM

▶ Minimum 500MB to 1GB free disk space (more required if the database is on the same computer)

▶ Minimum graphics resolution of 256 colors at 800x600 pixels

Cisco Secure ACS Solution Engine and Cisco Secure ACS Express 5.0 Comparison

One immediate advantage of these devices is that the software comes pre-installed on a 1U, rack-mountable server form factor with a security-hardened Windows Server pre-installed. Table 3.3 compares the specifications and capabilities of these devices.

TABLE 3.3 Rack-Mount ACS Solutions Comparison Matrix

	Cisco Secure ACS Solution Engine	Cisco Secure ACS Express
Processor	Intel Pentium 4, 800MHz FSB, 2MB cache	Intel 352 Celeron D
RAM	1GB	1GB
Optical Drive	CD/DVD combo	CD/DVD combo
Ports	1 x RS-232, 3 x USB 2.0	1 x RS-232, 3 x USB 2.0
Hard Drive	80GB SATA	250GB, non-SATA
Number of Users	over 350	up to 350
NICs	2 x 10/100/1000 Ethernet	2 x 10/100/1000 Ethernet

TACACS+ or RADIUS?

Whether you use Terminal Access Control Access Control Server Plus (TACACS+) or Remote Dial-in User Services (RADIUS) in your AAA implementation depends very much on what you need to accomplish. For example, the business needs of a large ISP might dictate that they choose the RADIUS protocol for their AAA solution because of the detailed accounting that is needed for billing dial-up and DSL users. On the other hand, if yours is an enterprise that has many groups of users accessing your core network devices, a centralized means to deploy granular authorization policies on a per-user or per-group basis may be required. In that case, TACACS+ would be a good solution. Table 3.4 represents a summary of some of the important differences between the two protocols.

TABLE 3.4 TACACS+ vs. RADIUS Comparison

	TACACS+	RADIUS
Authentication and Authorization Processing	Separates authentication and authorization.	Combines authentication and authorization.
Transport	TCP port 49.	Authentication: UDP ports 1645 or 1812. Accounting: UDP ports 1646 or 1813 (see note).

(continues)

TABLE 3.4   TACACS+ vs. RADIUS Comparison   *Continued*

	TACACS+	RADIUS
Encryption	Encrypts all communication.	Password encrypted.
Origin / Future	Developed from (but not compatible with) TACACS and XTACACS.	Developed by Livingston. DIAMETER is the planned replacement.
Where Used	Everywhere except when detailed accounting is required, especially for command authorization.	Remote access (dial-up, DSL, VPNs). IEEE 802.1X EAP. SIP. Anywhere that detailed accounting is required (for example: ISP).
Closed or Open Source	Mostly Cisco.	Open Source / RFC.
CHAP	Bidirectional.	Unidirectional.
Customization	Yes. For example, command authorization can be configured at user or group level.	No. No option for command authorization on a per-user or per-group level.
Protocol Support	Yes, multi-protocol.	Yes, but no ARA or NetBEUI.
Per-user IP ACLs	No.	Yes.

NOTE

The Cisco default port numbers for RADIUS are UDP port 1645 for authentication / authorization (remember, these processes are combined in RADIUS; see Table 3.4) and UDP Port 1646 for accounting. This becomes important when working in a mixed-vendor environment where the non-Cisco NAS or AAA server may be using a different port number. This is a very common source of misconfiguration.

Prerequisites for Cisco Secure ACS

One of the main tasks in setting up Cisco Secure ACS is establishing communication between the AAA client(s) and the AAA server, Cisco Secure ACS. You must ensure that all the IP addresses and port numbers that are required to set up the TACACS+ or RADIUS link between the AAA devices are not blocked by other devices. You are not always lucky enough to have the devices physically co-located on the same IP subnet. Many security policies dictate that the AAA server be in a separate DMZ or other protected zone that implies that there may well be a firewall on the communication path between the AAA devices. (Firewalls are discussed in Chapter 5, "Using Cisco IOS Firewalls to Implement a Network Security Policy.") There are some other prerequisites for Cisco Secure ACS of which you should be aware, as follows:

▶ Cisco IOS Release 11.2 or later must be installed on the Cisco AAA clients.

▶ Non-IOS Cisco devices (or non-Cisco devices) must be configurable for standards-compliant RADIUS and/or TACACS+.

▶ A supported web browser must be installed on the Cisco ACS server (see the following note).

NOTE

If you are planning to administer Cisco Secure ACS right on the server where it is installed, you can use a supported web browser to browse to the loopback IP address of the device at http://127.0.0.1:2002. Alternatively, you may administer ACS remotely by browsing to **http://***IP-address-of-ACS***:2002** in a supported web browser. You will then be prompted to login with the username and password of an administrator. After you login on the ACS home page, the browser will be automatically redirected to another port number besides 2002. You will not be prompted for login credentials if you administer ACS right on the server, but you will be prompted for login credentials if you browse to the ACS home page from a remote workstation. The ability to administer ACS remotely would be useful if your security policy dictates that the AAA server can only be administered remotely. You should consider deploying ACS in a separate management VLAN.

Three Main Tasks for Setting Up External AAA

We're going to take a different approach from most texts to understanding how Cisco Secure ACS works. We start in a very task-oriented fashion. First, we focus on getting a working external AAA set up, and then we look at some of the features of Cisco Secure ACS that have not yet been examined, followed by some verification and debugging commands.

On Cisco Secure ACS, the starting point for setup will always be the navigation bar on the left side of the Cisco Secure ACS browser window. See Figure 3.15 for a screenshot. This screenshot was obtained by browsing to the Cisco Secure ACS home page using a web browser right on the server. Recall that when administering the ACS right on the hosting server, you browse to the local loopback IP address of the server.

FIGURE 3.15 The navigation bar in Cisco Secure ACS.

The three main tasks for setting up external AAA are the following:

Task 1: Configure the AAA network (client and server).

Task 2: Set up users (server).

Task 3: Identify traffic to which AAA will be applied (client). This has three subtasks:

- ▶ Configuring authentication
- ▶ Configuring authorization
- ▶ Configuring accounting

Figure 3.16 shows where these three tasks occur The numbered labels in the figure match up with the task list. These general tasks would be followed regardless of the external AAA solution. Of course, we will model our solution after Cisco Secure ACS.

This section now goes on to discuss each of these tasks in more detail.

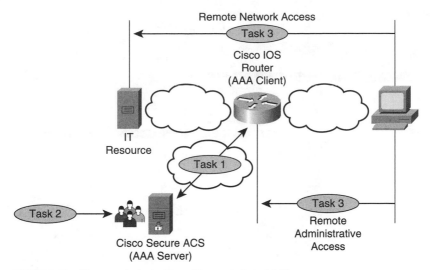

FIGURE 3.16 Three main tasks for setting up external AAA.

Task 1: Configuring the AAA Network (Client and Server)

Setting up the AAA network essentially consists of setting up a relationship between two peers, the AAA client and the AAA server. The server peers on the client and the client peers on the server. They perform mutual authentication using a pre-shared key and using the same protocol (RADIUS or TACACS+) to exchange AAA information. These main elements must be completed on both the AAA client and the AAA server:

▶ Set up the protocol (RADIUS or TACACS+).

▶ Specify the vendor of server (because port numbers used vary).

▶ Specify the IP address of the peer.

▶ Specify the pre-shared key (pre-shared because both client and server use the same key).

We perform these tasks first on the Cisco Secure ACS (the AAA server) and then on the IOS router (the AAA client).

Adding an AAA Client in Cisco Secure ACS

Figure 3.17 illustrates the fields that need to be filled out in adding an AAA client in Cisco Secure ACS.

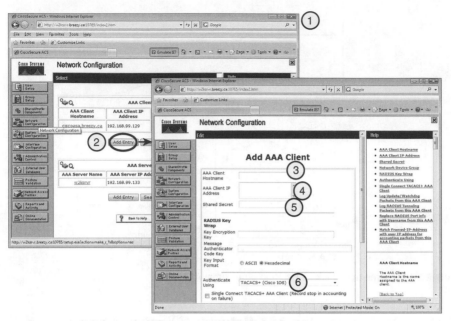

FIGURE 3.17 Adding an AAA client in Cisco Secure ACS.

The steps to add a Cisco IOS router as an AAA client in Cisco Secure ACS are as follows:

1. Click the **Network Configuration** button on the navigation bar. The Network Configuration page appears.

2. Click **Add Entry** in the AAA Clients section.

3. Enter the client hostname in the **AAA Client Hostname** field. This is the name of the router that will be the AAA client from Cisco Secure ACS's perspective.

> **NOTE**
>
> Here's a tip. You should take care when choosing the name for the AAA client in the AAA Client hostname field referenced in Figure 3.17. The hostname is actually a unique connection name and should reflect the hostname of the router and the protocol name so that we can use both TACACS+ and RADIUS between the ACS and the router (that is, "hostname-tacacs" and "hostname-radius").

4. Enter the router's IP address in the **AAA Client IP Address** field.

5. Enter the pre-shared secret key in the **Shared Secret** field (remember this value, as you will need it when you set up the router for AAA).

6. Choose the correct AAA protocol in the **Authenticate Using** drop-down list.

7. Complete any other parameters as required.

8. Click **Submit** and **Apply**.

Adding an AAA Server on the Cisco IOS Router

Now that we have configured the AAA client information on the AAA server, we can perform essentially the same steps, but now on the AAA client. Figure 3.18 illustrates the **Add AAA Server** dialog in Cisco SDM.

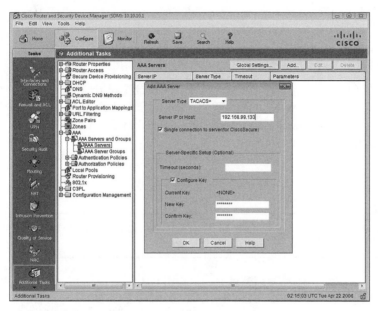

FIGURE 3.18 Adding a TACACS+ server to Cisco IOS router.

The following shows how to use SDM to add a TACACS+ AAA server to a Cisco IOS router (the CLI appears in a note at the end):

1. Open up the SDM, and choose **Configure->Additional Tasks->AAA->AAA Servers and Groups->AAA Servers**.

2. Click **Add** in the AAA Servers pane. The Add Server window appears. From the **Server Type** drop-down list, choose **TACACS+**.

3. Enter the IP address or hostname of the Cisco Secure ACS in the **Server IP or Host** field.

NOTE

Put in the hostname only if the router has been configured for Domain Name Service (DNS) lookups.

4. (Optional) You can choose to maintain a persistent connection to the server rather than opening and closing connections with every transaction. If this is what you want, check the **Single Connection to Server (for CiscoSecure)** check box. This is more efficient but only supported on Cisco Secure ACS version 1.0.1 or higher.

5. (Optional) If you want to set a timeout value specific to this server, enter a value in the **Timeout (seconds)** field in the Server-Specific Setup section. Otherwise, the router will use the value configured in the AAA Servers Global Settings window.

6. (Optional) If you want to set a pre-shared key specific to this server, enter a value in the **New Key** field in the Server-Specific Setup section. Otherwise, the router will use the value configured in the AAA Servers Global Settings window.

7. Click **OK**.

NOTE

The CLI command generated by the SDM will be of the form **tacacs-server host 192.168.99.133 key cisco123**.

Task 2: Setting Up Users in Cisco Secure ACS (Server)

The users are set up on Cisco Secure ACS, as illustrated in Figure 3.19.

Open up Cisco Secure ACS and follow these steps to set up users. The labels on Figure 3.19 correspond with the step numbers:

1. In the navigation bar, click **User Setup**.

2. To create a new user, simply enter a username in the **User** field and click **Add/Edit**. (If this user already exists, you will be editing that user.)

3. Enter data in the fields to define the user account in the Edit pane. You will probably want to set the user's password, as well as TACACS+ enable control, TACACS+ enable password, and TACACS+ shell authorized command. (Recall that command authorization is one of the features of TACACS+.)

4. Click **Submit**.

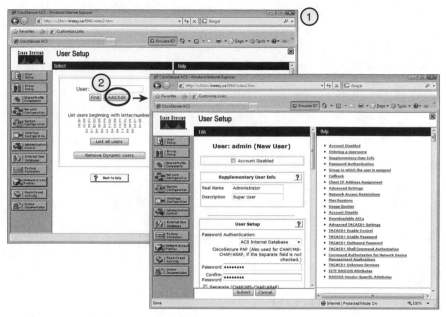

FIGURE 3.19   User setup in Cisco Secure ACS.

> **NOTE**
>
> What you see in the Edit pane in User Setup will depend on the interface configuration. "Interface" is this context means the user's interface to ACS. The interface is set up when ACS is installed, but if you want to modify it, you may customize what fields are visible by choosing **Interface Configuration->User Data Configuration** from the navigation bar.

Task 3: Identifying Traffic to Which AAA Will Be Applied (Client)

The identification of which traffic must have AAA service applied to it is done on the AAA client, which is the IOS router in our example. This task has three different elements to it, depending on which of the 3 A's in AAA we want to apply to the traffic. Recall that we must perform authentication at a minimum because authorization and accounting depend on authentication: To repeat, here are the subtasks that we examine separately and in order in the subsequent sections:

▶ Configuring authentication

▶ Configuring authorization

▶ Configuring accounting

Once the network is set up as in Task 1, this group of AAA server settings is modular and can be used for a number of purposes. For example, once you have set up a TACACS+ server for authentication, it could be used for both remote administrative access and remote network access purposes.

Creating an AAA Login Authentication Policy on the AAA Client

Figure 3.20 illustrates the steps that are required to create an AAA login authentication policy on the AAA client.

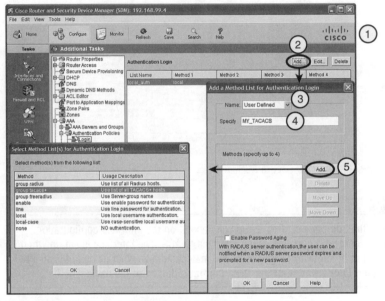

FIGURE 3.20 Adding a login authentication method in Cisco SDM.

Follow these steps to create an AAA login authentication policy using Cisco SDM on the IOS router, our AAA client:

1. Open up the Cisco SDM home page and choose **Configure->Additional Tasks->AAA->Authentication Policies->Login**.

2. Click **Add** from the Authentication Login pane.

3. From the **Name** drop-down list, choose **User Defined** to create a new authentication method.

4. In the **Specify** field, enter the authentication login method list name; MY_TACACS, for example.

5. To define the methods that this policy uses, click **Add**. The Select Method List(s) for Authentication Login window appears.

6. From the method list, choose **group tacacs+**.

7. To add group tacacs+ to the method list, click **OK**. This will return you to the Add a Method List for Authentication Login window. The just-added method will now appear in this list.

8. To add a backup method for this policy, click **Add**. The Select Method List(s) for Authentication Login window appears.

9. This time, choose **enable** from the method list. This will cause the enable password to be used as the backup login authentication method.

10. To add enable to the method list, click **OK**. This will return you to the Add a Method List of Authentication Login window. Both group tacacs+ and enable should show up in the window. To make the enable password a back up to the group tacacs+ authentication method, make sure it appears below the group tacacs+ authentication method.

11. To add the authentication login method list, click **OK**.

NOTE

The CLI command that is generated by the Cisco SDM is **aaa authentication login MY_TACACS group tacacs+ enable**.

Applying the Authentication Method

The authentication login method list, like any policy, has no effect by itself once created. It must be applied to an entity on the device. This is a handy rule of thumb on Cisco devices. You create a policy; then you have to apply it somewhere. Keeping in mind that we have set up a *login* authentication method (and using your intuition), this authentication method most likely needs to be applied to one of the line interfaces on the router. In this scenario, we apply the authentication method MY_TACACS, to the five default vty lines on the router.

The Cisco SDM dialog to apply the authentication method *MY_TACACS* to the vtys is illustrated in Figure 3.21.

To apply the authentication method to the vtys using the SDM, follow these steps:

1. Choose **Configure->Additional Tasks->Router Access->VTY->Edit**.

2. In the Edit VTY Lines window, choose the **MY_TACACS** login authentication method from the **Authentication Policy** drop-down list.

3. Click **OK** to deliver the commands to the router.

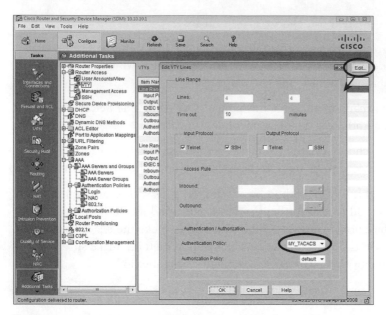

FIGURE 3.21 Applying the authentication method to the vtys using the Cisco SDM.

The CLI command to apply the authentication policy to the vtys would look like this:

```
CiscoISR#configure terminal
CiscoISR(config)#line vty 0 4
CiscoISR(config-line)#login authentication MY_TACACS
```

Now when administrators log in to the Cisco IOS router via the vtys, they will be prompted for a username and password. These credentials will be validated using the TACACS+ protocol against the user database on the Cisco Secure ACS. It should be noted that this will not affect SDM login, only access via Telnet or SSH.

Thus, we have completed the tasks to perform the first A in AAA, authentication. Let's turn our attention to the second A in AAA, authorization. Leveraging on our TACACS+ server, we will:

▶ First, create and apply an authorization policy for exec (character mode).

▶ Second, create and apply an authorization policy for network (packet mode).

Creating and Applying an AAA Exec Authorization Policy

The method to create an exec authorization policy is illustrated in Figure 3.22.

NOTE

The following steps assume that we have already configured an authorization policy on the Cisco Secure ACS (we have!). If you create and apply an AAA exec authorization policy before you have configured one on the authorization server, you will lock yourself out of the router. This is very embarrassing.

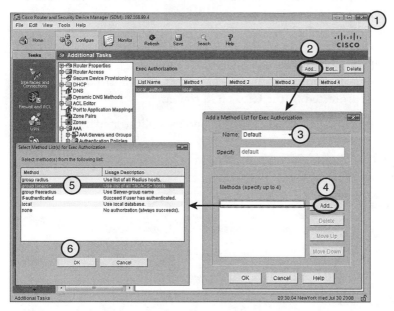

FIGURE 3.22 Creating and applying an AAA exec authorization policy.

Using the Cisco SDM and starting at the home page, follow these steps to create and apply the default authorization method list for exec (character mode) access. Figure 3.22 is labeled to correspond to the numbers in the following list of steps:

1. Choose **Configure->Additional Tasks->AAA->Authorization Polices->Exec**.

2. Click **Add** in the Exec Authorization pane.

3. Choose **Default** from the **Name** drop-down list in the Add a Method List for Exec Authorization window.

4. To define the methods that this policy uses, click **Add**.

5. Choose **group tacacs+** from the method list in the Select Method List(s) for Exec Authorization window.

6. Click **OK** on the next two windows in succession to return to the Exec Authorization pane.

NOTE

The Cisco SDM will generate this CLI command:

```
aaa authorization exec default group tacacs+
```

Now, when administrators access the CLI, they will only be allowed to execute the commands they are authorized to use as defined in the user's authorization policy on the Cisco Secure ACS.

Creating and Applying an AAA Network Authorization Policy

Let's now turn our attention to defining what a user is authorized to do on the network segment protected by the Cisco IOS router.

The method to create a network authorization policy is illustrated in Figure 3.23.

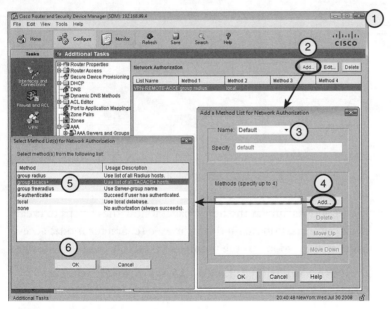

FIGURE 3.23 Creating and applying an AAA network authorization policy.

Starting on the Cisco SDM home page, complete the following steps to configure the default authorization method list for network (packet mode) access. Figure 3.23 has labels corresponding to the numbers of the following steps:

1. Choose **Configure->Additional Tasks->AAA Authorization Policies->Network**.

2. Click **Add** in the Network Authorization pane.

3. Choose **Default** from the **Name** drop-down list in the Add a Method List for Network Authorization window.

4. To define the methods that this policy uses, click **Add**.

5. Choose **group tacacs+** from the method list in the Select Method List(s) for Network Authorization window.

6. Click **OK** on the next two windows in succession to return to the Network Authorization pane.

NOTE

The Cisco SDM will generate this CLI command:

```
aaa authorization network default group tacacs+
```

AAA Accounting Configuration

When properly configured, Cisco Secure ACS acts as a central repository of tracked events as they occur on the network. For example, our comprehensive network security policy might stipulate that all failed login attempts to (and through) the routers are to be tracked, with detailed information about the attempt such as user credentials, time of day, and date. Without keeping track of this information, we might not be able to provide data to aid in a forensic investigation should our network be compromised or otherwise attacked.

As with authentication and authorization, you must first create a method list (the policy), and then apply it to the right entity. As we have seen, method lists can be multi-purpose, so a method list may support all three As in AAA.

AAA involves six different types of accounting, as follows:

▶ **Network.** Runs accounting for all network-related service requests, including Serial Line Internet Protocol (SLIP), PPP, PPP Network Control Protocols (NCPs), and AppleTalk Remote Access Protocol (ARAP).

▶ **Connection.** Provides information about all outbound connections made from the network access server, such as Telnet.

▶ **Exec.** Runs accounting for the EXEC shell session.

▶ **System.** Performs accounting for all system-level events not associated with users, such as reloads.

▶ **Commands.** Runs accounting for all commands at the specified privilege level.

▶ **Resource.** Performs accounting for resource use by remote users of the system. (The command syntax for setting resource accounting is different than the other items listed.)

These different types of accounting are reflected in the command syntax of the **aaa accounting** command:

```
aaa accounting { system ¦ network ¦ exec ¦ connection ¦ commands level }
{default ¦ list-name} {start-stop ¦ stop-only ¦ none} [method1 [method2]]
```

Use the following form of the command to perform accounting for system resource use by remote users:

```
aaa accounting resource method-list start-stop [broadcast] group groupname
```

To set up accounting using the CLI, follow these basic steps (with examples):

1. Create an accounting method list and enable accounting.

```
CiscoISR(config)#aaa accounting connection default start-stop group
tacacs+
```

2. Enter line configuration mode or interface configuration mode for the lines or interface to which the accounting method list will be applied.

```
CiscoISR(config)#line vty 0 4
```

3. Apply the account method list to the line(s) or interface(s).

```
CiscoISR(config-line)#accounting connection default
```

Troubleshooting/Debugging Local AAA, RADIUS, and TACACS+

Here are a handful of useful commands for troubleshooting and debugging local AAA, RADIUS, and TACACS+.

For a high-level view of login activity, use the following CLI command:

```
debug aaa authentication
```

Here is an example of the output of the **debug aaa authentication** command. The highlighted output indicates that someone logged on to this ISR and that the authentication method used was *local_auth*:

```
ciscoISR#debug aaa authentication
AAA Authentication debugging is on
443521: Aug  7 08:56:19.498 NewYork: AAA/BIND(000032C8): Bind i/f
443522: Aug  7 08:56:20.110 NewYork: AAA/BIND(000032C9): Bind i/f
443523: Aug  7 08:56:22.117 NewYork: AAA/BIND(000032CA): Bind i/f
443524: Aug  7 08:56:24.628 NewYork: AAA/BIND(000032CB): Bind i/f
443525: Aug  7 08:56:24.628 NewYork: AAA/AUTHEN/LOGIN (000032CB): Pick
method list 'local_auth'
```

For more detailed debugging of TACACS+ in particular, use the following CLI command:

```
debug tacacs
```

For even more detailed information about the TACACS+ helper process, you can use the following CLI command. Be careful with its use, because it generates copious amounts of output.

```
debug tacacs event
```

For more detailed debugging of RADIUS in particular, use the following CLI command:

```
debug radius
```

For even more detailed information about the RADIUS helper process, you can use the following CLI command. Be careful with its use, because it generates copious amounts of output:

```
debug radius event
```

AAA Configuration Snapshot

Here is a snapshot of a partial configuration with the commands in Tasks 1, 2, and 3 for setting up external AAA and including the preceding AAA accounting configuration. If the commands don't make sense, review them in the preceding sections:

```
aaa new-model
!
aaa authentication login MY_TACACS tacacs+ local
aaa authorization exec tacacs+
aaa authorization network tacacs+
aaa accounting connection default start-stop group tacacs+
!
tacacs-server host 192.168.99.133
tacacs-server key cisco123
!
line vty 0 4
 login authentication MY_TACACS
 accounting connection default
```

Exam Prep Questions

1. Match the following deployment scenarios for a Cisco IOS router with the correct description:

   1. Single Perimeter: ___

   2. Two Perimeters: ___

   3. Screen Subnet: ___

   Descriptions:

   A. The router establishes the trusted network boundary at the Internet and protects a single LAN.

   B. A DMZ is established on a firewall that, in turn, is deployed inside the Cisco IOS router.

   C. A firewall establishes a second perimeter behind the router.

2. Which of the following is not a feature of Cisco Integrated Services routers? (Choose all that apply.)

   ○ A. USB Port (most models)

   ○ B. Unified Network Services

   ○ C. Integrated PoE VoIP port

   ○ D. Integrated Security

   ○ E. Firewire port

3. True or false. By default, Cisco router passwords must contain at least 10 characters.

4. Which statement about the service password-encryption command is correct?

   ○ A. It encrypts all passwords in the router's configuration file with an AES (Advanced Encryption Standard) 256-bit level encryption.

   ○ B. With the exception of the hashed enable secret, all passwords on the router are encrypted.

   ○ C. All passwords on the router are encrypted.

   ○ D. It has no effect unless the service password secret-encrypt command is also issued.

   ○ E. None of the above.

5. You have entered the following commands to create a view called ISP:

```
CiscoISR(config)parser view ISP
CiscoISR(config-view)#secret 0 hardtoguess
```

Which one of the following commands enable users of this view to access the configure mode from a terminal?

○ **A.** commands configure include all terminal

○ **B.** commands exec include all configure

○ **C.** commands include exec configure

○ **D.** commands exec include configure terminal

○ **E.** None of the above.

6. Referring to the following list, select the five items that comprise the five basic services that SDM manages:

○ **A.** Wireless

○ **B.** Intrusion Protection Services (IPS)

○ **C.** Routing

○ **D.** Switching

○ **E.** Security

○ **F.** Interfaces

○ **G.** AAA

○ **H.** QoS

7. What (in the right order) does AAA stand for?

○ **A.** Access, accountability, administration

○ **B.** Administration, access, accounting

○ **C.** Accounting, access, administration

○ **D.** Authentication, authorization, accounting

○ **E.** Authorization, accounting, administration

○ **F.** None of the above.

8. Which of the following is true about the Cisco Secure ACS Solution Engine? (Choose all that are correct.)

   ○ **A.** Must be installed on an existing installation of Windows Server.

   ○ **B.** Must be installed on an existing installation of Windows Server or Sun Solaris.

   ○ **C.** An appliance-based solution that supports up to 50 AAA clients, as well as 350 unique user logons in a 24-hour period.

   ○ **D.** An appliance-based solution.

   ○ **E.** TACACS+ only

   ○ **F.** None of the above.

9. Fill in the blanks with the correct words from the list:

   When designing an AAA solution, remote administrative access is also known as _____ mode. Another name for remote network access is _____ mode.

   ○ **A.** Packet, character

   ○ **B.** Character, network

   ○ **C.** Network, character

   ○ **D.** Character, packet

   ○ **E.** Packet, network

10. What command will display a list of all local AAA users who have been locked out?

    ○ **A.** show aaa local user lockout

    ○ **B.** show aaa user all

    ○ **C.** show aaa sessions

    ○ **D.** show aaa local lockout

    ○ **E.** None of the above.

11. Which protocols are supported in the AAA dialog between a Cisco IOS router and Cisco Secure ACS? (Choose all that apply.)

    ○ **A.** LDAP

    ○ **B.** Active Directory

    ○ **C.** OBDC

    ○ **D.** RADIUS

    ○ **E.** TACACS+

    ○ **F.** Kerberos

12. Which of the following statements is most correct concerning RADIUS and TACACS+?

   ○ **A.** RADIUS has rich accounting and TACACS+ is capable of customizable user-level policies such as command authorization.

   ○ **B.** RADIUS encrypts the whole communication between the AAA client and server, whereas TACACS+ only encrypts the password.

   ○ **C.** RADIUS uses UDP for transport and TACACS+ uses TCP.

   ○ **D.** RADIUS is a proprietary standard, whereas TACACS+ is Open Source.

   ○ **E.** RADIUS uses UDP ports 1645 and 1646 exclusively

13. Which of the following are not included in the three main task areas in setting up for external AAA? (Choose all that apply.)

   ○ **A.** Configure the AAA network.

   ○ **B.** Install AAA supplicant software on IP hosts that will authenticate to the IOS router.

   ○ **C.** Identify traffic to which AAA is applied.

   ○ **D.** Set up users.

   ○ **E.** Install Cisco Secure ACS Solution Engine module on the Cisco IOS router.

14. Select the one answer with the correct two terms to fill in the following blanks.

   There are two distinct types of AAA authorization policies:

   ▶_____ policies that define access rules to the router.

   ▶_____ policies that define access rules *through* the router.

   Choices:

   ○ **A.** Network, Exec

   ○ **B.** Packet, Character

   ○ **C.** Character, Packet

   ○ **D.** Exec, Network

   ○ **E.** Administrative, User

Answers to Exam Prep Questions

1. 1—A; 2—C; 3—B.

2. The answers are C and E. Cisco ISRs do not contain integrated Power over Ethernet (PoE) ports or VoIP ports or Firewire ports. Some of the features are available as option cards on modular ISRs.

3. False. It is also a trick question! Cisco recommends that passwords should be at least 10 characters in length, but there is no default rule. Passwords can be blank. That is why this chapter stresses basics such as best practices for passwords.

4. Answer B is correct. Answer D is a trick because that command doesn't exist and answer A is just plain wrong. Answer C is tricky too because we learn in this chapter that passwords on the router are not encrypted unless we use the service password-encryption command.

5. The correct answer is B. This is a bit of a trick question because answer B enables configuration from not only the terminal but also from other sources. The syntax of the other (but wrong) answers is all mixed up.

6. Choices A, C, D, E, and H are correct. The other items can be configured in the SDM, but they are not considered one of the five basic services that the SDM manages.

7. The correct answer is D.

8. The correct answer is D. Answer C is meant to confuse because Cisco Secure ACS Express is being described and is also an appliance-based solution. Answers A, B, and E are simply wrong.

9. The correct answer is D.

10. Answer A is the correct answer. Answer B is the command that displays detailed statistics of all logged in users. Answer C is used to display current sessions of users who have been authenticated, authorized, or accounted by the AAA module. The command in answer D doesn't exist.

11. This is a trick question. The question is not which protocols does Cisco Secure ACS work with to authenticate to an external database. If that was the question, you could choose everything in the list. Answers D and E are correct because only RADIUS and TACACS+ are choices for protocols that work between the AAA client (the Cisco IOS router) and the AAA server (Cisco Secure ACS).

12. Answers A and C are correct. Answer B is backwards. It's TACACS+ that encrypts the whole communication, whereas RADIUS encrypts only the password. Answer D is incorrect but for a tricky reason. Although RADIUS is open source, TACACS+ isn't quite a proprietary standard because Cisco has published it as an RFC (Request for Comment), part of the IETF standards track. Answer E is incorrect because RADIUS can use either ports 1645 and 1646 or ports 1812 and 1813 for authentication/authorization and accounting, respectively.

13. Answers B and E are correct. Answer B is correct because you do not need special software on an IP host in order to enable AAA for the network. Answer E is correct because the Cisco Secure ACS Solution Engine is an appliance that comprises a self-contained AAA server solution. It is not an add-on module for a router, and the router is the AAA client in this scenario anyway.

14. Answer D is correct. The use of the terms "packet" and "character" are deliberately misleading because these refer to types of access in general (see Figure 3.10), but not specific types of AAA authorization policies. Answer E is simply wrong but sounds like it might be right to someone who hasn't read the Exam Cram.

CHAPTER FOUR

Implementing Secure Management and Hardening the Router

Terms You'll Need to Understand:

✓ Syslog Protocol (syslog)

✓ Out-of-band (OOB)

✓ In-band

✓ Simple Network Management Protocol (SNMP)

✓ Secure Shell (SSH) daemon

✓ Network Time Protocol (NTP)

✓ Simple Network Time Protocol (SNTP)

✓ Gratuitous Address Resolution Protocol (GARP)

✓ Proxy Address Resolution Protocol (ARP)

✓ AutoSecure

Exam Topics Covered in This Chapter:

✓ Secure Cisco routers using the SDM Security Audit feature

✓ Use the One-Step Lockdown feature in SDM to secure a Cisco router

✓ Secure the Cisco IOS image and configuration file

✓ Use CLI and SDM to configure SSH on Cisco routers to enable secured management access

✓ Use CLI and SDM to configure Cisco routers to send Syslog messages to a Syslog server

---

NOTE

These exam topics are from cisco.com. Check there periodically for the latest exam topics and info.

Secure management and reporting is an integral part to a comprehensive security policy. This chapter outlines some methods to protect the confidentiality of remote sessions to the router, either by encrypting the communication or ensuring that these remote administrative sessions do not cross the cables of a hostile network. In security terms, we look at methods to separate the *data plane* from the *management plane*. We also look at ways to implement reporting in such a way as to guarantee the integrity and confidentiality of the events logged.

In the last chapter, Chapter 3, "Security at the Network Perimeter," we took a large step toward securing the login system on the IOS router from both access and DoS attacks. We assumed that because the router was a perimeter device and, therefore, the first device that an attacker would see as they tried to crack the network, that security would start there. We didn't finish the tasks necessary to completely harden the router from attack, choosing to defer these steps until now. Using an analogy, if our router is a knight that we deploy on the battlements of a fortress to ward against attack, doesn't it make sense that we equip him with armor so he can protect himself as well? If he is felled by the first arrow that an attacker fires at him, we should rethink our security architecture. To that end, we will look at interactive and automated ways to both audit the router for security vulnerabilities and, more importantly, fix them based on best practices and Cisco's recommendations.

Planning for Secure Management and Reporting

Secure management and reporting is too often applied on top of a secure architecture as an afterthought rather than being designed into the solution from the beginning. Some hard questions need to be asked early on in the design because they bear on the implemented secure architecture. These questions are typically asked during the *Initiation* phase and answered during the *Acquisition and Development* phase of the Cisco Secure Network Life Cycle first introduced in Chapter 2, "Building a Secure Network Using Security Controls." In general, what types of activity need to be logged and what protocols and devices are required to perform these functions will determine the technology deployed during the *Implementation* phase of the Cisco Secure Network Life Cycle.

EXAM ALERT

The context of this discussion, as well as others throughout this book, is determined by the Cisco Secure Network Life Cycle. The steps of the lifecycle are listed next with the secure management and reporting topics to be discussed (in parentheses beside it):

Initiation (What to log? How to log?).

Acquisition and Development (Guidelines for secure management and reporting).

Implementation (Cisco solutions for secure management and reporting).

Operations and Maintenance.

Disposition.

Use the Cisco Secure Network Life Cycle as a framework for memorizing this information for the exam. For example, syslog as a management protocol is presented as a possible answer to the question, "How to log?" (Initiation). Recommendations are then made as to how to use syslog (Acquisition and Development), followed by outlining Cisco products that use syslog as a centerpiece for secure management and reporting (Implementation).

Planning for secure management and reporting is based on guidelines set out by the comprehensive security policy. Several questions need to be answered before secure management and reporting can be integrated into the network security architecture design and then configured. The questions that need to be answered can be grouped into two broad categories, as follows:

▶ "What to log (or report)?" questions.

▶ "How to log (or report)?" questions.

Let's break this down a bit further.

What to Log

Issues that bear heavily on the first question would be whether the data collected might be used for forensic purposes in investigating a possible network compromise or possibly for criminal prosecution. Rules of evidence, chain of custody, timestamps on log entries, and so on would need to be laid out. The answers to these questions will lead to administrative controls. Some helpful questions include the following:

▶ What are the most critical events to log?

▶ What are the most important logs?

▶ What log data may be required for forensic investigation and prosecution?

The answers to these questions are specific to the organization and thus vary. For example, an organization that is planning to prosecute a possible network compromise in criminal court would be well advised to log all successful and unsuccessful network login attempts, as well as users' activity once logged on and place timestamps on the events logged with a common clock synchronized from a recognized time source. On the other hand, an Internet Service Provider (ISP) that simply needs to keep track of login activities for billing purposes might simply need logs that reflect accurate network login and logoff by users.

How to Log

After the administrative controls have been put in place that set out what needs to be logged, then the mostly technical controls that define how the events will be logged can be laid out.

We saw in Chapter 2, "Building a Secure Network Using Security Controls," that Cisco has a number of solutions as part of the Cisco Integrated Security Portfolio. These solutions include security management products for multiple devices like Cisco Security MARS, with integral logging and report generation facilities for large networks. Here are some useful questions to ask when deciding on the technical controls needed to report and log events in the network:

▶ How can the integrity of both the logs, as well as the communication channels in which the log messages flow, be assured?

▶ How can the confidentiality of both the logs, as well as the communication channels in which the log messages flow, be assured?

▶ How do you deal with the copious amounts of log messages?

▶ How do you ensure that logs all use timestamps from the same clock to properly correlate events with logs, as well as logs with other logs?

▶ How can messages be prioritized so that critical messages are separated from routine messages?

▶ How can changes be reported when network outages or attacks occur?

▶ How do you log events from several devices in one central place?

These questions will be answered in the subsequent sections using the Cisco Secure Life Cycle as a guideline.

Reference Architecture for Secure Management and Reporting

So many questions! Nevertheless, these types of questions must be answered before the acquisition and integration of technology is considered. We will not try to answer these questions now, so we will take a shortcut and assume that they have been adequately answered in the reference architecture that we will be using for the subsequent sections in this chapter.

Figure 4.1 represents a typical architecture for secure management and reporting. It leverages on technologies that the reader would have examined in their CCNA studies, particularly in its use of VLANs to separate the traffic inside the network perimeter into different planes. It will serve as a simple visual tool to provide context for several of the *Implementation* phase guidelines that will be recommended presently.

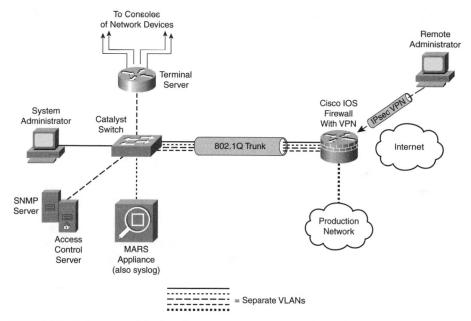

FIGURE 4.1 Reference architecture for secure management and reporting.

The following is a quick explanation of the reference architecture in Figure 4.1. A Cisco IOS firewall with VPN is protecting an organization's network.

The firewall has three interfaces on it. The interfaces are connected to the following:

▸ The Internet

▸ An inside production network

▸ An IEEE 802.1Q trunk to a Cisco Catalyst layer 2 Ethernet switch

Here is an explanation of some of the other security features found in the reference architecture:

▶ Ports on the Cisco Catalyst switch are configured in several VLANs (four pictured).

▶ The Cisco IOS firewall is routing among these VLANs (router-on-a-stick).

▶ ACLs on the Cisco IOS firewall manage traffic between the different VLANs. (See Chapter 5, "Using Cisco IOS Firewalls to Implement a Network Security Policy.")

▶ The firewall is stateful (see Chapter 5) and supports a remote access IPsec VPN for management (see Chapter 7, "Virtual Private Networks with IPsec").

▶ Deployed in different VLANs are the following:

    ▶ Cisco Security MARS Appliance

    ▶ SNMP Server

    ▶ Cisco Secure Access Control Server (ACS)

    ▶ System Administrator PC

    ▶ Terminal Server (Used to connect to the console ports of all the network devices.)

    ▶ Production Network

NOTE

This is a simplified secure network design for the sake of the discussion of the secure management and reporting topics throughout this chapter. It will serve the purpose of demonstrating secure management and reporting but it is lacking depth-of-defense for one thing and intrusion prevention/detection for another. IPS and IDS are discussed in Chapter 8, "Network Security Using Cisco IOS IPS."

EXAM ALERT

The communication between management hosts and the devices they manage can take two different paths, either by accident or design:

▶ Out-of-band (OOB). The traffic flows within a network separate from the production network. It is not in the data plane.

Example: A management VLAN.

▶ In-band. The traffic flows across the production network, the Internet (or other hostile network), or both. It is in the data plane.

Solution: Protect it inside a VPN, either site-to-site or remote access.

Secure Management and Reporting Guidelines

Recall the five steps of the Cisco Secure Network Life Cycle. Clearly, we had some productive meetings and answered the "how to log" and "what to log" questions during the *Initiation* and *Acquisition and Development* phases. Here are some of the guidelines that will be followed in the *Implementation* phase of Cisco's Secure Network Life Cycle:

- ▶ **General Management Guidelines:**

    - ▶ Synchronize clocks on hosts and network devices.

    - ▶ Document changes and make backups of configurations.

- ▶ **OOB Management Guidelines:**

    - ▶ Find solutions that mitigate the risk of transmitting unsecure management protocols over production networks.

- ▶ **In-Band Management Guidelines:**

    - ▶ Only manage devices that require monitoring or managing

    - ▶ Use encryption (IPsec, SSL, SSH) whenever possible.

    - ▶ Determine if management channel has to be open at all times.

The remaining material in this section addresses these guidelines in detail.

Logging with Syslog

Referring to Figure 4.1, you could deploy a syslog server in one of the private VLANs on the inside of the network. The *syslog server* would accept messages from any device that is configured as a *syslog client*—the Cisco IOS firewall, for example. Other network devices and other IP hosts like a public web server or a mail server could be set up to be syslog clients. There are several advantages to having a central syslog server logging events from a number of different sources. As previously discussed, care has to be taken to ensure that the integrity of the log files is assured, and that the communication path between the syslog server and its clients is not compromised. This is where OOB management and in-band management decisions are made. Also, best practices dictate that the devices' clocks should be synchronized to a recognized time source using the Network Time Protocol (NTP).

> **NOTE**
>
> If the syslog server is accepting messages from several clients, it is crucial that all the devices' clocks are synchronized from the same source. For example, if an IPS detects an attempted privilege escalation attack on a web server and sends a message to the log server, it might be necessary to correlate this event with the login logs on the web server itself. If the timestamps on the logs cannot be correlated because the devices' clocks are not synchronized, it might be difficult to prove that the two events are linked.
>
> Device synchronization is covered in the section, "Configuring Time Features," later in this chapter.

Cisco Security MARS

Logging to a central syslog server is not only part of the solution but potentially also part of the problem. The biggest issue is the enormity of the task of sifting through the resulting information, correlating the events from several different network devices and application servers and taking different types of actions based on a vulnerability assessment of the incident.

This is what Cisco Security MARS can do. Because Cisco Security MARS understands the complete network topology, MARS can intelligently analyze security events and help focus security staff's efforts in solving the potential problems. For example, false positives are more accurately detected. For example, MARS is used as a reporting and event correlation tool in Chapter 8, "Network Security Using Cisco IOS IPS." MARS sees the entire security architecture and thus sees security events in their complete context. It is a very complex and useful tool for reporting on security events. MARS is introduced in Chapter 2, "Building a Secure Network Using Security Controls."

> **EXAM ALERT**
>
> The MARS appliance is examined only at a high level in this Exam Cram. It is, however, a pivotal device in Cisco's comprehensive Self-Defending Network blueprint for network security. Memorizing MARS's features is recommended!

Where to Send Log Messages

Syslog is a key security policy component, but routers should also be configured to send log messages to one or more of these items:

- ▶ **Console.** Physical terminal lines.
- ▶ **Vtys.** Virtual terminal lines.

- ▶ **Buffered Logging.** Internal router circular buffer.

- ▶ **SNMP Traps.** Event-triggered messages to SNMP server.

- ▶ **Syslog.** External syslog server.

Log Message Levels

Not all messages are as important as others. Some messages are simple system level warnings, whereas others may denote real system emergencies that require immediate human intervention as the system is unusable. For example, an attacker may craft an attack that creates a DoS on a router system, resulting in emergency log messages. If no one's listening, no one knows!

Table 4.1 lists and explains the log severity levels. The "Log String" denotes how the log level appears in a log message.

> **NOTE**
>
> When you specify a level of syslog messages that you want to log, all levels below that level will be logged as well. For example, if the logging level specified is 4 (Warnings), levels 0–3 will also be sent.

TABLE 4.1   Cisco Log Severity Levels

Level	Log String	Name	Description
0	LOG_EMERG	Emergencies	Router unusable
1	LOG_ALERT	Alerts	Immediate action required
2	LOG_CRIT	Critical	Condition critical
3	LOG_ERR	Errors	Error condition
4	LOG_WARNING	Warnings	Warning condition
5	LOG_NOTICE	Notifications	Normal but important event
6	LOG_INFO	Informational	Informational message
7	LOG_DEBUG	Debugging	Debug message

> **EXAM ALERT**
>
> Memorize Table 4.1. Memorization tip: The lower the level number, the more severe the event.

Log Message Format

See Figure 4.2 for the log message format. The example is a level 4 syslog message from an IOS IPS, indicating that a user is attempting to communicate using the MSN Messenger instant messenger (IM) application. The organization's security policy might forbid the use of IM from its workstations, in which case this potential breach may constitute useful evidence for disciplinary purposes.

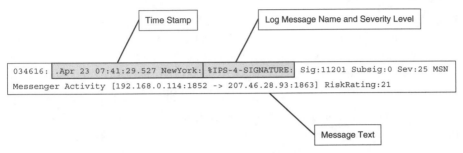

```
034616: .Apr 23 07:41:29.527 NewYork: %IPS-4-SIGNATURE: Sig:11201 Subsig:0 Sev:25 MSN
Messenger Activity [192.168.0.114:1852 -> 207.46.28.93:1863] RiskRating:21
```

FIGURE 4.2 Log message format.

Enabling Syslog Logging in SDM

Cisco Security Device Manager (SDM) is introduced and examined in Chapter 3, "Security at the Network Perimeter." Figure 4.3 illustrates how to navigate to the screen to configure syslog on the router.

Starting at the Cisco SDM homepage, follow these steps to enable and configure syslog logging on the Cisco IOS router:

1. Choose **Configure->Additional Tasks->Router Properties->Logging**.

2. Click **Edit** in the logging pane.

3. Check the **Enable Logging Level** check box in the Logging Window and choose the logging level desired from the Logging Level list box.

4. Click **Add**. In the resulting IP Address/Hostname field, enter the IP address of a logging host (syslog server).

5. Click **OK** and then **OK** again to return to the Logging pane.

> **NOTE**
>
> The CLI commands that result are as follows:
> ```
> logging buffered 4096
> logging trap debugging
> logging host 192.168.99.130
> logging on
> ```

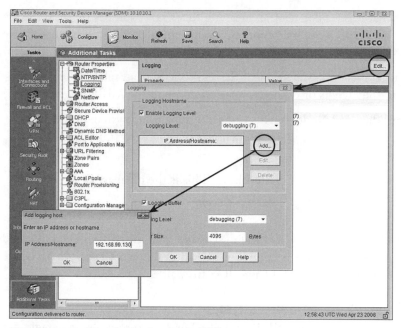

FIGURE 4.3 Enabling Syslog logging in SDM.

You can use Cisco SDM to monitor the internal buffer log, as well as messages that have been sent to syslog servers by choosing **Monitor->Logging** and selecting the **Syslog** tab in the Logging window.

> **NOTE**
>
> You can accomplish the same task by using the **show logging** CLI command.

Using SNMP

The Simple Network Management Protocol (SNMP) has long been deployed in networks to provide for central management of many types of network devices. There are, however, some notable security flaws in the original implementations of this very important protocol, SNMP version 1 and version 2. The protocol remains a valuable tool, and there will likely be a business case for its use. The vulnerabilities of the protocol will be outlined and discussed, as well as strategies for mitigating them, including the use of (the much newer) SNMP version 3.

SNMP Version 1 and 2 Architecture

The Simple Network Management Protocol (SNMP) enables an administrator to configure, manage, and view information on devices and IP hosts. One advantage of SNMP is that it is vendor-neutral, meaning that a common SNMP architecture can be used for many vendors' products. There are three main elements to the SNMP architecture:

- **Manager.** Network Management System (NMS). Can retrieve (*get*) information from agents or change (*set*) information in the MIB on agents.

- **Agent.** Managed Node. Agents can send traps when system events occur and respond to *sets* (configuration commands) and *gets* (information queries).

- **MIB.** Management Information Base. This is the database of information contained on the agent.

Referring to Figure 4.1, the Cisco Catalyst switch and Cisco IOS firewall could be SNMP agents. The NMS is configured OOB in its own VLAN on an inside network protected by the stateful Cisco IOS firewall.

SNMP v1 and v2 Community Strings

One of the vulnerabilities of SNMP v1 and v2 architecture is that messages are authenticated using cleartext community strings. Community strings have the following attributes:

- Essentially used for password-only authentication of messages between the NMS and the agent.

- Read-only (RO) strings are used to *get* information only from an agent's MIB.

- Read-write (RW) strings are used to *set* and *get* information on an agent.

SNMP Version 3 Architecture

SNMP Version 3 has the following improvements relative to SNMP Version 1 and 2:

- Messages may be encrypted to ensure confidentiality.

- Messages may be hashed to ensure integrity.

- Messages may be authenticated to ensure authenticity.

SNMP v1, v2, and v3 Security Models and Levels

Here is some other useful terminology that should be understood when deploying SNMP:

▶ **Security Model.** The security strategy used by an SNMP agent.

▶ **Security Level.** Provides a level of granularity within the security model. It is the permitted level of security within the security model.

Let's look at an example: Referring to Table 4.2, find the *noAuthNoPriv* security level within SNMPv3.

TABLE 4.2   SNMP Security Models and Levels

SNMP Ver	Security Level	Authentication	Encryption	Note
1	noAuthNoPriv	Community String	No	Authenticates with community string.
2c	noAuthNoPriv	Community String	No	Authenticates with community string.
3	noAuthNoPriv	Username	No	Authenticates with username.
3	authNoPriv	MD5 or SHA	No	Authenticates with HMAC-SHA or HMAC-MD5.
3	authPriv	MD5 or SHA	Yes	Authenticates with HMAC-SHA or HMAC-MD5.
				Encrypts with DES, 3DES, or AES ciphers.

At the *noAuthNoPriv* security level, SNMP v3 uses a username. SNMP v3 is downward-compatible with SNMP v1 and v2 if the username only is used. The username remains cleartext, as is the case with the community string in SNMP v1 and v2.

NOTE

HMAC = Hashing Message Authentication Code. SHA (Secure Hashing Algorithm) and MD5 (Message Digest 5) are examples. DES (Date Encryption Standard), 3DES (Triple-DES), and AES (Advanced Encryption Standard) are all examples of encryption algorithms or ciphers. We examine these in Chapter 6, "Introducing Cryptographic Services."

Enabling and Configuring SNMP with Cisco SDM

To enable the SNMP agent on the IOS router and configure it to respond to SNMP gets, follow these steps in the Cisco SDM:

1. Choose **Configure->Additional Tasks->Router Properties->SNMP** starting at the SDM homepage.

2. Click the **Edit** button, as shown in Figure 4.4.

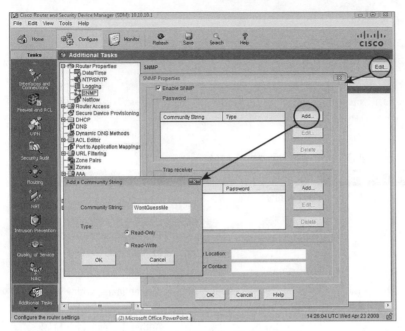

FIGURE 4.4 Enabling and configuring SNMP with Cisco SDM.

3. Check the **Enable SNMP** checkbox in the SNMP Properties pane.

4. As shown in Figure 4.4, click **Add** and fill in the Community String in the **Community String** dialog box. Click either the **Read-Only** or **Read-Write** radio buttons.

5. Click **OK**.

> **NOTE**
>
> SNMP v3 cannot be configured with the Cisco SDM.

Adding an SNMP Trap Receiver

While we're at the SNMP settings page, we can set up a trapping receiver for unsolicited SNMP messages to an SNMP server:

1. Starting at the SNMP pane in Cisco SDM, click **Edit**. The SNMP Properties window displays, as shown in Figure 4.5.

2. Click **Add** to add a new trap receiver in the Trap Receiver section of the SNMP Properties window.

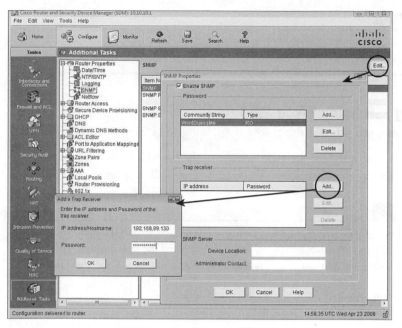

FIGURE 4.5   Adding an SNMP trap receiver using Cisco SDM.

3. Enter the IP address (or hostname) and password of the NMS, which is acting as the trap receiver.

4. Click **OK** to finish adding the trap receiver.

> **NOTE**
>
> The following CLI command results from following the preceding steps:
> ```
> snmp-server host 192.168.99.130 WontGuessMe
> ```

Configuring the SSH Daemon

In order to ensure that management sessions to the router are confidential, Secure Shell (SSH) is recommended. With respect to the reference architecture in Figure 4.1, SSH could be used to the Catalyst switch and the IOS firewall.

SSH is essentially encrypted Telnet. As such, it should be used instead of Telnet wherever possible, particularly where in-band management of a device is required. There are two versions of SSH:

- ▶ **Version 1.** Cisco IOS Release 12.1(1)T and later.

- ▶ **Version 2.** Cisco IOS Release 12.3(4)T and later. This is more secure than version 1.

> **NOTE**
>
> Beginning with Cisco IOS Release 12.1(3)T, the router can act both as a server and a client. The **ssh** command can be used to launch a client SSH session to an SSH server.

Enabling SSH Using Cisco SDM

The following are prerequisite tasks for enabling SSH using Cisco SDM:

▶ Ensure that you have the right release of the Cisco IOS Software image. Only images that contain the IPsec feature set will support the SSH daemon.

> **NOTE**
>
> Typically, IOS images whose names have the string "k8" or "k9" in them are crypto images that support cryptosystems such as IPsec VPNs and the SSH daemon. There are a number of ways that you can determine the image name. One way is the **show flash** command:
>
> ```
> ciscoISR#show flash
> 28672K bytes of processor board System flash (Intel Strataflash)
>
> Directory of flash:/
>
>   2 -rwx  18929780 May 15 2008 21:15:14 -04:00 c870-advipservicesk9-
> mz.124-15.T5.bin
> ```

▶ The target systems must be configured with AAA (either local or external) because SSH requires the use of a username and password.

▶ Ensure that target systems have unique fully-qualified domain names (FQDNs) if you are using the device's FQDN to SSH to.

▶ The domain name must also be set on any device running the SSH daemon because the RSA keys (see the following steps) will not generate without the domain name set.

Using the Cisco SDM, follow these steps to enable SSH on the IOS router:

1. Choose **Configure->Additional Tasks->Router Access->SSH**.

2. If the **Generate RSA Key** button is grayed out (as shown in Figure 4.6), this means that the RSA key exists and SSH is enabled on the router. If the **Generate RSA Key** button is available, press it and follow the prompts to generate a key with a modulus between 512 and 2048 in 64-bit increments. The larger the modulus, the longer it will take to generate the key.

Press this button to generate the RSA keys.

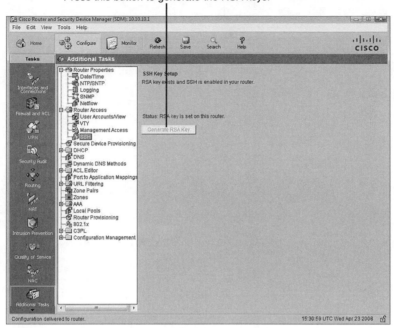

FIGURE 4.6   Enabling the SSH daemon using the Cisco SDM.

3. Click **OK**.

NOTE

SSH is enabled by default on the LAN interface on Cisco IOS routers that ship with the Cisco SDM pre-installed.

Rivest-Shamir-Addleman (RSA) keys are discussed in Chapter 6.

4. Now that we have the SSH daemon operational, we should be able to SSH to it, right? Wrong! Remember what we do with policies; we have to apply them somewhere. SSH has to be enabled on the vty lines. This is accomplished in the Cisco SDM by choosing **Configure->Additional Tasks->Router Access->VTY**. Figure 4.7 shows the Edit VTY Lines dialog box.

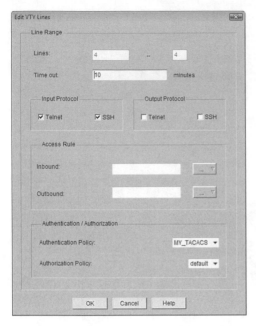

FIGURE 4.7 Edit VTY lines in the Cisco SDM.

Here are the equivalent CLI commands:

```
CiscoISR(config)#ip domain-name example.com
CiscoISR(config)#crypto key zeroize rsa

% All RSA keys will be removed.
% All router certs issued using these keys will also be removed.
Do you really want to remove these keys? [yes/no]: yes

CiscoISR(config)#crypto key generate rsa general-key modulus 1024
The name for the keys will be: CiscoISR.example.com

% The key modulus size is 1024 bits
% Generating 1024 bit RSA keys, keys will be non-exportable...[OK]

CiscoISR(config)#ip ssh time-out 120
CiscoISR(config)#ip ssh authentication-retries 4
CiscoISR(config)#line vty 0 4
CiscoISR(config-line)#transport input ssh
CiscoISR(config-line)#end
CiscoISR#
```

Configuring Time Features

The Cisco SDM enables you to manually:

▶ Synchronize the router's clock to the local PC clock.

▶ Edit the router's date and time.

Network Time Protocol

Assuming that our security policy requires that all of our network devices have their clocks synchronized to a single, recognized time source, manual setting of the router clock is not an option. We will choose to set the router's clock with a Network Time Protocol (NTP) source. An organization can set up its own master time source (preferably OOB) or synchronize from a public time server on the Internet.

A few important notes:

▶ NTP uses UDP port 123 and is considered secure.

▶ Simple Network Time Protocol (SNTP) is a simpler and less secure version of NTP.

▶ NTP version 3 (NTPv3) and above implement cryptography and authentication between NTP peers (client and server).

You must be careful when synchronizing from an NTP server. Rules of evidence might require you to prove that you are using an unimpeachable source of information to synchronize your devices' clocks if you want to use your logs in the course of a criminal proceeding. This makes using Internet time sources problematic. This might be mitigated somewhat by using your own master time server, but if you are synchronizing it from an Internet time source, you are back to where you started. Therefore, your master time server may need to be synchronized by radio or satellite to meet the security standards required by the security policy.

Figure 4.8 illustrates the steps to add an NTP server using the SDM. Starting at the Cisco SDM homepage, here are the steps required to add an NTP server:

1. Choose **Configure->Additional Tasks->Router Properties->NTP/SNTP**.

2. Click **Add** to add a new NTP server. The Add NTP Server Details window appears.

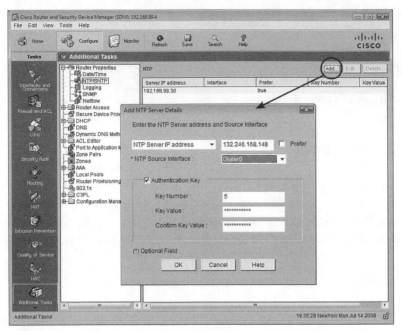

FIGURE 4.8 Configuring NTP in the Cisco SDM.

3. Fill in the details about your NTP server in the Add NTP Server Details window.

   ▶ (optional) You can select the source interface for your NTP packets from the **NTP Source Interface** drop-down box.

   ▶ (optional) If this is the preferred NTP server, check the **Prefer** check box. This server will be checked before other servers. You can have more than one preferred server.

4. Check the **Authentication Key** check box if the NTP server requires authentication and fill in the values.

5. To finish adding the server, click **OK**.

NOTE

The CLI command generated by the Cisco SDM in the preceding example would be as follows:

```
ntp server 192.168.99.30 key cisco123 source vlan2 prefer
```

Using Cisco SDM and CLI Tools to Lock Down the Router

Cisco routers come with services enabled on them by default that make them great routers, but not necessarily great security devices. The reasons for these default services are various, but generally speaking, they are there more for historical reasons than anything else and would not likely be the defaults were these devices to be given a rethink in the context of current security knowledge. In this section, we quickly summarize some of these default services, their security risk in the context of the router's responsibilities as a perimeter defense device, and (more importantly) what to do about it. As we will see, the router has a number of CLI and SDM tools that can first audit and secondly secure these vulnerabilities.

Router Services and Interface Vulnerabilities

The following is a list of general recommendations for router services and interfaces that are vulnerable to network attacks. They can be grouped into seven categories, as follows:

- ▶ Disable unnecessary services and interfaces.
- ▶ Disable commonly configured management services.
- ▶ Ensure path integrity.
- ▶ Disable probes and scans.
- ▶ Ensure terminal access security.
- ▶ Disable gratuitous and proxy ARP.
- ▶ Disable IP directed broadcasts.

Table 4.3 outlines Cisco's recommendations for disabling vulnerable router services and interfaces.

TABLE 4.3   Recommendations for Vulnerable Router Services and Interfaces

Disable these unnecessary services and interfaces:

Unused router interfaces	Cisco Discovery Protocol
BOOTP server	Configuration autoloading
FTP server	TFTP server
NTP service	PAD service
TCP and UDP minor services	DEC MOP service

Disable commonly configured management services:

SNMP	HTTP or HTTPs configuration and monitoring
DNS	

Ensure path integrity:

ICMP redirects	IP source routing

Disable probes and scans:

Finger	ICMP unreachable notifications
ICMP mask reply	

Ensure terminal access security:

IP identifications service	TCP keepalives

Disable gratuitous and proxy ARP:

GARP	Proxy ARP
Disable IP directed-broadcast	

A detailed explanation of the vulnerabilities presented by these features will not be attempted. What follows is a quick summary of the services and their respective vulnerabilities as well as security recommendations.

Disable Unnecessary Services and Interfaces

The following are Cisco's recommendations for disabling unnecessary services and interfaces:

▶ **Router Interfaces.** Disabling unused router interfaces will limit unauthorized access to both the router and the network.

Recommendation: Disable unused open router interfaces.

▶ **Bootstrap Protocol (BOOTP).** This service is enabled by default. It allows other devices to obtain IP addresses and other configuration information automatically.

Recommendation: This service is rarely needed and should be disabled.

► **Cisco Discovery Protocol.** Enabled by default. This protocol allows the router to discover information about directly connected neighbor Cisco devices.

Recommendation: This service is not required once a network has been constructed and tested. Disable.

► **Configuration Autoloading.** Disabled by default. It allows the autoloading of configuration files from a network server.

Recommendation: Disable unless needed.

► **FTP Server.** Disabled by default. Allows the router to act as an FTP server and serve files from flash memory to FTP clients.

Recommendation: Disable unless needed.

► **TFTP Server.** Disabled by default. Allows the router to act as a TFTP server and serve files from flash memory to TFTP clients.

Recommendation: Disable unless needed

► **Network Time Protocol (NTP) Service.** This protocol was discussed in the last section, as were recommendations for its use.

Recommendation: Disable unless needed.

► **TCP and UDP Minor Services.** These services are disabled by default in Cisco IOS Software Release 11.3 and later. They are small daemons that have a diagnostic purpose but are rarely needed.

Recommendation: Disable this service explicitly.

► **Maintenance Operation Protocol (MOP) Service.** Enabled by default on most Ethernet interfaces. It is a legacy Digital Electronic Corporation (DEC) maintenance protocol.

Recommendation: Disable this service explicitly when it is not in use.

Disable and Restrict Commonly Configured Management Services

The following are Cisco's recommendations for disabling and restricting commonly configured management services:

► **Simple Network Management Protocol (SNMP).** Enabled by default. This protocol's vulnerabilities (SNMP versions 1 and 2) were discussed in a previous section in this chapter.

Recommendation: Disable this service when it is not required.

▶ **HTTP or HTTPS Configuration and Monitoring.** Default operation is device-dependent. Used for monitoring and configuring the device using a web browser and/or Cisco SDM.

Recommendation: Disable if not in use or restrict access using ACLs.

▶ **Domain Name System (DNS).** Enabled by default. Also by default, the DNS client broadcasts its request to destination IP address 255.255.255.255. This makes it vulnerable to spoofed responses, possibly leading to session-hijacking.

Recommendation: Disable if not required. If it is required, set the DNS lookup service with the unicast address of specific DNS servers.

Ensure Path Integrity

The following are Cisco's recommendations for ensuring path integrity. Path integrity ensures that the path that data packets take through the network is not somehow redirected or otherwise compromised by an exploit:

▶ **Internet Control Message Protocol (ICMP) redirects.** Enabled by default. When a router receives an ICMP redirect on an interface, it is required to resend the packet out the same interface that it was received. If this is an Internet-facing interface, an attacker could use the resent information to redirect packets to an untrusted device, a classic session hijacking exploit.

Recommendation: Disable this service if it is not required.

▶ **IP source routing.** Enabled on interfaces by default. Routing is normally destination-based, but a IP host can indicate which path it would prefer to take through a network by specifying IP source-routing options in the IP packet header. Routers would be forced to honor this path. This can be exploited by an attacker as a carefully crafted attack that would take the attacker's choice of path through an unprotected network rather than the best path indicated in the routing table.

Recommendation: Disable this service on all interfaces unless it is required.

Disable Probes and Scans

The following are Cisco's recommendations for disabling probes and scans of the network and the router itself:

▶ **Finger Service.** Enabled by default. Finger service allows a reconnaissance of the router to determine a list of users currently using a particular device, among other information.

Recommendation: Disable this service if it is not required.

▶ **ICMP Unreachable Notifications.** Enabled by default. This service notifies users of unreachable IP hosts and networks. It can be used during a reconnaissance attack to map out a network's topology because if the attacker doesn't receive an ICMP unreachable notification in reply to an ICMP request, they can infer that the network is reachable.

Recommendation: An attacker can infer all they want! Turn off ICMP unreachable notifications on all interfaces facing untrusted networks unless they are required.

▶ **ICMP Mask Reply.** Disabled by default. Same general vulnerabilities as ICMP unreachables.

Recommendation: Turn off ICMP mask replies on all interfaces facing untrusted networks unless they are required.

Ensure Terminal Access Security

The following are Cisco's recommendations for ensuring terminal access security. These recommendations will mitigate the possibility that an attacker can identify the device and launch certain DoS attacks against the device itself:

▶ **IP Identification (IDENT) Service.** Enabled by default. Useful in reconnaissance attacks. When TCP port 113 is probed, the identity of the device is obtained.

Recommendation: Disable explicitly.

▶ **TCP Keepalives.** Disabled by default. This service is a reaper service that polls TCP sessions to see if they are still active. If a response isn't received, the connection is closed, thereby freeing up resources on the router and preventing certain DoS attacks.

Recommendation: Should be enabled globally.

Disable Gratuitous and Proxy Address Resolution Protocol (ARP)

The following are Cisco's recommendations for disabling gratuitous and proxy address resolution protocol (ARP) messages.

▶ **Gratuitous ARP (GARP).** Enabled by default. It is commonly used in ARP poisoning attacks. It is gratuitous in that they are ARP replies that don't match ARP requests. The intent is to fool IP hosts to cache these replies in their ARP tables so that the host will send packets to the attacker versus the legitimate hosts whose IP addresses and MAC addresses the attacker has spoofed.

Recommendation: Should be disabled on each interface unless it is needed.

▶ **Proxy ARP.** Enabled by default. This service allows the router to reply to an ARP request by proxy with its own MAC address where an IP address resolves to a remote segment.

Recommendation: Should be disabled unless the router is acting as a layer 2 LAN bridge.

Disable IP Directed-broadcasts

This service is disabled by default in Cisco IOS Release 12.0 and later. IP directed-broadcasts are used in smurf and other related DoS attacks.

Recommendation: This service should be disabled if not required.

Performing a Security Audit

Now that we have identified the specific vulnerabilities that may be present on the router, we will perform a security audit of the router using the Cisco SDM, as well as some CLI tools.

The Cisco SDM Security Audit, shown in Figure 4.9, is based on the Cisco IOS AutoSecure feature (also accessible by the CLI, as we will see later), which is an automated, interactive script that checks for vulnerabilities and recommends how they might be remediated. As we will see, the Cisco SDM Security Audit has *almost* all the feature of the Cisco AutoSecure functions.

The Security Audit Wizard can be reached by choosing **Configure->Security Audit** from the Cisco SDM homepage. There are two modes of operation, as indicated in Figure 4.9:

▶ **Security Audit Wizard.** Once vulnerabilities are discovered, the wizard gives you a choice as to which vulnerabilities you want to secure. Press the **Perform security audit** button if you want this.

▶ **One-Step Lockdown.** This configures the router with a set of defined security features with recommended settings in one step and without further user interaction. Press the **One-step lockdown** button if you want this.

Let's examine the Cisco SDM Security Audit Wizard first.

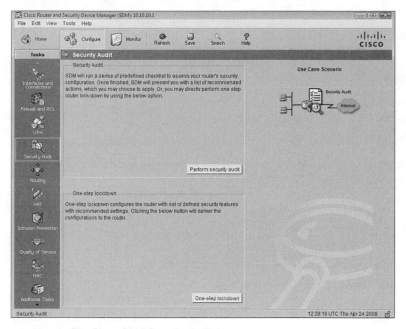

FIGURE 4.9   The Cisco SDM Security Audit homepage.

Cisco SDM Security Audit Wizard

In the last section, we identified the specific vulnerabilities that may be present on the router. Now we will use the Cisco SDM Security Audit Wizard to determine whether they are present and give us the option to remedy them.

To perform a security audit, follow these steps from the Cisco SDM homepage:

1. Choose **Configure->Security Audit**.

NOTE

The figures in this series of steps are based on a Cisco 800 Series ISR whose inside interface is *Vlan1* and whose outside interface is *FastEthernet4*.

2. Click the **Perform Security Audit** button. The Welcome Page of the Security Audit Wizard appears.

3. Click **Next** to bring up the Security Audit Interface Configuration page as shown in Figure 4.10.

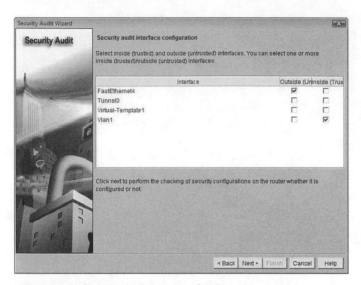

FIGURE 4.10 Security Audit Interface Configuration.

4. Before the audit proceeds, the Security Audit Wizard needs to know which interfaces connect to the outside and which interfaces connect to the inside. Beside each interface listed, check the **Inside** or **Outside** check box. (This makes sense because some of the vulnerabilities listed previously depend on whether the interface is connected to a hostile network or not.)

5. Click **Next**.

   The Security Audit report window appears, which runs an audit, finishing with an itemized report detailing the number, item name, and status of the potential vulnerabilities, as shown in Figure 4.11. A check mark will appear if the item has passed. An X will appear if the item has not passed.

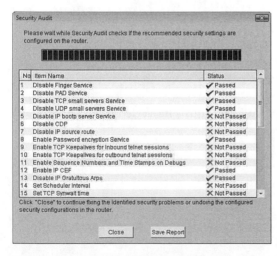

FIGURE 4.11 Security Audit report window.

6. If you want to save the report to a file, click **Save Report**.

7. To continue with fixing the identified security issues, click **Close**.

8. The Security Audit Wizard window appears, as shown in Figure 4.12. If you want to fix the security problems identified, you can either check the **Fix it** check box in the Action column beside each identified security problem you want to fix, or you can click the **Fix All** button, which checks all the boxes for you.

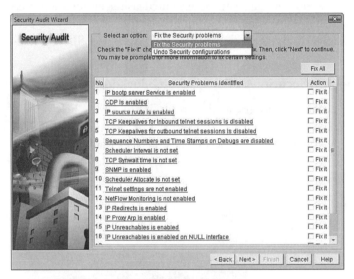

FIGURE 4.12   Security Audit Wizard window.

If you want to undo security problems that have been identified as "Passed" in the Security Audit report window (refer to Step 5), you can choose **Undo Security configurations** in the **Select an option** drop-down list at the top of the Security Audit window. The resulting Security Audit Wizard window will allow you to check off **Undo** in the Action column beside each enabled security configuration you want to undo.

NOTE

Interestingly, each security problem identified is a hyperlink that, if selected, will pop up a description of the problem from the SDM's built-in context-sensitive help feature. This will help the administrator decide on a course of action for that specific vulnerability.

9. Click **Next**.

10. Depending on which security vulnerabilities you have chosen to fix, you might be asked to enter more information on the subsequent screens. Enter the required information and click **Next** as indicated until you arrive at the Summary screen.

11. Click **Finish** to deliver the changes to the router.

Cisco SDM One-Step Lockdown

The Cisco one-step lockdown feature can be executed using either the Cisco SDM or the CLI command, **auto secure**. Complete the following steps to perform a one-step lockdown using the Cisco SDM, starting at the SDM homepage:

1. Choose **Configure->Security Audit->One-step lockdown**.

2. An SDM Warning dialog appears, as shown in Figure 4.13. Click **Yes** if you are sure you want to lock down the router. A one-step lockdown window appears with a check mark beside all the items that will be fixed.

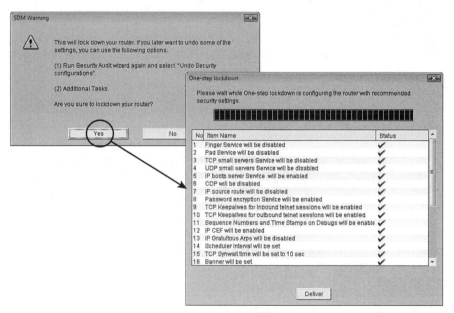

FIGURE 4.13 Cisco SDM one-step lockdown.

3. Click **Deliver** to deliver the configuration changes to the router.

4. Click **OK** to exit back to the Security Audit window.

Using the Cisco AutoSecure Feature to Lock Down a Router

Cisco AutoSecure is a feature that is initiated from the CLI and executes a script, which first makes recommendations for fixing security vulnerabilities, and then modifies the security configuration of the router. The syntax of the command is as follows:

```
auto secure [no-interact]
```

It can be executed in either of two modes:

▶ **Interactive Mode.** Prompts the user with recommendations for enabling and disabling specific services. This is the default mode. Use the **auto-secure** command with no options.

▶ **Non-Interactive Mode.** Automatically executes the Cisco AutoSecure command with Cisco's recommended default settings. Use the **auto secure no-interact** form of the command.

Here is what the opening dialog looks like. This example is using the interactive mode:

```
ciscoISR#auto secure
        —- AutoSecure Configuration —-

***AutoSecure configuration enhances the security of
the router, but it will not make it absolutely resistant
to all security attacks***

AutoSecure will modify the configuration of your device.
All configuration changes will be shown. For a detailed
explanation of how the configuration changes enhance security
and any possible side effects, please refer to Cisco.com for
Autosecure documentation.
At any prompt you may enter '?' for help.
Use ctrl-c to abort this session at any prompt.

Gathering information about the router for AutoSecure

Is this router connected to internet? [no]:yes
[output omitted]
Securing Management plane services...

Disabling service finger
Disabling service pad
Disabling udp&tcp small servers
Enabling service password encryption
Enabling service tcp-keepalives-in
Enabling service tcp-keepalives-out
```

```
Disabling the cdp protocol

Disabling the bootp server
Disabling the http server
Disabling the finger service
Disabling source routing
Disabling gratuitous arp
Configure NTP Authentication? [yes]:no
Configuring AAA local authentication
Configuring Console, Aux and VTY lines for
local authentication, exec-timeout, and transport
Securing device against Login Attacks
Configure the following parameters

Blocking Period when Login Attack detected: 120
```

At the end of the AutoSecure interactive dialog, the recommended running-config with the changes to be applied is displayed. You are then asked:

```
Apply this configuration to running-config? [yes]:yes
```

> **NOTE**
>
> Once applied to the running-config, if you lose connectivity to the router or something stops working, you can always reboot the router because the changes will not have been saved to the startup-config. This sounds strange, but many security texts recommend this procedure. Essentially if you don't know what a service does, turn it off. If something important stops working as a result, you now know what it does. Locking down a network device, despite the excellent features such as AutoSecure, is often a trial-and-error approach.
>
> You should consider testing these changes in a lab environment first, and only make changes on a production network when you are absolutely sure of what you are doing.

Caveats: Cisco AutoSecure Versus Cisco SDM Security Audit

There are some notable limitations and differences between Cisco AutoSecure and the Cisco SDM Security Audit:

- ▶ Cisco SDM does not implement the following Cisco AutoSecure features:
  - ▶ Disabling NTP
  - ▶ Configuring AAA
  - ▶ Setting SPD values
  - ▶ Enabling TCP intercepts
  - ▶ Configuring anti-spoofing ACLs on outside-facing interfaces

- ▶ Cisco SDM implements some Cisco AutoSecure features differently:

    - ▶ SNMP is disabled but will not configure SNMPv3 (varies with router).

    - ▶ SSH is enabled and configured with Cisco IOS images that support this feature.

    - ▶ Curiously, Secure Copy Protocol (SCP) is not enabled and unsecure FTP is.

Exam Prep Questions

1. Which of the following is *not* a consideration for setting up technical controls in support of secure logging?

   ○ **A.** How can the confidentiality of logs as well as communicating log messages be assured?

   ○ **B.** How do you log events from several devices in one central place?

   ○ **C.** What are the most critical events to log?

   ○ **D.** What are the most important logs?

   ○ **E.** None of the above.

2. Fill in the blank with the correct term from the choices.

   One communication path between management hosts and the devices they manage is _____, meaning that the traffic flows within a network separate from the production network.

   ○ **A.** In-band

   ○ **B.** Inter-vlan

   ○ **C.** Private

   ○ **D.** Out-of-band

   ○ **E.** Intranet

3. True or false. A general management guideline is to ensure that clocks on network devices are not synchronized with an external time source because this is a known vulnerability.

4. Indicate the number for each logging level:

   ▶ Debugging: ____

   ▶ Alerts: ____

   ▶ Emergencies: ____

   ▶ Notifications: ____

   ▶ Critical: ____

   ▶ Informational: ____

   ▶ Warnings: ____

5. To what menus do you have to navigate to setup logging in the SDM?

   ○ **A.** Configure->Router Management->Additional Tasks->Logging

   ○ **B.** Configure->Additional Tasks->Router Properties->Logging

○ **C.** Monitor->System Properties->Configure->Syslog

○ **D.** Configure->Additional Tasks->Router Properties->Syslog

○ **E.** Monitor->Logging Options->Syslog Setup

6. Match the following SNMP terms with their definitions:

    1. MIB: ___

    2. Agent: ___

    3. NMS: ___

    A. Responds to sets and gets

    B. Sends sets and gets

    C. Information database

7. True or false. Secure Network Time Protocol (SNTP) is more secure than regular NTP as it requires authentication.

8. Which of the following is part of Cisco's list of seven categories of vulnerable router services and interfaces? (Choose all that apply.)

○ **A.** Disable unnecessary services and interfaces.

○ **B.** Disable commonly configured management services.

○ **C.** Ensure path integrity.

○ **D.** Disable probes and scans.

○ **E.** All of the above.

9. Fill in the blank with the correct term from the choices.

The Cisco SDM Security Audit Wizard and One-Step Lockdown tools are based on the Cisco _____ feature.

○ **A.** Auto-Initiate

○ **B.** SafeAudit

○ **C.** AuditMany-SecureOnce

○ **D.** AutoSecure

○ **E.** None of the above.

10. True or false. SNMPv3 is implemented in the Cisco SDM Security Audit Wizard but not in the auto secure CLI command.

Answers to Exam Prep Questions

1. Answer E is correct because all the choices are valid considerations.

2. The right answer is D, out-of-band (OOB). A design goal for a secure network is to try to separate management traffic from the production networks wherever possible. Answer A is the opposite. The other answers are incorrect because they are not used in this context.

3. False. This is a bit of a trick question. Yes, there are some known vulnerabilities with synchronizing clocks with external time sources, but these are outweighed by the advantage of having all network devices' clocks synchronized to a single time source.

4. The logging levels are the following:

   ▶ Debugging: 7

   ▶ Alerts: 1

   ▶ Emergencies: 0

   ▶ Notifications: 5

   ▶ Critical: 2

   ▶ Informational: 6

   ▶ Warnings: 4

5. The correct answer is B. The other choices, although they look vaguely correct, do not represent real choices.

6. The correct answers are: 1—C; 2—A; 3—B. MIB stands for Management Information Base and resides on an agent. The information in this database can be queried (get) or configured (set) by a Network Management System (NMS).

7. False. SNTP stands for Simple Network Time Protocol and is considered less secure than NTP. NTPv3, on the other hand, is more secure because it implements cryptography and authentication between NTP peers.

8. Answer E is correct. The complete list is as follows:

   ▶ Disable unnecessary services and interfaces.

   ▶ Disable commonly configured management services.

   ▶ Ensure path integrity.

   ▶ Disable probes and scans.

   ▶ Ensure terminal access security.

   ▶ Disable gratuitous and proxy ARP.

   ▶ Disable IP directed broadcasts.

9. Answer D is correct. The other choices are made up and don't appear in any context with Cisco network security.

10. False. SNMPv3 is not part of the Cisco SDM Security Audit Wizard.

PART III

Augmenting Depth of Defense

CHAPTER FIVE

Using Cisco IOS Firewalls to Implement a Network Security Policy

Terms You'll Need to Understand:

✓ Firewall

✓ Perimeter

✓ Static and dynamic packet-filtering firewalls

✓ Application inspection firewalls

✓ Application layer gateways

✓ Transparent firewalls

✓ Inbound versus outbound

✓ Protocol numbers of common protocols

✓ Cisco Common Classification Policy Language (C3PL)

✓ ZPF terms: zone, zone pair, class maps, policy maps, self zone

Exam Topics Covered in This Chapter:

✓ Explain the functionality of standard, extended, and named IP ACLs used by routers to filter packets

✓ Configure and verify IP ACLs to mitigate given threats (filter IP traffic destined for Telnet, SNMP, and DDoS attacks) in a network using CLI

✓ Configure IP ACLs to prevent IP address spoofing using CLI

✓ Discuss the caveats to be considered when building ACLs

✓ Describe the operational strengths and weaknesses of the different firewall technologies

✓ Explain stateful firewall operations and the function of the state table

✓ Implement Zone Based Firewall using SDM

NOTE

These exam topics are from cisco.com. Check there periodically for the latest exam topics and info.

At this juncture, it would be easy to say something like, "Now that we have secured the network perimeter (see Chapter 3, "Security at the Network Perimeter," and Chapter 4, "Implementing Secure Management and Hardening the Router"), we can now implement firewall technologies on our router." After all, everyone knows what a firewall is, right? Most people would be fine with this and just ... do it. But we're not "most people." To be totally comfortable with the subject of implementing IOS firewalls in support of a network security policy, we should start by defining what is meant by a firewall in the first place. This question will lead to more questions:

- ▶ Just what is a firewall?

- ▶ What types of firewalls are there?

- ▶ Can any one definition suffice?

- ▶ What kind of firewall technologies do I need to deploy to protect the perimeter?

- ▶ What do I need firewalls for in the first place?

This chapter answers these questions.

In Chapter 4, we introduced a reference design to give us a design context for secure management and reporting. For consistency, we will use the same reference architecture in this chapter as presented in Figure 5.1.

We will refer to this reference design from time to time when examining, defining, and implementing firewall technologies.

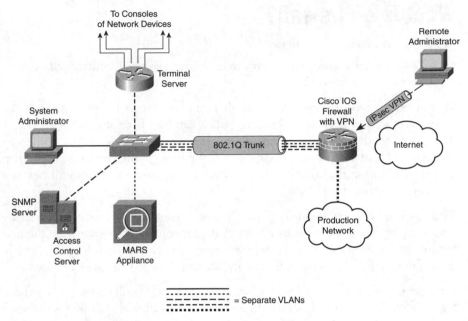

FIGURE 5.1 Reference architecture for firewall technologies.

Examining and Defining Firewall Technologies

This section covers the following topics:

- ▶ What is a firewall?

- ▶ Characteristics of a firewall

- ▶ Firewall advantages

- ▶ Firewall disadvantages

- ▶ Role of firewalls in a layered defense strategy

- ▶ Types of firewalls

- ▶ Cisco family of firewalls

- ▶ Firewall implementation best practices

What Is a Firewall?

According to Cisco, a firewall is:

> "a system or a group of systems that enforce an access control policy between two networks."

With a definition this loose, anything that controls access between parts of the network, at whatever layer of the OSI model, can be a firewall! Although vague, the preceding definition is essentially accurate but we could define some key characteristics of a firewall. In Chapter 4, we look at the means to lockdown default services on the router in the context of the router's responsibilities as a perimeter security device.

The key word here is "perimeter." In Chapter 3, we find that it is typically at the perimeter, or edge, of a network where we deploy routers. They are often the first bastion of defense against attack because many enterprises, both large and small, use routers as their first connection to an Internet Service Provider's IP cloud.

If we can define the word "perimeter," and accept that a firewall defends this perimeter, then we have a good appreciation for what a firewall does. Chapter 3 defines a perimeter as a "trusted network boundary." The context is the discussion of the three deployment scenarios for a router acting as a firewall. (Pretty dangerous stuff, considering we're only now defining the word firewall!) Putting these thoughts together into a working definition, we arrive at this definition of a firewall:

> A firewall is a system or a group of systems that establish a trusted network boundary (a perimeter) and then manages traffic across that boundary.

Implicit in this definition is a sense of direction. In Chapter 2, "Building a Secure Network Using Security Controls," we observe that establishing the perimeter made it fairly simple to define ingress and egress flows of traffic because ingress (or inbound) would be defined as traffic that flows from a less-trusted to a more-trusted security zone. Egress (or outbound) traffic would be the opposite direction.

So there you have it! A firewall doesn't even have to be a device. It could be software deployed on an application server, the perimeter being the point of ingress and egress to the application stack served by that device. It could be software installed on a network device that inspects application layer traffic as it flows across to ensure that it is protocol-compliant. Find the perimeter, and you find the firewall.

> **NOTE**
>
> The Cisco material mixes its metaphors, so this Exam Cram is forced to do likewise to a certain extent. The word "perimeter" is used in some contexts as the network's edge, and in the context of network security as a trusted network boundary. (Remember the "blurring of the perimeter" in Chapter 2?) Make sure you understand that in some contexts, the network edge and the trusted network boundary are one and the same thing.

Characteristics of a Firewall

Now that we have defined what constitutes a firewall, let's look at some common characteristics of firewalls:

- ▶ **Enforces the Access Control Policy of an Organization.** The security policy's access control policy component defines what is permitted or denied across the firewall.

- ▶ **Must Be Hardened Against Attacks.** Compromising the firewall itself should be remotest of all possibilities because compromising the firewall would compromise its enforcement of access control policies.

- ▶ **Must Be the Only Transit Point Between Networks.** How can a firewall enforce ingress and egress policies when not all traffic is forced to flow through it?

> **NOTE**
>
> An improperly configured or badly oversubscribed firewall may create an inadvertent network performance problem because of its deployment at a network chokepoint.

Firewalls can aid in the design of secure network architecture because their incorporation creates natural zones of security with differing levels of trusts.

Firewall Advantages

First, the good news. In addition to the characteristics presented in the previous section, other advantages of firewalls include the following:

- ▶ Firewalls defend networks against the exploitation of protocol flaws and sanitize the protocol in some cases.

- ▶ Firewalls defend sensitive hosts and applications against exposure to untrusted users.

- ▶ Firewalls defend against attackers sending malicious code or data to clients and servers.

- ▶ With proper design, a firewall makes policy enforcement visual, simple, robust, and scalable.

- ▶ Network access control can be simplified by offloading security management to a few points in the network.

Firewall Disadvantages

Now, the bad news. Firewalls aren't a perfect solution, sometimes because the people who design and configured them aren't. Besides the aforementioned traffic bottlenecks, here are some other disadvantages:

▶ Firewall misconfiguration can cause single points of failure.

▶ Many applications are not firewall-friendly because their specific attributes are not well understood and are therefore hard to securely pass through a firewall.

▶ End-users may try to find ways around an overly restrictive firewall.

▶ Tunneled traffic (covert channels) is difficult to detect and protect against.

Role of Firewalls in a Layered Defense Strategy

According to Cisco, a firewall has three basic roles in the Cisco Self-Defending Network:

▶ **Perimeter Security.** Secures the boundaries between zones.

▶ **Communications Security.** Provides information assurance (C-I-A).

▶ **Core Network Security.** Ensures that only compliant traffic traverses the perimeter:

  ▶ Protects against malicious software.

  ▶ Protects against traffic anomalies.

  ▶ Enforces network security policies.

  ▶ Ensures survivability.

▶ **Endpoint Security.** Enforces compliance to identity and device security policies.

Types of Firewalls

According to Cisco, there are five main categories of firewalls:

▶ Static Packet-Filtering Firewalls

▶ Application Layer Gateways

▶ Dynamic (or Stateful) Packet-Filtering Firewalls

▶ Application Inspection Firewalls

▶ Transparent Firewalls

We will look at all five, devoting most of our attention to the first three.

Static Packet-Filtering Firewalls

Figure 5.2 illustrates the basic functionality of a static packet-filtering firewall. Static packet-filtering firewalls work at layers 3 and 4 and filter packets one at a time.

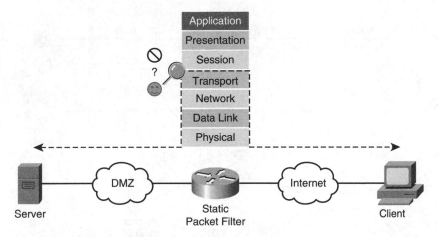

• Static packet filtering works at layers 3 and 4.
• Packets are looked at (and filtered) one at a time.

FIGURE 5.2 Static packet-filtering firewall.

Static packet-filtering routers are relatively unintelligent. By using ACLs, they can either permit or deny traffic up to the layer 4 of the OSI model, but they don't see the PDUs (Protocol Data Units) that carry the data as part of a dynamic conversation. For example, they can permit traffic if it matches the well-known TCP port number for HTTP, port 80, but they can only filter the packets singly and have no appreciation for how a TCP connection is built, carries and re-transmits data as required, and is torn down.

A static packet-filtering firewall is like unknowledgeable fans at a tennis match. They can watch single volleys go across the net, but they don't see the ball in the context of game, set, and match. If you think of the tennis ball as a TCP segment, for example, the analogy is complete. These fans may be qualified to let volleys with the green-colored (destination port 80) balls across the net, but the finer points of how the game is started (begin TCP session), played (data flow),

and ended (session torn down) is beyond them. You could even give the fans further responsibilities, telling them that the green ball (TCP port 80) is only
allowed from player A (source IP address) to player B (destination IP address),
but they will still only be able to examine each volley separately.

Static packet-filtering firewalls are very useful for simple, not particularly granular, rules … "big chunk" rules like, "Absolutely no TCP Port 80 traffic is
allowed inbound past the perimeter."

Be careful how you use ACLs, however. In Figure 5.3, a static packet filtering firewall is configured to permit Internet users to access the web server in the DMZ.

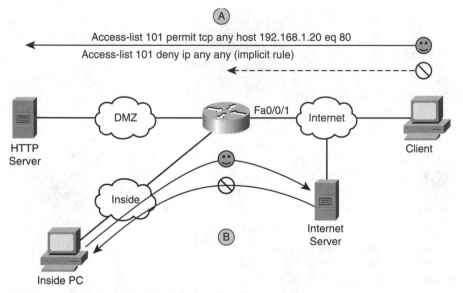

FIGURE 5.3 Example static packet-filter configuration.

Refer to "A" in Figure 5.3. The ACL is applied inbound on the Internet facing
interface, FastEthernet 0/0/1 in the figure.

```
access-list 101 permit tcp any host 192.168.1.20 eq 80
interface FastEthernet 0/0/1
ip access-group 101 in
```

Recall from your CCNA studies that when you create an ACL, you also create an
implicit rule at the very end of the ACL, whether you enter it or not:

```
access-list 101 deny ip any any
```

All traffic that doesn't match the access control list entries (ACE) before this last statement will therefore be implicitly denied. This also means that you have to have at
least one permit somewhere in the ACL; otherwise, all traffic is doomed for failure!

The effect is that only destination port 80 traffic will be allowed in through the firewall and only to IP address 192.168.1.20, the public IP address of the web server in the DMZ. Replies from the web server will be allowed out, because there is no interface ACL applied outbound on the Internet-facing interface. "Great!" you say. Mission accomplished. But what about the inside PC? Can it make connections out to the Internet server (point "B" in Figure 5.3)? Yes, but replies will be blocked on the implied rule in access-list 101. This happens because the firewall is only looking at packets one at a time. It doesn't see the return packets from the Internet server as part of a conversation that was started from the inside PC and allowed outbound. Stupid firewall! How could you solve this problem with the existing network topology? You could do one of the following:

▶ Add ACEs to access-list 101, allowing the source port number of every conceivable Internet application that your users are allowed to access inbound through the firewall.

▶ Apply access-list 101 outbound on the DMZ interface instead of inbound on the Internet interface.

▶ Upgrade to a dynamic packet filtering firewall.

The first choice is impractical, not to mention it creates a large vulnerability. The second choice is feasible, but the effort would have to be replicated for every internal interface on your network, and might create a management nightmare. The third choice might be the best one and might even be accomplished with a Cisco IOS software upgrade and some small re-configuration and without the need for additional hardware.

So, where would you deploy a static packet-filtering firewall? A good example would be a Cisco IOS router configured with ACLs as a static packet-filtering firewall at the network edge. This customer-managed Internet router, connected to an ISP router, could enforce *perimeter security* as part of a layered defense strategy. It wouldn't be very good at *communications security*, *core network security*, or *endpoint security* (of the four firewall roles covered previously), but that isn't its intended role.

Advantages and Disadvantages of Static Packet-Filtering Firewalls

Advantages of static packet-filtering firewalls include the following:

▶ Simple permit/deny rules

▶ Little or no impact on network performance

▶ Simple to configure

▶ Supported on most routers

▶ Good first level of defense at a lower OSI layer ("big chunk" rules)

▶ 90% of effectiveness of high-end firewalls at an appreciably lower cost

Disadvantages of static packet-filtering firewalls include the following:

► Difficult to catch IP spoofing

► Filtering fragmented IP packets is problematic

► Implementation and maintenance of complex ACLs

► Some applications/services cannot be filtered

► Stateless (only one packet at a time)

Application Layer Gateways

Figure 5.4 illustrates the basic operation of an application layer gateway.

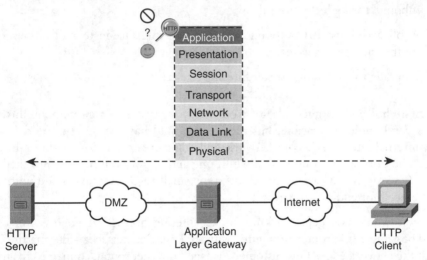

• Works at OSI layers 3, 4, 5, and 7.
• Also known as proxy servers and application gateways.

FIGURE 5.4 Application layer gateway (proxy server) firewall.

An application layer gateway (or proxy server) is a firewall that proxies a client's connection to a server at layers 5 and 7 (session and application) of the OSI model.

> **NOTE**
>
> When describing layered network architecture, it is often convenient to group layers 5, 6, and 7 of the OSI model into a single application layer. Thus, the TCP/IP protocol stack can line up, layer-by-layer, with the OSI model for layers 1 to 4, with a single layer 5. It is at this single, composite application layer that application layer gateways operate.

Referring to Figure 5.4, here are the steps that illustrate the operation of an application layer gateway:

- ▶ At the application layer, the client first connects to the application layer gateway.

- ▶ (Optional) The user is authenticated to the proxy at the application layer.

- ▶ The application layer gateway proxies (acts on behalf of) the client's connection to the application server.

- ▶ The application layer gateway accepts replies from the application server.

- ▶ The application layer gateway forwards the replies to the client.

If the proxy server is not operational, the client will not be able to connect. No proxy = no service.

Advantages and Limitations of Application Layer Gateways

Advantages of application layer gateways include the following:

- ▶ Persons, and not devices, are authenticated.

- ▶ DoS attacks are made more difficult because it is harder for hackers to spoof as theirs isn't a direct path to the target system.

- ▶ Option to monitor and filter application data.

- ▶ Option to configure detailed logging.

Limitations of application layer gateways include the following:

- ▶ Software processing of packets can be CPU-intensive.

- ▶ Can be memory and disk-intensive, too. (We have to store the cached connection information somewhere!)

- ▶ Requires a proxy per application.

- ▶ Limited number of application supported.

- ▶ Sometimes requires additional client configuration or software.

As a general recommendation, only use application layer gateways in key situations where increased security is an acceptable tradeoff for less performance.

> **NOTE**
>
> Recall that there are six bits in a TCP segment header that, depending on which combination of bits is set, describe the state of a TCP session. TCP defines rules for the combinations of bit settings that are allowed. A stateful packet-filtering firewall will also understand these rules. The bits are as follows:
>
> ▶ URG = Urgent
>
> ▶ ACK = Acknowledge
>
> ▶ PSH = Push
>
> ▶ RST = Reset
>
> ▶ SYN = Synchronize
>
> ▶ FIN = Finish (or finalize)

Dynamic (or Stateful) Packet-Filtering Firewalls

Figure 5.5 illustrates the basic operation of a dynamic (or stateful) packet-filtering firewall.

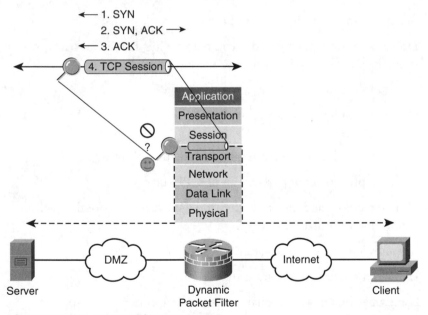

FIGURE 5.5 Dynamic packet-filtering firewall.

• Stateful filtering works at OSI layers 3 and 4.
• Packets are examined as part of a TCP session.

A dynamic packet-filtering firewall is like a knowledgeable tennis fan or umpire. They understand all the rules of the game and can permit or deny volleys that don't follow the rules. They can filter all the way up to layer 4 of the OSI model like the static packet-filtering firewall can, but they also understand that:

▶ A game starts with an opening serve from the player who has service (requester send SYN).

▶ The in-bounds serve is supposed to be returned by the opponent (responder sends SYN, ACK), but sometimes it is rejected (responder sends RST) because the opponent is not ready.

▶ If the initial player receives the ball back from the opponent (SYN, ACK), they will return the ball (thank you very much!) with an (ACK) and the volley continues. The initial three-way handshake (SYN; SYN, ACK; ACK) is complete.

▶ Either the initial server or the opponent can tear down the volley (the TCP session) at any time by sending a (FIN) to their opponent, beginning a four-way handshake that culminates in the session's (the volley's) termination.

In this manner, the firewall builds a database of connections that are built across it and the state that they are in. This is called the *state table*. Here's what a stateful firewall does with every packet that is lobbed across it:

▶ The packet is checked first to see if there is a pre-existing connection between the end systems' (client and server) sockets.

> **NOTE**
>
> A socket is made up of an IP address + a port number. The two sockets (source and destination) uniquely identify the circuit between the connection partners.

▶ If the state table indicates that there is an existing connection between the sockets, the state table is further referenced for that connection and the flags (SYN, ACK, RST, and so on) in the packet are checked to see if they are valid for that connection. For example, once a connection is set up, the firewall would refuse any further SYNs between the sockets, as they are used only when the connection is first being set up.

▶ If a connection doesn't already exist, the firewall will allow it to be built as long as no ACL denies the initial SYN. The connection state is put into the state table (see the following note).

> **NOTE**
>
> It is important to note that stateful firewalls only consult an interface ACL once: when the connection is being set up with the initial SYN. All subsequent packets are checked against the state table. As long as the packet matches the correct state per the state table, as well as other information like sequence numbers, the packet is allowed through the firewall.
>
> Therefore, unlike static packet-filtering firewalls, an interface ACL on a stateful firewall only needs to permit that first SYN. There is no need to have another ACL to allow the correct response (for example, SYN, ACK, or RST), as would likely be the case with a static packet-filtering firewall.
>
> In this fashion, the stateful firewall is plug-and-play. You only need to permit a connection to be initiated in one direction, and the firewall will dynamically create a rule to allow the return flow. This makes configuration that much simpler. Referring again to Figure 5.3, the network would function as designed if the static packet-filtering IOS router/firewall was replaced with a dynamic packet-filtering firewall.

Dynamic packet-filtering firewalls can enforce *perimeter security*. They also can ensure *core network security* insofar as they can detect anomalies in traffic patterns. Often they employ VPN technologies and can therefore manage some of C-I-A implicit in *communications network security*.

Uses and Limitations of Dynamic Packet-Filtering Firewalls

Uses of dynamic packet-filtering firewalls include the following:

- ▶ Intelligent first level of defense
- ▶ Primary defense mechanism
- ▶ Augmenting static packet filtering
- ▶ Improving routing throughput
- ▶ Proof against spoofing and DoS attacks

Limitations of dynamic packet-filtering firewalls include the following:

- ▶ Doesn't filter at the application layer.
- ▶ Not all protocols are stateful like TCP (for example: ICMP, UDP, some routing protocols).
- ▶ Some applications use multiple channels and dynamic port numbers negotiated above the transport layer (for example: FTP, RealAudio, some multimedia).
- ▶ Cannot authenticate users to connections (because this occurs at a higher layer of the OSI model).

As a general recommendation, deploy stateful firewalls as the premier defense mechanism of a secure network architecture.

Application Inspection Firewalls

Figure 5.6 illustrates a firewall that works at the application layer.

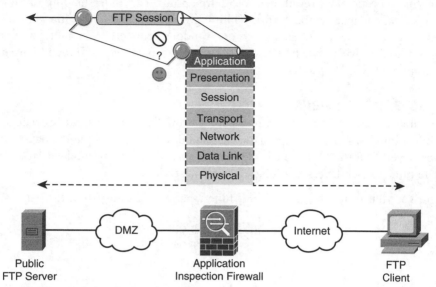

FIGURE 5.6 Application inspection firewall.

At first glance, you might assume that application layer gateways and application inspection firewalls are synonymous. They are not. Though they both work at the application layer (really, layers 5, 6, and 7) of the OSI model, an application inspection firewall will perform deep packet inspection at the application layer in order to determine that protocols that are proceeding across the firewall are compliant with the organization's security policy. At the same time, the application inspection firewall can ensure that the protocol is standards-compliant and also look for signs of unauthorized protocols tunneled inside the application session. For example, the eDonkey protocol that is used by the popular P2P application, Kazaa, could be blocked when it appears inside an HTTP session.

Here's another example. Refer to Figure 5.6. The network security policy says that anonymous FTP is allowed to the FTP server in the DMZ, but that no one is allowed to alter, move, create, copy, or delete files or directories. This would be typical of a public mirror site supporting a Linux distribution, perhaps on a university's network. We could instruct the computer science student who is managing the FTP server, that the server's patch revision must be up-to-date and that it is configured correctly to allow only anonymous FTP with access control per the security policy. The application inspection firewall could be configured to inspect the FTP command channel (recalling that FTP uses two channels: one for command/control and another for data) and block unauthorized activity at the application layer.

For this to occur, the firewall needs to have an intrinsic understanding of how the application layer protocol works. This higher intelligence is not found on all firewall products and can distinguish one vendor's products from another. It is often bundled with dynamic packet filtering as part of a Unified Threat Management (UTM) product.

Transparent Firewalls

The final category of firewalls is transparent firewalls. A transparent firewall, as its name implies, starts making forwarding and filtering decisions at the data link layer (layer 2) of the OSI model. It works in a secure bridging mode at layer 2, while offering rich layers 2 through 7 security services.

Figure 5.7 illustrates the basic layer 2 functionality of a transparent firewall.

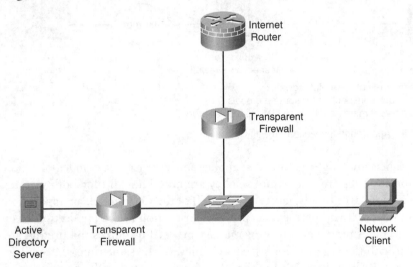

• Rich layer 2 through 7 security services.
• No readdressing of the network required.
• Protects against many layer 2 attacks.

FIGURE 5.7 Transparent firewall.

The four other firewall categories mentioned previously are all fundamentally IP firewalls. A transparent firewall, on the other hand, can filter and forward other protocol suites (such as AppleTalk, Novell IPX, DEC VMS, and so on) based on identifying information in the Ethernet frame header. It can also guard against some common layer 2 attacks such as ARP table poisoning, DHCP spoofing, and MAC flooding by virtue of its layer 2-aware design.

Like a switch, the transparent firewall is invisible at layer 3, requiring no readdressing of the network.

Cisco Family of Firewalls

The Cisco family of firewalls includes the following:

- Cisco IOS firewalls
- Cisco PIX 500 Series firewalls
- Cisco ASA 5500 Series Adaptive Security appliances

The following are features of Cisco IOS firewalls:

- Zone-based policy framework
- Application layer firewalling for email, web, and other traffic
- IM and P2P application filtering
- VoIP inspection and firewalling
- Virtual Routing and Forwarding (VRF) support
- Wireless integration (if equipped)
- Stateful failover
- Local URL filtering: whitelist and blacklist support
- National Institute of Science and Technology (NIST) Federal Information Processing Standard (FIPS) 140 and Common Criteria certifications
- Dynamic Multipoint VPN (DMVPN)

The following are features of Cisco PIX 500 Series firewalls:

- Advanced application-aware firewall services
- VoIP and multimedia security
- Site-to-site and remote access IPsec VPN
- Five models:
  - PIX 501 (SOHO / ROBO)
  - PIX 506E (ROBO / SMB)
  - PIX 515E (SMB / Enterprise)
  - PIX 525 (Enterprise)
  - PIX 535 (Enterprise / SP)

The following are features of Cisco ASA 5500 Series Adaptive Security appliances:

▶ Intelligent threat defense

▶ Secure Sockets Layer (SSL) and IPsec VPN

▶ IPS

▶ Content Security Services

▶ Cisco Unified Communications (voice and video)

▶ Key component of the Cisco Self-Defending Network

▶ Five models:

  ▶ ASA 5505 (SOHO / ROBO)

  ▶ ASA 5510 (ROBO / SMB)

  ▶ ASA 5520 (SMB / Enterprise)

  ▶ ASA 5540 (Enterprise)

  ▶ ASA 5550 (Enterprise / SP)

Firewall Implementation Best Practices

According to Cisco, this is a summary of the most important best practices for integrating firewalls into a comprehensive security policy:

▶ Place firewalls at key network security boundaries.

▶ Although firewalls are the primary security device, it is unrealistic to assume that the firewall is all that is needed for security.

▶ Adopt a "deny all" strategy by default. Deny all traffic except that which is expressly needed. (See Chapter 2, "Building a Secure Network Using Security Controls.")

▶ Do not forget physical controls on firewall access.

▶ Regularly monitor firewall logs for signs of intrusion. (See Chapter 4, "Implementing Secure Management and Hardening the Router.")

▶ Make sure that changes to the firewall's configuration occur within an overall change management policy.

▶ Firewalls are primarily technical controls against outside attack. Do not let internal security lapse as a result.

▶ Adopt strong administrative controls and physical controls to complement the firewall's technical controls.

Creating Static Packet Filters with ACLs

You should already have an understanding of the basics of ACLs as covered in CCNA material. This being the case, we can forgo the basics of creating and applying access lists to interfaces (and also vtys) in favor of focusing on examples and recommendations for their use. We will look at some specific examples of their use, both using the CLI and the Cisco SDM.

In this section, we examine the use of interface ACLs in the context of creating a static packet-filtering firewall and examining the relative strengths and weaknesses of this type of firewall. Remember, these are not particularly intelligent firewalls but, as we see, they do have an important role in the Cisco Self-Defending Network.

> **EXAM ALERT**
>
> ACLs will be on the exam. Understand them thoroughly in the context of static packet filtering per the prerequisite courses ICND1 and ICND2.

Threat Mitigation with ACLs

ACLs can mitigate the following types of threats:

- Inbound IP address spoofing
- Outbound IP address spoofing
- DoS and DDoS TCP SYN attacks
- DoS smurf attacks
- Inbound and outbound ICMP messages (used for DoS attacks and reconnaissance)
- Traceroute (used for reconnaissance)

Inbound Versus Outbound

There are two different meanings for "inbound" and "outbound," depending on the context in which they are used:

- **Definition One—Security Zone Context.** The words "inbound" and "outbound" are used in the preceding list. What do they mean? Do they indicate directions of packet flow relative to security zones? In this context, yes. Outbound traffic is traffic flowing from a more-trusted zone to a less-trusted zone. Inbound traffic is traffic flowing from a less-trusted zone to a more-trusted zone.

> ► **Inbound.** For example, IP packets arriving inbound on an Internet-facing interface should never have a source address of an internal network. Configuring an ACL to check the source addresses would be relatively simple.

> ► **Outbound.** Similarly, packets arriving on a LAN interface (or leaving an Internet-facing interface) would constitute outbound traffic, and should only contain source addresses from the organization's own address space, whether they are network address translated or not.

► **Definition Two—Interface ACL Context.** "Inbound" and "outbound" can also be relative to the interfaces themselves. This is an important distinction because after you create an interface ACL, you have to apply it either *in(bound)* or *out(bound)* on an interface.

> ► **Inbound ACLs.** These ACLs check packets as they arrive on an interface from a connected network. For example, a packet that arrives on a LAN interface from the physical network that it is connected to would be inbound. Thus, this traffic has not been routed yet and, in fact, the router hasn't decided whether to route it or not. Inbound ACLs are more efficient in terms of processing because if a packet is denied by the ACL, no CPU time has been wasted performing a routing table lookup. A permitted packet will be routed.

> ► **Outbound ACLs.** These ACLs check the packets after they have been dispatched to the correct interface per the routing table and prior to being forwarded to the connected network. A *permitted* packet will be sent to the output buffer and a *denied* packet will be discarded.

EXAM ALERT

Make sure you understand what context these terms are being used in when taking the exam. Misunderstanding the context is a sure recipe for confusion.

NOTE

Encrypted packets are tested on the ACL twice. If a packet is encrypted, it will first be tested on the inbound ACL to determine whether encrypted packets are allowed. If it is allowed, the packet is decrypted before it is again tested on the inbound ACL.

Identifying ACLs

Let's review how to identify ACLs on Cisco IOS routers:

- ▶ **Numbered ACL:**

    - ▶ The number indicates the protocol that is being filtered.

    - ▶ The ranges 1–99 and 1300–1999 indicate standard ACLs (filter all of IP, source address only). Cannot create a layer 4 firewall with these.

    - ▶ The ranges 100–199 and 2000–2699 indicate extended ACLs (filter IP, protocols encapsulated in IP, source and destination socket [address and port] as applicable). Can create a layer 4 firewall with these.

- ▶ **Named ACL:**

    - ▶ Can use custom name for ACL (available from Cisco IOS Release 11.2).

    - ▶ Rules: Names contain alphanumeric characters but no spaces or punctuation. Must begin with an alphabetic character.

    - ▶ Can be either standard or extended.

    - ▶ Can add or delete entries within the ACL.

NOTE

An interface ACL will not filter traffic that originated from the router itself.

ACL Examples Using the CLI

We look at two examples of ACLs in action using the CLI. This will be a useful review of basic ACL concepts, as first we create and apply a numbered extended ACL and second, examine the use of *established* parameters in ACLs, as well as how to edit an existing ACL.

Example 1: Numbered IPv4 ACL

Figure 5.8 illustrates the goals of the ACL we are creating.

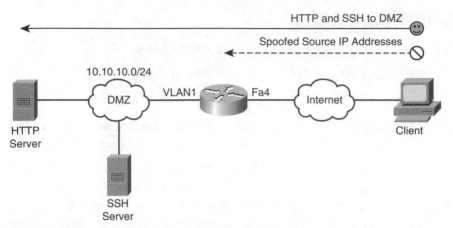

FIGURE 5.8 Allow HTTP and SMTP, block IP spoofing.

The following CLI commands match Figure 5.8. First, we create the ACL and then apply it to the Internet-facing interface, FastEthernet 4. This is a very common and practical use for an ACL. ACLs are usually applied on perimeter devices, such as routers, where simple rules can be used. The idea is to get rid of traffic that is absolutely not allowed as early as possible, leaving whatever is left over for other devices further inside our network. This concept of nesting of perimeters is discussed in Chapter 4. In this example, we create an anti-spoofing rule, ensuring that the source address of any inbound packets to our network do not match our internal network. Then we explicitly permit the traffic that is allowed, namely traffic to the HTTP and SSH servers in the Demilitarized Zone (DMZ).

```
CiscoISR(config)#access-list 101 remark -- anti-spoofing rule
CiscoISR(config)#access-list 101 deny ip 10.10.10.0 0.0.0.255 any
CiscoISR(config)#access-list 101 remark -- permit HTTP and SSH to inside
CiscoISR(config)#access-list 101 permit tcp any 10.10.10.0 0.0.0.255 eq 80
CiscoISR(config)#access-list 101 permit tcp any 10.10.10.0 0.0.0.255 eq 22
CiscoISR(config)#interface FastEthernet 4
CiscoISR(config-if)#ip access-group 101 in
```

You can review the access-list and the matches against the ACEs with the **show access-list** command. Note that the remarks do not display with the **show access-list** command output. You can only see them when you view the *running-config*:

```
CiscoISR#show access-list 101
Extended IP access list 101
    10 deny ip 10.10.10.0 0.0.0.255 any (109 matches)
    20 permit tcp any 10.10.10.0 0.0.0.255 eq www (11532 matches)
    30 permit tcp any 10.10.10.0 0.0.0.255 eq 22 (23453 matches)
CiscoISR(config)#
```

> **NOTE**
>
> Strictly speaking, the anti-spoofing rule is not necessary because the non-HTTP and SSH traffic is denied by the implicit deny-all statement at the end of the access-list. Best practices dictate that explicit rules will allow for the logging of specific attacks (note there are 109 matches in the preceding ACL), and by putting the anti-spoofing ACE early in the ACL, the attack is thwarted early on and there's no possibility that it might accidentally be permitted by a later ACE.

Note that the **show access-list 101** command displays sequence numbers (10, 20, 30, and so on) in the numbered ACL. As of Cisco IOS Software Release 12.3, you can delete and insert ACEs using these sequence numbers. For example, if we wanted to delete sequence 10 (the anti-spoofing ACE), we could enter these CLI commands:

```
CiscoISR(config)#ip access-list extended 101
CiscoISR(config-ext-nacl)#no 10
CiscoISR(config-ext-nacl)#
```

This deletes ACE 10, but does *not* re-sequence the ACL:

```
CiscoISR#show access-list 101
Extended IP access list 101
    20 permit tcp any 10.10.10.0 0.0.0.255 eq www (11989 matches)
    30 permit tcp any 10.10.10.0 0.0.0.255 eq 22 (23492 matches)
CiscoISR(config)#
```

You can use similar logic to insert ACEs too. Let's combine that thought with the **established** parameter in the next example.

Example 2: Established Command and Inserting ACEs

The second example covers the two concepts of established command and inserting ACEs. A static packet filtering router will never be stateful. That said, what if you want to make sure that applying an ACL to an interface does not drop existing TCP sessions? The **established** parameter in an ACE allows the router to examine the flags in the TCP header and permit TCP segments that have the RST or ACK bit set because only active TCP sessions would have at least one or the other of these bits set. Continuing with the previous example (also refer to Figure 5.8), if you wanted to ensure that all existing TCP sessions remain active, you could enter this CLI command to put it at the beginning of access-list 101:

```
CiscoISR(config)#ip access-list extended 101
CiscoISR(config-ext-nacl)#5 permit tcp any any established
CiscoISR(config-ext-nacl)#do show access-list 101
Extended IP access list 101
    5 permit tcp any any established (96 matches)
    20 permit tcp any 10.10.10.0 0.0.0.255 eq www (12032 matches)
    30 permit tcp any 10.10.10.0 0.0.0.255 eq 22 (25000 matches)
CiscoISR(config-ext-nacl)#
```

Of course, we don't know what existing TCP sessions are being permitted across our firewall, so best practices dictate that we would specify minimally the port number of the established protocol that is being permitted. For example, if the HTTP server in the DMZ were somehow hijacked by a hacker, it might try to initiate a connection out to the Internet using some other protocol, perhaps Telnet (TCP Port 23). If we left ACL 101 as is, the hijacked server could initiate a Telnet connection (SYN) outbound to the Internet and the reply (SYN, ACK) would be allowed back through the firewall on the **established** ACE in the ACL. Not good!

You can verify that an ACL is applied on an interface and what direction it is applied in by using the **show ip interface** command:

```
CiscoISR#show ip interface FastEthernet 4
FastEthernet4 is up, line protocol is up
  Internet address is 192.168.99.218/25
  Broadcast address is 255.255.255.255
  Address determined by non-volatile memory
  MTU is 1500 bytes
  Helper address is not set
  Directed broadcast forwarding is disabled
  Outgoing access list is not set
  Inbound  access list is 101
  Proxy ARP is disabled
[output omitted]
```

ACL Guidelines

Table 5.1 outlines Cisco's general best practices for the use of ACLs.

TABLE 5.1 ACL Pointers

Item	Guideline
Implicit deny all	Statement is there at the end of the ACL whether you enter it or not.
Standard ACLs	Not particularly granular. May need an extended ACL to enact a security policy.
Order of Operation	ACEs are parsed top to bottom. Place more specific tests at the top. Ensure that ACEs do not contradict/negate one another.
Inbound vs. Outbound	Check the direction in which the ACL is applied to an interface. This will determine source/destination addresses and port numbers to use.
Modifying Numbered ACLs	Prior to Cisco IOS Software Release 12.3, the whole ACL would have to be recreated.
Router-Generated Traffic	Interface ACLs cannot filter this traffic. If it needs to be filtered, it must be done on other routers or using other router filter mechanisms with ACLs (not discussed here).
Extended ACLs	Consider placing on routers as close as possible to source being filtered.
Standards ACLs	Consider placing on routers as close as possible to destination being filtered.

Using the Cisco SDM to Configure ACLs

Using the Cisco SDM to configure ACLs follows the same rules as using the CLI. First, you create the ACL, and then you apply it to the interface in the correct direction.

> **EXAM ALERT**
>
> By this chapter, you will have noticed that much of the manual configuration of the device is performed in the Cisco SDM starting at Configure->Additional Tasks.

In this example, we create an extended ACL (if you master this, you can easily do a standard ACL) called "inside-servers" that will permit HTTP and SSH to the DMZ. In fact, this ACL will follow the example we just completed in the CLI.

1. Choose **Configure->Additional Tasks->ACL Editor->Access Rules**.

2. Click **Add**. The Add a Rule window appears.

3. Enter a name or number for the ACL in the Add a Rule window (following the rules for names and number ranges, of course!). We'll give it the name inside-servers.

4. Confirm that **Extended Rule** is selected in the drop-down list. You can also put in a rule description (optional).

5. Click **Add**. The Add an Extended Rule Entry window appears.

Figure 5.9 illustrates the addition of an extended ACL entry using the Cisco SDM.

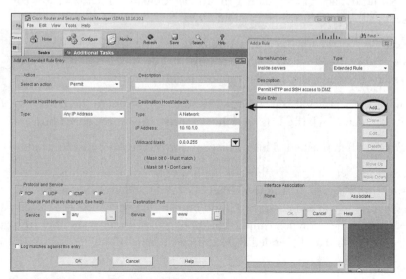

FIGURE 5.9 Adding an extended rule entry in the Cisco SDM.

6. Choose **Permit** or **Deny** from the **Select an action** drop-down list. You can also add a description (fewer than 100 characters) in the **Description** field. We will choose **Permit**.

7. You have a choice of either using **Any IP Address** (that is, the default) for the address, or you can construct the IP addresses by selecting the address type in the **Type** drop-down list. The **Type** drop-down list gives you three choices:

   ▶ A Network

   ▶ A Host Name or IP Address

   ▶ **Any IP Address** (selected by default)

   In the Destination Host/Network list, we choose **A Network** in this example. Enter the IP address of the network and a wildcard mask as required (**10.10.1.0** and **0.0.0.255**, respectively, in our example).

8. For the Source Host/Network, we choose **Any IP Address** because we don't know what the source address will be of the Internet users of our DMZ servers.

9. We're not done yet! Click the radio button in the Protocol and Services section that corresponds to the protocol that is being filtered—**TCP**, in our case.

10. Again, we can't be too specific about the source port because we don't know what dynamic port number the Internet client will choose, so we'll leave it at the default, which is **=** and **any**.

11. We can be specific for the destination port because it is a WWW server, so we choose **=** and **www**, respectively, for the destination port. You can also manually enter the destination port number or name.

12. If our security policy dictates that we need to log access to the DMZ server, we can check the **Log matches against this entry** check box.

13. Click **OK** when finished. This will return you to the **Add a Rule** window.

14. Repeat the preceding steps, but for the SSH server too (which is at Destination Port = 22). You can either click **Add** and go through all the steps again, or you can click the **Clone** button that will clone the selected entry and then you can simply edit the Destination Port number in the resultant Add an Extended Rule Entry window.

15. The ACL doesn't do anything by itself. It now must be associated with an interface. Click the **Associate** button and select the interface and direction in the Associate with an Interface window.

Figure 5.10 illustrates the dialog box for associating an ACL to an interface in the Cisco SDM.

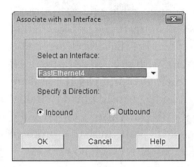

FIGURE 5.10 Associating an ACL to an interface in the Cisco SDM.

16. Alternatively you can choose **Configure->Interfaces and Connections** and select the interface you want to associate the ACL with. In the Interface Feature Edit Dialog window, put in the ACL name or number in the **Inbound** or **Outbound** access rule fields, as shown in Figure 5.11.

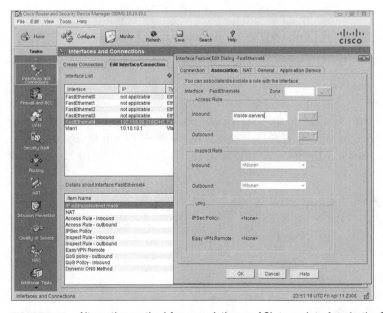

FIGURE 5.11 Alternative method for associating an ACL to an interface in the Cisco SDM.

Using ACLs to Filter Network Services

You may recall from Chapter 4 that there were a number of services that run on the router by default, which would be useful to lock down. Some of these services could be used by an attacker for reconnaissance. Some others might make the router vulnerable to DoS attacks. In this example, we are configuring the router so it will only accept RIP, EIGRP, and OSPF routing table updates from IP address 192.168.99.129, a neighbor router. This will mitigate the possibility that a knowledgeable attacker could engineer routing packets that inject erroneous routing table information into the router. Neither OSPF nor EIGRP use TCP or UDP for transport. They are services that use their own protocol IDs and are encapsulated directly into the IP packet header. The protocol ID field in the IP packet header identifies what protocol is inside the IP packet. An OSPF router, for example, would ignore IP packets with protocol ID 88 because that protocol ID identifies EIGRP. Some useful numbers to remember are as follows:

- ICMP: protocol ID 1

- TCP: protocol ID 6

- UDP: protocol ID 17

- GRE: protocol ID 47 (used by Microsoft VPNs and others)

- ESP: protocol ID 50 (used by IPsec VPNs)

- EIGRP: protocol ID 88 (proprietary Cisco routing protocol)

- OSPF: protocol ID 89 (open standard routing protocol)

While constructing an ACL in the Cisco SDM, you can click on the ellipse beside the IP Protocol field to see a list of the built-in protocol IDs in the Cisco SDM. You can also manually enter the protocol ID number if it is not in the list. Figure 5.12 shows the Protocol window in the Add an Extended Rule Entry window.

Here are the resulting CLI commands in the configuration generated by the Cisco SDM for the named extended IP ACL inbound-routing:

```
ip access-list extended inbound-routing
 remark SDM_ACL Category=1
 permit ospf host 192.168.99.129 any
 permit eigrp host 192.168.99.129 any
 permit udp host 192.168.99.129 any eq rip
interface FastEthernet 4
  ip access-group inbound-routing in
```

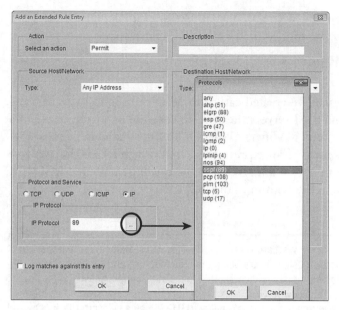

FIGURE 5.12 Protocol window in the Add an Extended Rule Entry window of the Cisco SDM.

Using ACLs to Mitigate IP Address Spoofing Attacks

As indicated in Figure 5.8 and in the accompanying subsection, "ACL Examples Using the CLI," ACLs can be very effective in mitigating IP address spoofing attacks. We will examine their use in mitigating both inbound IP address spoofing and outbound IP address spoofing.

Inbound IP Address Spoofing

In general, the source IP address in packets arriving inbound (that is, from a less-trusted network) should not be the same as an internal network's IP address range. That said, there are other source IP addresses that have no business being in these inbound packets. Here are guidelines for other IP addresses that normally should not be in the source address field, particularly when this Internet is connected to the Internet and therefore public, routable IP address space:

- ▶ **Local addresses.** 127.0.0.0/8 (used for loopback testing, for example).

- ▶ **Reserved private addresses.** Defined in RFC 1918, *Address Allocation for Private Internets.*

- ▶ **IP multicast addresses.** 224.0.0.0/4.

- ▶ **Any address starting with a 0.** 0.0.0.0/24 (for example, DHCP uses 0.0.0.0 in the source address field for DHCP requests).

- ▶ **All 1's source IP addresses.** 255.255.255.255.

Remember ACL 101 that we created earlier to permit traffic to the DMZ and only to the HTTP and SSH servers there? Let's take the opportunity to put a few key points together and modify it. We will follow the guideline of most specific ACEs first that we covered in a previous section, which means that we have a problem already. If we start adding ACEs to the existing numbered ACL 101, the new ACEs will go to the bottom of the ACL.

> **NOTE**
>
> Another tricky thing here is the wildcard masks used in the ACEs. Remember that the wildcard mask is an inverse mask, with 0's being the matching bits and 1's being the don't care bits. If you don't understand this, and the following example doesn't make any sense, then you have some review to do. For example, a /24 subnet mask would be represented as 255.255.255.0 with a regular mask, but as 0.0.0.255 as a wildcard mask.

First, use the **show access-list 101** command to verify the existing ACL:

```
CiscoISR(config)#do show access-list 101
Extended IP access list 101
    10 permit tcp any 10.10.10.0 0.0.0.255 eq www
    20 permit tcp any 10.10.10.0 0.0.0.255 eq 22
CiscoISR(config)#
```

Then, use the new features of Cisco IOS Software version 12.3 and later that enable you to use sequence numbers to add statements to an existing numbered ACL. We must insert these new lines ahead of the existing sequence number 10:

```
CiscoISR(config)#ip access-list extended 101
CiscoISR(config-ext-nacl)#1 deny ip 0.0.0.0 0.255.255.255 any
CiscoISR(config-ext-nacl)#2 deny ip 10.0.0.0 0.255.255.255 any
CiscoISR(config-ext-nacl)#3 deny ip 127.0.0.0 0.255.255.255 any
CiscoISR(config-ext-nacl)#4 deny ip 172.16.0.0 0.15.255.255 any
CiscoISR(config-ext-nacl)#5 deny ip 192.168.0.0 0.0.255.255 any
CiscoISR(config-ext-nacl)#6 deny ip 224.0.0.0 15.255.255.255 any
CiscoISR(config-ext-nacl)#7 deny ip host 255.255.255.255 any
```

Why stop there? Still following the guideline of most specific tests first, why don't we insert ACEs that will allow EIGRP and OSPF from 192.168.99.129/32, per the example in the section "Using ACLs to Filter Network Services," in this chapter (we would put RIP in there too, but we've run out of room if we want to insert it ahead of ACE 10!):

```
CiscoISR(config-ext-nacl)#8 permit eigrp host 192.168.99.129 any
CiscoISR(config-ext-nacl)#9 permit ospf host 192.168.99.129 any
```

Verify ACL 101:

```
CiscoISR(config-ext-nacl)#do show access-list 101
Extended IP access list 101
    1 deny ip 0.0.0.0 0.255.255.255 any (50 matches)
    2 deny ip 10.0.0.0 0.255.255.255 any
    3 deny ip 127.0.0.0 0.255.255.255 any
    4 deny ip 172.16.0.0 0.15.255.255 any
    5 deny ip 192.168.0.0 0.0.255.255 any
    6 deny ip 224.0.0.0 15.255.255.255 any (99937 matches)
    7 deny ip host 255.255.255.255 any
    8 permit eigrp host 192.168.99.129 any (2232 matches)
    9 permit ospf host 192.168.99.129 any (156 matches)
    10 permit tcp any 10.10.10.0 0.0.0.255 eq www (11345 matches)
    20 permit tcp any 10.10.10.0 0.0.0.255 eq 22
CiscoISR(config-ext-nacl)#
```

Outbound IP Address Spoofing

Generally speaking, the source address in IP packets that are leaving your network should belong to your address space, whether the addresses are RFC 1918 addresses or publicly routable. In this example, we create an ACL named no-spoof-out and apply it to the Vlan1 interface (default LAN interface on a Cisco 800 series ISR) in the inbound direction. Figure 5.13 illustrates the effects of the cumulative example we have been working on.

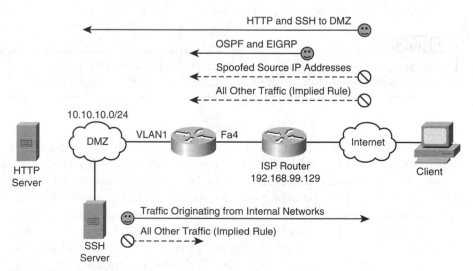

FIGURE 5.13 Complete solution.

Figure 5.13 illustrates the net, cumulative effect of all the previous ACL examples.

```
CiscoISR(config)#ip access-list extended no-spoof-out
CiscoISR(config-ext-nacl)#permit ip 10.10.10.0 0.0.0.255 any
CiscoISR(config-ext-nacl)#exit
CiscoISR(config)#interface Vlan 1
CiscoISR(config-if)#ip access-group no-spoof-out in
CiscoISR(config-if)#
```

> **NOTE**
>
> Cisco introduced the IP Unicast Reverse Path Forwarding (RPF) verification with IOS Release 12.0. This is an alternative to using ACLs and uses the **ip verify unicast reverse-path** interface configuration CLI command.

Using ACLs to Filter Other Common Services

If ACLs were only as straightforward in practice as our examples are so far! Chances are good that there are other services that will need to be allowed through the static packet-filtering firewall. For example, if your security policy allows it, you may need to be able to ping (that is, ICMP echo request) devices on the inside of your network in the DMZ from the outside for network management reasons. Speaking of network management, you may have some devices that need to be managed by SNMP. In the example that we have been working on, neither ICMP nor SNMP are allowed through the firewall because they are being denied by the implicit rules. Not only do you have to allow these protocols inbound, but their replies need to be allowed outbound. You have to ensure that existing ACLs will allow these responses.

> **NOTE**
>
> In our example, we needn't be worried about blocking the replies because the ACL no-spoof-out allows anything whose source address comes from the DMZ through the firewall.

ICMP

We could create an ACE in ACL 101 that would allow all ICMP inbound, but do we really want to do this? Our security policy dictates which protocols are required for business reasons. Because in the last chapter we agreed that ICMP (and other services) can be used for reconnaissance and DoS attacks, it makes good sense to only allow specific messages through the firewall. In this example, we would want to allow ICMP echoes through the firewall to the DMZ and allow the replies back out. Certainly this will allow an attacker to determine live IP hosts in the DMZ, and also engineer an ICMP flood. If we don't allow other ICMP commands through (such as ICMP redirects, which can be used for certain exploits), then this may be a reasonable tradeoff.

EXAM ALERT

Cisco specifically recommends against allowing ICMP echoes and ICMP redirects (as mentioned) inbound. We are allowing ICMP echoes through because it fits with the worked example, but when asked on an exam, always answer the Cisco way!

The following CLI command adds a rule that will allow ICMP echoes from any IP address to 10.0.0.0/8. Note the use of the inverse mask, 0.0.0.255, being the inverse of 255.0.0.0:

```
CiscoISR(config)#access-list 101 permit icmp any 10.10.10.0 0.0.0.255 echo
```

Because we didn't insert this command with a sequence number, it will be added to the end of the existing ACL 101 before the implicit deny.

Here's a list of some useful ICMP messages you may want to filter:

- ▶ **Echo.** Allows pinging to IP hosts.

- ▶ **Echo-reply.** Replies to pinging.

- ▶ **Unreachable.** Reply indicating that a host cannot be reached.

- ▶ **Redirect.** Command to alter a routing table.

- ▶ **parameter-problem.** Invalid/problem packet header.

- ▶ **Packet-too-big.** Required for Maximum Transmission Unit (MTU) path discovery.

- ▶ **Source-quench.** Throttles traffic as necessary.

EXAM ALERT

Cisco says that all ICMP types, with the exception of echo, parameter problem, packet too big, and source quench, should be blocked outbound as a rule. Memorize the ICMP types in the preceding list.

Filtering Other Miscellaneous Services

The CLI and the Cisco SDM have built-in keywords for the following common and router service traffic:

- ▶ **Common Services.** *domain, smtp, ftp.*

- ▶ **Router Service Traffic.** *telnet, syslog, snmptrap.*

EXAM ALERT

Curiously, SSH is not specified by keyword ssh in either the CLI or the Cisco SDM. You must use TCP port 22 when specifying it. SSH is preferred over Telnet wherever possible because it uses encryption.

Know the TCP and UDP port numbers for these common services.

Cisco Zone-Based Policy Firewall Fundamentals

The last section examines the configuration of a static packet-filtering firewall using interface ACLs. In this section, we leverage on Cisco's Zone-Based Policy Firewall (ZPF) to create a dynamic packet-filtering firewall. ZPF is not Cisco's first foray into dynamic packet filtering technology. Before ZPF, Cisco offered Context-Based Access Control (CBAC, pronounced "see-back"), later changing its name to IOS Classic Firewall. As we know, "classic" infers that it is older, so if you want the latest and greatest dynamic packet-filtering firewall technology, you will want to master the Cisco Zone-Based Policy Firewall.

NOTE

We will implement a stateful packet inspection and application layer firewall by leveraging on the Cisco IOS Zone-Based Policy Firewall. If you already understand the fundamentals of both, go ahead and read this section. If you don't, and you have skipped the earlier section, "Examining and Defining Firewall Technologies," now is the time to go back and carefully read it through. You have been warned!

As we have seen, when you only have a few interfaces on the firewall, configuring ACLs on a static packet-filtering firewall isn't an enormous task. However, even with a pair of interfaces, by the time you have sorted all the permutations and combinations of pairing reply traffic with requests, rule order logic, and inbound versus outbound, the need for a disciplined configuration management approach as well as much testing is crucial.

Now imagine that you had five interfaces on the firewall (see Figure 5.14). The number of permutations with just the choice of applying ACLs inbound vs. outbound on 5 interfaces = 2^5 = 32 possible interactions to troubleshoot.

This is one of the reasons for the Cisco Zone-Based Policy Firewall (ZPF). ZPF enables you to group interfaces into security zones and design rules using the Cisco Common Classification Policy Language (C3PL) for traffic moving between the different zones.

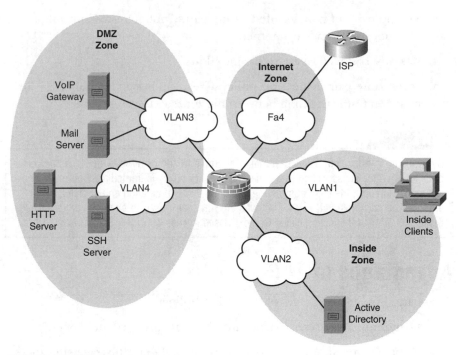

FIGURE 5.14 ZPF conceptual overview.

NOTE

C3PL is not to be confused with his distant cousin, C3PO, of Star Wars fame!

For example, using ZPF for access rules by grouping DMZ1 and DMZ2 into a DMZ zone, Inside1 and Inside2 into a INSIDE zone, and the Internet uplink into its own INTERNET zone, you could create and troubleshoot rule interaction between three different security zones equally as easily as you would use ACLs on a three-interface firewall. C3PL is the language that is used to classify (or differentiate) traffic that flows between the different zones and take different security, and QoS actions on the flows. Of course, this is a security course, so you know that the focus will be on security policies for the traffic!

It's not too early to look at a general overview of the workflow in configuring for ZPF. The following list is a high-level overview of the concepts, while trying to avoid Cisco terminology as much as possible:

1. **Create zones.** For example, DMZ, INSIDE, and INTERNET.

2. **Assign interfaces to a zone.** Vlan1 and Vlan2 in INSIDE zone; Vlan 3 and Vlan 4 in DMZ zone; FastEthernet 4 in INTERNET zone.

3. **Define pairs of zones called "zone pairs."** inbound-to-dmz, inbound-to-inside; outbound-to-internet.

4. **Classify traffic.** Classify traffic into flows.

5. **Inter-zone pair inspection policy.** Create an inspection policy for the classified traffic traveling between the zones in the zone pair.

> **NOTE**
>
> By grouping interfaces into zones, it makes it simple to add or remove interfaces because once an interface is associated to a zone, the security policy is immediately enforced without worrying about the extra abstraction and complexity of creating and applying ACLs and inspection (**ip inspect**) rules. That was the way that it used to be done with the legacy Cisco IOS Stateful Inspection called Context-Based Access Control (CBAC) firewall.

Advantages of ZPF

There are six main advantages of the ZPF, as follows:

- ▶ **Grouping.** Physical and virtual interfaces are grouped into zones.

- ▶ **Zone Traversal.** Firewall policies are applied to traffic traversing zones.

- ▶ **Simplicity.** Adding and removing interfaces into zones automatically integrates them into the firewall policy.

- ▶ **ACL Independence.** ZPF is not dependent on ACLs (see the following note).

- ▶ **Troubleshooting.** C3PL makes policies easier to visualize.

- ▶ **Security Posture.** ZPF turns the IOS router into a "deny unless explicitly permitted" firewall (reverse of the logic of the legacy stateful inspection model).

The other advantage is conceptual. Because ZPF is so visual, especially when using the Cisco SDM, it aids in learning how stateful firewalls operate and applying the rules in an intuitive fashion.

> **NOTE**
>
> Interface ACLs are still relevant and can be used to complement ZPF policies.
> - ▶ **Inbound ACL.** Applied before ZPF policies.
> - ▶ **Outbound ACL.** Applied after ZPF policies.

Features of ZPF

The six main supported features of ZPF are as follows:

- ▸ Stateful (Dynamic) packet inspection
- ▸ Application layer firewall
- ▸ URL filtering
- ▸ Transparent firewall
- ▸ Per-policy parameter
- ▸ Virtual Routing and Forwarding (VRF)-aware firewall

ZPF Actions

There are three main categories of actions that the ZPF can take on traffic:

- ▸ **Inspect.** Stateful inspection. Monitor outbound traffic and statefully inspect the return traffic to ensure that it matches session table entries.
- ▸ **Drop.** Analogous to a deny ACE in an ACL.
- ▸ **Pass.** Analogous to a permit ACE in an ACL (not stateful as is the inspect action).

Zone Behavior

Refer to Figure 5.15. Note that the network zone topology has changed from Figure 5.14. Interfaces Vlan2 and Vlan4 are no longer members of zones. Vlan5 has been added to the INSIDE zone. This is just the kind of situation that will drive you crazy! Perhaps the INSIDE, DMZ, and INTERNET zones were configured previously and you have just added two interfaces without yet putting them in zones. If you let your intuition guide you (and remembering that the firewall will err on the side of caution), you could probably figure this out for yourself, but let's look at the possible combinations of results.

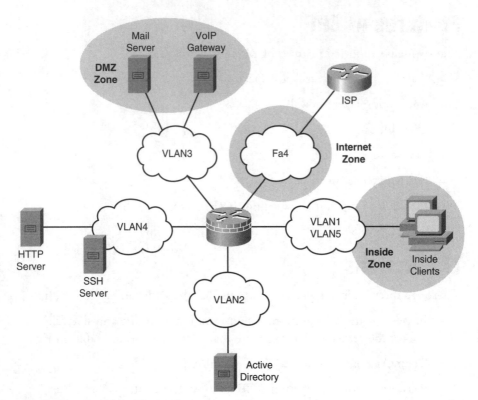

FIGURE 5.15 Zones partially implemented.

Traffic Flowing Through the Router

What will happen to traffic that would be routed between two interfaces when ZPF is fully or partially configured? Here are the possible results with examples:

▶ **Vlan2 to Vlan4.** Inter-interface traffic is permitted (normally routed) if neither interface is a member of a zone.

▶ **Vlan1 to Vlan3.** If the interfaces are in two different zones, and there is a ZPF policy configured for that zone-pair, the policy actions (inspect, drop, or pass) will dictate what to do with the traffic.

If the interfaces are in two different zones, and there is no ZPF policy configured, the traffic will be dropped. (The firewall errs on the side of caution!)

▶ **Vlan2 to FastEthernet4.** If one interface is in a zone and the other one isn't, the traffic is dropped.

▶ **Vlan1 to Vlan5.** If the interfaces are in the same zone (zone-pair is therefore not applicable) the traffic is passed.

Traffic Originating from the Router and Destined to the Router

What about traffic that either originates from or is destined to the router itself? By default, this traffic is permitted. The exception is where the traffic flows in a zone-pair in which the router's zone is a member (see note about the "self" zone below). In this latter case, the traffic either from or to the router will be subject to the actions (inspect, drop, or pass) specified in the ZPF policy. Figure 5.16 illustrates the self zone.

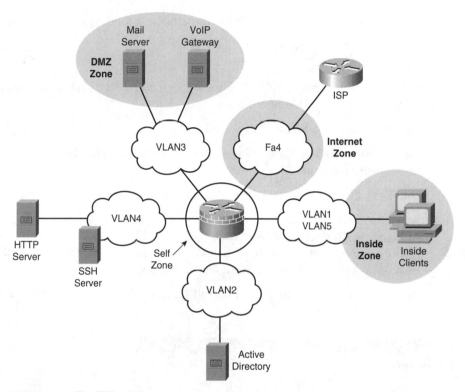

FIGURE 5.16   The ZPF self-zone.

NOTE

The router is automatically put in a special zone called the "self" zone when ZPF is configured. Figure 5.16 illustrates this.

Using the Cisco SDM Basic Firewall Wizard to Configure ZPF

A basic firewall is essentially a firewall that has two zones: inside (trusted) and outside (untrusted). The Cisco SDM Basic Firewall wizard enables you to do the following:

- ▶ Create a stateful firewall policy between these zones, inspecting outbound TCP, UDP, and router-generated ICMP traffic.

- ▶ Block all IM (MSN, AOL, and Yahoo!) whether its tunneled in HTTP or not.

- ▶ Deny traffic from outside to inside zones.

Follow these steps to configure ZPF using the Cisco SDM Basic Firewall Wizard. Starting from the Cisco SDM home page:

1. Select **Configure->Firewall and ACL**.

2. Ensure that the **Basic Firewall** radio button is selected and then push the **Launch the selected task** button.

3. The Basic Firewall Configuration Wizard window appears. Click **Next**.

4. Select the interface(s) that will be in the outside zone and the inside zone. At least one interface must be in each zone in order to continue. Check the **Allow secure SDM access from outside interfaces** check box if you will be accessing the SDM from an interface in the untrusted zone.

   Figure 5.17 illustrates the Basic Firewall Interface Configuration window in the Firewall Wizard.

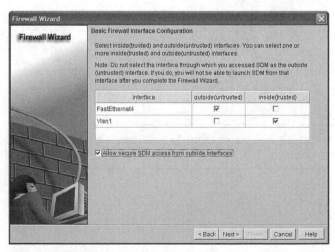

FIGURE 5.17   Basic Firewall Interface Configuration window.

5. Click **Next**.

6. If you have selected the **Allow secure SDM access from outside inter-faces** check box in the previous step, you will be prompted to set a policy for which range of IP addresses will be allowed to access the SDM from the outside zone. (Sound like a zone-pair that includes the self zone?) In the **Type** drop-down box, choose either **Network address**, **Host IP address**, or **any**. This dialog is illustrated in Figure 5.18.

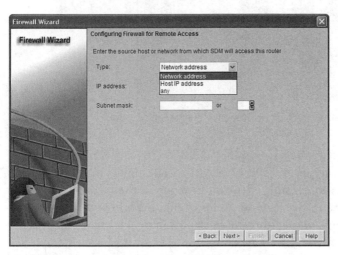

FIGURE 5.18 Configuring firewall for remote access.

7. Click **Next**. An Information window appears, indicating that the SDM connection will be dropped when the configuration is delivered to the firewall. Click **OK** on this window.

8. The Basic Firewall Security Configuration window appears. A slider control gives you a choice of applying either a high, medium, or low security policy. The default is high security. Click **Next** to accept the default.

9. The Basic Firewall Domain Name Server Configuration window appears, as illustrated in Figure 5.19. DNS is needed for application security, mainly because the domain names for IM services have to be resolved and the High Security policy (per the last step) will block IM. Fill in at least the **Primary DNS Server** and click **Next**.

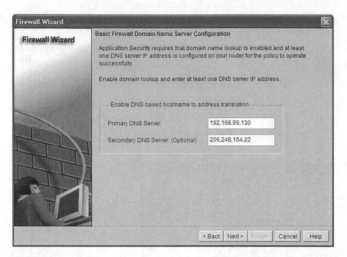

FIGURE 5.19 Basic Firewall Domain Name Service Configuration window.

10. The Firewall Configuration Summary window appears. This window presents a summary of the ZPF rules that will be applied to the router. The following is an example of the information in the Firewall Configuration Summary window. Refer to Figures 5.14 and 5.15 because the interfaces and zones in this summary match up with that example. This is not a preview of the CLI commands per se; it is just a summary of the policies that will be applied when the wizard is finished:

```
Note: Do not select the interface through which you accessed SDM as the
outside (untrusted) interface. If you do, you will not be able to launch
SDM from that interface after you complete the Firewall Wizard.

Inside(trusted) Interfaces:
    Vlan1 (10.10.10.1)

Outside(untrusted) Interface:
    FastEthernet4 (192.168.99.218)

Service Policy Configuration:

In-zone -> Out-zone:
    Inspect TCP,UDP,H323,SIP,SCCP and other protocols
    Deny packets with invalid ip address as source
Application Inspection for HTTP:
    Block HTTP port-misuse for IP,P2P
    Block HTTP protocol violation
    Block HTTP request methods other than post,head,get
    Block http request response containing non-ascii characters
Application Inspection for Instant Messaging:
    Block all services of msn,yahoo,aol with log action
```

```
Application Inspection for P2P:
    Block file transfer over edonkey,fasttrack,gnutella and kazaa2
    Block text-chat over edonkey
Application Inspection for Email:
    Block invalid command for imap,pop3
    Block SMTP session with data length over 5 MB

Self -> Out-zone:
    Inspect router generated ICMP traffic
Out-zone -> Self:
    Permit secure SDM Access to router (HTTP,SSH,RCP) from specified
source.
    Deny all other traffic.

DNS Configuration:
    Primary DNS:192.168.99.130
    Secondary DNS:206.248.154.22
```

11. Click **Finish**. The SDM delivers the configuration to the router. This is illustrated in Figure 5.20.

FIGURE 5.20 Cisco SDM commands delivery status.

Recall Step 4. If you were accessing the SDM from the outside (untrusted) zone, you will lose the connection. Reconnect to the router using a secure http connection.

12. Navigate to the home page of the Cisco SDM and verify that the ZPF has been applied by looking for a green check mark beside the Firewall Policies menu. Expand the menu with the down arrow on the right-hand side. This is illustrated in Figure 5.21.

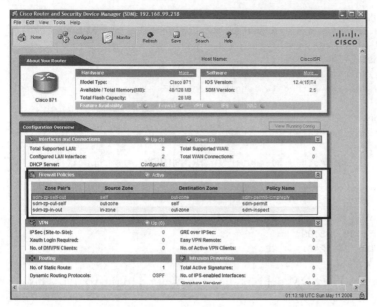

FIGURE 5.21 Cisco SDM home page with active Firewall Policies.

13. Navigate to **Configure->Firewall and ACL->Edit Firewall Policy** to see a visual representation of the rule flow, as indicated in the bottom of the window illustrated in Figure 5.22.

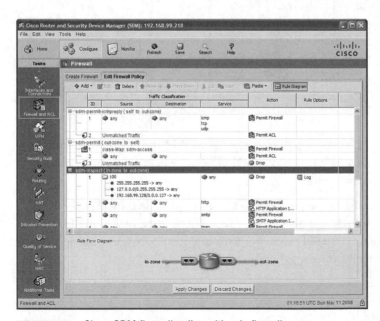

FIGURE 5.22 Cisco SDM firewall policy with rule flow diagram.

The following CLI commands match the preceding example of using the SDM Basic Firewall Wizard.

```
!----------
!1. CREATE CLASS MAPS
!----------
class-map type inspect smtp match-any sdm-app-smtp
 match  data-length gt 5000000
class-map type inspect match-any SDM_HTTPS
 match access-group name SDM_HTTPS
class-map type inspect match-any SDM_SSH
 match access-group name SDM_SSH
class-map type inspect match-any SDM_SHELL
 match access-group name SDM_SHELL
class-map type inspect match-any sdm-cls-access
 match class-map SDM_HTTPS
 match class-map SDM_SSH
 match class-map SDM_SHELL
class-map type inspect http match-any sdm-app-nonascii
 match  req-resp header regex sdm-regex-nonascii
class-map type inspect imap match-any sdm-app-imap
 match  invalid-command
class-map type inspect match-any sdm-cls-protocol-p2p
 match protocol edonkey signature
 match protocol gnutella signature
 match protocol kazaa2 signature
 match protocol fasttrack signature
 match protocol bittorrent signature
class-map type inspect match-any SDM_OSPF
 match access-group name SDM_OSPF
class-map type inspect match-any sdm-cls-insp-traffic
 match protocol dns
 match protocol https
 match protocol icmp
 match protocol imap
 match protocol pop3
 match protocol tcp
 match protocol udp
class-map type inspect match-all sdm-insp-traffic
 match class-map sdm-cls-insp-traffic
class-map type inspect match-any SDM-Voice-permit
 match protocol h323
 match protocol skinny
 match protocol sip
class-map type inspect match-any SDM_OSPF_TRAFFIC
 match class-map SDM_OSPF
class-map type inspect match-all sdm-protocol-pop3
 match protocol pop3
class-map type inspect match-any sdm-cls-icmp-access
 match protocol icmp
```

```
 match protocol tcp
 match protocol udp
class-map type inspect match-any sdm-cls-protocol-im
 match protocol ymsgr yahoo-servers
 match protocol msnmsgr msn-servers
 match protocol aol aol-servers
class-map type inspect pop3 match-any sdm-app-pop3
 match  invalid-command
class-map type inspect match-all sdm-access
 match class-map sdm-cls-access
 match access-group 101
class-map type inspect match-all SDM_OSPF_PT
 match class-map SDM_OSPF_TRAFFIC
class-map type inspect match-all sdm-protocol-p2p
 match class-map sdm-cls-protocol-p2p
class-map type inspect http match-any sdm-http-blockparam
 match  request port-misuse im
 match  request port-misuse p2p
 match  request port-misuse tunneling
 match  req-resp protocol-violation
class-map type inspect match-all sdm-protocol-im
 match class-map sdm-cls-protocol-im
class-map type inspect match-all sdm-icmp-access
 match class-map sdm-cls-icmp-access
class-map type inspect match-all sdm-invalid-src
 match access-group 100
class-map type inspect http match-any sdm-app-httpmethods
 match  request method bcopy
 match  request method bdelete
 match  request method bmove
 match  request method bpropfind
 match  request method bproppatch
 match  request method connect
 match  request method copy
 match  request method delete
 match  request method edit
 match  request method getattribute
 match  request method getattributenames
 match  request method getproperties
 match  request method index
 match  request method lock
 match  request method mkcol
 match  request method mkdir
 match  request method move
 match  request method notify
 match  request method options
 match  request method poll
 match  request method post
 match  request method propfind
 match  request method proppatch
```

```
 match   request method put
 match   request method revadd
 match   request method revlabel
 match   request method revlog
 match   request method revnum
 match   request method save
 match   request method search
 match   request method setattribute
 match   request method startrev
 match   request method stoprev
 match   request method subscribe
 match   request method trace
 match   request method unedit
 match   request method unlock
 match   request method unsubscribe
class-map type inspect match-all sdm-protocol-http
 match protocol http
class-map type inspect match-all sdm-protocol-smtp
 match protocol smtp
class-map type inspect match-all sdm-protocol-imap
 match protocol imap
!
!—————————————
!2.   CREATE POLICY MAPS
!—————————————
policy-map type inspect sdm-permit-icmpreply
 class type inspect sdm-icmp-access
  inspect
 class class-default
  pass
policy-map type inspect http sdm-action-app-http
 class type inspect http sdm-http-blockparam
  log
  reset
 class type inspect http sdm-app-httpmethods
  log
  reset
 class type inspect http sdm-app-nonascii
  log
  reset
 class class-default
policy-map type inspect smtp sdm-action-smtp
 class type inspect smtp sdm-app-smtp
  reset
 class class-default
policy-map type inspect imap sdm-action-imap
 class type inspect imap sdm-app-imap
  log
  reset
 class class-default
```

```
policy-map type inspect pop3 sdm-action-pop3
 class type inspect pop3 sdm-app-pop3
  log
  reset
 class class-default
policy-map type inspect sdm-inspect
 class type inspect sdm-invalid-src
  drop log
 class type inspect sdm-protocol-http
  inspect
  service-policy http sdm-action-app-http
 class type inspect sdm-protocol-smtp
  inspect
  service-policy smtp sdm-action-smtp
 class type inspect sdm-protocol-imap
  inspect
  service-policy imap sdm-action-imap
 class type inspect sdm-protocol-pop3
  inspect
  service-policy pop3 sdm-action-pop3
 class type inspect sdm-protocol-p2p
  drop log
 class type inspect sdm-protocol-im
  drop log
 class type inspect sdm-insp-traffic
  inspect
 class type inspect SDM-Voice-permit
  inspect
 class class-default
  pass
policy-map type inspect sdm-permit
 class type inspect sdm-access
  inspect
 class type inspect SDM_OSPF_PT
  pass
 class class-default
!
!------------
!3. CREATE SECURITY ZONES
!------------
zone security out-zone
zone security in-zone
!------------
!4. CREATE ZONE PAIRS
!------------
zone-pair security sdm-zp-self-out source self destination out-zone
 service-policy type inspect sdm-permit-icmpreply
zone-pair security sdm-zp-out-self source out-zone destination self
 service-policy type inspect sdm-permit
```

```
zone-pair security sdm-zp-in-out source in-zone destination out-zone
 service-policy type inspect sdm-inspect
!


!_____
!5. ASSOCIATE INTERFACES WITH ZONES
!_____

interface FastEthernet4
 zone-member security out-zone
!
interface Vlan1
 zone-member security in-zone
```

Manually Configuring ZPF with the Cisco SDM

To configure ZPF manually, here are the four basic steps:

1. Create zones.

2. Create class maps.

3. Create policy maps (and actions: inspect, drop, or pass).

4. Create zone pairs and assign policy maps to zone pairs.

These steps are summarized in Figure 5.23 and are covered in more detail in the following sections through an example of manually configuring ZPF with the Cisco SDM. Refer to Figure 5.14 for the network diagram that this example follows.

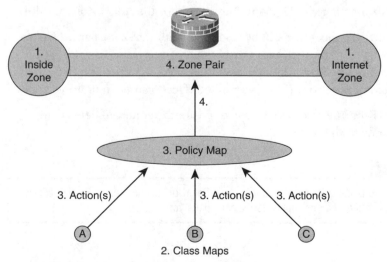

FIGURE 5.23 Summary: Manually configuring ZPF.

Step 1: Create Zones

Follow these steps to create a zone:

1. Select **Configure->Additional Tasks->Zones**.

2. Click **Add** to create a new zone in the Zone panel, which is illustrated in Figure 5.24.

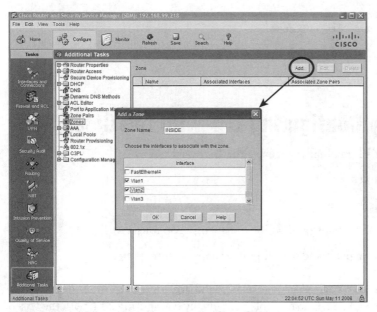

FIGURE 5.24 Adding a security zone in the Cisco SDM.

3. Enter a zone name in the **Zone Name** field of the Add a Zone window.

4. Select the interfaces that will be associated with that zone name by placing a check mark in the check box beside the interface name. Physical interfaces can be placed in only one zone, whereas virtual interfaces (such as dialer interfaces or bridged virtual interfaces) can be in multiple zones.

5. Click **OK** on the next two dialogs to create the zone and deliver the commands to the router.

NOTE

Be mindful of zone behavior per the earlier "Zone Behavior" section, because the policies have not been configured nor applied to the zone pairs yet!

Step 2: Create Class Maps

The next step to creating a ZPF policy is to define a Layer 3-4 class map. The class map will identify traffic that will have actions applied to it by policy maps (next step). For example, you might want all TCP traffic to be statefully inspected from the INSIDE zone to the INTERNET zone, with additional deep packet inspection (see the following note) applied to HTTP to ensure that it is both protocol-compliant and that IM traffic isn't tunneled inside it. In Figure 5.25, a class map is created that will eventually be used to 1) identify, then 2) inspect outbound traffic (that is, from the INSIDE zone to the INTERNET zone) for IM protocols MSN, Yahoo, and AOL as well as for miscellaneous P2P (Peer to Peer) traffic such as BitTorrent and Kazaa. Remember, the class map doesn't do anything but identify the traffic.

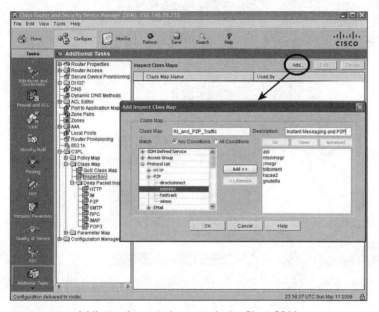

FIGURE 5.25 Adding an inspect class map in the Cisco SDM.

In order to identify the traffic, one or more distinguishing characteristics must be determined and based on the following criteria:

- ▶ **Access-group.** An ACL (standard or extended) can be applied to a class map.

- ▶ **Protocol.** TCP, UDP, ICMP, and application layer protocols such as HTTP, SMTP, IM, and P2P can be used as distinguishing characteristics. Any protocol (either user-defined or well-known) understood by Port-to-Application Mapping (PAM) can be specified.

- ▶ **Class-map.** Class maps can be nested inside another class map to provide additional match criteria.

NOTE

ZPF also supports advanced layer 7 application inspection. This is not covered in the Cisco Introduction to IOS Network Security v1.0 course, on which this Exam Cram is based.

Step 3: Create Policy Maps

Once the class maps are created, create policy maps and associate class maps to them along with actions (inspect, drop, or pass). See Figure 5.26 for the steps in the Cisco SDM.

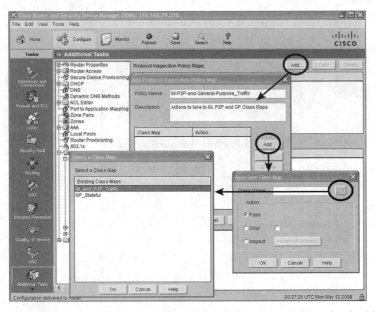

FIGURE 5.26   Creating a policy map and associating class map(s) and action(s) to the policy map.

When you are done, Figure 5.27 shows what your policy map should look like when class maps and actions are associated to it. In this example, the policy map has two class maps associated to it with Drop/Log and Inspect actions, respectively.

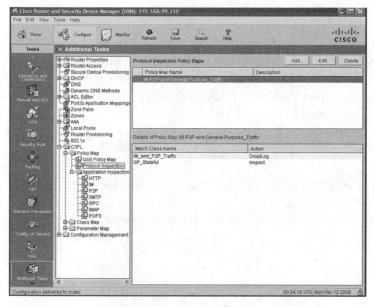

FIGURE 5.27　Example of policy map with two class maps and actions applied.

Step 4: Create Zone Pairs

Create a zone pair to which the policy map will be assigned. Assign the policy map to the zone pair in the same dialog, as illustrated in Figure 5.28.

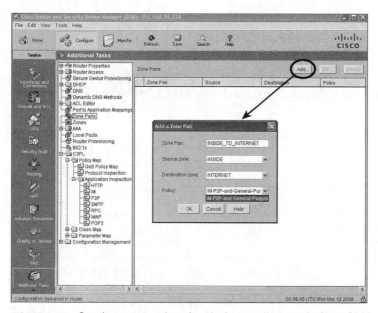

FIGURE 5.28　Creating a zone pair and assigning a policy map in Cisco SDM.

Monitoring ZPF

Zone-Based Policy Firewall can be monitored using either the CLI or the Cisco SDM. To monitor ZPF with the Cisco SDM, choose **Monitor->Firewall Status**. Select the firewall policy from the list of policies and choose either: **Active Sessions**, **Dropped Packets**, or **Allowed Packets**, from the list on the left-hand side, as illustrated in Figure 5.29.

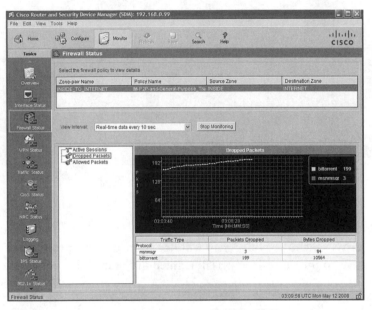

FIGURE 5.29 Monitoring the firewall status in Cisco SDM.

The equivalent CLI command is **show policy-map type inspect zone-pair session**. The output of this command is shown a little later. See if you can identify these items:

▶ The zone pair name.

▶ The service policy that was applied to the zone pair.

▶ The class maps that are associated to the service policy.

▶ The actions that the policy map takes for each class map.

> **NOTE**
>
> Hint: The command's output is indented to show objects nested within others. Shading has been added to the output of the **show policy-map type inspect zone-pair session** command later to make it easier for you to identify the items in the previous list.

Not so fast! Before issuing the **show policy-map type inspect zone-pair session** command, first verify that the zones are set up per Figure 5.14:

```
CiscoISR#show zone security INSIDE
zone INSIDE
  Member Interfaces:
    Vlan1
    Vlan2
CiscoISR#show zone security INTERNET
zone INTERNET
  Member Interfaces:
    FastEthernet4
CiscoISR#show zone security DMZ
zone DMZ
  Member Interfaces:
    Vlan3
    Vlan4
```

Now, look at the CLI output of the **show policy-map type inspect zone-pair session** command for detail of the traffic that was inspected, dropped, or passed by the policy map *IM-P2P-and-General-Purpose_Traffic* that was applied to the zone pair *INSIDE_TO_INTERNET*.

▶ Traffic that matches on class-map *IM_and_P2P_Traffic* will be dropped. Thus, IM (MSN Messenger) and P2P traffic (BitTorrent) will be dropped.

▶ Traffic that matches on class-map *GP_Stateful* will be inspected. Thus, TCP and UDP traffic will be statefully inspected.

▶ Traffic that matches on class-map *class-default* will be dropped. Thus, all other traffic will be dropped.

Note that some of the output was omitted to ensure comprehension:

```
CiscoISR#show policy-map type inspect zone-pair session
Zone-pair: INSIDE_TO_INTERNET

  Service-policy inspect : IM-P2P-and-General-Purpose_Traffic

    Class-map: IM_and_P2P_Traffic (match-any)
      Match: protocol msnmsgr
        3 packets, 84 bytes
        30 second rate 0 bps
      Match: protocol bittorrent
        1 packets, 28 bytes
        30 second rate 0 bps
      Drop
```

```
          4 packets, 112 bytes

  Class-map: GP_Stateful (match-any)
     Match: protocol tcp
        127 packets, 3916 bytes
        30 second rate 0 bps
     Match: protocol udp
        390 packets, 29217 bytes
        30 second rate 2000 bps
     Inspect
       Established Sessions
        Session 8394B708 (192.168.0.101:5762)=>(72.247.244.32:80) tcp
SIS_OPEN
           Created 00:01:39, Last heard 00:00:49
           Bytes sent (initiator:responder) [4661:3726]
          Session 83944270 (192.168.0.101:5757)=>(72.247.244.32:80) tcp
SIS_OPEN
           Created 00:01:39, Last heard 00:00:37
           Bytes sent (initiator:responder) [5734:3299]
          Session 839472C8
(192.168.0.101:50454)=>(68.40.182.79:19313) udp SIS_OPENING
           Created 00:00:09, Last heard 00:00:09
           Bytes sent (initiator:responder) [67:0]


  Class-map: class-default (match-any)
     Match: any
     Drop (default action)
        0 packets, 0 bytes
```

Exam Prep Questions

1. Which of the following is the best description of a firewall? (Choose one.)

   ○ **A.** Firewalls statefully inspect reply packets to determine whether they match the expected state of a connection in the state table.

   ○ **B.** Firewalls statically inspect packets in both directions and filter on layer 3 and layer 4 information.

   ○ **C.** A firewall is a system or a group of systems that enforce an access control policy between two networks.

   ○ **D.** A firewall is any device that blocks access to a protected network.

   ○ **E.** None of the above.

2. Which of the following define characteristics of a firewall? (Choose all that apply.)

   ○ **A.** Enforces the access control policy of an organization.

   ○ **B.** Must be hardened against attacks.

   ○ **C.** Must be the only transit point between networks.

   ○ **D.** Completely eliminates the risk of network compromise.

   ○ **E.** All of the above.

3. True or false. Transparent firewalls mitigate the risk of attack by applying rich layer 3 through 7 inspection services to the traffic transiting the firewall.

4. Consider the following output for your answer: What sequence of commands would you enter to add a line at the beginning of the ACL that permits packets for established TCP sessions?

```
CiscoISR# show access-list 101
Extended IP access list 101
    10 permit tcp any 10.10.10.0 0.0.0.255 eq www (12032 matches)
    20 permit tcp any 10.10.10.0 0.0.0.255 eq 22 (25000 matches)
```

   ○ **A.** `configure terminal`
        `ip access-list extended 101`
        `5 permit tcp any any established`

   ○ **B.** `configure terminal`
        `ip access-list name 101`
        `5 permit tcp any any established`

   ○ **C.** `configure terminal`
        `ip access-list extended 101 line 5 permit tcp any any`
        `established`

○ **D.** `configure nacl`
`10 permit tcp any any established`

○ **E.** `configure extended-nacl permit line 5 session-established`

○ **F.** None of the above.

5. Fill in the blank in the sequence below for editing an existing access control list in the Cisco SDM.

`Configure->_____->ACL Editor->Access Rules`

○ **A.** Firewall rules

○ **B.** Additional tasks

○ **C.** Policy editor

○ **D.** Perimeter security

○ **E.** None of the above.

6. Match the protocols in the numbered list below with the letter corresponding to their protocol ID in an IP packet.

1. EIGRP

2. UDP

3. ICMP

4. GRE

5. ESP

6. TCP

A. 1

B. 6

C. 17

D. 47

E. 50

F. 88

7. Certain source IP addresses should be filtered using ACLs to prevent IP spoofing attacks. Which of the following list should be filtered? (Choose all that apply.)

   ○ **A.** All 1's source IP addresses

   ○ **B.** Any address starting with a zero

   ○ **C.** IP multicast addresses

   ○ **D.** Reserved private IP addresses

   ○ **E.** All of the above.

8. True or false. Cisco specifically recommends against allowing ICMP echoes and ICMP redirects inbound.

9. True or false. The Cisco IOS Zone-Based Policy Firewall (ZPF) is not used solely to implement a Stateful Packet Inspection (SPI) firewall.

10. Consider the following scenario: A firewall has five interfaces, two of which are not associated with security zones:

   ▶ Two interfaces are in the INTERNET zone.

   ▶ One interface is in the INSIDE zone.

   ▶ Two interfaces are not in any zone.

   What is the default rule for traffic that originates from one of the two interfaces that are not in any zone and is destined for an interface in the INTERNET security zone?

   ○ **A.** The traffic is dropped.

   ○ **B.** The traffic is passed because it's going to the Internet.

   ○ **C.** The traffic is either permitted or denied based on the actions in the policy map if it has been applied to the zone pair.

   ○ **D.** The traffic is passed because the default policy map action is to pass traffic that doesn't have a specific match.

   ○ **E.** None of the above.

244

Chapter 5: Using Cisco IOS Firewalls to Implement a Network Security Policy

Answers to Exam Prep Questions

1. The correct answer is C. Answers A and B define types of firewalls. Answer D is incorrect.

2. Answers A, B, and C are correct. Answer D is incorrect because no firewall can eliminate risk. Firewalls mitigate risk.

3. False. Transparent firewalls mitigate the risk of attack by applying rich inspection services from layer 2 through 7 of the OSI model. They are "transparent" in the same way that a LAN switch is transparent to layer 3 devices.

4. Answer A is correct. With version 12.3 of the Cisco IOS, you can insert and delete lines in numbered ACLs, both standard and extended. The other answers are made up and use a mix of existing and nonexistent commands to try to trick you.

5. Answer B is correct.

6. 1—F; 2—C; 3—A; 4—D; 5—E; 6—B.

7. The answer is E, All of the above. IP ACLs should also filter local addresses in the 127.0.0.0/8 range.

8. True. Cisco recommends against ICMP echoes because this would be useful for network reconnaissance. ICMP redirects are recommended against because this might allow an attacker to hijack routing as part of a Man-in-the-Middle (MiM) attack.

9. True. ZPF policy maps can take inspect, drop, or pass actions on traffic. The drop and pass actions are analogous to deny and permit actions on an ACL and are not stateful.

10. Answer A is correct. Recall that one of the advantages of ZPF is that the firewall becomes a "deny all" firewall for all traffic that doesn't have an explicit action that will permit it to pass.

CHAPTER SIX

Introducing Cryptographic Services

Terms You'll Need to Understand:

✓ Cryptography

✓ Cryptanalysis

✓ Cryptosystem

✓ Encryption keys

✓ Encryption algorithms

✓ Block and stream ciphers

✓ Hashing, Hashing Message Authentication Codes (HMACs)

✓ DES, 3DES, and AES ciphers

✓ Message Digest 5 (MD5) and Secure Hashing Algorithm -1 (SHA-1) hashes

✓ Digital signatures

✓ Symmetric and asymmetric key algorithms

✓ Public Key Infrastructure (PKI)

✓ Certificate Authority (CA)

✓ Digital certificates

✓ X.509

✓ Public Key Cryptography Standard (PKCS)

✓ Simple Certificate Enrollment Protocol (SCEP)

Exam Topics Covered in This Chapter:

✓ Explain the different methods used in cryptography

✓ Explain IKE protocol functionality and phases

✓ Describe the building blocks of IPSec and the security functions it provides

> **NOTE**
>
> These exam topics are from cisco.com. Check there periodically for the latest exam topics and info.

This chapter provides an overview of the art and science of cryptography. Emphasis is on key points, especially where this knowledge is important in understanding cryptography's implementation in virtual private networks (VPNs) and other IOS services that require cryptography. Chapter 7, "Virtual Private Networks with IPsec," has more information on configuring VPNs. This chapter has a practical emphasis, with specific reference to examples of where cryptographic technology might be implemented in a modern cryptosystem, such as those found in Cisco Self-Defending Networks.

Cryptology Overview

The first thing you need to know is that cryptology and cryptography are not the same things. *Cryptology* is the overall art and science of making and breaking codes. *Cryptography* and *cryptanalysis* are disciplines *within* cryptology.

> **NOTE**
>
> The second thing you need to know is that in attempting to define any one term in the field of cryptology, a floodgate of other new terminology, many starting with the letter "c," is opened!

Here are some basic definitions of words that start with "crypt":

- **Cryptography.** Code *making*. It is the art of creating and using simple word or character substitutions to hide the original meaning.

- **Cryptanalysis.** Code *breaking*. It is the process of analyzing a cryptographic algorithm for weaknesses and exploiting them to break the code.

- **Cryptosystem.** Any system that implements codes to encrypt and decrypt messages.

- **Cipher.** A cryptographic algorithm (or "encryption algorithm") used to encrypt and decrypt files and messages.

- **Ciphertext.** An encrypted message or file. Code.

- **Cleartext (or plaintext).** An unencrypted message or file.

- **Encryption (Enciphering).** Cryptosystems encrypt by rendering cleartext into ciphertext. Encoding.

- **Decryption (Deciphering).** The message recipient's cryptosystem decrypts by rendering the ciphertext back into cleartext. Decoding.

NOTE

The terms *enciphering* and *deciphering*, while technically accurate, are not commonly used anymore.

Let's talk about a common misuse of terminology. There is no such action as *unencryption* because there is no verb "unencrypt." Encrypted messages are *decrypted*, not *unencrypted*, by a cryptosystem. *Unencrypted* is an adjective that refers to a message that is sent in cleartext.

An example of a real-time use of cryptology would be an IPsec VPN cryptosystem, which uses cryptographic algorithms (ciphers) to encrypt messages into ciphertext and decrypt those same messages back to cleartext. A cryptanalyst (a hacker, for example) would use the science of cryptanalysis as a form of man-in-the-middle attack to try to break the code. There, we've used all the terms in the list of definitions that we've created so far!

Figure 6.1 illustrates the elements of a cryptosystem. The data flow is left to right. All the traffic from the A network to the B network is encrypted by router A and becomes ciphertext for transmission inside an IPsec VPN to router B. Attackers (cryptanalysts!) would not be able to read the ciphertext because they possess neither the encryption key nor the encryption algorithm, both of which would be needed to decrypt this coded transmission. When the ciphertext arrives at router B, it is decrypted using the same encryption algorithm and encryption keys as were used by router A to encrypt it. When the message is forwarded by router B to network B, its final destination, it has been rendered back into cleartext.

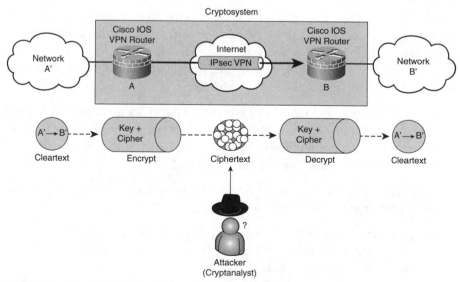

FIGURE 6.1   IPsec VPN: Example of a real-time cryptosystem.

Theoretically, it is possible to break any code because an attacker would only need to try by brute force every possible key (a large universe of possibilities) in combination with all known ciphers (a small universe of possibilities). The emphasis, of course, is on the word *theoretical*. Part of the art of encryption in a Cisco network, or any network security architecture, is to find the balance between usability and security. In this case, the encryption algorithms may be well known and therefore guessable, but we must make the keys reasonably difficult to break such that a knowledgeable attacker cannot access our sensitive information. You can read the specifics of how to implement an IPsec VPN cryptosystem in Chapter 7, but it would be useful to look at some of the building blocks first.

EXAM ALERT

Understanding the fundamentals of a cryptosystem at a high level will aid you greatly in understanding, rather than simply memorizing, the concepts. In turn, you will find it much easier to configure the crypto features of the Cisco IOS, including IPsec VPNs. If that isn't motivation enough, troubleshooting issues that deal with cryptography requires a high-level understanding at a minimum.

Historically, earlier efforts in creating cryptosystems relied on the secrecy of the cipher itself to achieve confidentiality. Examples of this would be the Caesar cipher or the Enigma machine used by the German military during World War II. With most modern cryptosystems, secrecy relies on the strength of the keys because knowledge of the crypto algorithms themselves is largely in the public domain.

We hadn't used the term *key* until the last two paragraphs. Basically, there are two main elements in a cryptosystem that are used to turn cleartext into ciphertext: ciphers, defined earlier, and keys. A key (also known as an encryption key or cryptographic key) is a collection of bits, usually stored in a file, that are used with a cipher to encrypt and decrypt a message.

Fair to say, the larger the number of bits in your bit collection, the stronger the resulting encryption. There is more about keys in the sections "Exploring Symmetric Key Encryption" and "Exploring Asymmetric Key Encryption and Public Key Infrastructure" later in this chapter.

To place all this into a networking context, encryption can occur at several layers of the OSI model, including the following:

▶ **Data Link Layer (OSI Layer 2).** Proprietary link layer encryption devices; examples include Ethernet NICs with encryption chips, which encrypt the payload of frames.

- **Network Layer (OSI Layer 3).** Protocols such as the IPsec framework, which create encrypted payload in network layer packets.

- **Transport Layer (OSI Layer 4).** Protocols such as Transport Layer Security (TLS) and Secure Sockets Layer (SSL), which create encrypted payload in transport layer segments.

- **Application Layer (OSI Layers 5–7).** Protocols such as Microsoft's Remote Desktop Protocol (RDP) for remote terminal sessions or secure messaging applications, such as Lotus Notes, and secure database applications, such as Oracle's SQL*Net, which create encrypted payload at the application layer.

NOTE

There are examples of both IPsec and SSL in Chapter 7 because they are useful in setting up the vendor-neutral, real-time network cryptosystems called virtual private networks (VPNs).

Cryptanalysis

It's a question of perspective. If you're a hacker, you're not attacking, you're cryptanalyzing, right? At least, that's what you tell the judge. If you are the victim, it's a cryptographic attack. Table 6.1 explains some examples of cryptographic attacks.

TABLE 6.1   Examples of Cryptographic Attacks

Attack	Explanation
Brute force	An attacker tries every possible key combination with a specific decryption algorithm. Theoretically, all encryption algorithms are vulnerable to a brute force attack. A modern cryptosystem will create keys of sufficient size and complexity that breaking the code is too expensive to accomplish both in terms of money and time (see the following note).
Ciphertext-only	Several examples (the more the better) of ciphertext created by the same cryptosystem are statistically analyzed to deduce the underlying plaintext by pattern analysis. This is not practical with modern ciphers because they use pseudorandom output to resist statistical analysis.
Known-plaintext	Another type of brute force attack. The attacker knows some of the underlying plaintext and, when used in combination with knowledge of the file types and protocols being used, can brute-force guess keys until meaningful plaintext is produced from ciphertext. This is a very practical attack because, unlike a pure brute force attack, the attacker can use his knowledge to direct the guesswork for the keys, greatly reducing the universe of possible values (see also Meet-in-the-Middle attack).

(continues)

TABLE 6.1   Examples of Cryptographic Attacks   *Continued*

Attack	Explanation
Meet-in-the-Middle	A type of known-plaintext attack. The attacker obtains a portion of plaintext and its corresponding ciphertext.
	1. The plaintext is brute-forced encrypted with every possible key; these values being stored for comparison.
	2. The ciphertext is brute-force decrypted with every possible key until a result is found that matches one of the values stored in step 1.
Chosen-plaintext	If the attacker is able to break into the cryptosystem, they can choose the plaintext that is encrypted. Careful analysis of the resulting ciphertext may yield important information that leads to cracking the keys. Good physical security (see Chapter 2 and the following note) can make this attack impractical.
Chosen-ciphertext	Similar to a chosen-plaintext attack. The attacker captures ciphertext and observes the result after it has been decrypted. Because they don't have access to the key directly (it may be tamperproof, perhaps on an embedded cryptosystem device), they need to deduce the key.
Birthday	Makes use of an incredible statistical fact that there is a greater than 50% probability that two people in a group of 23 persons will share the same birthday. This attack is a form of brute-force attack leveraged against hash functions. Hashes are examined in a later section, "Exploring Cryptographic Hashing Algorithms and Digital Signatures," in this chapter.

NOTE

You may recall from Chapter 2, "Building a Secure Network Using Security Controls," that encryption, and thus cryptosystems, are examples of technical controls. The organization's security policy will dictate what constitutes "reasonable security," hopefully after using industry-standard metrics to measure the organization's vulnerability to the threat of certain exploits. Physical controls must be defined and implemented to safeguard the technical controls.

In January of 1999, the Data Encryption Standard (DES) cipher developed by IBM, and which uses 56-bit keys, was cracked in just over 22 hours as part of the RSA Data Security's "DES Challenge III" (see http://www.networkworld.com/news/1999/0120cracked.html).

It is estimated that using the same method, the Advanced Encryption Standard (AES) could be cracked in 149 trillion years.

Encryption Algorithm (Cipher) Desirable Features

A good encryption algorithm should be resistant to the attacks outlined in Table 6.1. Table 6.2 lists other key features desirable in an encryption algorithm.

TABLE 6.2   Encryption Algorithm Desirable Features

Feature	Explanation
Resistance to cryptographic attack	Make cracking the code unfeasible/impractical (see attacks in Table 6.1).
Long and variable key length and flexibility	The more bits in the key, the harder it is to break, but more processor overhead is required to encrypt and decrypt messages. Scalability is ensured by allowing the flexibility of keys of varying lengths depending on the speed versus strength tradeoff required.
Avalanche effect	A good encryption algorithm will yield dramatically different ciphertext when only a few bits of cleartext are changed.
No export or import restrictions	Ideally, there should be no export or import restrictions placed on the cipher that is being used in the cryptosystem. Laws for the use of ciphers vary widely by country. Some governments put severe legal restrictions on the grade of encryption algorithms that its citizens are allowed to use.

Symmetric Key Versus Asymmetric Key Encryption Algorithms

Encryption keys work with encryption algorithms to turn cleartext into ciphertext. But be careful with our terminology because it isn't the keys that are symmetric or asymmetric; it is the method in which they are used by encryption algorithms that determines their symmetry. There are two broad categories of use for encryption keys:

- ▶ **Symmetric Encryption Algorithm.** Uses the same key to encrypt and decrypt data.

- ▶ **Asymmetric Encryption Algorithm.** Requires different keys—one key to encrypt the cleartext, and another to decrypt the ciphertext.

Complete sections later in this chapter explore examples of each in more detail.

NOTE

"I want examples!" you say. OK, here's one. As was noted earlier, since the focus on modern cryptosystems is the strength of the encryption key, safeguarding the key is of primary importance. A related issue is key distribution. For example, if the modern cryptosystem is an IPsec VPN using symmetric keys, generating a shared secret key for encryption between two VPN gateways over a hostile network such as the Internet is a critical issue. For example, the keys could be distributed out-of-band using a courier service or a phone call and then manually inputted on the devices. This is probably secure but hardly convenient. The Diffie-Hellman (DH) key exchange solves this issue. It defines an in-band (and slightly magical!) way of securely creating a shared key using the same hostile network that the data will eventually be encrypted and transmitted across. This is explained in Chapter 7.

Symmetric Key Algorithms

Because symmetric key algorithms are based on simple mathematical operations, they are quite fast and often used for encryption services; they are easily accelerated by hardware. We will see examples of hardware acceleration in Cisco hardware in Chapter 7.

Key management algorithms, such as Diffie-Hellman mentioned in the previous note, provide secure key exchange. Examples of symmetric key algorithms and their key lengths include the following:

▶ **DES (Data Encryption Standard).** 56 bits.

▶ **3DES (Triple DES).** 112 and 168 bits.

▶ **AES (Advanced Encryption Standard).** 128, 192, and 256 bits.

▶ **IDEA (International Data Encryption Algorithm).** 128 bits.

▶ **RC (Rivest Cipher or Ron's Code) Series:**

    ▶ RC2: 40 and 64 bits.

    ▶ RC4: 1 to 256 bits.

    ▶ RC5: 0 to 2040 bits.

    ▶ RC6: 128, 192, and 256 bits.

▶ **Blowfish.** 32 to 448 bits.

▶ **SEAL (Software Encryption Algorithm).** 160 bits.

EXAM ALERT

Know the names of all the ciphers in the previous list, as well as the key length that they each require.

> **NOTE**
>
> AES, also known as Rijndael after the last names of the co-inventors, resulted from a competition by the National Institute of Standards and Technology (NIST) for a successor to the pervasive DES cipher. RC6 was one of the finalists in that same competition. AES was adopted in November 2001 and approved by NIST as FIPS 197. It is remarkable for its speed, relative ease of use, and little memory requirement. Since its adoption, it has quickly become the de facto standard for encryption worldwide and not just for the U.S. federal government.

Asymmetric Key Algorithms

Asymmetric key algorithms are more commonly referred to as public key algorithms. For example, in an IPsec VPN, a device such as an IOS router will use its peer's public key to encrypt data to that peer and decrypt data from that same peer using its own private key. The asymmetry is found in the fact that each peer requires a key pair consisting of a private key and public key. The private key is almost never transmitted to the peer, but the public key can be freely exchanged because only the holder of the matching private key will be able to decrypt messages encrypted with that public key. This makes the resulting cryptosystem highly resistant to attacks … assuming that a key of sufficient length and complexity is chosen of course.

Examples of encryption algorithms that make use of asymmetric keys (usually in lengths of 512 to 4096 bits) include the following:

▶ Diffie-Hellman (DH)

▶ Rivest Shamir Adleman (RSA)

▶ Elliptic Curves Cryptography (ECC)

▶ ElGamal Encryption System (ElGamal)

Asymmetric encryption algorithms are slower than symmetric encryption algorithms because they are based on complex computations.

Also, the lengths of the encryption keys, while longer than symmetric keys, do not equate to equivalent security bit-to-bit, according to the following key equivalency:

▶ RSA with 1024-bit key equal to 80-bit symmetric key

▶ RSA with 2048-bit key equal to 112-bit symmetric key

▶ RSA with 3072-bit key equal to 128-bit symmetric key

Block Versus Stream Ciphers

Now that we've categorized encryption algorithms by their use of keys (symmetric or asymmetric), let's look at categorizing ciphers by the way they organize data prior to encryption. Encryption algorithms can be either block ciphers or stream ciphers.

Block ciphers have the following characteristics:

- ▶ A data stream is parsed into fixed-length units (blocks) of plaintext data and then transformed into ciphertext of the same length.

- ▶ The size of the block used varies with the cipher (DES uses 8 bytes = 64 bits).

- ▶ Block sizes have to be uniform so padding is common.

- ▶ The resulting ciphertext is typically longer than the plaintext (see the last bullet in the following stream cipher characteristics list for comparison).

Stream ciphers have the following characteristics:

- ▶ Stream ciphers work at a more granular level, using smaller units of plaintext data; bits, for example.

- ▶ Because blocking is not used, padding is not needed, and therefore the size of the messages does not change when they are transformed to ciphertext.

> **NOTE**
>
> Do not confuse the number of bits in a block used by a block cipher with the number of bits in its key. For example, 3DES uses a 168-bit key, but 64-bit blocks.

Stream ciphers can be much faster than block ciphers because they do not need to block and pad the data and can encrypt an arbitrary number of bits.

Common block ciphers include the following:

- ▶ DES and 3DES when used in Electronic Code Book (ECB) or Cipher Block Chaining (CBC) mode

- ▶ AES

- ▶ IDEA

- ▶ Secure and Fast Encryption Routine (SAFER)

- ▶ Skipjack

- ▶ Blowfish

- ▶ RSA

Common stream ciphers include the following:

- DES and 3DES when used in Output Feedback (OFB) or cipher feedback (CFB) mode

- RC4

- Software Encryption Algorithm (SEAL)

Which Encryption Algorithm Do I Choose?

We've categorized encryption algorithms by whether they use block or stream ciphers and whether they use symmetric or asymmetric keys. At a high level, we have looked at some of the features of these categories. This still doesn't answer the over-arching question as to which encryption algorithm we should choose. Is there a body of industry best practices that will help? According to Cisco, it is a matter of trust and an algorithm's resistance to brute force attack.

Two basic criteria for choosing an encryption algorithm are as follows:

- The algorithm provides sufficient protection against brute force attacks. (For more about who defines "sufficient," see Chapter 2 and the following note.)

- The algorithm is trusted by the greater cryptographic community.

With respect to the last point, symmetric algorithms that are considered trusted are DES, 3DES, IDEA, RC4, and AES.

Asymmetric algorithms that are considered trusted are RSA and DH.

NOTE

Practically speaking, the organization's security policy will determine whether a cipher provides sufficient protection against attack based on such factors as the likelihood of an exploit and the cryptosystem's vulnerability against specific threats. One would think that the most secure cipher should always be the one to choose, as long as it doesn't introduce unacceptable tradeoffs in terms of performance and latency. In reality, it is the trustworthiness and not just the security of a cipher that may tip the balance when deciding the cipher to use in a cryptosystem such as an IPsec VPN. Trust is hard to quantify, but the idea of trust is easier to quantify with industry data. For example, because they are trusted by industry, an IPsec VPN might be configured to use the following:

- AES as a symmetric algorithm for protecting data and the negotiations between the peers.
- DH for automating the generation and exchange of encryption keys between the peers.

Other encryption algorithms might not be trusted. For example, ECC is considered to be relatively immature. However, depending on the cryptosystem's requirements, it might be an acceptable tradeoff, especially if the devices in the cryptosystem do not possess much processing power.

Cryptographic Hashing Algorithms

A cryptographic hash is sometimes described as a one-way encryption—encryption where there is no possibility of decryption. Hashing algorithms, like encryption algorithms, take cleartext data and using an encryption key, transform the cleartext data into something different and unreadable by an attacker. But what comes out of the hashing process is not ciphertext as with encryption algorithms, but rather a fixed-length hash. The implication with ciphertext is that it will be deciphered. With a hash, the whole purpose is that it *cannot* be deciphered.

Hashes are most commonly used as a method of integrity assurance. (Recall C-I-A from Chapter 1.) When a device in a cryptosystem wants to ensure that the data that it is sending to its peer is not being tampered with, it can append a hash of a message with the original message. The receiving device can create its own hash of the received message and compare it with the hash that is appended to the message. If they are the same, then the message has not been tampered with.

What prevents an attacker from altering a message and then altering the hash to reflect the altered message's new contents? Nothing actually, except both the sender and the receiver are not only using the same hashing algorithm, but they are hashing the message with a shared secret key added. Only the devices that knows the key (and they're not sharing it with an attacker) will be able to create and compare the hashes correctly. There's another use of keys, again underlining how important it is to properly manage and secure these keys.

> **NOTE**
>
> Hashing algorithms are described in more detail in the "Exploring Cryptographic Hashing Algorithms and Digital Signatures" section of this chapter.

Principles of Key Management

A recurring thread has been the necessity of proper key management because attacks against modern cryptosystems are not against the encryption algorithms, but against the keys.

Principles of key management include the following:

▶ Key management policies describe the *secure* generation (or issuance), verification, exchange, storage, and destruction of keys.

> **NOTE**
>
> Getting way ahead of ourselves for a moment, Public Key Infrastructure (PKI) is a good example of the principles of key management. PKI defines a whole protocol for the secure issuance, exchange, revocation, destruction, storage, and backup of digital certificates and integral asymmetric keys used for device and individual authentication and encryption, typically in an enterprise setting. PKI is examined later in the section, "Exploring Asymmetric Key Encryption and Public Key Infrastructure."

▸ Key management is often considered the most difficult task of designing, implementing, and maintaining cryptosystems.

▸ Secure key management is vitally important in a cryptosystem.

▸ Compared to encryption algorithms, key management is a more common avenue of attack on modern cryptosystems.

Following is a summary of the component tasks in a key management policy. A key management policy manages key:

▸ Generation

▸ Verification

▸ Storage

▸ Exchange

▸ Revocation

▸ Destruction

Other Key Considerations

Because we have established that attackers will pry away at a modern cryptosystem's keys, it stands to reason that we should do nothing to aid the attackers in their tasks. Two considerations with respect to keys stand out: the concept of keyspaces and the issue of key length.

Keyspaces

A *keyspace* is the set of all possible values that a key might draw from. This is the "universe of choices." The larger the keyspace, the more difficult it will be for a brute force attack to be successful. An effective comprehensive network security policy will recognize these keyspace concepts:

▶ The keyspace of an encryption algorithm is the set of all possible key values.

▶ Each bit has two possible values, 1 or 0; thus, an n-bit key has 2^n possible key values.

▶ Most encryption algorithms can be configured to use weak (easily guessable and repeating) keys.

▶ Manual definition of keys can be difficult because care must be taken to avoid the use of known weak keys.

Key Length

The longer the key length, the larger the keyspace, the more difficult it is to crack the code. If an encryption algorithm is considered trustworthy (see the earlier section, "Which Encryption Algorithm Do I Choose?"), then the only way that an attacker can crack the code is by attempting to brute-force the keys. The goal is to make this kind of attack unfeasible.

NOTE

A largely unspoken axiom of network security is that you are making your network unattractive to attackers. The more unattractive you make your network, the more likely that an attacker will move on to another network. This is the philosophy that many people use in burglar-proofing their homes. It's not so much that they are burglar-proof; rather, that there is often a visible deterrent that makes the burglar move on to a neighbor's house. Remember from an earlier chapter, network security is not a risk *elimination* exercise; it is a risk *mitigation* exercise. Long keys are unfeasible to crack. A sufficiently long key with a modern cryptosystem could conceivably take millions or billions of years to crack. The sun will have exploded and the earth turned to dust by that time.

EXAM ALERT

On average, cryptanalysis by brute force will crack the code after searching through half the keyspace.

The length of your keys should be dictated by the tradeoff between security and usability. Knowing your attackers (including how well-funded they are) through a proper risk assessment will indicate the encryption algorithm to use and the length of encryption keys to use with that algorithm.

SSL VPNs

SSL VPNs are becoming increasingly common. SSL is also a good way to demonstrate some of the encryption algorithms, hashing algorithms, and the use of encryption keys that we have looked at so far. Chapter 7 contains a quick overview of some of Cisco's SSL VPN solutions. Here we will do a quick overview of what SSL is and then use it to glue some of the ideas we have come across to our synapses. SSL is a cryptosystem that was invented by Netscape Corporation in the mid 1990s.

SSL characteristics include the following:

▶ Symmetric key algorithms for encryption.

▶ Asymmetric key algorithms for authentication and key exchange.

▶ Hashes during the authentication process. Cleartext passwords are never exchanged.

▶ Similar to IPsec in that it specifies methods to negotiate encryption algorithms and then uses the negotiated algorithms to transform data.

▶ Used worldwide by many e-commerce sites (at least the ones we trust!).

▶ Secures not only web communication but is also popular to secure email protocols such as SMTP, FTP, IMAP, and POP3.

▶ Gaining rapid acceptance as an alternative to IPsec for remote-access VPNs.

▶ Transport Layer Security (TLS) is the newer, standards-based, replacement for SSL. (But we still call the whole paradigm SSL.)

▶ Employs key lengths between 40 and 256 bits for encryption algorithms.

Figure 6.2 illustrates Cisco's new remote-access AnyConnect SSL VPN client establishing a VPN to a central site ASA 5500 Series adaptive security appliance using SSL. As noted, SSL defines methods for negotiating the ciphers, as well as authenticating the peers and performing a secure key exchange. This is the same exchange as would occur if a user were to visit a secure e-commerce site such as would be established for online banking.

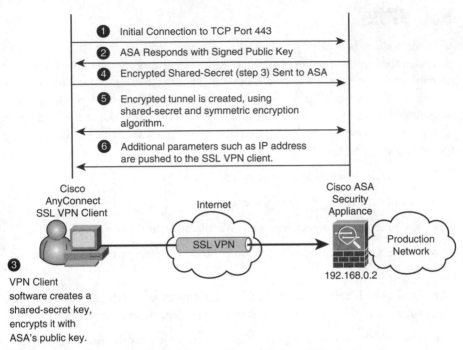

FIGURE 6.2 SSL tunnel establishment using Cisco AnyConnect SSL client.

NOTE

Step 6 in Figure 6.2 is included for the sake of completeness, however it is not part of a standard SSL tunnel establishment process.

After the secure SSL tunnel is established, the VPN client obtains an IP address, subnet mask, default gateway, and other information from the VPN server, the ASA. The result is illustrated in Figure 6.3. Look for these two things on Figure 6.3:

A. The client has obtained IP address 192.168.20.8.

B. An RSA_AES_128_SHA1 cipher has been negotiated to protect the data in the VPN tunnel.

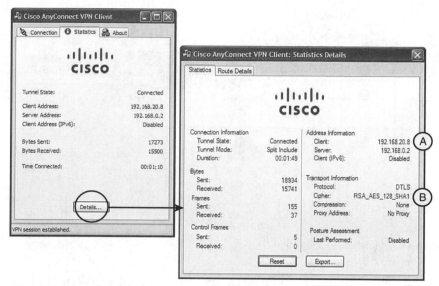

FIGURE 6.3 Parameters obtained from VPN server by AnyConnect SSL VPN client.

Exploring Symmetric Key Encryption

The simplest, most scalable cryptosystems to implement are those that use symmetric key encryption. Ciphers that use symmetric keys use the same key to encrypt and decrypt the data. We will examine the principles and operation of symmetric key encryption algorithms and look at examples of its implementation while weighing its strengths and weaknesses.

Figure 6.4 represents a typical symmetric key cryptosystem. The data flow is from left to right. Cleartext data is rendered into ciphertext by the sender by encrypting the data with an encryption key and a cipher. The ciphertext is turned back into cleartext when the receiver in the cryptosystem uses the same encryption algorithm with an identical key to decrypt the data.

Here are some facts about the key lengths used with symmetric key encryption algorithms:

▶ 40 to 256 bits are typical key lengths.

▶ Trusted key lengths are 80 bits or greater.

▶ Regardless of which encryption algorithm employs them, key lengths of less than 80 bits are considered obsolete and should not be used.

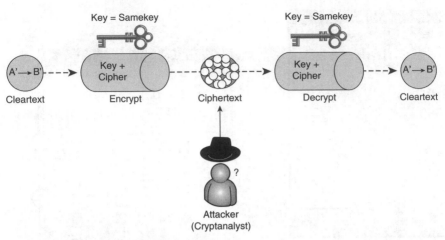

FIGURE 6.4 Symmetric key encryption.

Now that we've established that 80 bits or greater is acceptable, let's speak about the longevity of the keys' protection. What length of key should be used, grouped by the algorithm that employs it and longevity of protection? Table 6.2 explores those parameters as they relate to longevity of protection. The assumption made in Table 6.2 is that we are protecting against brute force attack. Also, when you look at the table, recall that symmetric algorithms are considered the strongest type of algorithms, thus they necessitate a shorter key length than asymmetric encryption algorithms.

TABLE 6.2 Key Length Longevity

Protection	Key Use			
	Symmetric Key Encryption Algorithm	Asymmetric Key Encryption Algorithm	Digital Signature	Hashing Algorithm
Up to 3 years	80	1248	160	160
Up to 10 years	96	1776	192	192
Up to 20 years	112	2342	224	224
Up to 30 years	128	3248	256	256
Protects against even quantum computers	256	15424	512	512

The remainder of this section explores the details of the most common Symmetric Key Encryption algorithms individually.

DES

The following are the main characteristics of DES:

▶ Fixed key length of 64 bits, though only 56 bits are always used for encryption.

▶ Hardware acceleration is relatively simple because of its logical (binary) operation.

▶ 40-bit DES is still 56-bits: 40-bit key plus 16 known bits to pad the key out to 56 bits.

▶ Block cipher modes include the following:

  ▶ ECB (Electronic Code Block) mode.

  ▶ CBC (Cipher Block Chaining) mode. IPsec VPNs mostly choose this.

▶ Stream cipher modes include the following:

  ▶ CFB mode (Cipher Feedback). Similar to CBC.

  ▶ OFB mode (Output Feedback).

EXAM ALERT

Cisco IPsec VPNs use DES and 3DES in CBC mode.

Although DES is considered obsolete, mostly because of its small key size, it can be used for small amounts of data where no alternative exists. It is susceptible to brute force attacks on its keys, having been cracked in 2001 in 22 hours.

Here are some other guidelines to make a DES cryptosystem as secure as possible:

▶ Change keys frequently.

▶ Use a secure channel to exchange keys between the sender and receiver. (Diffie-Hellman is one method.)

▶ Use CBC if possible. In CBC block cipher mode, encryption of one 64-bit block depends on the previous blocks.

▶ Use 3DES if possible.

3DES

The following are the main characteristics of 3DES:

- ▶ Basic algorithm is identical to DES, just applied three successive times.

- ▶ Can use two or three 56-bit keys to achieve 112- or 168-bit key strength. (See the next Exam Alert.)

- ▶ 3DES is not significantly more processor-intensive than DES, making it a good choice for software-based encryption.

- ▶ 3DES is considered the most trusted of symmetric encryption algorithms by virtue of how long it has been used, as well as its key length.

> **NOTE**
>
> Don't confuse the trustworthiness of an encryption algorithm with its strength. Although AES is considered cryptographically stronger than 3DES, it has only been a NIST standard since 2001 and an official U.S. government standard since May 2002, whereas 3DES has been tested in the field for more than 35 years and has not been found to possess any flaws. Brute force attacks are considered to be unfeasible against 3DES.

> **EXAM ALERT**
>
> Cisco IPsec VPNs use the 168-bit 3DES implementation in the CBC block cipher mode.

If you use DES as a verb, 3DES has sometimes (and rather lazily) been described as producing ciphertext from cleartext that has been DES'd three times. Strictly speaking this is true, but it also implies that the cleartext is encrypted three times. This is incorrect. In fact, Figure 6.5 illustrates how 3DES operates. The numbering in the figure matches the following steps:

1. The cleartext data is first encrypted with a 56-bit key creating ciphertext.

2. This ciphertext is then *decrypted* (not encrypted!) with a second 56-bit key. Because the second key is *always* different than the first key, actual decryption doesn't occur, so effectively the result is also ciphertext.

3. The ciphertext from step 2 is again encrypted, either with a third different key or with the same one that was used in step 1.

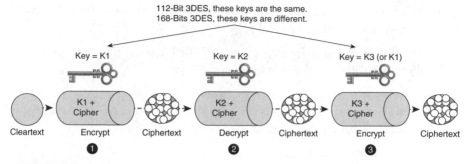

FIGURE 6.5 3DES operation.

> **NOTE**
>
> If three different keys are used, (K1, K2, and K3 in Figure 6.5), then the total key length is said to be 168 bits. If only two keys are used (that is, K1 and K3 are the same and K2 is different), then the total key length is said to be 112 bits. Cisco does not use 112-bit 3DES in its IPsec VPN implementation.

Surprisingly, if you use the three different keys, and all three steps encrypted in succession from the original cleartext, the composite key strength would be only 58 bits! The encrypt-decrypt-encrypt (EDE) process that 3DES uses is known as 3DES-EDE.

AES

It might take several years before AES is as trusted as 3DES, but it is considered a stronger algorithm. In 1997, NIST announced a competition that was open to the public, inviting them to submit a proposal for an encryption algorithm that would eventually replace DES. Of the fifteen proposed candidates, the Rijndael algorithm was chosen to become AES. Twofish and RC6 were two other candidates. Rijndael is a combination of the names of the inventors, Vincent Rijmen and Joan Daemen.

The following are the main features of AES:

- AES uses a variable block length and variable key length. Blocks can be 128, 192, or 256 bits in length and encryption keys can be 128, 192, or 256 bits in length.

- AES is future-proof because both block and key lengths can be added to in 32-bit increments.

- AES is much faster than 3DES, making it ideal for software encryption.

- AES is specifically designed for efficient implementation in software or hardware on a number of processor platforms.

- ▸ AES is gaining trust in the security community because it has exhibited no known flaws in 10 years of review.

- ▸ AES is considered to be stronger than 3DES because it is faster and it allows 192- and 256-bit key lengths.

The default encryption algorithm on Cisco platforms remains 3DES, probably because of its maturity relative to AES.

AES is supported on the following Cisco platforms:

- ▸ Cisco IOS Software Release 12.2(13)T and later

- ▸ Cisco PIX Firewall Software Version 6.3 and later

- ▸ Cisco ASA Software Version 7.0 and later

- ▸ Cisco VPN 3000 Software Version 3.6 and later

SEAL

The Software Encryption Algorithm (SEAL) was first published in 1994. The current version, 3.0, was published in 1997.

The following are the main features of SEAL:

- ▸ SEAL is a stream cipher and is considered very fast.

- ▸ SEAL was first supported in IOS with Release 12.3(7)T.

- ▸ SEAL uses a 160-bit encryption key.

- ▸ SEAL is less processor-intensive than equivalent encryption algorithms.

EXAM ALERT

Routers that have hardware-accelerated encryption do not support SEAL. Also, the VPN peers must support IPsec and have the K9 subsystem.

You can use the **show version** CLI command to confirm whether your version of IOS has the K9 subsystem required to run SEAL:

```
CiscoISR-A#show version
Cisco IOS Software, C870 Software (C870-ADVIPSERVICESK9-M), Version
12.4(15)T5, RELEASE SOFTWARE (fc4)
Technical Support: http://www.cisco.com/techsupport
Copyright (c) 1986-2008 by Cisco Systems, Inc.
```

```
Compiled Thu 01-May-08 02:31 by prod_rel_team

ROM: System Bootstrap, Version 12.3(8r)YI2, RELEASE SOFTWARE

CiscoISR-A uptime is 21 hours, 6 minutes
System returned to ROM by power-on
System restarted at 20:45:39 UTC Mon May 26 2008
System image file is "flash:c870-advipservicesk9-mz.124-15.T5.bin"
```

Rivest Ciphers (RC)

These encryption algorithms are called Rivest Ciphers, as they were written by Ron Rivest of RSA fame. They are sometimes also called Ron's Code. They are popular encryption algorithms because of their relative speed and variable key-length.

The following are the main features of Rivest Ciphers:

- **RC2.** Block cipher that features a variable-length key.

  - It was designed as a plug-in replacement for DES.

- **RC4.** Stream cipher that features a variable length key.

  - RC4 uses the Vernam cipher, but is not considered a one-time pad (OTP) because it uses a pseudo-random key.

  - RC4 Runs very quickly in software.

  - RC4 is often used to secure real-time communications such as e-commerce sites that use SSL or SSL VPNs like Cisco's SSL VPN solution. (See the example in Figure 6.6.)

  - Wired Equivalent Privacy (WEP) is an example of how RC4 can be implemented poorly.

- **RC5.** Block cipher that features speed and a variable block size and a variable key length.

- **RC6.** Block cipher that lost out to Rijndael in the AES competition. Based on RC5.

Figure 6.6 illustrates a website certificate for a Cisco Content Engine CE-590 indicating a 128-bit RC4 encrypted SSL link.

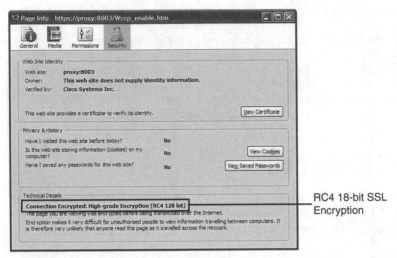

RC4 18-bit SSL Encryption

FIGURE 6.6 Website certificate for Cisco Content Engine indicating RC4 128-bit SSL encryption.

Exploring Cryptographic Hashing Algorithms and Digital Signatures

Recall from the previous discussion in this chapter that a cryptographic hash is sometimes described as one-way encryption—encryption where there is no possibility of decryption. Hashing algorithms, like encryption algorithms, take cleartext data and, using an encryption key, transform the cleartext data into something different and unreadable by an attacker. But what comes out of the hashing process is not ciphertext as with encryption algorithms, but rather a fixed-length hash or digest. The implication with ciphertext is that it will be deciphered. With a hash, the whole purpose is that it essentially *cannot* be deciphered as it is extremely infeasible to do so. The two most popular hashing algorithms are Message Digest 5 (MD5) and Secure Hashing Algorithm 1 (SHA-1). These will be discussed separately in their own sections shortly.

> **NOTE**
>
> The output of the hashing functions is a fixed-length hash or "digest." Think of a hashing function as a hungry beast into whose mouth you pour in data of variable lengths. The animal digests it and then outputs it (the analogy gets a bit ugly here) into fixed-length digests. The digestion algorithm of the animal can be either of the following:
>
> ▶ **Message Digest 5 (MD5).** Creates 128-bit digests.
>
> ▶ **Secure Hashing Algorithm 1 (SHA-1).** Creates 160-bit digests.
>
> In both cases, the output is completely unrecognizable from the input. It is important to realize that the hashing function does not define the formatting of the output, but rather the *process* to completely disassociate it from the input.

Hashing functions are most commonly used as an integrity check, similar to a frame check sequence (FCS) in a frame. When data is transmitted, a hash of that transmitted data is appended to the data to be checked by the receiver. If the receiver determines that the computed hash is different than the hash appended to the message, the receiver assumes that the data has been tampered with. The key here is the word *computed*. The receiver computes the hash using the same algorithm that was used with the appended hash.

It is common to represent a hashing algorithm as a mathematical function (because that's what it is!):

$h = H(x)$

Where:

h = The computed hash.

H = The hashing function (MD5 or SHA-1).

x = The data of variable length fed into the hashing function.

Figure 6.7 represents a simple hashing cryptosystem.

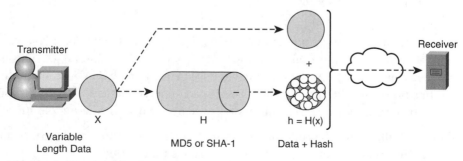

FIGURE 6.7 Simple hash cryptosystem.

NOTE

In general, hashing functions should be "collision resistant," meaning that two messages with the same hash are very unlikely.

If that was all there was to it, an attacker could launch a man-in-the-middle attack that would go something like this:

1. Seize the data with the original hash.

2. Alter it.

3. Compute and append a new hash by making an educated guess as to which of the two popular hashing algorithms (MD5 or SHA-1) was used.

4. Transmit the altered data with the new hash to the receiver.

So, how good is the hash as an integrity check if we left it right there? Not very good, right? The reason standalone hashing functions were designed this way was to serve as a lightweight, simple, but effective way to guarantee the integrity of transmission over telecommunication circuits of sometimes dubious quality. If a receiving station finds that a message fails the integrity check, it can ask for a retransmission from the transmitting station. The assumption is that the communication links between the transmitter and receiver are not hostile, which would be true in the case of closed networks such as leased-line, circuit-switched, or packet-switched networks.

HMACs

If, however, the intermediate network is the Internet or some other network that is considered hostile by our security policy, we should find a way to assure the authenticity of the hash itself. The transmitter would create a hash made of the following:

▶ A shared-secret encryption key.

▶ + the variable-length data.

Thus, only if the receiver possesses the same shared-secret encryption key would it be able to compute the same hash with the same variable-length data. This is how Hashing Message Authentication Codes (HMACs) work. HMACs are hashing functions with the addition of a shared-secret encryption key. This makes for a hashing cryptosystem that is much more resistant to a man-in-the-middle attack.

Figure 6.8 illustrates the addition of a shared-secret encryption key to create an HMAC instead of a simple hash before the data is transmitted.

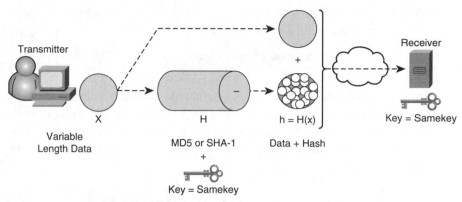

FIGURE 6.8 Hashing cryptosystem with HMACs.

Cisco uses two popular HMACs:

▶ Keyed MD5

▶ Keyed SHA-1

They are based respectively on MD5 and SHA-1 hashing functions.

NOTE

If you're keeping track, we have now achieved the I and A in C-I-A. IPsec VPNs use HMAC functions to assure data *integrity* and to provide origin *authentication*. Only the holder of the same shared-secret key could create a hash that can be matched by the receiver.

EXAM ALERT

The use of HMACs is the same procedure that is used in the generation and verification of secure fingerprints.

Message Digest 5 (MD5)

The following are the main features of the MD5 hashing algorithm:

▶ MD5 is very common (ubiquitous).

▶ MD5 was derived from its predecessor, MD4.

▶ MD5 uses a complex sequence of logical (binary) operations that result in a 128-bit message digest.

- ▶ MD5 is not recommended for new cryptosystems because SHA-1 is preferred for its theoretically higher security.

- ▶ MD5 was invented by Ron Rivest.

MD5 is less trusted than SHA-1 because of some theoretical weaknesses in some of its building blocks. This kind of speculation makes the cryptology world somewhat uneasy. Thus, although it has not been proven in the real world that MD5 is any less safe than SHA-1, SHA-1 is preferred over MD5 because any risk should be avoided.

Secure Hashing Algorithm 1 (SHA-1)

Theoretically, SHA-1 should be marginally slower than MD5 on the same platform because it works with a 32-bit longer buffer than MD5, but it should be more resistant to a brute force attack for that very reason.

The following are the main features of the SHA-1 hashing algorithm:

- ▶ Similar to MD4 and MD5 in that it takes an input message, x, of no more than 2^{64} bits.

- ▶ Produces a 160-bit message digest.

- ▶ Slightly slower than MD5.

- ▶ SHA-1 corrects an unpublished flaw in its predecessor, SHA.

- ▶ SHA-1 is published as an official NIST standard as FIPS 180-1.

> **NOTE**
>
> As with any modern cryptosystem, the most important best practice with HMACs is to protect the secret keys. Realistically, an attacker has a 1 in 2 chance of guessing the hashing algorithm used, but they should never be able to guess the keys!

Digital Signatures

Another way of securing messages among devices and people in a cryptosystem is the use of a digital signature. Digital signatures are usually derived from digital certificates, which are part of a Public Key Infrastructure (PKI). As their name suggests, when digital signatures are used instead of hashes and HMACs in transactions, the sender cannot disavow themselves from the transaction. This is called *non-repudiation*, and simply means that the data came uniquely (and could only have originated) from the holder of the digital signature.

Here are the most common uses for digital signatures:

- Non-repudiation
- Authenticating users
- Proving both the authenticity and integrity of PKI-generated certificates
- Signed timestamps

In Figure 6.9, a user is composing an email message to Bob's email address, CCNASecurity@abc.com, telling him to take the day off. The user clicks the button (1) in the email message, indicating that it should be digitally signed and when (2) the message is sent, a message (3) pops up, indicating that the message is about to be signed by the user's private key.

1. User indicates message should be digitally signed.

2. User sends message.

3. Popup indicating that the message is about to be signed by the user's private key.

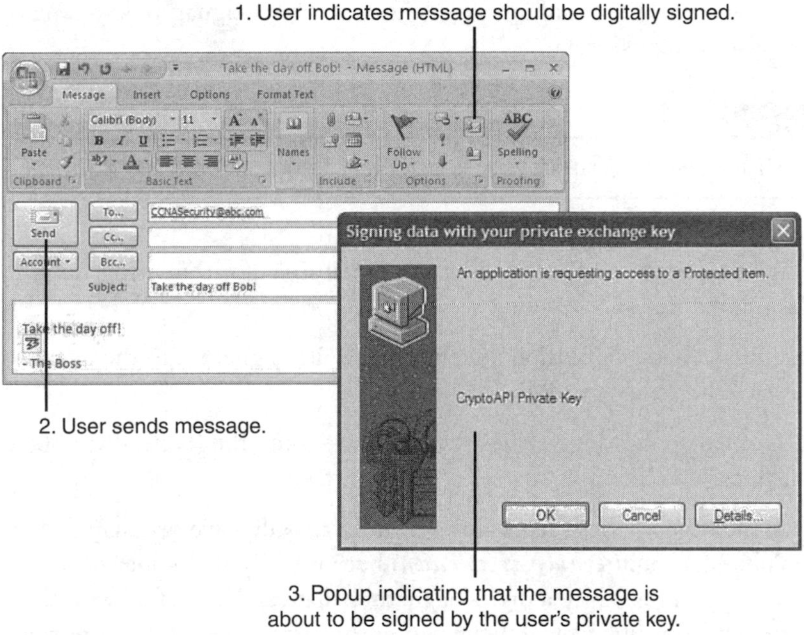

FIGURE 6.9 Signing and sending an email with a digital signature.

The question is whether the email message really came from Bob's boss. Clearly, Bob should only take the day off if the message actually originated from his boss and Bob can verify the message upon receipt. If he verifies the message successfully, then only the boss or someone with access to the boss's computer (and private key) could have sent it. The message source is non-reputable.

Figure 6.10 shows the process of sending a digitally signed email message.

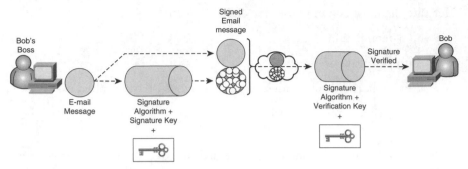

FIGURE 6.10 Digital signature process example.

Here's how it works. The assumption is that Bob and Bob's boss have agreed upon a signature algorithm:

1. Bob's boss signs the email message with her private signature key. This key must be kept secret.

> **NOTE**
>
> If the boss's signature key is not kept secret and private, there can be no non-repudiation.

2. A digital signature is generated by the signature algorithm using Bob's boss's signature key.

3. The boss's email application attaches the digital signature to the email message and sends it to Bob.

4. Bob's email application verifies the signature using the (typically publicly available) verification key.

5. If the message verifies successfully, then it can only have originated from Bob's boss's computer (*non-repudiation*) because only the holder of the private key can produce a digital signature that can be verified with the corresponding public key. Furthermore, the verification check confirms that the data has not changed in transit, thus assuring its *integrity*.

> **NOTE**
>
> Technically, the sender's private signature key and the receiver's public verification keys can be any agreed-upon keys, but the use of Public Key Infrastructure (PKI) is recommended to manage the keys; this will ensure their safeguarding and improve the scalability of the solution.

Digital Signature Standard (DSS)

The whole process hinges on the digital signature algorithm used, so it only makes sense that there should be a Digital Signature Standard. DSS was first issued in 1994 by NIST. Originally, there was only one standard, but now DSS incorporates three, as follows:

- **Digital Signature Algorithm (DSA):**

  - The original standard.

  - Not as flexible as RSA.

  - Slow verification of signatures.

- **Digital Signature Using Reversible Public Key Cryptography (RSA).** An RSA digital signature algorithm. This is commonly referred to as simply "RSA," although this is technically incorrect.

- **Elliptic Curves Digital Signature Algorithm (ECDSA).** Also added to the DSS.

Exploring Asymmetric Key Encryption and Public Key Infrastructure

One of the main issues with symmetric key cryptosystems is that they don't scale very well. Asymmetric key cryptosystems, where different keys are used for encrypting and decrypting, scale well. This is mainly because the management of these asymmetric keys is integral to the same infrastructure that is used to generate and issue them in the first place. In this section, we examine the principles behind asymmetric key encryption and look at popular encryption algorithms that use asymmetric keys including Rivest Shamir Adleman (RSA), Diffie-Hellman (DH), and public key infrastructure (PKI).

Asymmetric algorithms are slower than symmetric algorithms because they are more mathematically complex. Because they are slower, they are not typically used in real-time encrypted data flows and are instead used as key exchange protocols. Symmetric algorithms are discussed in the section, "Exploring Symmetric Key Encryption."

Asymmetric encryption algorithms provide for both confidentiality and authentication. They are often called public key algorithms. They are asymmetric in that each party to the cryptosystem has two keys, contained in a "key pair" consisting of a private key and a corresponding public key:

▶ **Private key.** This key is not freely distributed, and is closely guarded, thus ensuring confidentiality.

▶ **Public key.** Usually freely available, and distributed to any entity that wants to enter into confidential communication with the system that holds the corresponding private key.

Both keys are capable of encrypting data. If the private key is used for encrypting data, the corresponding public key is used to decrypt the data and vice versa.

Examples of public key encryption algorithms include the following:

▶ **RSA:**

  ▶ Invented in 1997 by Rivest, Shamir, and Adleman.

  ▶ Often used in digital signatures for authentication and non-repudiation.

  ▶ 100 times slower than DES in hardware and 1,000 times slower than DES in software.

  ▶ Consequently, it can be used for encryption but not typically for large quantities of data.

▶ **DSA.** Digital Signature Algorithm (part of DSS).

▶ **DH.** Diffie-Hellman key exchange algorithm. Describes a method for generating a shared secret encryption key in a secure fashion over an unsecure network. The DH key exchange uses the peers' public and private key pairs as part of its algorithm. Very commonly used by Internet Key Exchange (IKE) Phase I during the establishment of an IPsec VPN session. See the next chapter for more information.

▶ **ElGamal.** An asymmetric key encryption algorithm based on the DH key agreement. First described by Taher Elgamal in 1984.

▶ **Elliptic Curve.** Used for both encryption and also part of DSS.

Encryption with Asymmetric Keys

In order to encrypt a message to an entity (a box or a person), you need their public key. The transmitter encrypts the message with an agreed-upon encryption algorithm and the receiver's public key. The receiver decrypts the message with the receiver's private key. Confidentiality is assured because only the holder of the private key can decrypt the message. Thus:

Encrypt (public key) + Decrypt (private key) = confidentiality

Authentication with Asymmetric Keys

We discussed digital signatures in the last section. This is an example of how authentication works with asymmetric keys. Remember how Bob's boss signed the email message with her private key, and Bob verified the email message with the boss's public key? Authentication is assured because only Bob's boss could have encrypted a message that is verified with the boss's public key. Thus:

Encrypt (private key) + Decrypt (public key) = authentication

> **NOTE**
>
> As with any modern cryptosystem, the most common attack will be on the encryption keys. Safeguarding of the private keys in an asymmetric key cryptosystem is absolutely critical.

Public Key Infrastructure Overview

In large-scale asymmetric encryption cryptosystems, Public Key Infrastructure (PKI) is often used to manage the keys. The integrity of the cryptosystem itself revolves around the trust inherent in the PKI employed. Because the cryptosystem's private keys are managed by the framework of the PKI, a badly managed PKI would lead to an untrustworthy cryptosystem. All the devices, users, and other entities within the cryptosystem leverage on this trust. If their credentials (certificates, keys, and so on) can be proved to be issued by the same, trusted third-party authority, then the entities will trust one another.

Thus, in a PKI, it is all about trust. Here is some terminology providing a framework for a discussion of PKI:

- ▶ **PKI.** A trust framework that supports technologies in a Public Key technology implementation.

- ▶ **Certificate Authority (CA).** The trusted third party that signs public keys.

- ▶ **Certificates.** Documents that associate names to the public keys that have been signed by the CA.

> **NOTE**
>
> User's certificates are always signed by a CA; otherwise, they lack validity and are not trustworthy. CAs have certificates themselves that contain their public key. Who does the CA trust? Itself, of course! These so-called CA certificates are self-signed by the CA because hierarchically the CA is at the top of the trust "org chart."

PKIs don't just happen. Neither are they just users and certificates. PKIs comprise five main areas, as follows:

▶ **CAs.** Address key management and issuance.

▶ **PKI Users.** Some examples are VPN gateways, routers, people, and e-commerce servers

▶ **Storage and Protocols:**

    ▶ How are credentials (keys, certificates) safely stored and distributed?

    ▶ Some of the enrollment and issuance procedures can be automated.

▶ **Supporting Organizational Framework.** Practices and procedures and user authentication using Local Registration Authorities (LRAs), integrated into the organization's comprehensive security policy.

▶ **Supporting Legal Framework.** Acceptable Use Policy (AUP), incident response, policies for lost or stolen keys, and so on.

PKI Topologies

There are two basic PKI topologies, central (single-root) and hierarchical. These are illustrated in Figures 6.11.

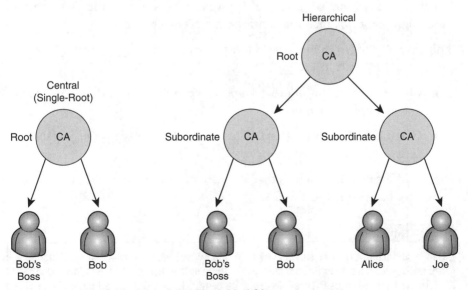

FIGURE 6.11   Central (single-root) and hierarchical CAs.

Central (Single-Root) CA

This is the simplest way to implement a PKI. Certificates are issued by one CA. Its most obvious advantage is its simplicity, but having one root CA has some disadvantages:

- ► Not scalable to large environments; for example, across several departments within a federal government.

- ► Topology requires one centralized administration where all the trust decisions are made.

- ► Single point of failure. If the single root CA is compromised, then the whole PKI is, because all the public keys have been signed by the same CA.

Hierarchical CA

A hierarchical CA delegates the root CA's authority to subordinate CAs, thereby distributing trust. A compromise of a subordinate CA's private key only compromises the public keys that it has signed. Ultimately, all subordinate CAs' public keys have been signed by the same root CA; no matter the depth of the hierarchy, there is only one root. Thus, users trust certificates issued to other users within the same hierarchy. In Figure 6.11, even though Alice and Bob are in different departments of the same company, their CA's certificates were issued by the same root CA, and thus Alice trusts Bob.

This chain of logic is called the *certification path*.

Cross-Certified CAs

With cross-certified CAs, two or more separate organizations' root CAs are configured to trust or "cross-certify" each other. In this manner, all entities within each organization's PKI trust entities in the other organization's PKI. This is another approach to hierarchical CAs.

PKI and Usage Keys

Some Public Key Infrastructures are designed such that users are required to possess two key pairs: one for encryption and another one for signing. These key pairs can be different strengths. This necessitates two certificates for the user: one for encryption and another for signing. (Recalling that the certificate contains the user's public key.)

PKI Server Offload and Registration Authorities (RAs)

Many organizations require that the CA be kept under lock and key and, in some cases, powered down until it is needed to sign certificates. This is because the security of the CA defines the security and trustworthiness of the whole PKI. Depending on the scale of the solution, some of the day-to-day management tasks in a PKI can be offloaded (delegated) to a Registration Authority (RA), minimizing the CA's exposure. Some of these tasks may include the following:

▶ User authentication during enrollment.

▶ User key generation. (If required, normally the client will create its own public key, which is signed by the CA when the enrollment request is approved and the certificate issues.)

▶ Certificate distribution.

NOTE

In general, PKI is a good fit for an IPsec VPN because if a VPN peer is compromised and its certificate quickly revoked by a PKI administrator, that peer can no longer use that certificate to connect to the VPN. This is very effective if the VPN peers check the Certificate Revocation List (CRL), which is issued by the CA, whenever authentication occurs.

PKI Standards

Standardization of PKI protocols is crucial, especially when interoperability of PKI protocols is required. One example of this that we've already seen is in cross-certification of CAs. PKI also should work with other standards, such as the following:

▶ X.500 directory services

▶ Public Key Cryptography Standards (PKCS)

▶ Lightweight Directory Access Protocol (LDAP)

Some of these standards define user information databases and information repositories. It is very convenient (especially when these other services already exist) that PKI interoperates with them.

X.509 v3

The most common standard for the PKI framework is X.509 v3. X.509 defines the certificate structure. Its use is widespread in the following:

- **Servers.** Web, email, LDAP, and other servers using SSL and TLS.

- **Web Browsers.** SSL and TLS.

- **Email Programs.** Secure Multipart Internet Mail Extension (S/MIME) attachments.

- **IPsec VPNs.** Used for authentication instead of simple pre-shared keys (PSKs) during the IKE Phase I negotiation. (See Chapter 7.)

Public Key Cryptography Standards (PKCS)

PKCS defines the formatting of data that is exchanged between the different elements within a PKI. It was developed to promote interoperability, as well as standardize PKI APIs. Some important examples of these standards include the following:

- PKCS #1: RSA Cryptography.

- PKCS #2: DH Key Agreement.

- PKCS #7: Cryptographic Message Syntax (see note below).

- PKCS #10: Certificate Request Syntax (see note below).

NOTE

Think of PKCS #7 and #10 as standards for encapsulation of information between elements in a PKI. In this way, it is similar to network protocols because these standards define rules for communicating information between PKI peers. For example, a certificate enrollment request may be contained in a PKCS #10 envelope and transmitted in turn as the payload of PKCS #7 message to the CA. The issued X.509 v3 certificate is encapsulated as the payload of a PKCS #7 message.

Simple Certificate Enrollment Protocol (SCEP)

SCEP automates the procedure of enrolling in a CA and the issuing of certificates. It is most commonly used in IPsec VPNs where the VPN peers use certificate-based authentication and where manual enrollment is not practical. SCEP not only automates the secure issuance of certificates, but it manages the whole PKI life cycle, including automatic renewal of certificates that are close to their expiry date.

Figure 6.12 shows a simple depiction of this process using the reference network design introduced with Figure 4.1 in Chapter 4, "Implementing Secure Management and Hardening the Router."

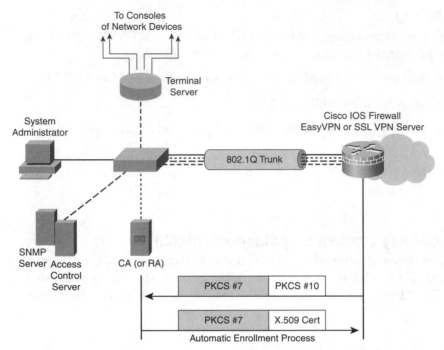

FIGURE 6.12 SCEP process.

Certificate Enrollment Process

There are three basic steps involved in enrolling in a CA. Naturally, the first step is making sure that the participants in the PKI trust the CA. This is done by retrieving and validating the CA's certificate. At a high-level, the three steps are as follows:

1. **Retrieving the CA Certificates.** The PKI participants retrieve the CA's certificate and validate (authenticate) it. Cisco recommends using some out-of-band (relative to the network) channel for the most secure solution. For example, validation of the CA certificate may be as simple as faxing the information found in the CA's X.509 certificate and the CA's public key to the CA administrator and asking that they validate it by return fax.

2. **Certificate Enrollment.** Assuming that the CA's certificate is validated successfully, the PKI participants now trust the CA to issue identity certificates. The PKI participants enroll in the CA by sending a certificate request to the CA. This request contains the user's self-generated public key; the user's corresponding private key is retained on the user's device. (The PKI can also be configured so the CA generates the private and public key pair.) The CA issues the certificate after validating the user's enrollment request. Like the validation of the CA's certificate on the part

of the user, Cisco recommends that the user's certificate request is validated using an out-of-band method by the CA. (Only seems fair!)

> **NOTE**
>
> Note the terminology in step 2. The participants *enroll in the Certificate Authority*. This process can be automated (SCEP) or it can be a manual process. When SCEP is used, steps 1 through 3 are all automated, though the CA administrator will likely reserve the right to manually issue the pending enrollment requests before they can be retrieved.
>
> The participants in a PKI can be people or machines.

3. **Certificate Issuance/Retrieval.** The certificate is *issued* by the CA. As noted, this process is typically manual for security reasons. The PKI participants can now *retrieve* the issued certificates from the CA. This might involve visiting a special web page on the CA or some other method, such as an attachment to an email message from the CA administrator.

When steps 1 through 3 are complete, each participant in the PKI will possess the following:

- ▶ The CA's certificate.

- ▶ Participant's identity certificate (containing the participant's signed public key) signed by the CA.

- ▶ A key pair:

  - ▶ Participant's public key.

  - ▶ Participant's corresponding private key.

Certificate-Based Authentication

Now that the participants have the CA's certificate, their own identity certificate and a key pair, they can authenticate to one another without the involvement of the CA. Because they possess identity certificates that have been signed by the same CA, they should naturally trust one another. The PKI participants could be IPsec VPN peers, as in Figure 6.13.

> **NOTE**
>
> If you have skipped to this part of the chapter and are not familiar with the concept of digital signatures, you owe it to yourself to go to the section "Digital Signatures" in this chapter before reviewing the following steps. Recall that the digital signature is derived from the certificate.

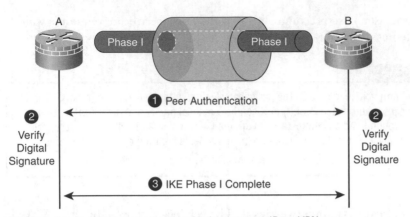

FIGURE 6.13 Certificate-based authentication between IPsec VPN peers.

The actual mechanics of certificate-based authentication are as follows:

1. The PKI participants exchange certificates.

2. The participants verify each other's digital signatures. This step consists of each participant:

   a. Hashing the plaintext portion of the other participant's certificate.

   b. Decrypting the other participant's digital signature using the CA's public key (contained in the CA's certificate).

   c. Comparing the results in steps a and b. If they match, the participant's certificate has been issued by the same CA.

3. Internet Key Exchange (IKE) Phase I completes. (The mechanics of what happens inside IKE Phase I beyond this authentication process will be examined in Chapter 7.)

Certificate Applications

We've mentioned IPsec, SSL VPN servers and application layer servers (such as email and web servers) as common applications of certificates. One CA server can issue certificates that can be used for all these types of authentication, as long as the participants in the PKI support the same procedures for enrollment, issuance, and installation.

Certificates are often seen at the application layer of the OSI model in the following ways:

- ▶ SSL
- ▶ TLS
- ▶ S/MIME (Secure Multi-part Internet Mail Extension)
- ▶ PGP (Pretty Good Privacy)

The most common Cisco uses of certificates include:

- ▶ IPsec—certificate-based authentication during IKE Phase I
- ▶ 802.1X using EAP-TLS (Extensible Authentication Protocol-TLS)
- ▶ TN3270 over SSL (IBM Telnet protocol using SSL encryption)
- ▶ SSL VPN Servers (WebVPN solution; see Chapter 7)

Exam Prep Questions

1. Fill in the blanks with the best choice from the list.

   Cryptography is the art of code _____ and cryptanalysis is the art of code _____.

   - ○ **A.** Graphing, analyzing
   - ○ **B.** Generation, cracking
   - ○ **C.** Making, breaking
   - ○ **D.** Breaking, making
   - ○ **E.** None of the above.

2. Read the following sentence and choose the type of attack that is being described from the list of choices.

   Several examples of ciphertext created by the same cryptosystem are statistically analyzed to deduce underlying plaintext by pattern analysis.

   - ○ **A.** Known-Plaintext
   - ○ **B.** Meet-in-the-Middle
   - ○ **C.** Brute Force
   - ○ **D.** Ciphertext-Only
   - ○ **E.** Chosen-Ciphertext

3. Match the following crypto algorithms with the letter corresponding to its key length.

   AES: ___

   3DES: ___

   DES: ___

   RC4:   ___

   Blowfish: ___

   Your choices are:

   - **A.** 1 to 256 bits
   - **B.** 112 and 168 bits
   - **C.** 56 bits
   - **D.** 128, 192, and 256 bits
   - **E.** 32 to 448 bits

4. True or false. AES is considered a trusted encryption algorithm by virtue of its strong 128-bit encryption keys and its 20+ years of use in crypto systems.

5. What is the best choice of category of encryption algorithm for situations where large volumes of data are transmitted and speed is important? (Choose one from the list.)

    A. Block cipher

    B. Stream cipher

    C. Symmetric key encryption

    D. Asymmetric key encryption

    E. DES

6. Figure 6.14 illustrates what type of PKI topology? (Choose the one best answer.)

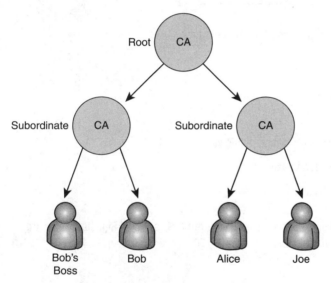

FIGURE 6.14 What PKI technology is this?

    A. Subordinate-Tiered CA

    B. Cross-Certified CA

    C. Central CA

    D. Hierarchical CA

    E. Independent-Mesh CA

7. Figure 6.15 illustrates the part of the enrollment process that occurs after a PKI participant has retrieved and validated the CA's certificate. What is always contained in the
PKCS #7 message that the PKI participant is retrieving from the CA? (Choose all the
correct answers.)

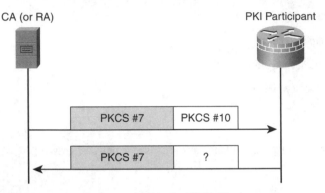

CA (or RA)   PKI Participant

| PKCS #7 | PKCS #10 |

| PKCS #7 | ? |

FIGURE 6.15   What is contained in the PKCS #7 message?

    A. X.509 certificate

    B. CA's private key

    C. CA's public key

    D. PKI participant's signed public key

    E. CA's encryption usage keys

    F. None of the above.

8. Which of the following list of protocols are part of NIST's Digital Signature Standard
(DSS)? (Choose all that apply.)

    A. DSA

    B. Digital Signatures using Reversible Public Key Cryptography

    C. SEAL

    D. Blowfish

    E. ECDSA

9. Fill in the blanks in the following sentence with the letter corresponding to the best
choice. (Choose three.)

Hashing functions are used to validate a message's _____ but do not provide for _____ like HMACs. If _____ is required, the use of digital signatures is specified.

    A. Confidentiality

    B. Integrity

    C. Authentication

    D. Non-repudiation

    E. Origin authentication

10. Which one of the following statements best compares MD5 and SHA-1 as hashing algorithms?

    A. MD5 theoretically has higher security than SHA-1; however, SHA-1 remains more commonly used.

    B. MD5 is not recommended for new cryptosystems because SHA-1 is preferred for its theoretically higher security.

    C. SHA-1 is less resistant to a brute force attack than MD5, and its 32-bit longer buffer makes it faster than MD5.

    D. SHA-1 and MD5's security is not based on encryption keys.

    E. None of the above.

Answers to Exam Prep Questions

1. The correct answer is C. Cryptography is the art of creating and using cryptosystems, whereas cryptanalysis is the process of analyzing a cryptographic algorithm for weaknesses and exploiting them to break the code. They are essentially opponents in the security arena.

2. The correct answer is D. This kind of attack is not practical with modern ciphers because they use pseudorandom output to resist statistical analysis.

3. The answers are as follows:

AES:	D
3DES:	B
DES:	C
RC4:	A
Blowfish:	E

4. False. AES has not yet reached the level of trustworthiness of ciphers such as DES and 3DES precisely because it has not been tested in the field nearly as long. Although AES is cryptographically stronger and a simpler algorithm computationally, DES and 3DES have been in use for over 35 years and found not to possess any flaws.

5. Answer C is correct. Answers A and B are both incorrect because they define categories of ciphers that may be used both for symmetric and asymmetric key encryption. Answer D is incorrect because asymmetric key encryption is best employed for small amounts of data and where speed isn't as important. Answer E is incorrect since DES is 1) an example of an obsolete symmetric key encryption algorithm, and 2) not a category of encryption algorithm.

6. The correct answer is D. Answers A and E are incorrect because they are made-up terms.

7. Answers A and D are correct. At this point in the enrollment process, the PKI participant retrieves the certificate that contains its CA-signed public key. Answer B is incorrect because the private key is always retained on the CA and is never transmitted at any time during enrollment. The security of the whole PKI depends on safeguarding the CA's private key. Answer E is incorrect because this is made-up terminology.

8. Answers A, B, and E are correct. Answers C and D are incorrect because they are examples of encryption algorithms.

9. The correct choices, in order, are B, E, and D. Answer A is incorrect since hashes, HMACS, and digital signatures do not encrypt. Answer C is incorrect because HMACs' strength is that they authenticate the origin of the data in a cryptosystem.

10. The correct answer is B. Answers A and C are exactly opposite to correct. Answer D is incorrect because the security of a hashing cryptosystem is completely based on the safeguarding of the encryption keys that, together with the hash, create the message digest.

7

Virtual Private Networks with IPsec

Terms You'll Need to Understand:

✓ Virtual Private Network (VPN)

✓ IPsec

✓ Remote access VPNs

✓ Site-to-site VPNs

✓ Secure Sockets Layer (SSL) VPN

✓ Easy VPN

✓ Web VPN

✓ Encryption algorithms and keys

✓ Hashing Media Authentication Code (HMAC)

✓ Diffie-Hellman (DH) Key Exchange

✓ Rivest Shamir Adleman (RSA) signatures

✓ Pre-shared keys (PSK)

✓ Hash, Authentication, Group, Lifetime, Encryption (HAGLE) memory aid

✓ Internet Key Exchange (IKE) policy set

✓ IPsec transform set

✓ Crypto Access Control List (ACL)

✓ Crypto map

Exam Topics Covered in This Chapter:

✓ Explain IKE protocol functionality and phases

✓ Describe the building blocks of IPSec and the security functions it provides

✓ Configure and verify an IPSec site-to-site VPN with pre-shared key authentication using SDM

NOTE

These exam topics are from cisco.com. Check there periodically for the latest exam topics and info.

IPsec is often described as a framework for real-time, secure communications. When properly configured, IPsec can scale to large networks, and in some cases, replace the requirement for dedicated WAN circuits. Organizations can leverage on existing high-speed Internet connections to provide reliable and secure transport of communications between the organization's sites, as well as to its mobile workforce using IPsec. Understanding the systems that go into IPsec is critical to both configuring as well as troubleshooting the solution. Although this chapter will not go into great depth about the underlying theory of IPsec, it examines the separate components of the IPsec framework to the extent that this understanding will aid the reader in configuring IPsec. Toward the end of the chapter, we use first the CLI, then the Cisco SDM to configure a site-to-site IPsec VPN in order to cement the theory.

Overview of VPN Technology

Virtual Private Networks (VPNs) are "virtual" in that they can either replace or, at least, complement existing network circuits, whether dial-in or between sites. VPNs are virtual in that sense, but hopefully there is nothing virtual about their privacy! According to Cisco, a good working definition of a VPN is as follows:

> "A VPN [is] an encrypted connection between private networks over
> a public network, usually the Internet."

NOTE

This is the definition that we use in this Exam Cram; although there are a number of other technologies that are called VPNs, they don't provide for encryption and are thus hardly private. Historically, anything that created an IP tunnel was called a VPN. With such a loose definition, technologies that don't provide encryption, such as Generic Routing Encapsulation (GRE) and IPsec tunnels using Authentication Header (AH), are still considered VPNs.

Any kind of network connection over a hostile network could benefit from implementing a VPN. Even on the inside of an organization's perimeter, there are often places where a VPN is required to create a secure channel between network devices, as well as between people and network devices.

Cisco VPN Products

Table 7.1 lists the *primary* products in the Cisco product portfolio that can be used to deploy VPNs.

TABLE 7.1 Cisco VPN Products

VPN Scenario	Best Cisco Product Choice
Dedicated VPN	Cisco VPN 3000 Series concentrators
	Cisco 7200 Series routers
VPN-enabled routers	Cisco SOHO 70 Series
	Cisco 1700 Series Modular Access Routers and Cisco 2600 Series
	Cisco 800, 1800, 2800, and 3800 Series Integrated Services routers
	Cisco 3700 Series Multiservice Access routers and Cisco 3600 Series Multiservice platforms
	Cisco 7200 and 7300 Series routers
	Cisco Catalyst 6500 Series switches and 7600 Series routers
Firewall VPN	Cisco PIX 500 Series Security appliances
	Cisco ASA 5500 Series Adaptive Security appliances

VPN Benefits

VPNs have many benefits, including the following:

▶ **Cost Savings.** The use of cost-effective, high-speed Internet technologies versus dedicated WAN links makes VPNs attractive.

▶ **Security.** Advanced encryption, integrity, and authentication protocols provide for the highest protection against unauthorized access and data loss.

▶ **Scalability.** VPNs can grow seamlessly without the need to add extra infrastructure, particularly when using the Internet.

▶ **Compatibility with Broadband Technology.** VPN technology is largely independent of the underlying infrastructure, meaning that organizations can leverage on the most convenient broadband technology for the greatest flexibility.

There are two main types of VPNs:

▶ Site-to-site

▶ Remote-access

Site-to-Site VPNs

With a site-to-site VPN, host devices operate behind network devices, such as IOS routers, which act as VPN gateways. This is an evolution of WAN technology. The host devices do not need any special software because the fact that there is a VPN between sites is immaterial to them, as the VPN is established between other devices, possibly their own default gateway in the simplest case.

For example, if we configure IOS routers to be VPN gateways, the IP hosts in the production network behind the router would only have to attempt to establish a connection with a device on the inside of a peer network's router. The host's own VPN router would recognize that this site-to-site traffic from the local site to the remote site needs to be protected by the VPN and it would launch a tunnel (that is, the VPN) to its peer if one doesn't already exist. This is illustrated with a small modification to the reference network layout that was first introduced in Figure 5.1 of Chapter 5, "Using Cisco IOS Firewalls to Implement a Network Security Policy."

In Figure 7.1, all traffic between the A and B networks is protected inside a site-to-site VPN between router A and router B.

FIGURE 7.1 Site-to-site VPN.

A device inside network A'—the system administrator PC, for example—would already have router A as its default gateway. Something magic happens from that PC's perspective because when it tries to communicate with the private (RFC 1918) addresses in network B', it gets a response. Breaking it down just a little bit, this is what happens:

> ▶ **Confidentiality.** The IP packet from the system administrator's PC, from network A' to network B', is encrypted before it is encapsulated in another IP packet to router B. Similarly, upon receipt, router B decrypts the A' to B' packet before delivering it to the destination host on the B network.

> ▶ **Integrity.** As we see in the section, "Conceptualizing a Site-to-Site IPsec VPN," it's possible that when the encrypted packet is sent to router B from router A, there is some integrity information added to the packet to add some assurance that the packet has not been tampered with in transit.

▶ **Authentication.** Additionally, some authentication information might have been added to the encrypted IP packet to add assurance that it actually came from router A. Remember the C-I-A triad from Chapter 1, "Network Insecurity"? The "A" in the VPN C-I-A triad stands for authentication.

The optional integrity and authentication information will add some extra overhead per unit of data transmitted. It is up to the guidelines contained in the organization's comprehensive security policy as to whether an acceptable tradeoff has been achieved between security and performance. Many VPN implementations implement confidentiality only, relying on other layers of the OSI model to provide for integrity and authentication outside the context of the VPN.

> **NOTE**
>
> Router B (or router A, for that matter) in Figure 7.1 could be any appropriate Cisco VPN product from Table 7.1.

Remote-Access VPNs

In the same way that site-to-site VPNs evolved from traditional WANs, remote-access VPNs are an evolution of dial-up networking technology. Certainly the same principles of C-I-A apply here. The two most evident differences between remote-access and site-to-site VPNs are the following:

▶ Remote-access VPN clients initiate the VPN on demand.

▶ The remote-access client (whether a PC or a Cisco hardware device) requires Cisco VPN client software to connect.

When implemented as a software solution on a remote user's PC, this can be a very flexible solution. The teleworker can benefit from the same confidentiality, integrity, and authentication services of a site-to-site VPN, while using whatever Internet technologies are at their immediate disposal.

Referring to Figure 7.2, a corporate knowledge worker could be sipping designer coffee at their local coffee shop's wireless hotspot while protecting corporate secrets on network A' from hackers and the merely curious.

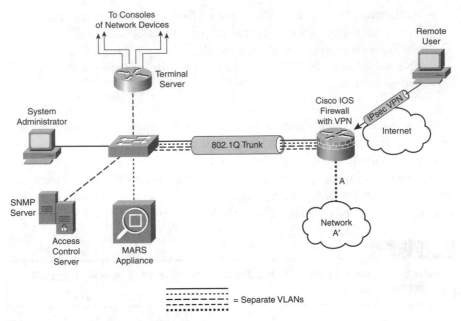

FIGURE 7.2 Remote Access IPsec VPN.

Cisco IOS SSL VPN

Cisco specifies another type of VPN that uses a web browser's built-in Secure Sockets Layer (SSL) encryption to encrypt at the transport layer of the OSI model. One advantage of this solution is that in its simplest form, it doesn't require the installation of additional software on a client PC. SSL VPN offers two modes of operation:

▶ **Clientless.** Uses a web portal to access hosts behind the gateway. Access to file and print shares, email servers, web servers, and other services is provided by the web portal's interface.

▶ **Client.** Uses a thin client that provides an IP address and thus the ability to access applications with their native interface.

The SSL VPN solution is an emerging technology that complements Cisco's IPsec VPN offerings.

Some disadvantages of the SSL VPN solution are as follows:

▶ **Software-Only.** One disadvantage is that it is a software-only solution in IOS routers; thus, it doesn't take advantage of the hardware-accelerated onboard encryption in many router models. The router (and the client) CPU processes all the encryption.

> ▶ **Cryptographic Security.** Does not currently support the same level of encryption security as IPsec.

SSL VPNs have compatibility advantages. SSL VPNs can be configured and operate alongside other features on Cisco network devices. SSL VPNs are compatible with the following:

- ▶ Dynamic Multipoint VPNs (DMVPNs)

- ▶ Cisco IOS Firewalls

- ▶ IPsec

- ▶ Intrusion Protection Systems (IPSs)

- ▶ Cisco Easy VPN (Cisco's remote-access IPsec VPN solution)

- ▶ Network Address Translation (NAT)

Cisco VPN Product Positioning

Cisco has a number of devices in its product portfolio that provide VPN services. Some of these devices are end-of-sale (EOS) and are marked as such in Table 7.2. EOS does not mean end-of-life! For example, there are literally hundreds of thousands of PIX firewalls in the field, and Cisco continues to support these devices with new OS updates and technical support.

EXAM ALERT

You should memorize Table 7.2, as Cisco just loves asking questions that refer to information found in tables.

TABLE 7.2   Cisco VPN Product Positioning

VPN Type		
Product	Remote-Access	Site-to-Site
VPN 3000 Series concentrator (EOS)	Primary role	Secondary role
VPN-Enabled IOS router	Secondary role	Primary role
PIX 500 Series Security appliance (EOS)	Complements firewall role	Yes, but IT Security manages the VPN
ASA 5500 Series Adaptive Security appliance	Supports VPN 3000 Series Concentrator features	Yes, but IT Security manages the VPN

> **NOTE**
>
> The VPN 3000 Series Concentrator was end-of-sale (EOS) in February 2007. The PIX 500 Series Security Appliances were recently announced EOS, with the last order date being July 28, 2008. They are not end-of-life (EOL) until July 27, 2013. Our focus will be on VPN-enabled IOS routers and the ASA 5500 Security Appliances. It's also worth noting that Cisco recently announced (Q1 2008) two new ASA 5500 Series models: the ASA 5580-20 and 5580-40. These devices are positioned at the service provider level and have option cards that augment the ASA's built-in hardware encryption by providing VPN hardware acceleration of 10,000 IPsec and 10,000 SSL connections simultaneously. Here is a link to a product matrix for the complete ASA 5500 Series portfolio: http://www.cisco.com/en/US/products/ps6120/prod_models_comparison.html.
>
> Here is a link to Cisco's Q&A about the EOS PIX firewalls:
>
> http://www.cisco.com/en/US/prod/collateral/vpndevc/ps5708/ps5709/ps2030/qa_eos_for_sale_for_cisco_pix_products_customer.html.

VPN-Enabled IOS Router Features

Here are some of the VPN features of the Cisco VPN-enabled IOS routers:

- ▶ **Voice and Video Enabled VPN (V3PN).** Integration of QoS, IPsec, and VoIP (IP telephony).

- ▶ **IPsec Stateful Failover.** Provides for network resiliency in site-to-site VPN configurations, in both stateless and stateful failover solutions. Options include the following:

  - ▶ Dead Peer Detection (DPD)

  - ▶ Hot Standby Router Protocol (HSRP)

  - ▶ Reverse Route Injection (RRI)

  - ▶ Stateful Switchover (SSO)

- ▶ **DMVPN.** Enables automatic provisioning of site-to-site IPsec VPNs, putting together three Cisco IOS features:

  - ▶ Next Hop Resolution Protocol (NHRP)

  - ▶ Multipoint GRE

  - ▶ IPsec VPN

- ▶ **Cisco Easy VPN.** Cisco's common framework for remote-access IPsec VPNs.

ASA 5500 Series Adaptive Security Appliance

As you can infer from Table 7.2, the primary purpose of the ASA 5500 Series security appliances is as a perimeter security device that implements the organization's comprehensive security policy. Because the IT security staff own the policy, they also own the security appliance and any policies, including the VPN, which are configured on it. In the context of VPN technology, the ASA 5500 Series of security appliances is Cisco's direct replacement for the 3000 Series VPN concentrators, of which many tens of thousands still exist in the field. Here are some of the features of the ASA 5500 Series of security appliances:

▶ **Flexible Platform.** IPsec and SSL VPN solutions on one platform that also supports application inspection firewall and IPS.

▶ **Resilient Clustering.** VPN load balancing and backup server in a mixed environment of ASAs and VPN concentrators.

▶ **Cisco Easy VPN.** Cisco's common framework for remote-access IPsec VPNs. Also supports automatic Cisco VPN Client updates.

▶ **Cisco IOS SSL VPN.** Both clientless and client-based solutions.

▶ **Web-Based Management.** The Cisco Adaptive Security Device Manager (ASDM) configures and manages all the security and VPN features of the appliance.

VPN Clients

Let's eliminate confusion here before it even begins! Cisco's product planners have been hard at work coming up with worthy names for their VPN remote-access solutions, both IPsec and SSL:

▶ **Easy VPN.** If it's a remote-access IPsec VPN solution, regardless of whether the client uses Cisco software on a PC or the client is a device such as a router, it is called Easy VPN. Of course, it would be too easy if the client was called a client! The client is called an Easy VPN Remote. The VPN server is called an Easy VPN Server. See how easy that is?

▶ **WebVPN.** If it's a remote-access SSL VPN solution, it is called WebVPN, regardless of whether the client is a web browser accessing servers behind the server's web portal, or a thin client such as the SSL VPN Client (SVC) or the newer standalone AnyConnect VPN Client (currently only supported on the ASA 5500 Series Adaptive Security Appliance).

Here are some Cisco VPN clients. See if you can determine which broad category, Easy VPN or Web VPN, they fall into (the answers are after the list):

- **Certicom Client.** IPsec VPN client software that runs on wireless PDAs with either the Palm OS or Windows Mobile operating systems.

- **Cisco VPN 3002 Hardware Client.** (EOS February 2007) Dedicated remote-access VPN client appliance. Connects SOHO LANs to the VPN.

- **Cisco VPN Software Client.** Software loaded on an individual's PC or laptop that initiates an IPsec VPN to a central site VPN server. Comes in versions for Linux, Mac, and Windows OSs.

- **Cisco AnyConnect VPN Client.** SSL VPN client software loaded on an individual's PC or laptop that initiates an SSL VPN to a central site VPN server. Currently supports Windows Vista, XP, and 2000 OSs, as well as MAC OS X (version 10.4 or later) and Red Hat Linux (version 9 or later).

Answers: Certicom Client = Easy VPN; Cisco VPN 3002 Hardware Client = Easy VPN; Cisco VPN Software Client = Easy VPN; Cisco AnyConnect VPN Client = WebVPN.

Hardware-Accelerated Encryption

Cisco offers hardware modules for modular routers, security appliances, and concentrators that will offload encryption processing from the device's CPU and thus increase encrypted throughput:

- **AIM-VPN (Advanced Integration Module).** Certain modular IOS router models.

- **Cisco IPsec VPN SPA (Shared Port Adapter).** Catalyst 6500 Series switches and 7600 Series routers.

- **SEP-E (Scalable Encryption Processor–Enhanced).** VPN 3000 Series concentrators.

- **VAC+ (VPN Accelerator Card +).** Modular PIX Firewalls.

NOTE

All ASA security appliances have onboard hardware encryption for both IPsec and SSL VPNs.

IPsec Compared to SSL

Cisco's VPN product portfolio consists of both IPsec and SSL VPN solutions in order to give the most choices to their customers. Whether you choose IPsec or SSL for your VPN solution, there are some tradeoffs between usability and security. The AnyConnect SSL VPN solution, for example, is simple to use and tolerates very well NAT devices on the path between the client and the server. In IPsec VPN's favor is the strong authentication that can be used to secure the communication path.

> **EXAM ALERT**
>
> Table 7.3 is a summary that compares the two VPN technologies (SSL and IPsec) in the areas of: applications, encryption, authentication, ease of use, and overall. Memorize this table. It is sure to be on the exam. If you are reading this chapter before Chapter 6, "Introducing Cryptographic Services," you may want to review the definitions for encryption algorithms, key length, and authentication.

TABLE 7.3 IPsec Compared to SSL

Area	SSL VPN	IPsec VPN
Applications	Web-based applications, file and print sharing, email (IMAP, POP3, and SMTP).	All IP-based applications with native interface.
Encryption (Not cipher; key length. See Chapter 6 for this distinction.)	Moderate—key lengths of 40-bit to 128-bits.	Stronger—key lengths range from 56-bit to 256-bit.
Authentication	Moderate—one-way or two-way (mutual) authentication.	Strong—two-way (mutual) authentication using pre-shared secrets (PSKs) or digital certificates.
Ease of Use (setup and use)	Very high for the user, especially using the clientless Web VPN portal. Also, the AnyConnect client can be downloaded, installed, and the session established from the Web VPN portal.	Moderate—the initial setup means that nontechnical users may find it to be challenging.
Overall Security	Moderate—any device with a web browser (clientless portal) or with the appropriate software (AnyConnect) can connect.	Strong—only specific devices with specific Cisco software configurations can connect.

> **NOTE**
>
> There is an inconsistency in the Applications comparison in Table 7.3. As we have seen, one of Cisco's SSL VPN solutions is the AnyConnect client. When using the AnyConnect SSL VPN client, you can have your cake and eat it too! The AnyConnect client obtains an IP address from the VPN gateway (an IOS router, for example), and you can then access applications on the VPN gateway's network using their native interfaces. It also supports the use of digital certificates for authentication, and data can be protected up to a 256-bit AES cipher. Cisco is probably trying to incorporate the clientless Web VPN portal in their comparison because that technology has integral support for web servers, file sharing, and email.

You can see IPsec's many strengths in Table 7.3. We will now turn our focus to IPsec VPNs, specifically site-to-site configurations.

Conceptualizing a Site-to-Site IPsec VPN

One of the advantages of a site-to-site IPsec VPN is that the clients whose traffic is being protected by the VPN don't need to know anything about VPNs. All the users know is that something magic happens, and they can access an HQ server on its native IP address, even if that server is on the other side of a hostile network like the Internet. In this section, we look at the separate components of *all* IPsec VPNs, and then reinforce these concepts by constructing a site-to-site IPsec VPN, using both the CLI and the SDM.

IPsec Components

IPsec is an Internet Engineering Task Force (IETF) standard that defines a framework of open standards for secure, real-time communication using IP. Like IP, it works at the network layer, and while it is deliberately security algorithm-independent, it does provide an environment into which various encryption, authentication, and keying algorithms can be plugged in. It is described in RFCs 2401–2412 and was designed as a native component of IPv6, but has been ported to IPv4, where our focus lies. IPsec can be recognized inside an IP packet by its protocol IDs, 50, and 51, which are reserved for ESP (Encapsulating Security Payload) and AH (Authentication Header), respectively.

IPsec's framework provides its own C-I-A triad (actually C-I-A-A):

- ▶ **Confidentiality.** Uses encryption algorithms (encryption is optional with IPsec VPNs. See the following note).

▶ **Integrity.** IPsec policies must implement hashing algorithms to assure date integrity.

▶ **Authentication.** Peers must authenticate during tunnel establishment. Optionally, origin authentication is specified to verify that packets come from an authenticated peer. Authentication is managed by the Internet Key Exchange (IKE) and can take different forms.

▶ **Anti-Replay.** IPsec must provide assurance of each packet's uniqueness and that it hasn't been duplicated through sequencing and the use of a sliding window.

EXAM ALERT

Know what the IPsec C-I-A stands for. (C)onfidentiality through encryption, (I)ntegrity through hashing algorithms, and (A)uthentication using PSKs and digital certificates and RSA encrypted nonces, as well as origin authentication using HMACs (Hashing Media Authentication Codes), has been discussed in Chapter 6. We are now taking those tools out of the toolbox and constructing an IPsec VPN with them.

NOTE

Anti-replay is the last A in C-I-A-A and will not be further discussed in this book. Besides, C-I-A is a lot easier to remember than C-I-A-A, right?

NOTE

Our focus will be on encryption; or else how *private* are our Virtual Private Networks? That said, IPsec provides for either ESP or AH inside IP packets. ESP specifies encryption, whereas AH does not. Do not be surprised if you see little or no discussion about ESP's forgotten cousin, AH.

IPsec is versatile as it allows for new and better security protocols in every facet of IPsec's C-I-A because it is security algorithm-independent. Think of the different components that fit into IPsec as modular, hot-swappable plug-ins. Let's look at the different elements of C-I-A separately.

Confidentiality: Encryption Algorithms

Confidentiality is assured through the use of encryption algorithms (or ciphers) and encryption keys. Only the VPN peers know what encryption algorithms they have negotiated and which keys they have arrived at (calculated). This information is never transmitted with the encrypted payload, so good luck breaking the code if you're an attacker! Of course, the shorter the key, the easier it is to guess.

The longer the key, the harder it is to guess, and the longer it takes to create encrypted data because the key is used with the encryption algorithm to create encrypted data, or ciphertext. This is where it would be useful for the VPN peer to possess hardware-accelerated encryption as this can be burdensome on the CPU, again pointing at the classic tradeoff between security and usability. This becomes a critical issue when the VPN peer supports hundreds or thousands of VPN connections simultaneously.

Figure 7.3 gives a high-level overview of the relationship between cleartext, ciphertext, encryption, decryption, and encryption algorithms and encryption keys.

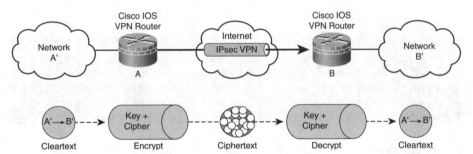

FIGURE 7.3 Overview of the relationship between encryption algorithms, encryption keys, and VPNs.

Where do these keys come from? How long are they? We're getting a bit ahead of ourselves because we haven't considered how the encryption algorithms and encryption keys are negotiated between the peers. As we will see in the later section, "IKE Phase I: The IKE Protocol," the keys are either manually configured or dynamically negotiated (calculated) when the VPN is being established during the Diffie-Hellman (DH) key exchange phase. See the next section for a bit more information on DH.

Here are some encryption algorithms and their associated key lengths that VPNs use:

▶ **DES (Data Encryption Standard).** This cipher uses 56-bit keys. It is a symmetric key crypto system.

▶ **3DES ("Triple" or "Three" DES).** Using DES as a verb, 64-bit blocks of data are DES'd three times. The base key is still 56 bits. Often described as a 168-bit cipher, but we know better, right? 3DES is a symmetric key crypto system.

▶ **AES (Advanced Encryption Standard).** 128-, 192-, or 256-bit keys. AES has stronger security than DES and is computationally more efficient than 3DES. It was adopted by the National Institute of Standards and Technology (NIST) as a replacement for DES and as a result of a competition.

- ▶ **RSA (Rivest, Shamir and Adleman).** Not used by IPsec for encryption (C), though RSA encryption can be used during peer authentication (A). RSA uses 512-, 768-, 1024-bit, or larger keys. It is an asymmetric key crypto system.

- ▶ **SEAL (Software-Optimized Encryption Algorithm).** Stream cipher that uses a 160-bit key for encryption.

Creating an Encryption Key: The Diffie-Hellman Key Exchange

Again, we will put off the discussion for where and how the DH key exchange occurs during IPsec tunnel establishment. For now, it is important to know that it is a necessary component of IPsec and is a way for VPN peers to arrive at a share-secret encryption key for symmetric protocols, such as DES and 3DES, which require it. It describes a secure method for VPN peers to calculate a shared-secret key over a public network without having to resort to some out-of-band method such as a courier or a phone call for transmission. This sounds impossible, and was in fact considered as such by cryptographic experts for many years. DH makes VPNs more practical because the shared encryption key is negotiated on demand during the VPN setup.

DH algorithms supported on Cisco IOS routers include DH Groups 1, 2, 5, and 7 (DH1, DH2, DH5, and DH7 for short).

Integrity: Hashing Algorithms

If you want to make sure the 1's and 0's you put in one end of the VPN are the same 1's and 0's that come out the other end, you need to employ a Hashed Message Authentication Code (HMAC), or "hash" for short. Here are the two common HMAC algorithms that are supported on the Cisco IOS router:

- ▶ **Message Digest 5 (MD5).** HMAC-MD5 uses a 128-bit shared-secret encryption key.

- ▶ **Secure Hash Algorithm 1 (SHA-1).** HMAC-SHA-1 uses a 160-bit shared-secret encryption key.

The idea is fairly straightforward. Looks like we're going to use those encryption keys again! Here are the three steps in insuring the integrity of messages:

1. The VPN peers agree upon the hash they will use, either MD5 or SHA-1, while the VPN is being set up.

2. When a message is transmitted from one peer to the other, a hash is made up using the original message and the shared-secret encryption key, and is appended to it.

3. When the receiving peer receives the message, it hashes the message with the agreed-upon hash and the shared encryption key and compares it with the hash that is appended to the message. If the computed hash differs from the one that is appended to the message, the peer infers that the message must have been altered in transit.

Authentication: PSKs, RSA Signatures, or RSA Encrypted Nonces

This completes the IPsec C-I-A triad. Again, we have yet to look at how these separate elements, Confidentiality, Integrity, and (now) Authentication are brought into play during the VPN establishment. Suffice it to say, they constitute the categories of modular, swappable plug-ins that can fit in the IPsec framework and that the VPN peers negotiate while the VPN is being set up.

Peers can be authenticated (their identity verified) using one of three methods:

▶ **Pre-Shared Key (PSK).** A simple password, manually configured in the VPN peers. This is the simplest form of authentication and therefore quite common, but is not very scalable.

▶ **RSA Signature.** Peers are authenticated through the exchange of digital certificates. Each peer has a key pair made up of a private and public key contained in a certificate that has been issued by a certificate authority. Peer A creates a hash and encrypts it with its private key. This encrypted hash signature is appended to a message. Peer B decrypts the encrypted hash with Peer A's public key (it is public after all!). The decrypted hash is compared with a recomputed hash. If they are the same, the signature is genuine.

▶ **RSA Encrypted Nonces.** Least common of the three authentication methods. Public keys of every peer have to be manually configured on all the peers as part of the configuration process. These keys are used with a nonce, which is a random number generated by the peer to create an encrypted value that is used to validate a peer's identity.

NOTE
The pre-shared key (PSK) has nothing whatsoever to do with the shared-secret encryption key that we discussed in the preceding two sections.

IPsec Strengths

In every mode of operation, the payload of the IP packets transmitted between the peers is encrypted and not the IP packet header, where the routing information resides. Because IPsec is just cargo (same as TCP, UDP, ICMP, and so on) from the perspective of an IP network, implementing IPsec is transparent.

Other strengths of IPsec include the following:

▶ **Data Link Layer independent and Application Layer independent.** Because IPsec operates at the network layer, it is supported by all data link layer protocols.

▶ **Extremely scalable.** With careful design, IPsec can scale to very large networks.

Constructing a VPN: Putting it Together

Before we start looking at the details, we should look at IPsec at a high level. It's easy to over-simplify and speak of a single VPN tunnel. In reality, IPsec constructs two tunnels called Internet Key Exchange (IKE) security associations (SAs):

▶ **IKE Phase I SA.** All negotiation and authentication between VPN peers occurs in this security association.

▶ **IKE Phase II SA.** Data is transformed (encrypted, verified, authenticated) and transmitted in this security association.

Figure 7.4 depicts a high-level overview of IKE Phase I and IKE Phase II security associations.

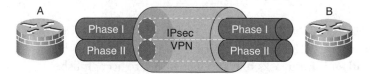

FIGURE 7.4 High-level view of IKE Phase I and IKE Phase II.

If you understand how the File Transfer Protocol (FTP) works, then you also have a good idea about how IPsec VPNs work. As with FTP, IPsec creates two security associations; one that manages the control plane (Phase I) and another which manages the data plane (Phase II).

IKE Phase I: The IKE Protocol

Negotiating what? Authenticating what? No surprise that IKE Phase I is where all the separate components of the IPsec framework are negotiated between the peers. Encryption algorithms, encryption keys, HMACs, authentication method, and other parameters are negotiated between the peers. Even how to negotiate is negotiated! Once the peers agree on the parameters for the Phase I SA, the peers authenticate to one another and Phase I completes. Phase II negotiation can now occur. A good way to remember the separate IPsec policy elements, which are negotiated during Phase I, to remember the acronym HAGLE. Of course, this is a (misspelled) play on words because "haggle" is slang for negotiate and that's what happens during Phase I.

Table 7.2 explains the separate elements of the HAGLE acronym.

EXAM ALERT

This is an excellent memory aid. Make sure you memorize it and the choices inferred by each of the letters in HAGLE.

TABLE 7.2   HAGLE During IKE Negotiation

Letter	Policy Element	Choices
H	HMAC	MD5 SHA-1
A	Authentication	PSKs RSA signatures RSA encrypted nonces
G	Group	DH1, DH2, DH5, DH7
L	Lifetime	Time and/or Data
E	Encryption	DES 3DES AES: 128-, 192-, or 256-bit

The IPsec policy elements in the table should look familiar by now. Let's break down what happens during IKE Phase I a bit further by looking at a list of the negotiation and authentication tasks that IPsec uses IKE to accomplish:

▸ Automating the encryption key exchange process by:

   ▸ Negotiating SA parameters.

   ▸ Automating key generation.

   ▸ Automating key refreshing.

   ▸ Providing for manual configuration.

▸ IKE specifies three modes (in order) for negotiating parameters and establishing security associations:

   ▸ Main mode (MM): Negotiating IKE Phase I SA (see the following note).

▶ Aggressive mode (AM): Negotiating IKE Phase I (see the following note).

▶ Quick mode (QM): Negotiating IKE Phase II.

> **NOTE**
>
> As was pointed out a bit earlier, IKE is responsible for determining the rules that will be followed during negotiation. Main mode and aggressive mode are two different protocols for negotiating Phase I parameters and leading to the forming of a IKE Phase I SA. They are like Robert's Rules of Order for IPsec. One or the other is chosen at the beginning of IKE Phase I negotiation and establishes the rules that subsequent negotiation are bound to follow.
>
> Some vendors conduct their own, proprietary, exchanges after MM or AM complete. Cisco's *Mode Configuration*, which is used with Easy VPN, is an example of this. This is outside the scope of this Exam Cram.

> **NOTE**
>
> As its name implies, aggressive mode specifies fewer exchanges than main mode. Each exchange has fewer packets so more negotiating is done in a shorter timeframe that equates to more efficiency. The security tradeoff is that aggressive mode is considered less secure than main mode by some security experts.

Figure 7.5 diagrams a main mode exchange between two VPN peers, Peer A and B, which in this example are both IOS VPN routers.

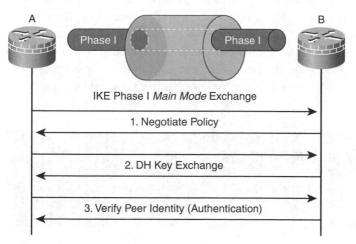

FIGURE 7.5   IKE Phase I main mode exchange.

As can be seen, main mode uses three two-way exchanges:

▶ **Exchange One.** VPN peers propose and agree upon encryption algorithms, authentication method, and HMACs that will be used to secure
subsequent IKE communications. This is where HAGLE occurs. The
elements of HAGLE are called policy sets.

▶ **Exchange Two.** VPN peers employ Diffie-Hellman (DH) to create
share-secret encryption keys. This share-secret encryption key is the base
for generation of all other encryption and authentication keys. A secure
channel (the SA) is now established.

▶ **Exchange Three.** Authentication occurs. If successful, the SA remains
up; otherwise, it is torn down by the initiator.

After these three exchanges complete successfully, a secure and authenticated
communication path (that is, the Secure Association) is established that is used for
all subsequent exchanges between the peers. It's useful to note that exchange three
is secure because the initiator will not send its own authenticators (PSK, RSA digital signature, or RSA encrypted nonce) until it has verified the responder's.

Breaking it down a bit more, here is additional information you need to know
about what happens inside main mode exchanges one and two.

Exchange One

The separate elements of the IKE proposals (HAGLE) are grouped in policy
sets. A VPN peer may have several policy *sets*, numbers indicating their priority, in a policy *suite*. Why not just one policy set, you might ask? A single VPN
peer might need several policy sets because it is configured to support several
other VPNs, both site-to-site and remote-access. Each one of those other VPN
peers may require a different policy set for successful VPN establishment.

> **EXAM ALERT**
>
> You will need to know what a policy set is and also two things about the policy set
> numbers:
>
> ▶ They are locally significant to the VPN peer and not exchanged during Phase I;
> therefore, they do not need to match between two VPN peers.
>
> ▶ The lower the number, the higher the priority.

Exchange Two

One of the things agreed upon in the policy sets during exchange one was the
size of the key exchange (that is, the DH groups). This is a good thing because
the Diffie-Hellman key exchange results in keying "material." The DH groups

refer to the amount of keying material that results. The more keying material, the more secure (unbreakable) the encryption keys are that are generated for use with encryption algorithms.

Cisco IOS software supports four DH groups:

▶ **DH Group 1 (DH1).** 768 bits, usually chosen with DES encryption algorithm.

▶ **DH Group 2 (DH2).** 1024 bits, usually chosen with 3DES encryption algorithm.

▶ **DH Group 5 (DH5).** 1536 bits, usually chosen with AES encryption algorithm.

▶ **DH Group 7 (DH7).** 163-bit elliptic curve cryptography (ECC), usually chosen with low CPU-powered devices such as PDAs and therefore typically only remote-access VPNs.

IKE Phase II: Quick Mode

At a high level, IKE Phase II performs these functions:

▶ Negotiates IPsec Transform sets.

EXAM ALERT

Transform Sets Versus Policy Sets
IKE Phase II Encryption algorithms and HMACs are grouped in something called a transform set. Because the *transform* set dictates how the data is *transformed* through the Phase II SA, this should be easy to remember for an exam. This also implies something quite correct, which is that the encryption algorithm and HMACs in Phase II transform sets are independent (and are often different) than those negotiated in IKE Phase I policy sets.

▶ Establishes IPsec SAs (at least two; see Figure 7.6).

▶ Periodically renegotiates IPsec SAs.

▶ (Optional) Performs an additional DH key exchange.

Remember that all negotiating and authentication occurs within IKE Phase I. So, where do you think IKE Phase II negotiations occur? They are conducted in the secure channel established during IKE Phase I negotiations (AM or MM) and use Quick Mode (QM). For example, during QM, policies such as the following are negotiated:

▶ Which networks will be protected by the VPN (for example, Net A' <—> Net B').

▶ Encryption algorithm for the Phase II SA.

▶ HMACs.

▶ Transport mode versus tunnel mode (discussed in the "Transport Mode Versus Tunnel Mode" section later).

▶ ESP versus AH.

Figure 7.6 depicts IKE Phase II SAs. Using the FTP analogy again, this is the data plane of the IPsec VPN and is protected by the encryption algorithms contained in the transform sets.

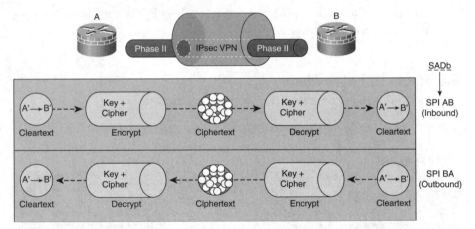

FIGURE 7.6 IKE Phase II SAs

Interestingly, an IKE Phase II SA is unidirectional, meaning that you need two SAs for bidirectional data flow between VPN peers. This is indicated in Figure 7.6. The SAs are identified by their Security Parameter Index (SPI) numbers. For example, once the VPN was established, Peer B would have SPI AB as an inbound SPI and SPI BA as an outbound SPI in its Security Association Database (SAD).

We now examine some of IPsec's data transport features, protocols, and algorithms.

Authentication Header (AH)

If your VPN solution does not require confidentiality, you can choose Authentication Header (AH) alone for transport of IPsec data. AH enables you to choose algorithms to assure data integrity and data authentication but not confidentiality. No C-I-A here if you use AH alone! AH is most often used by ESP to provide for optional data integrity and data authentication and not used by itself. If AH is used by itself, AH is encapsulated in an IP packet as protocol 51.

AH features are as follows:

- ▶ Assures data integrity.
- ▶ Origin authentication (ensures that all the 1's and 0's came from an authenticated peer).
- ▶ Uses a keyed-hash mechanism.
- ▶ No provision for encryption.
- ▶ Anti-replay protection.

Encapsulating Security Payload (ESP)

If your VPN solution requires confidentiality, you must choose Encapsulating Security Payload (ESP) for transport of IPsec data. As indicated previously, AH can be used with ESP to provide for data integrity and data authentication; thus covering all the letters in C-I-A. ESP is encapsulated in an IP packet as protocol 50.

ESP features are as follows:

- ▶ Data confidentiality through encryption.
- ▶ Assures data integrity.
- ▶ Origin authentication.
- ▶ Anti-replay protection.

Referring to Figure 7.7, an IP packet with source address A' and destination address B' arrives at peer A. Peer A applies C-I-A services to the packet as required

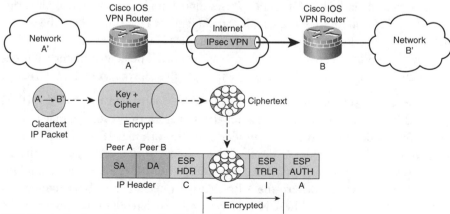

FIGURE 7.7 Syntax of tunnel mode IPsec packet.

Depending on the transform sets negotiated between the peers, not all the facets of C-I-A will be applied to the packet that will travel in the IPsec VPN between the peers. Assuming that confidentiality will be applied as a minimum, then we must use ESP for encapsulation. This also enables us to optionally apply integrity and authentication services to the packet. If you were to look at the IPsec packet on a protocol analyzer, you will see that the order of the extra fields added while encapsulating the original IP packet are C (ESP Header), I (ESP Trailer), and A (ESP Authentication Trailer) = C-I-A.

> ▶ **C.** Peer A encrypts the packet and places it into a new IP packet, prepending the encrypted payload with an ESP header. This provides for confidentiality.

> ▶ **C and I.** If integrity assurance is required, Peer A will add an integrity checksum (a hash) in the form of an ESP trailer before encrypting the original packet and placing it in the payload of the new IP packet.

> ▶ **C and I and A.** If origin authentication is required, an authentication checksum (similar to a frame check sequence in a data link layer frame) will be added to the payload of the new IP packet but will not be encrypted.

EXAM ALERT

Have you noticed that the order of the fields in the IPsec payload of the IP packet is C-I-A, making it simple to remember?

Tunnel Mode Versus Transport Mode

The example described with Figure 7.7 uses tunnel mode. Simply put, all the original IP packet from A' to B' is encrypted, including the IP header where the source and destination addresses reside, before it is tunneled inside a new IP packet. Thus, we have layer 3 inside layer 3 and that equals a tunnel. The new (or outer) IP packet has the routing information necessary to route the packet across the Internet.

In some circumstances, it is either not desirable or needed to wrap the IPsec payload (either AH or ESP) inside a new IP packet. In this case, you may opt for transport mode. With transport mode, only the original IP packet's payload (example: TCP) is encrypted, leaving the original IP header intact. If the IP addresses in the original IP packet are private, RFC 1918, addresses this might be problematic, except where the VPN between peers A and B are connected across a private intranet. There is less overhead associated with transport mode, but it isn't very common, particularly where the VPN peers are connected across the Internet, where tunnel mode is pretty much mandatory.

Implementing IPsec on a Site-to-Site VPN Using the CLI

We will set up an IPsec site-to-site VPN using first the CLI and then second (next section) with the Cisco SDM. Using the CLI is a very good way to demonstrate how IPsec VPNs work because manual configuration of the protocols, policies, and rules reinforces much of the theory.

The basic tasks for implementing IPsec on a site-to-site VPN using the CLI can be broken into five steps, as follows:

Step 1. Ensure that existing ACLs are compatible with the IPsec VPN.

Step 2. Create ISAKMP (IKE Phase I) policy set(s).

Step 3. Configure IPsec transform set(s).

Step 4. Create crypto ACL that defines traffic that will be in the IPsec VPN (for example, Net A' <—-> Net B').

Step 5. Create and apply the crypto map (IPsec tunnel interface).

EXAM ALERT

The missing step is Step 6: Test! That small fact aside, memorize the *five* steps for the exam.

Figure 7.8 illustrates the reference design for the following worked example of the steps for implementing IPsec on a site-to-site IPsec VPN using the CLI.

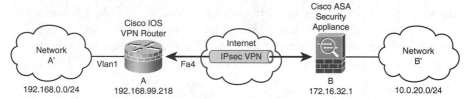

FIGURE 7.8 Reference diagram for site-to-site IPsec VPN.

Step 1: Ensure That Existing ACLs Are Compatible with the IPsec VPN

Use the commands that you learned in Chapter 5 to ensure that ISAKMP, ESP, or AH traffic will not be blocked by an existing interface ACL.

ISAKMP is the Internet Security Association Key Management Protocol and uses UDP for transport. It uses both source and destination UDP port 500. IKE messages use ISAKMP for transport. The Cisco IOS software denotes ISAKMP with keyword **isakmp**.

ESP is defined as IP protocol number 50. The Cisco IOS software denotes ESP with the keyword **esp**.

AH is defined as IP protocol number 51. The Cisco IOS software denotes ESP with the keyword **ahp**.

Assuming that you have an ACL 101 applied on interface FastEthernet4 on Peer A, you would need to add these lines to it in the correct place:

```
access-list 101 permit ahp host 172.16.32.1 host 206.248.168.15
access-list 101 permit esp host 172.16.32.1 host 206.248.168.15
access-list 101 permit udp host 172.16.32.1 host 206.248.168.15 eq isakmp

CiscoISR-A#show access-list 101
Extended IP access list 101
    10 permit ahp host 172.16.32.1 host 206.248.168.15
    20 permit esp host 172.16.32.1 host 206.248.168.15
    30 permit udp host 172.16.32.1 host 206.248.168.15 eq isakmp
    40 permit tcp any any eq 22
    50 permit tcp any any eq www
    60 permit tcp any any eq 443
CiscoISR#
```

Step 2: Create ISAKMP (IKE Phase I) Policy Set(s)

Recall that IKE policies group all the separate elements of HAGLE into a policy set. If you need more than one IKE policy, you can create a policy suite. The **crypto isakmp policy** command creates the policy set. In this example, we leverage on the HAGLE acronym and create policy set 99 with the following:

H = SHA-1

A = PSK

G = DH5

L = 86,400 seconds

E = 128-bit AES

```
CiscoISR-A(config)#crypto isakmp policy 99
CiscoISR-A(config-isakmp)#hash sha
CiscoISR-A(config-isakmp)#authentication pre-share
CiscoISR-A(config-isakmp)#group 5
```

```
CiscoISR-A(config-isakmp)#lifetime 86400
CiscoISR-A(config-isakmp)#encryption aes
CiscoISR-A(config-isakmp)#
```

If we don't need to create any more policy sets for our policy suite, we are finished with this step. You may create other policy sets, but remember that the lower the number, the higher the priority. It is good practice to put the cryptographically strongest policies near the top of the policy suite by assigning numerically lower numbers.

Also, you must ensure that the Peer B has a policy set that matches Peer A's.

Table 7.5 shows a list of possible ISAKMP parameters when you construct a policy set. If you don't specify a parameter, the Cisco IOS will choose the default.

TABLE 7.5   ISAKMP Policy Set Parameters

Policy Element	Parameter	Keyword	Meaning	Default
H	hash	sha	SHA-1	sha
		md5	MD5	
A	authentication	rsa-sig	RSA signatures	rsa-sig
		rsa-encr	RSA encrypted nonces	
		pre-share	PSK	
G	group	1	DH1—768-bit	1
		2	DH2—1024-bit	
		5	DH5—1536-bit	
L	lifetime	seconds	Your choice	86400
E	encryption	des	56-bit DES-CBC	des
		3des	168-bit DES-CBC	
		aes	128-bit AES	
		aes 192	192-bit AES	
		aes 256	256-bit AES	

In our example, we specified that we would use a PSK for authentication. Because it is possible that we may have several tunnels to the same peer, the PSK is not tied to a specific policy set. To configure a PSK, use the **crypto isakmp key** global configuration command. Note that the PSK is case-sensitive:

```
CiscoISR-A(config)#crypto isakmp key Cisc0R0ck5! Address 172.16.32.1
```

Alternatively, if you know the fully-qualified domain name (FQDN) of Peer B, you could type:

```
CiscoISR-A(config)#crypto isakmp key Cisc0R0ck5! Hostname peerB.abc.com
```

NOTE

With the **crypto isakmp key** command, if you use hostname or IP address to identify a VPN peer, then that peer's configuration must identify your device using the same method.

Verify your configuration of both the ISAKMP policy set you created and the default policy set with the **show crypto isakmp policy** command. Effectively, you now have a policy suite with two policy sets in it: policy set 99, and the default Cisco IOS policy set.

```
CiscoISR-A#show crypto isakmp policy

Global IKE policy
Protection suite of priority 99
encryption algorithm:   AES - Advanced Encryption Standard (128 bit keys).
hash algorithm:         Secure Hash Standard
authentication method:  Pre-Shared Key
Diffie-Hellman group:   #5 (1536 bit)
lifetime:               86400 seconds, no volume limit
Default protection suite
encryption algorithm:   DES - Data Encryption Standard (56 bit keys).
hash algorithm:         Secure Hash Standard
authentication method:  Rivest-Shamir-Adleman Signature
Diffie-Hellman group:   #1 (768 bit)
lifetime:               86400 seconds, no volume limit
```

NOTE

The terminology in the output of the CLI command is inconsistent. What we know to be policy *sets* the CLI is labeling policy *suites*. This is incorrect, but short of asking Cisco to reengineer the CLI, we can't change it.

Assuming we have configured a similar policy set on Peer B, the peers have all the information they need to successfully negotiate an IKE Phase I SA.

Step 3: Configure IPsec Transform Set(s)

Now we configure the transform sets that will be used to protect (transform) the data in the IKE Phase II SA. Recall that transform sets are made up of an encryption algorithm and an HMAC. We create a transform set, giving it a case-sensitive name in this step. We will apply it to the policy defining the Phase II SA to Peer B in Step 5. Here are two things to remember about transform sets:

▶ A transform set is a combination of IPsec transforms that enact a security policy (transformation) for traffic.

▶ A transform set can have one AH transform and up to two ESP transforms

Use the **crypto ipsec transform-set** CLI command to create the transform:

```
CiscoISR-A(config)#crypto ipsec transform-set CantHackMe ?
ah-md5-hmac    AH-HMAC-MD5 transform
ah-sha-hmac    AH-HMAC-SHA transform
comp-lzs       IP Compression using the LZS compression algorithm
esp-3des       ESP transform using 3DES(EDE) cipher (168 bits)
esp-aes        ESP transform using AES cipher
esp-des        ESP transform using DES cipher (56 bits)
esp-md5-hmac   ESP transform using HMAC-MD5 auth
esp-null       ESP transform w/o cipher
esp-seal       ESP transform using SEAL cipher (160 bits)
esp-sha-hmac   ESP transform using HMAC-SHA auth
CiscoISR-A(config)#crypto ipsec transform-set CantHackMe esp-sha-hmac
esp-aes 128
```

Recall that transforms are negotiated during QM in IKE Phase I.

Step 4: Create Crypto ACL Defining Traffic in the IPsec VPN

Create an ACL that will define the traffic that will be transmitted inside the IPsec VPN. Of course, the ACL doesn't do anything by itself. It will be applied to the configuration in Step 5. From Peer A's perspective, this is any packet from the A' network to the B' network:

▶ Permit = Encrypt.

▶ Deny = Do not encrypt.

```
access-list 102 permit ip 192.168.0.0 0.0.0.255 10.0.40.0 0.0.0.255
```

NOTE
Watch those wildcard masks in the ACL. Remember that a 0 is a match bit and a 1 is an ignore bit.

Try to be as specific as possible with the crypto ACL. In our example, all IP traffic will be sent to Peer B if it is source address for the A' network and destination address for the B' network. If you only want VoIP traffic, for instance, to travel between the sites, say it in the ACL. Any packets that don't match a permit statement in the ACL will be sent out of the router in cleartext.

Ensure that the crypto ACL on the other peer is symmetric with this one. Peer A's ACL says that all IP traffic from A' to B' shall be in the VPN; thus, Peer B's ACL must say the symmetric opposite. If this is not the case, VPN tunnel establishment will fail during quick mode, as this is where the policies as to what traffic is to be in the VPN are negotiated.

Step 5: Create and Apply the Crypto Map (IPsec Tunnel Interface)

Conceptually, the crypto map is a virtual IPsec tunnel interface. The crypto ACL that was created in Step 4 defines the traffic that will flow into this interface toward Peer B. Here are all the elements that go into a crypto map:

- ▶ Crypto ACL to be used

- ▶ Address or hostname of remote VPN peer(s)

- ▶ Transform set

- ▶ Key management method (remember, this is optional in IKE Phase II)

- ▶ SA lifetime

Heads up! There can be only one crypto map on a router interface. This one crypto map must support as many VPN peers, both remote-access and site-to-site as you may have to that interface. Priority numbers (just like with IKE Phase I policy sets) will group the elements together and dictate their relative priority. The lower the number, the higher the priority. Use the **crypto map** global configuration command to create and modify the crypto map. First, you must create the crypto map. In the following example, a crypto map called "multipurpose" is created and sequence number 999 is attached to it. Note the output from the following command, indicating that the crypto map is disabled until a peer and ACL are assigned to it:

```
CiscoISR-A(config)#crypto map multipurpose 999 ipsec-isakmp
% NOTE: This new crypto map will remain disabled until a peer
and a valid access list have been configured.
CiscoISR-A(config-crypto-map)#
```

Let's add some parameters to sequence 999. Certainly we will want to add the transform set that we created in Step 3 and the crypto ACL that we created in

Step 4. We will also want to identify the IP address or hostname of Peer B. We'll look at an example, and then talk about some of the other parameters we can add:

```
CiscoISR-A(config-crypto-map)#set peer 172.16.32.1
CiscoISR-A(config-crypto-map)#set transform-set CantHackMe
CiscoISR-A(config-crypto-map)#match address 102
CiscoISR-A(config-crypto-map)#set security-association lifetime seconds
86400
CiscoISR-A(config-crypto-map)#set security-association lifetime kilobyte
4000000
CiscoISR-A(config-crypto-map)#set pfs group2
```

At this point, we have created the crypto map, but we must also apply it to a router interface—FastEthernet 4, in this example. Use the **crypto map** interface configuration mode command to do this:

```
CiscoISR-A(config)#interface fa4
CiscoISR-A(config-if)#crypto map multipurpose
```

You can verify the completeness of the crypto map and that it has been applied to the correct interface with the **show crypto map** CLI command:

```
CiscoISR-A#show crypto map
Crypto Map "multipurpose" 999 ipsec-isakmp
  Peer = 172.16.32.1
  Extended IP access list 102
access-list 102 permit ip 192.168.0.0 0.0.0.255 10.0.40.0 0.0.0.255
        Current peer: 172.16.32.1
        Security association lifetime: 4000000 kilobytes/86400 seconds
        PFS (Y/N): Y
        DH group:  group2
        Transform sets={
CantHackMe,
        }
        Interfaces using crypto map multipurpose:
                FastEthernet4
```

Verifying and Troubleshooting the IPsec VPN Using the CLI

The commands in Table 7.6 can be used to verify and troubleshoot the IPsec VPN. We have already looked at the first two while configuring the site-to-site IPsec VPN during Step 2 and Step 5, respectively.

TABLE 7.6 IPsec VPN Troubleshooting Commands

Command	Description
show crypto isakmp policy	Displays configured and default IKE policies.
show crypto map	Displays configured crypto maps.
show crypto ipsec transform-set	Displays configured IPsec transform sets.
show crypto ipsec sa	Displays established IKE Phase II SAs (IPsec tunnels).
show crypto isakmp sa	Displays established IKE Phase I SAs (ISAKMP) tunnels.
debug crypto isakmp	Debugs IKE Phase I events. (This command creates a lot of output, and you will not be responsible for analyzing the output on the exam, so this command will not be explained further.)
debug crypto ipsec	Debugs IKE Phase II (IPsec) events. (This command creates a lot of output, and you will not be responsible for analyzing the output on the exam, so this command will not be explained further.)
show access-list	Displays matches for packets that have been assigned to the VPN by the crypto ACL.

The following sections look at the output of the commands in Table 7.6 not yet examined. Look at the output and verify that it matches the reference network diagram in Figure 7.8.

Verify the IPsec Transform Set(s)

This command verifies the configured IPsec transform sets. Recall that previously we created an IPsec transform set called CantHackMe with an AES 128-bit for the encryption algorithm and SHA for the HMAC:

```
CiscoISR-A#show crypto ipsec transform-set
Transform set CantHackMe: { esp-aes esp-sha-hmac  }
will negotiate = { Tunnel,  },
```

Verify/Display the Established IKE Phase II SAs (IPsec Tunnels)

The **show crypto ipsec sa** command is used to verify the operation of the IKE Phase II data tunnels. The following command output is from Peer A's perspective. Among other things, it can verify the following:

▶ The inbound and outbound Security Parameter Indices (SPIs) in Peer A's Security Association Database (SAD).

▶ The type of IKE Phase II SAs created (ESP, AH, or other).

> **NOTE**
>
> The following output was captured from a Cisco ISR that was behind a NAT router and connecting to a Cisco ASA 5505 security appliance with a public IP address and that was not behind a NAT router. The two VPN devices negotiated RFC-compliant NAT Traversal (NAT-T), which wraps IKE Phase II's ESP inside a UDP port 4500 wrapper so that it will traverse what might be a Port Address Translation (PAT) router. This is because PAT cannot tolerate stateless, portless ESP without a bit of help! This will not be on the exam, but it helps explain some of the parameters you see in the output. For example, the inbound SA's in use settings include this pearl:
>
> *in use settings ={Tunnel UDP-Encaps, }*
>
> This indicates that the peers have negotiated tunnel mode (versus transport mode) for IKE Phase II but inside a UDP wrapper.

Refer to the following command output. The shaded output indicates the following things that we can observe:

- The IKE Phase II SAs are formed between local peer, Peer A (192.168.99.218), and remote peer, Peer B (172.16.32.1).

- The transform set applied to both the outbound and inbound IKE Phase II IPsec VPN SAs is the contains esp-aes and esp-sha-hmac as the encryption algorithm and HMAC, respectively.

- The IKE Phase II SAs are being encrypted and decrypted using onboard hardware acceleration (Motorola processor on this Cisco 871 ISR).

- Both inbound and outbound IKE Phase II IPsec VPN SAs are active.

- All traffic between 192.168.0.0/24 and 10.0.20.0/24 is being protected in the VPN.

```
CiscoISR-A#show crypto ipsec sa

interface: FastEthernet4
    Crypto map tag: multipurpose, local addr 192.168.99.218

    protected vrf: (none)
    local  ident (addr/mask/prot/port): (192.168.0.0/255.255.255.0/0/0)
    remote ident (addr/mask/prot/port): (10.0.20.0/255.255.255.0/0/0)
    current_peer 172.16.32.1 port 4500
      PERMIT, flags={origin_is_acl,}
     #pkts encaps: 3, #pkts encrypt: 3, #pkts digest: 3
     #pkts decaps: 3, #pkts decrypt: 3, #pkts verify: 3
     #pkts compressed: 0, #pkts decompressed: 0
     #pkts not compressed: 0, #pkts compr. failed: 0
     #pkts not decompressed: 0, #pkts decompress failed: 0
```

```
#send errors 13, #recv errors 0

 local crypto endpt.: 192.168.99.218, remote crypto endpt.:
172.16.32.1
    path mtu 1500, ip mtu 1500, ip mtu idb FastEthernet4
    current outbound spi: 0xBB1E0DBD(3139308989)

    inbound esp sas:
     spi: 0x9D5D2EC7(2640129735)
       transform: esp-aes esp-sha-hmac ,
       in use settings ={Tunnel UDP-Encaps, }
       conn id: 1, flow_id: Motorola SEC 1.0:1, crypto map: multipurpose
       sa timing: remaining key lifetime (k/sec): (3843604/27899)
       IV size: 16 bytes
       replay detection support: Y
       Status: ACTIVE

    inbound ah sas:

    inbound pcp sas:

    outbound esp sas:
     spi: 0xBB1E0DBD(3139308989)
       transform: esp-aes esp-sha-hmac ,
       in use settings ={Tunnel UDP-Encaps, }
       conn id: 2, flow_id: Motorola SEC 1.0:2, crypto map: multipurpose
       sa timing: remaining key lifetime (k/sec): (3843604/27896)
       IV size: 16 bytes
       replay detection support: Y
       Status: ACTIVE

    outbound ah sas:

    outbound pcp sas:
```

Verify/Display Established IKE Phase I SAs (ISAKMP) Tunnels

Look at the output of the **show crypto isakmpsa** command. Note that the tunnel is in a state *QM_IDLE* indicating that quick mode (QM) completed successfully and is currently in an idle state.

```
CiscoISR-A#show crypto isakmp sa
IPv4 Crypto ISAKMP SA
dst              src              state           conn-id slot status
172.16.32.1   192.168.99.218   QM_IDLE           2005    0 ACTIVE

IPv6 Crypto ISAKMP SA
```

Verify/Display the Crypto ACL

ACL 102 defines the traffic that is supposed to be in the IPsec VPN. Note that there are 19 matches, indicating that traffic is flowing into the VPN subject to the policy defined in the ACL.

```
CiscoISR-A#show access-list 102
Extended IP access list 102
    10 permit ip 192.168.0.0 0.0.0.255 10.0.20.0 0.0.0.255 (19 matches)
```

Implementing IPsec on a Site-to-Site VPN Using Cisco SDM

Configuring a site-to-site VPN with the SDM should be fairly straightforward, now that we have examined the fundamentals of how IPsec VPNs work and grounded the theory by configuring a site-to-site IPsec VPN with the CLI.

When using the SDM to configure a site-to-site IPsec VPN, you can either manually configure the VPN or employ the Cisco SDM VPN Wizard. We will choose the wizard and see that the wizard will give us a choice of the following:

▶ **Quick setup.** Uses pre-built settings (useful for a brand-new VPN configuration with another Cisco IOS router that is being configured with the quick setup versus the step-by-step wizard).

▶ **Step-by-step wizard.** For more granular, detailed configuration control.

Let's look at these two wizards, one at a time.

Site-to-Site VPN Wizard Using Quick Setup

To launch the Site-to-Site VPN Wizard and enter Quick Setup, complete the following steps:

1. Navigate to **Configure->VPN** in the SDM.

2. Select **Site-to-Site VPN** from the left navigation pane.

3. Make sure that the **Create Site to Site VPN** tab is selected in the main navigation window.

4. Check the **Create a Site to Site VPN** radio button, as indicated in Figure 7.9.

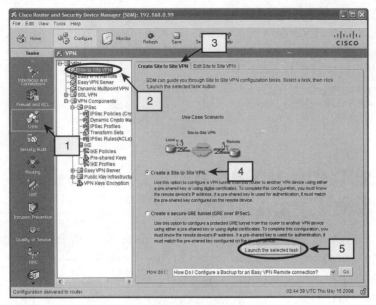

FIGURE 7.9 Launching the Site-to-Site VPN Wizard.

5. Press the **Launch the selected task** button. The Site-to-Site VPN Wizard window appears.

6. Note the choices indicated in Figure 7.10. You can choose either **Quick setup** or **Step by step wizard**. Press the **Quick setup** radio button; then click **Next**. A window appears in which you can enter some basic information about the VPN. Note that it doesn't ask you what encryption algorithms, hashes, or DH groups you want to use.

7. The VPN Connection Information window pops up, as indicated in Figure 7.11. Look at this window while referring to the reference network diagram in Figure 7.8. We know exactly what to fill in. From top to bottom:

VPN Connection Information:

▶ Select the interface for this VPN connection: FastEthernet4.

▶ Select the type of peer(s) used for this VPN connection: Peer with static IP address.

▶ Enter the IP address of the remote peer: 172.16.32.1.

Authentication:

▶ Pre-Shared Keys or Digital Certificates radio button: Press the Pre-shared keys radio button. Fill in the pre-shared key in the pre-shared key and Re-enter key fields.

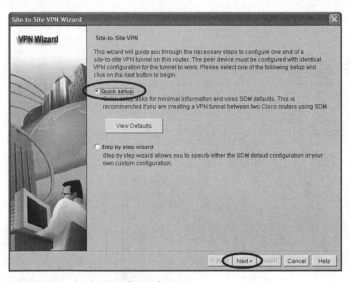

FIGURE 7.10 Launching Quick Setup.

Traffic to Encrypt:

▶ Source: Choose Vlan1 as the source interface in the drop-down list. This is the interface that the net A' to net B' traffic will arrive on.

▶ Destination: Enter 10.0.20.0 in the IP Address field and 255.255.255.0 in the Subnet Mask field. (Alternatively, you can put the number of bits (24) in the "or" field.)

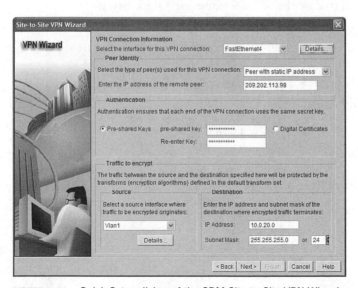

FIGURE 7.11 Quick Setup dialog of the SDM Site-to-Site VPN Wizard.

8. Click **Finish**. The Summary of the Configuration window appears. It will look something like Figure 7.12.

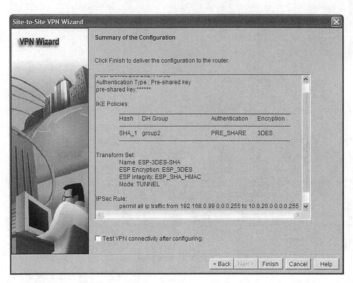

FIGURE 7.12   Summary of the Configuration window in the SDM Site-to-Site VPN Wizard.

If you don't like the IKE policies and IPsec transform sets that are created for you, then Quick Setup is not a good choice. Chances are good that 3DES for a cipher for both Phase I and Phase II will not match the organization's comprehensive network security policy. Here are the parameters selected by the SDM when using Quick Setup:

IKE Policy Set (HAGLE):

>H = SHA-1

>A = PSK

>G = DH2

>L = 86,400 (default, since doesn't appear)

>E = 3DES

IPsec Transform Set:

>Transport = ESP

>Tunnel Mode

>Encryption = 3DES

>Hash = SHA-1

9. If you like what you see, click on **Finish** to deliver the commands to the router. You might have noticed the Test VPN connectivity after configuring check box. We examine this feature when we (next) configure the VPN with the SDM Site-to-Site VPN Wizard, but choosing step-by-step this time.

Site-to-Site VPN Wizard Using Step-by-Step Setup

The five tasks of the wizard using Step-by-Step setup are as follows:

Task 1: Define Connection Settings:

- ▶ Outside interface
- ▶ Peer address
- ▶ Authentication credentials

Task 2: Define IKE Proposals:

- ▶ Priority
- ▶ Encryption algorithm
- ▶ HMAC
- ▶ Mode of operation (AM, MM)

Task 3: Define IPsec Transform Sets:

- ▶ Encryption algorithm
- ▶ HMAC
- ▶ Mode of operation (tunnel, transport)
- ▶ Compression

Task 4: Define Traffic to Protect (Crypto ACL):

- ▶ Single source and destination subnets

or

- ▶ Create ACL (can use existing if already created)

Task 5: Review and Complete the Configuration

To begin the step-by-step setup of the Cisco SDM Site-to-Site VPN Wizard:

1. Navigate to **Configure->VPN** and select **Site-to-Site VPN** in the list box on the left side.

2. Ensure the **Create Site to Site VPN** tab is selected and push the **Create a Site to Site VPN** radio button.

3. Click the **Launch the selected task** button. The Site-to-Site VPN Wizard window appears, as indicated in Figure 7.13.

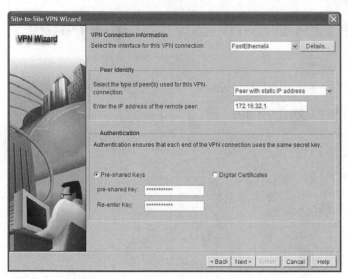

FIGURE 7.13   Step-by-Step VPN Wizard: Define connection settings.

4. Push the **Step by step wizard** radio button and click the **Next** button. A window appears, prompting you to define the connection settings.

Task 1: Define Connection Settings

Follow these steps to define basic connection settings:

1. Fill in the information per the reference diagram in Figure 7.8. If this was the real world, you would have all this information at your fingertips as part of a well-executed security policy.

2. Click **Next**. A window appears, as indicated in Figure 7.14, prompting you to define an IKE proposal for the site-to-site VPN.

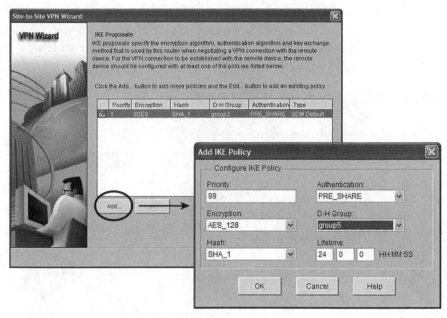

FIGURE 7.14 Step-by-Step VPN Wizard: Define IKE proposals.

Task 2: Define IKE Proposals

The next step is to define the IKE proposals to be used. You can use either the built-in, default proposal or create your own. Follow these steps to define the IKE proposal:

1. The list of IKE proposals will have at least the SDM default (look under the Type column). Click **Add** and the Add IKE Policy window appears.

2. Fill in the information for the IKE proposal using the HAGLE values that you have already determined. In this example, we are creating an IKE proposal with these parameters:

   ▶ **Priority: 99**

   ▶ **Authentication: PRE_SHARE**

   ▶ **Encryption: AES_128**

   ▶ **D-H Group: group5**

   ▶ **Hash: SHA_1**

   ▶ **Lifetime: 24:00:00** (HH:MM:SS)

3. Click **OK** when finished. The IKE proposal appears highlighted in the list of IKE proposals. Leave it selected and click **Next**. A window appears, as indicated in Figure 7.15, prompting you to define an IPsec transform set for the site-to-site VPN.

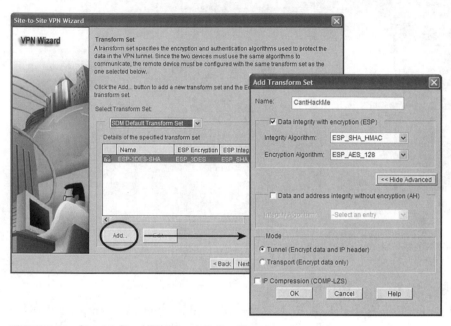

FIGURE 7.15   Step-by-Step VPN Wizard: Define IPsec transform sets.

Task 3: Define IPsec Transform Sets

Follow these steps to define an IPsec transform set for use in the site-to-site VPN:

1. The list of IPsec transform sets will have at least the SDM default (selected in the **Select Transform Set** drop-down list). Click **Add**, and the Add Transform Set window appears. Click the **Show Advanced** button to reveal advanced options.

2. Fill in the information for the IPsec transform set. Because we have selected the advanced options, we can verify that:

   ▸ The **Tunnel** radio button is selected in the Mode section of the advanced options.

   ▸ The **Data and address integrity without encryption (AH)** box is unchecked.

   ▸ The **IP Compression (COMP-LZS)** box is unchecked.

We will fill in the following parameters:

- **Name: CantHackMe**
- **Data Integrity with encryption (ESP):** checked
- **Integrity Algorithm: ESP_SHA_HMAC**
- **Encryption Algorithm: ESP_AES_128**

3. Click **OK**. The transform set we just added appears highlighted in the Transform Set window. Leave it selected; then click **Next**. A new window appears, as indicated in Figure 7.16, prompting you to define the traffic to protect in the site-to-site VPN.

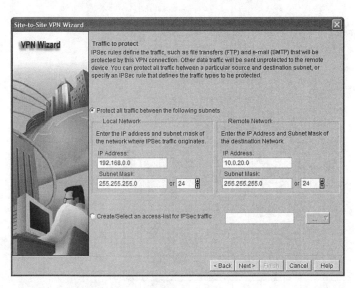

FIGURE 7.16 Step-by-Step VPN Wizard: Define traffic to protect (Crypto ACL).

Task 4: Define Traffic to Protect (Crypto ACL)

Follow these steps to define the traffic that will be protected by the VPN. These steps create a crypto ACL:

1. Fill out the IP address and subnet mask of the local and remote networks that will be protected by the site-to-site VPN. Alternatively, if you already have an ACL created or want to create an ACL for this purpose, you can press the **Create/Select an access-list for IPSec traffic** radio button and follow the prompts. In this example, we press the **Protect all traffic between the following subnets** radio button and fill out the following information:

Local Network:

- ▶ **IP Address**: 192.168.0.0
- ▶ **Subnet Mask**: 255.255.255.0

Remote Network:

- ▶ **IP Address**: 10.0.20.0
- ▶ **Subnet Mask**: 255.255.255.0

2. Click **Next**. The Summary of the Configuration window appears, as indicated in Figure 7.17.

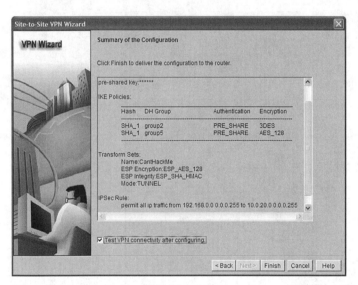

FIGURE 7.17   Step-by-Step VPN Wizard: Review and complete the configuration.

Task 5: Review and Complete the Configuration

Follow these steps to review and complete the configuration:

1. We're almost done. Review the information in the Summary of the Configuration window. Note that this VPN peer will propose two IKE policy sets: the SDM default, and the one we created earlier in the wizard. For IKE Phase II, it will propose only the IPsec transform set that we created in task 3.

2. Check the **Test VPN connectivity after configuring** box because we will want to test the VPN when we are finished.

3. Click **Finish**. The commands are delivered to the router.

4. Click **OK**. Because we indicated that we wanted to test the VPN, the VPN Troubleshooting window appears, as shown in Figure 7.18. Verify under Tunnel Details at the top of this window that the interface that we are using to connect to our VPN peer appears beside the Interface section.

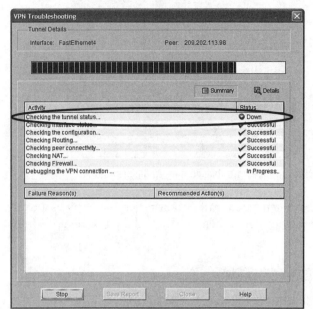

FIGURE 7.18 Step-by-Step VPN Wizard: VPN troubleshooting.

5. Click **Start** to initiate the test.

NOTE

Don't be surprised if the tunnel doesn't come up during the test because there is no reason for the tunnel to be constructed unless traffic is generated from the A' to B' networks. This is indicated in Figure 7.18, where the first step, "Checking the tunnel status..." fails. If this occurs, the SDM will prompt you to allow either the SDM or you to generate traffic to attempt to bring up the VPN. Figure 7.19 shows this dialog preceded by a warning (that we have to click through) written by Cisco's lawyers that indicates that generating the traffic may create router performance issues.

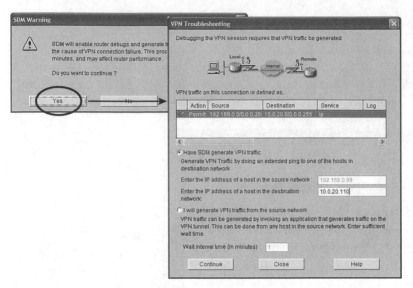

FIGURE 7.19 Step-by-Step VPN Wizard: VPN troubleshooting traffic generation.

If the VPN fails and you have generated traffic to bring up the VPN as a troubleshooting step (see the previous note), then the VPN should come up as indicated in Figure 7.20.

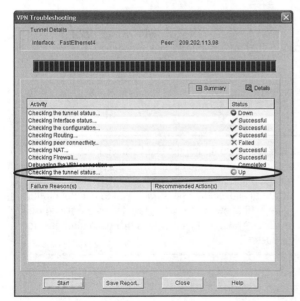

FIGURE 7.20 Step-by-Step VPN Wizard: VPN troubleshooting tunnel status up.

For more advanced troubleshooting, Cisco recommends using the CLI commands covered in the section, "Implementing IPsec on a Site-to-Site VPN Using the CLI." They are found in Table 7.6.

Exam Prep Questions

1. True or false. Site-to-site IPsec VPNs are an evolution of dial-up networking.

2. Which of the following is not considered a feature that can be configured as part of an IPsec VPN? (Choose all that apply.)

   ○ **A.** Authorization

   ○ **B.** Auditing

   ○ **C.** Confidentiality

   ○ **D.** Integrity

   ○ **E.** Authentication

3. What are two disadvantages of Cisco IOS SSL VPNs when compared with IPsec VPNs?

   ○ **A.** Hardware-only. The solution is implemented in hardware on either the VPN gateway or the client making the solution Cisco-proprietary.

   ○ **B.** Software-only. The solution is implemented in software on the VPN gateway and client.

   ○ **C.** Cryptographic security. Does not support the same level of encryption security as IPsec.

   ○ **D.** Incompatibility. Creating rules to allow SSL VPN traffic over intermediate routers and other gateways is difficult.

   ○ **E.** None of the above.

4. Fill in the following table with the letter corresponding to the most correct answer for devices' role in the context of remote-access and site-to-site VPNs. (The same letter can be used more than once.)

VPN Type

Product	Remote-Access	Site-to-Site
VPN 3000 Series concentrator (EOS)		
VPN-Enabled IOS router		
PIX 500 Series Security appliance		
ASA 5500 Series Adaptive Security appliance		

Choices:

   A. Primary role

   B. Secondary role

   C. Complements firewall role

   D. Yes, but IT Security manages the VPN

   E. Supports VPN 3000 Series Concentrator features

5. Which of the following list is not considered to be a VPN feature of Cisco VPN-enabled IOS routers? (Choose all that apply.)

   ○ **A.** Stateful Switchover (SSO)

   ○ **B.** AnyConnect standalone SSL VPN client

   ○ **C.** IPsec Stateful Failover

   ○ **D.** Voice and Video Enabled VPN (V3PN)

   ○ **E.** Cisco Easy VPN Remote

6. Fill in the blanks in the description below with choices from the list. (A choice may only be used once.)

   At a high-level, IKE Phase I handles all _____ and _____ between VPN peers, whereas the main task of IKE Phase II is the transmission and _____ of data by applying confidentiality, integrity, authentication, and anti-replay services to it.

   Choices:

   A. Transformation

   B. Authentication

   C. Negotiation

   D. Verification

7. Which of the following encryption algorithms (ciphers) is supported on VPN-enabled Cisco IOS routers? (Choose all that apply.)

   ○ **A.** Blowfish

   ○ **B.** DUAL

   ○ **C.** SEAL

   ○ **D.** 3DES

   ○ **E.** AES

   ○ **F.** RSA

8. Fill in the blanks in the paragraph below with a letter corresponding to the correct choice from the list:

   IKE Phase I uses a _____ to group elements together, whereas IKE Phase II groups ciphers and HMACs and other parameters in a _____.

   Choices:

   ○ **A.** Negotiation set

   ○ **B.** Encryption set

○ **C.** HMAC (Hashing Media Authentication Code) set

○ **D.** Transform set

○ **E.** Policy set

9. Which of the following is true about a crypto map? (Choose all that apply.)

○ **A.** You can only have one crypto map per interface.

○ **B.** You can only have one crypto map per router.

○ **C.** A single crypto map can support multiple peers.

○ **D.** A single crypto map can support only one peer.

○ **E.** Crypto maps group all the policy elements of a transform set.

10. Which of the following statements is true about using the Cisco SDM VPN Wizard? (Choose one.)

○ **A.** You cannot configure to the same level of granularity as with the CLI.

○ **B.** There is no SDM item to test the VPN once it is created, and you must use the CLI to generate traffic to launch the VPN.

○ **C.** You can test the VPN once it is created and use the SDM to generate traffic to launch the VPN if needed.

○ **D.** The SDM cannot create a site-to-site VPN. This must be accomplished through the CLI, though a new version of the SDM is planned that will have wizards to accomplish this task.

○ **E.** None of the above.

Answers to Exam Prep Questions

1. The correct answer is false. Site-to-site IPsec VPNs are an evolution of WAN technology.

2. The correct choices are A and B. Authorization and auditing (accounting) are considered parts of a AAA solution. IPsec VPNs provide for Confidentiality, Integrity, Authentication, and Anti-replay (C-I-A-A).

3. Answers B and C are correct. Answer A is incorrect because, although the Cisco IOS SSL VPN solution is proprietary to Cisco, the solution is implemented as a software-only solution as of the course material's (and this Exam Cram's) publishing date. The new Cisco 5500 Series ASA adaptive security appliance platforms do support hardware-accelerated encryption. Answer D is incorrect because one of SSL's biggest strengths is that it uses stateful TCP for transport, making it easier to tolerate across Port Address Translation (PAT) devices, and uses the standard TCP port number for HTTPS.

4. The correct answers are as follows:

VPN Type

Product	Remote-Access	Site-to-Site
VPN 3000 Series concentrator (EOS)	A	B
VPN-Enabled IOS router	B	A
PIX 500 Series Security appliance	C	D
ASA 5500 Series Adaptive Security appliance	E	D

5. The correct choice is B. Currently, the AnyConnect SSL VPN client is only supported on the Cisco ASA 5500 Series adaptive security appliances. All of the other choices are VPN features of the Cisco VPN-enabled IOS routers.

6. The first two blanks should be B and C, in any order. The last blank is A. Verification is a subset of transformation; therefore, answer D cannot be used.

7. Blowfish is a cipher but is not supported on the router. DUAL is the name for the algorithm that Cisco's proprietary Enhanced Interior Gateway Routing Protocol (EIGRP) employs and is not a cipher. All the other choices (C, D, E, and F) are supported ciphers for IPsec VPNs.

8. The correct choices are E and D. The other choices are made up.

9. Answers A and C are correct. You can have as many crypto maps as you have interfaces, but only one crypto map per interface. This being the case, that one crypto map may need to support multiple remote-access and site-to-site VPNs.

10. The correct answer is C. One of the strengths of the SDM is that you can perform all the configuration tasks for a VPN with the SDM wizards. For comprehensive troubleshooting, Cisco recommends using certain CLI commands, but the SDM wizard can generate traffic in order to launch the VPN.

CHAPTER EIGHT

Network Security Using Cisco IOS IPS

Terms You'll Need to Understand:

✓ Intrusion Protection System (IPS)

✓ Intrusion Detection System (IDS)

✓ Sensor

✓ Inline

✓ Promiscuous

✓ Host Intrusion Protection System (HIPS)

✓ Network Intrusion Protection System (IPS)

✓ Signatures

✓ Alerts

✓ Micro-engine

✓ Signature alarms

✓ Signature Definition File (SDF)

✓ Secure Device Event Exchange (SDEE)

Exam Topics Covered in This Chapter:

✓ Define network based vs. host based intrusion detection and prevention

✓ Explain IPS technologies, attack responses, and monitoring options

✓ Enable and verify Cisco IOS IPS operations using SDM

> **NOTE**
>
> These exam topics are from cisco.com. Check there periodically for the latest exam topics and info.

Cisco has many solutions for Intrusion Protection and Detection Systems (IPS and IDS). These solutions run the gamut from purpose-built rackmount appliances for the enterprise to host-based solutions such as Cisco Security Agent (CSA) to provide intrusion protection right to the endpoint. Deploying these solutions as part of the Cisco Self-Defending Network is a challenge and a deep subject all of itself. In this chapter, we do a high-level overview of the different solutions, starting with defining the systems and terminology involved. The chapter culminates with using the Cisco Security Device Manager (SDM) IPS Wizard to configure the Cisco IOS IPS.

Exploring IPS Technologies

In this section, we examine the fundamentals of IPS and IDS technologies, as well as ways to categorize them. We determine where they fit into Cisco's Self-Defending Network and introduce some exemplary solutions in Cisco's product portfolio. We conclude with some introductory comments about the Cisco IOS IPS router solution in order to set up for the next section, which concentrates on features of the Cisco IOS IPS.

IDS Versus IPS

It's simple, right? Intrusion Detection Systems (IDSs) monitor for signs of intrusion but do not take action, but Intrusion Prevention Systems (IPSs) monitor for signs of intrusion **and** take action, right? Actually ... not! Some vendors make this distinction, but Cisco does not. The following is a high-level description of Cisco's definition of what constitutes an IDS or IPS:

- ▶ **IDS.** According to Cisco, an IDS works offline to the data stream going through the network, analyzing copies of the traffic instead of forcing the data to flow through it. Specifically:

  - ▶ Monitors *copies* of the data flow.

  - ▶ Does not impede network traffic.

  - ▶ *Allows some* traffic deemed malicious to enter or leave the network.

- ▶ **IPS.** An IPS places itself in the data stream, thus seeing all the traffic that goes through that part of the network. Specifically:

- ▶ Monitors traffic and content from layers 2 through 7 in real-time.

- ▶ Must be capable of handling all ingress and egress traffic where it is deployed.

- ▶ *Prevents* traffic deemed malicious from entering or leaving the network.

Fundamentally, both an IDS and IPS monitor for signs of intrusion but because an IDS take copies of traffic from a data flow, it might miss trigger packets or single-packet attacks. A *trigger packet* is the very first packet in a malicious data flow. That aside, IDSs and IPSs are complementary in function and have their own strengths and weaknesses. An IDS will often require assistance from other devices such as routers or firewalls to perform the actions dictated by the security policy for the malicious traffic. As we will see, IDS/IPS systems can be deployed as a hardware or software solution depending on the requirement and can be deployed in a number of different solutions; an IDS/IPS can be:

- ▶ A separate network device

- ▶ An option card in a router or security appliance

- ▶ Integral software (as with the Cisco IOS IPS, pictured in Figure 8.1)

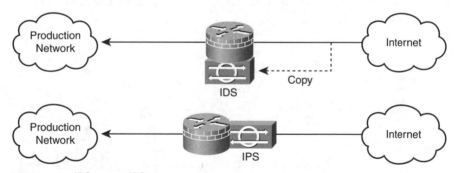

FIGURE 8.1 IDS versus IPS.

IDS and IPS Categories

As shown in Figure 8.1, where you deploy the system and how you configure it will determine whether it is an IDS or IPS. Here are some examples of Cisco IDS and IPS technologies:

- ▶ The AIP-SSM card can be configured on a Cisco ASA 5500 Series security appliance in either promiscuous (IDS) or inline (IPS) mode.

▶ Cisco IOS IPS is configured as a process on a Cisco IOS router.

▶ Cisco has a whole product line of rackmount IPS appliances that can be physically implemented in line with the network traffic or configured to look at copies of the traffic only.

▶ Software deployed on an IP host such as an application server or a client workstation.

NOTE

IDS and IPS technology is called a *sensor*. IDS and IPS technologies use policy-based rules called *signatures* to detect intrusions.

Where you deploy IDS and IPS technologies will dictate what they can see and how they can deal with intrusion attempts (and how quickly). You can deploy them in two places:

▶ **In the network.** Called network IDS and network IPS.

▶ **On a host.** Host-based IPS or HIPS.

In Figure 8.2, an attacker on the Internet launches a hack on the public HTTP server deployed in the DMZ.

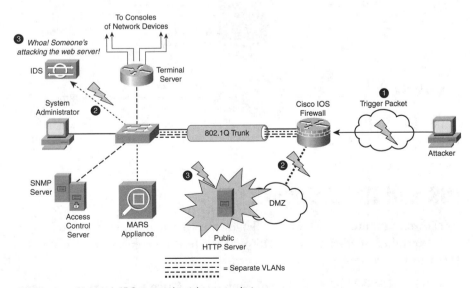

FIGURE 8.2 Network IDS may miss trigger packet.

As indicated in Figure 8.2, this attack might be missed by a network IDS because it is not deployed inline with the ingress packets to the network and will probably not be able to react to the trigger packet of the attack The following steps illustrate this logic. The numbers in the list refer to the labels in Figure 8.2:

1. The trigger packet of the attack arrives on the IOS firewall.

2. The router is configured to work with a network IDS. One packet is sent to the HTTP server in the DMZ and a copy is sent to the IDS, which is on a separate VLAN.

3. The packet arrives relatively simultaneously on both the server in the DMZ and the network IDS. The IDS recognizes that an attack is taking place.

4. (not pictured) The IDS tells the IOS firewall to block the attack and logs the attack via syslog or SDEE (see the following notes) messages to the MARS appliance.

NOTE

If you haven't heard about Cisco Security Monitoring Analysis and Reporting System (MARS) yet, you may want to read a description of MARS in Chapter 4, "Implementing Secure Management and Hardening the Router." MARS is also mentioned in Chapter 1, "Network Insecurity," and is referenced in Table 8.3.

NOTE

The network design in Figure 8.2 should look familiar. It is essentially the same as the reference design in Figure 5.1 from Chapter 5, "Using Cisco IOS Firewalls to Implement a Network Security Policy," with the addition of a new VLAN where the IDS resides. As mentioned in that chapter, the IOS firewall is capable of performing deep packet inspection and can mitigate a number of network-borne attacks, although this isn't discussed until another Cisco CCSP course, SNRS.

SDEE (Security Device Event Exchange) protocol is discussed later on in this chapter of the Exam Cram.

EXAM ALERT

Table 8.1 presents an overview of the relative pros and cons of IDS and IPS. Memorize this table—it's just the kind of thing that will be on the exam.

TABLE 8.1   Comparing IDS and IPS Technologies

Technology	Pros	Cons
IDS (Promiscuous)	No impact on network QoS (for example, delay and jitter). Sensor failure does not impact network. Sensor overload does not impact network.	Trigger packets are not blocked. More vulnerable than an IPS to certain network evasion techniques. Response actions require careful tuning. Requires a carefully constructed security policy.
IPS (Inline)	Blocks trigger packets. Stream normalization techniques can be employed.	A failed sensor may affect network traffic (fail-open or fail-closed?). Sensor overload may impact network. Requires a carefully constructed security policy. May impact network QoS because some applications like VoIP can be both delay and variable-delay (jitter) sensitive.

EXAM ALERT

Table 8.2 presents a broad overview of sensor types as well as their relative pros and cons. Memorize it for the exam.

TABLE 8.2   IDS and IPS Sensor Types

Sensor Type	Pros	Cons
Signature-Based	Simple to configure. Less false positives. Effective if good signature design.	Cannot detect unknown signatures. Lots of false positives until system is tuned. Signatures must be created or updated and possibly tuned.
Policy-Based	Easy and reliable. Policies can be customized. Therefore can detect unknown attacks.	Unspecific, generic output. Someone has to create the policies.
Anomaly-Based	Simple to configure. Can detect unknown attacks.	Large networks make it difficult to define a baseline of normal activity.

TABLE 8.2   IDS and IPS Sensor Types *Continued*

Sensor Type	Pros	Cons
		To be effective, baseline has to be constant. If the baseline constantly changes, many false positives will result.
Honey Pot-Based	Great place from which to observe attacks. Distraction to attackers. Can slow down and subvert attacks. Allow collection of attack taxonomy data.	Someone has to configure and maintain the honey pot server. Security policies have to allow for the honey pot server being untrusted.

NOTE

Do not infer from Table 8.2 that anomaly-based IDS/IPS sensors are easy to maintain. Yes, the initial configuration is no more complicated than a signature-based sensor, but much ongoing analysis and reconfiguration of what constitutes normal traffic patterns is required for them to be effective. One thing many enterprises have no real data for is what normal network activity actually is.

NOTE

A *honey pot* is a system that you have deployed in your network security architecture with the specific purpose to attract bees. A honey pot is an excellent place to analyze intrusion attempts to your network, and they are often used in conjunction with more mainstream technical solutions, such as Cisco IDS sensors. You must be careful how you deploy them in a legal context, too. Some legal jurisdictions may declare evidence of intrusion attempts on a honey pot as inadmissible for prosecution because of the fine line between *enticement* and *entrapment*. Enticement means that you have made it easier for the bees (the attackers) to conduct their normal activity, whereas entrapment means that you have coerced the bees into conducting an activity to which they are not normally predisposed. We'll let the lawyers argue over that one! See the "Law and Ethics" section in Chapter 1 for more information about the legal framework.

IPS Attack Responses

Putting the terms together, an example solution might be a network IPS that uses signatures and policies to detect and block attacks. This leads to the next question, which is: "What response and monitoring actions can be employed by IPS technologies?"

> **NOTE**
>
> From this point forward, we will focus on IPS technologies (thus the name of the chapter!) and the term IDS will hardly be breathed. This is mainly because the term IDS is falling somewhat out of favor, and IPS is often used interchangeably, though often incorrectly. Besides, what will sell more boxes, an intrusion *detection* system or an intrusion *protection* system?!

> **EXAM ALERT**
>
> So, what are you going to do about that attempted network compromise or intrusion attempt? What response and monitoring actions can be employed by an IPS? Memorize the following list! You may also want to review the theory of TCP sessions found in Chapter 5 before looking at some of these actions.

What follows is a list of some of the actions that we can configure on Cisco sensors:

- **Deny Attacker Inline.** Terminates current packet and shuns all subsequent packets from this attacker for a specified time period, regardless of whether they are part of new TCP connections.

- **Deny Connection Inline.** Terminates current and future packets in a specific TCP connection.

- **Deny Packet Inline.** Terminates the packet only.

- **Log Attacker Packets.** Logs all packets with an attacker's IP address.

- **Log Pair Packets.** Logs events in an attack pair that contains the attacker and victim address pair. This is useful for identifying specific flows.

- **Log Victim Packets.** Logs all packets with a victim's IP address.

- **Produce Alert.** Sends an alert to the Event Store (internal log buffer).

- **Produce Verbose Alert.** Sends an encoded dump (capture) of the offending packet in the alert.

- **Request Block Connection.** Sends a request to another device (router, switch, firewall) to block this connection.

- **Request Block Host.** Sends a request to another device (router, switch, firewall) to block this attacker.

- **Request SNMP Trap.** Instructs the sensor to send an SNMP trap.

- **Reset TCP Connection.** Sends TCP RSTs to terminate the TCP connection.

Every action that contains the words "log," "produce," or "SNMP" sends an alert to the Event Store (internal log buffer), regardless of whether Produce Alert is also selected as an action. This makes sense because they are all essentially alerting type of actions, even if they aren't called that.

Some actions can be combined. For example, the Deny Packet and Deny Flow actions do not reset the connection, preferring to silently discard traffic, making the IPS stealthy. If you do want to reset the connection, add the Reset TCP Connection action. Of course, the IPS is no longer invisible to the attacker, possibly provoking them. This said, the organization's security policy will dictate the action(s) to take.

Event Management and Monitoring

Back in Chapter 4, we discussed options for secure management and logging, focusing mainly on syslog and SNMP. So, we already have our mind around the concept of sending event-triggered alerts to the various reporting servers in our network. This is handy, because referring to Figure 8.2, the reference network diagram indicates that a MARS (Monitoring, Analysis, and Response System) appliance has been deployed in a separate VLAN inside the Cisco IOS firewall. This section isn't a discussion about how to log to these servers. It is a discussion of what to log and how to log (management) and real-time monitoring of events as they unfold in the traffic streams through our network. The scale of the solution has to match the scale of the network, both in the number of devices deployed, as well as the volume of traffic that is being moved across the monitored devices. As we have seen, some of those same metrics define whether the IPS is inline to the traffic or not.

We need to know the following:

- ▶ What is happening in real-time (monitoring)

- ▶ IPS actions and event information collection (management)

- ▶ Analysis of the archived information (reporting)

A little context is in order. You may recall that in Chapter 4, we discussed how secure management and logging needs to be integrated into the organization's security policy, and this doesn't just happen—it takes careful design. It was also pointed out that as much as possible, this traffic should be in a separate plane and preferably should not "cross the cables" of the production network. Similarly, monitoring and management should be OOB (out-of-band) with respect to the data plane, perhaps by putting it in a separate VLAN. Keep this in the back of your mind when you look at some of the subsequent high-level discussion about IPS deployment scenarios and technologies in the remainder of this section.

We will look at and implement the different logging protocol options The next section in this chapter, "Implementing Cisco IOS IPS," examines and implements the different logging protocol options.

Cisco makes the following points about event management and monitoring:

▶ Management and monitoring comprises two key functions:

▶ Real-time event monitoring and management

▶ Analysis of the archived event information (reporting)

▶ Depending on scale, management and monitoring can be deployed on a single server or on separate servers.

▶ Recommended maximum of 25 well-tuned sensors reporting to a single IPS management console (management consoles will be discussed shortly).

Cisco IPS Management Software

Table 8.3 outlines Cisco's portfolio of IPS management software.

TABLE 8.3 Cisco IPS Management Software

Software	Description
Cisco SDM	Cisco Router and Security Device Manager (SDM): Web-based tool used to manage a single router.
Cisco Security MARS	Cisco Security Monitoring, Analysis, and Response System (MARS): Discussed in Chapter 4. Allows network and security administrators to monitor, identify, isolate, and counter security threats. MARS has a complete picture of the network and can deploy responses to threats based on its integral knowledge of the devices and the interaction of security policies on the traffic through the network.
Cisco IEV	Cisco IPS Event Viewer (IEV): Lightweight, Java-based application that enables you to manage alarms (events) from up to five sensors.
Cisco CSM	Cisco Security Manager (CSM): Powerful centrally-managed solution to provision all aspects of device configuration, including security policies for Cisco firewalls, VPN concentrators, and IPS. Scales from small- to large-scale networks. Features include the following: ▶ Auto update for Cisco IOS Software Release 12.4(11)T2 or later. ▶ Custom signature templates. ▶ Signature wizards.
Cisco IDM	Cisco IPS Device Manager (IDM): Web-based configuration tool for network IPS appliances.

> **NOTE**
>
> The day after the IINS version 1.0 course was released, Cisco announced a new, freeware IPS management solution called IME (IPS Manager Express). It fully supports the newer 6.x version of the IPS signatures and also has limited support for version 5.x signatures. For more information on Cisco IME, navigate to this link: http://www.cisco.com/en/US/products/ps9610/index.html.

Figure 8.3 illustrates the Threat Analysis Console of the Cisco IPS Event Viewer (IEV)

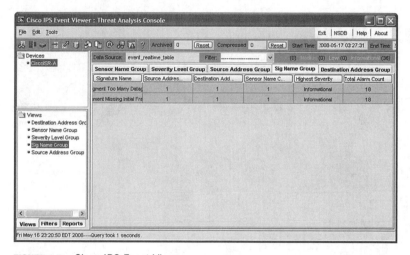

FIGURE 8.3   Cisco IPS Event Viewer.

Host IPS

Recall that IPS technology can be either network- or host-based, although they often co-exist as complementary solutions. With host-based IPS (HIPS), software is deployed right on the application server or client. Cisco's HIPS solution is the Cisco Security Agent (CSA). Here are some features and recommendations about HIPS:

▶ HIPS audits files systems, OS registries, log files, and system resources.

▶ CSA should be installed on every host that requires HIPS.

▶ CSA protects the individual host by detecting intrusion attempts.

▶ CSA does not require special hardware.

▶ Because CSA is behavior-based, it can stop even newer attacks in real-time whose behavior it identifies as malicious.

Referring to Figure 8.4, if we installed CSA on the public HTTP server that we first saw in Figure 8.2, it might obviate the need to configure the Cisco IOS firewall as a Network IPS. We could then manage the CSA with the CSA Management Center (CSA MC) on the Systems Administrator workstation. This might work on a small network, but imagine if you have a large network of thousands of IP hosts. You would need to install, configure, and manage all of those CSA instances. Often, CSA is deployed in parts of the network—on critical application servers, for instance—and used to complement Network IPS systems if possible.

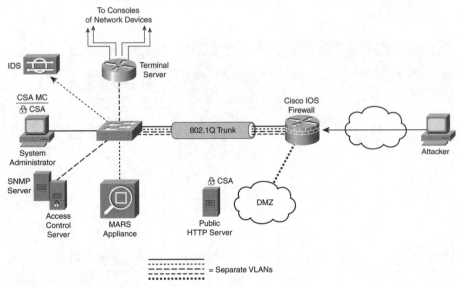

FIGURE 8.4   CSA deployment in the reference network.

Figure 8.5 illustrates how CSA works to protect an IP host from malicious applications directly at the kernel level.

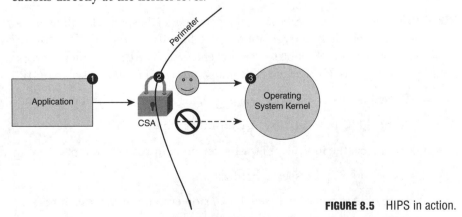

FIGURE 8.5   HIPS in action.

The steps in Figure 8.5 are as follows:

1. An application attempts to call the OS kernel for system resources.

2. The HIPS intercepts this call, and checks it against the policy.

3. The request for system resources is either allowed or denied.

Here are some other points about how HIPS operates:

- ▶ HIPS intercepts both operating system and application calls.

- ▶ Rules control application and network protocol stacks.

- ▶ Processor controls set limits on the following:

    - ▶ Buffer overflow.

    - ▶ Registry updates.

    - ▶ Writes to system directory.

    - ▶ Launching of installation programs.

- ▶ HIPS is behavior-based.

Table 8.4 outlines the pros and cons of Host Intrusion Prevention Systems (HIPS).

Table 8.4	HIPS Pros and Cons
Pros	Success or failure of an attack is obvious because CSA sits right on top of the application server or client. A network IPS cannot follow an attack right to its victim to determine whether it is successful.
	Network IPS cannot look inside an encrypted data stream, whereas the data is decrypted by the time it hits the HIPS.
	Fragmentation attacks or variable TTL (Time to Live) attacks cannot trick HIPS because these attacks are handled by the host's IP stack before it gets to HIPS.
Cons	HIPS does not have a picture of the whole network because it is deployed on individual hosts. Anomalous events that occur across an entire network are difficult to coordinate.
	HIPS has to support multiple operating systems. If HIPS is running on every system in the network, support will have to be verified for every different operating system used.

Network IPS

Figure 8.6 illustrates a network IPS deployed on the WAN side of a Cisco IOS firewall. It is deployed in such a way that it will see the inbound traffic (represented as an arrow) from an attacker on the outside. It is an IPS because it is inline with the flow of traffic from the outside. The features of a network IPS are explained more thoroughly next.

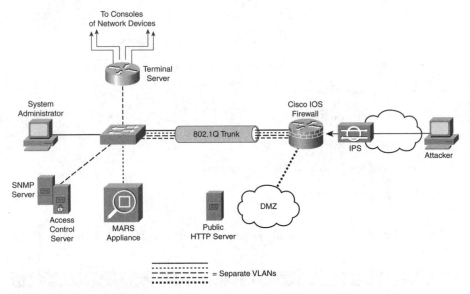

FIGURE 8.6   Network IPS.

Here are some features of a network IPS:

▶ Connected to the network where, if properly deployed, a single sensor can monitor traffic for many hosts or at least a small group of important hosts.

▶ Sensors are appliances with software that is tuned for its role in intrusion detection analysis:

  ▶ The underlying operating system is hardened.

  ▶ Hardware is optimized for intrusion detection analysis.

▶ Scalable—networks are easily protected as they grow:

  ▶ New end system hosts and devices can be added without the need for new sensors (unlike HIPS).

  ▶ New sensors can be easily added to new or existing networks.

> **NOTE**
>
> Network IPSs are not necessarily network appliances, although the appliance versions are rack mount blade servers with a hardened version of a Windows Server OS. Also, if you have an extra slot in your Catalyst 6500 series switch, you can add an IDSM-2 module. (see the "Cisco IPS Appliances" section of this chapter). When we implement Cisco IOS IPS using the SDM in the next section, we see that network appliances aren't Cisco's only network IPS solution.

Table 8.5 outlines the relative pros and cons of network IPS.

Table 8.5	Relative Pros and Cons of Network IPS
Pros	Network IPS can see traffic in an entire network.
	Network IPS does not have to support every operating system deployed on the IP hosts.
Cons	Encryption of the data stream can make for a blind IPS.
	As the network grows in size and complexity, it might be necessary to purchase additional network IPS because:
	▶ There may be multiple points of ingress and egress of traffic.
	▶ As traffic volumes increase, the throughput might eventually challenge the network IPS necessitating an upgrade.
	Reconstruction of fragmented traffic can be somewhat problematic due to the time and resources required to coalesce multiple fragments of a single conversation before it can be analyzed for intrusion or malicious content.

HIPS and Network IPS Comparison

Most of the points in Table 8.6 were already made, but it is useful to summarize them in one place to compare HIPS and network IPS.

Table 8.6	HIPS and Network IPS Comparison	
	Pros	Cons
HIPS	Host-specific. Sees post-decryption traffic. Application layer protection.	Operating system-dependent. Lower-layer network events not seen. Host is visible to attackers because the network layer is not protected.
Network IPS	Can be cost-effective in large networks. Invisible to attackers. OS-independent. Lower-layer network events are seen.	Cannot examine encrypted data streams. Can only monitor for signs of attack and cannot determine its success.

Cisco IPS Appliances

Figure 8.7 illustrates Cisco's portfolio of IPS appliance.

Cisco IPS 4200 Series Sensors

Cisco ASA 5520 with AIP-SSM-20

Cisco IDSM-2 Module for
Catalyst 6500 Series Switch

IPS AIM for Cisco 1841, 2800
and 3800 Series ISR

FIGURE 8.7 Cisco IPS appliances.

Here is a list of Cisco's four solutions for IPS appliances:

▶ **Cisco IPS 4200 Series Sensors.** Standalone rackmount appliance.

▶ **Cisco ASA AIP-SSM.** Advanced Inspection and Prevention Security Services Module for the ASA 5500 Series adaptive security appliances.

▶ **Cisco Catalyst 6500 Series IDSM-2.** Intrusion Detection System Services Module for the Catalyst 6500 Series switch.

▶ **Cisco IPS AIM.** IPS Advanced Integration Module for Cisco 1841, 2800, and 3800 Series Integrated Services routers.

All of these devices share the same code as the Cisco IPS 4200 Series IPS appliance. This was not an accident, as Cisco product planners wanted to ensure commonality of the configuration interface (and code base) as networks grow and needs change requiring more and different sensors. This makes it easier for IT security staff to grow with the product.

> **NOTE**
>
> There is a fifth choice of network IPS, and it is not an appliance. Cisco IOS IPS acts as an inline IPS sensor that can be turned on in Cisco IOS Software router platforms with security feature images. For example, Cisco 800 series Integrated Services routers must have the Advanced IP Services IOS image to enable this feature. We will be examining and configuring the Cisco IOS IPS in the next section, using the Cisco SDM.

IDS and IPS Signatures

IDS and IPS technologies use signatures to detect malicious network activity. This is similar to Anti-X products—virus scanners, for example. A good IPS solution enables you to update the signatures regularly as new threats emerge because the IPS is only as good as the ability of its signatures to detect intrusive activity. Here are the characteristics of IPS signatures:

- A network IPS signature is a set of rules used to detect intrusive activity.

- Sensors use signatures to test network packets for signs of known attacks. The signatures have predefined actions to respond to a detected attack.

- When a signature-based IPS is first installed, there will be false positives. You must fine tune the signatures to reduce the frequency of false positives by modifying certain signature parameters.

- Built-in signatures cannot be added or deleted, although they may be tuned to reduce false positives (see the following note).

- Some signatures have sub-signatures nested in them. These sub-signatures may be used by other signatures. Changing a sub-signature affects only that sub-signature and not the signature that uses it.

NOTE

Built-in signatures have been removed from Cisco IOS IPS starting from Cisco IOS Software Release 12.4(11)T (reference: http://www.cisco.com/en/US/prod/collateral/iosswrel/ps6537/ps6586/ps6634/prod_qas0900aecd806fc530.html).

Signature Micro-Engines

Conceptually, signatures are a database of patterns that match attacks. The signatures don't do anything by themselves, but they are read-in, cached, and parsed by real-time processing daemons called signature micro-engines (SME). A signature micro-engine is a self-contained parallel process that has the following characteristics:

- Signature micro-engines support IPS signatures.

- Signatures that are read into a micro-engine are scanned in parallel for efficiency and maximum throughput.

- Micro-engines group a category of signatures.

- Each micro-engine is customizable for the protocol and PDU fields that it is designed to inspect.

▶ Micro-engines specify permissible, legal ranges for the items that they are designed to inspect.

▶ Micro-engines use router memory to compile, load, and merge signatures (see the following note). These signatures use "regular expressions" (REGEXs) for pattern matching. This will be very familiar to readers from the Unix world where REGEXs are quite common in shell scripts. Signatures are customized or written with REGEX. Compiling takes more RAM than the finished signature, so you must be careful to stay within the RAM requirements of your platform for the number of signatures that will be used.

> **NOTE**
>
> Micro-engines use router memory to compile, load, and merge signatures only when Cisco IOS IPS is used as the IPS is a software process hosted on an IOS router in that case. The four appliances listed previously are self-contained environments with their own flash memory, RAM, and CPUs. It's not clear whether the exam makes this distinction, so the "right wrong answer" is above.

The third item in the list states that micro-engines group a category of signatures. Table 8.7 shows the list of supported micro-engines and the categories of signatures they group as of Cisco IOS release 12.4(6)T.

TABLE 8.7   Supported Signature Micro-Engine in IOS 12.4(6)T

Signature Micro-Engines	Signature Categories
Atomic	Signatures that examine simple packets, for example: IP, ICMP, and UDP (see the following note).
Service	Signatures that examine attacks on "services," such as application layer protocols like HTTP, FTP, and SMTP.
String	Signatures that use REGEX-based patterns to detect intrusive activity.
Multi-String	Supports flexible packet matching (FPM) and supports signatures by Trend Labs.
Other	Internal engine dedicated to miscellaneous signatures.

> **NOTE**
>
> Atomic signatures examine simple packets. "Simple" in this context means that the test is simple—for example, an ATOMIC.TCP signature micro-engine provides for simple TCP packet alarms based on source and destination port numbers and flags (SYN, RST, ACK, PSH, URG, FIN). For example, the ATOMIC.TCP SME would be able to analyze a TCP session and reset the session if the two connection partners aren't playing by the rules. Remember the Reset TCP Connection action in the "IPS Attack Responses" subsection earlier in the chapter?

Signature Alarms

When a signature is matched due to an attack or a policy violation, the SME in which the signature is compiled will raise an alarm, after which an action is taken to respond. The signature is said to "fire." The whole efficacy of the IPS solution hinges on the ability of the sensor to react quickly with an IPS action response using the action specified in the signature. Anyone fond of watching Hollywood dramas would quickly state that there are usually more false alarms than there are real ones. In the real world, reacting to false alarms can result in embarrassment, but no real damage is done. If a network IPS blocks legitimate traffic because of a false alarm (a so-called false positive), there might be real damage done to the throughput and quality of service offered by the network. Alarms are either false or true, negative or positive:

- **False Positive.** Normal traffic or a non-malicious action causes the signature to fire.

- **True Positive.** An attack is properly detected by the IPS.

- **False Negative.** An attack is not detected by the IPS.

- **True Negative.** Legitimate traffic does not cause signatures to fire.

Alarm Severity Levels

Some attacks can cause more damage than others. The alarm severity level assigned to the signature should match the severity of the event. Think of the SMEs as a group of patients vying for the attention of medical doctor, the IPS sensor. The IPS sensor (as well as a real-time monitoring, analysis, and reporting system, such as Cisco Security MARS) should be able to prioritize its responses to the attacks based on the alarms from the SMEs. Signatures should be fired by order of severity, not necessarily in the order in which they are received. The sensor triages the patients, treating the most severely ill first, regardless of when they walked into the emergency room of the hospital.

Here are some general principles with respect to implementing alarms in signatures:

- The alarm level assigned to the signature determines the alarm severity level.

- Alarm severity levels are: informational, low, medium, and high.

- The severity level of the signature should be made to be the same as the severity level of the alarm. (Remember this particularly when you create your own signatures.)

- Signatures should be tuned to recognize traffic patterns that are anomalous with respect to your normal network traffic patterns.

Here is a summary of the meaning of the four severity levels:

- **Informational.** Activity is not an immediate threat, but the information provided is useful.

- **Low.** Activity is not an immediate threat, but anomalous network activity could be perceived as malicious.

- **Medium.** Activity is likely an immediate threat, and the anomalous network activity is likely malicious.

- **High.** An immediate threat is extremely likely, and an access or DoS attack has been detected.

Best Practices for IPS Configuration

The following list of best practices is most appropriate in the context of a large network with multiple IPS sensors. Some of these ideas will be familiar to anyone who has had to set up a deployment of new code to client workstations within a large LAN domain. Even the bandwidth of a modern, high-speed Gigabit Ethernet core can be severely strained if some intelligent design is not employed when updating several devices simultaneously. From a security perspective, it makes good sense to perform your updates separate from the data plane of the production network, using the management network. To summarize:

- Set the sensors to automatically update their signature packs instead of doing a manual upgrade of individual sensors.

- Employ a dedicated FTP server in the management network from which the sensors can fetch the signature packs.

▶ Stagger the time of day for checking and downloading of the signature packs to prevent over-taxing network resources.

▶ Make the deployment of updates simpler by grouping IPS sensors together in a few larger profiles.

Figure 8.8 shows Autoupdate enabled in the Cisco SDM for an IOS IPS configuration. Note that in this example, autoupdate is set up to fetch the signature packs from a Trivial File Transfer Protocol (TFTP) server.

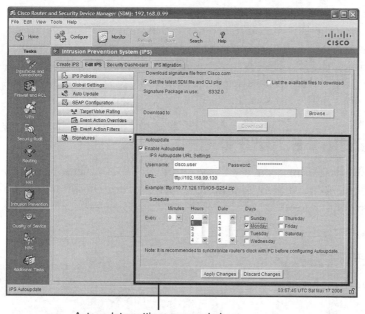

Autoupdate settings are made here.

FIGURE 8.8   Configuring Autoupdate in the Cisco SDM for IOS IPS.

NOTE

If you are deploying a dedicated server that uses a cleartext (not encrypted) protocol such as FTP or TFTP, it is critical that these servers be deployed in a dedicated VLAN or entirely separate physical network so that this traffic does not cross the cables with normal data traffic.

Implementing Cisco IOS IPS

In this section, we introduce the Cisco IOS IPS router solution and walk through a complete configuration using the Cisco SDM. We will also look at logging options available and methods in both the SDM and the CLI to verify the configuration.

Cisco states that the Cisco IOS IPS is an inline network IPS. Actually, it's a bit redundant saying this, since we have established that whether a device is inline to the traffic or analyzes copies of the traffic offline is what marks the difference between IPS and IDS technology in the first place. Regardless, one of the advantages of having the IPS run on the router is that, unlike IPS deployments where the sensor and the router are separate and must be configured to cooperate with one another, the IPS logic is integral to the router and can leverage on the router's firewall to take response actions to intrusions. We covered the various response actions in the last section.

Cisco IOS IPS Feature Blend

Cisco IOS IPS blends features from the Cisco IPS 4200 Series of sensors, as well as the IDSM module for the Cisco Catalyst 6500 Series of switches. It uses three main detection technologies:

▶ Profile-based

▶ Signature-based

▶ Protocol analysis-based

The first two were discussed in the last section. The third was not and bears some discussion. Protocol analysis-based technology simply means that the IPS analyzes the complete structure of the IP packets and their layer 4 through 7 payload to look for suspicious or abnormal activity. If this analysis was based solely on the protocols' standards, a lot of traffic would be flagged as anomalous. Instead, this is the Cisco IOS IPS signatures common practice rather than some ideal, reflecting the fact that many protocols violate standards in some fashion.

Cisco IOS IPS Primary Benefits

Cisco specifies the following benefits for the IOS IPS:

▶ **Attack Signatures.** Over 2,000 are supported, using a common database across Cisco IPS appliances.

▶ **Management Tool Support.** Supported by Cisco SDM, Cisco Security MARS, Cisco Security Manager, and Cisco IEV.

▶ **Cisco Self-Defending Network.** Integrates into a Self-Defending Network made up of Cisco IPS, Cisco IOS Firewall, Cisco VPN, and Cisco NAC solutions.

▶ **Inline IPS.** All inbound and outbound traffic has to flow through the IPS, meaning that malicious traffic can be detected both inside and outside the network.

▶ **Multi-Threat Detection.** Easily integrates into existing network infrastructure to protect against threats to network infrastructure, servers, and other endpoints.

▶ **Router Integration.** Cisco IOS IPS's use of the underlying router infrastructure adds an extra layer of security.

Cisco IOS IPS Signature Integration

As stated, the Cisco IOS IPS borrows heavily from the Cisco IPS 4200 Series of sensors and Catalyst 6500 IDSM IPS modules. Table 8.8 shows the features of the signatures in the Cisco IOS IPS.

TABLE 8.8   Cisco IOS IPS Signature Feature Summary

Signature Feature	Notes
REGEX	Matching of string patterns using regular expressions (used in creating/editing signatures).
Response Actions	Signatures contain default response actions when the signature has been matched (see the last section).
Alarm Summarization	When signatures are triggered, alarms of the same type are aggregated before they are sent to the sensor's event store (queue), making signature triggering more efficient and less CPU-intensive. (Remember, the IPS sensor is likely to be attacked, too!)
Threshold Configuration	False positives can be minimized by careful tuning of the threshold beyond which the signature is triggered and an alarm is sent.
Anti-Evasive Techniques	Signatures are intelligent enough to evade common evasive techniques by attackers.

Configuring Cisco IOS IPS with the Cisco SDM

We configure the Cisco IOS IPS using the Cisco SDM, starting with an IOS router with no IPS configuration on it.

> **NOTE**
>
> There's no requirement that the IOS IPS work in conjunction with either CBAC (Cisco IOS classic firewall) or the newer Zone-Based Policy Firewall (ZPF), both of which were discussed in Chapter 5, "Using Cisco IOS Firewalls to Implement a Network Security Policy." The Cisco IOS IPS could simply be added to basic router functionality on the edge of the network for network designers that subscribe to the separation of services philosophy, with a firewall configured with Cisco ZPF establishing a separate, inner perimeter.

Figure 8.9 illustrates the Cisco SDM home page, indicating an unconfigured IOS IPS.

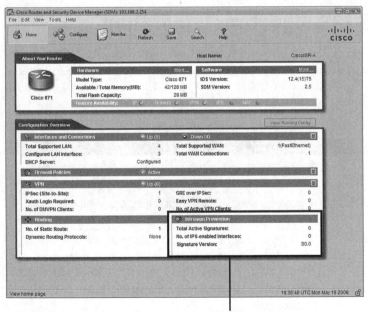

Unconfigured IOS IPS

FIGURE 8.9   Cisco SDM showing unconfigured IOS IPS.

Figure 8.10 illustrates the SDM Configure->Intrusion Prevention System (IPS) window.

Tabs

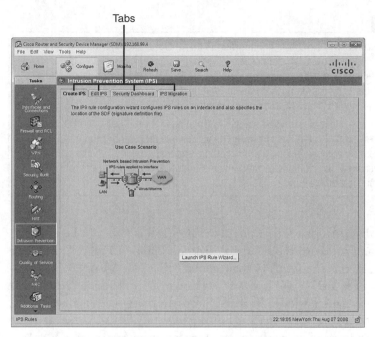

FIGURE 8.10   Cisco SDM Configure->Intrusion Prevention System (IPS) window.

Before we start configuring the IPS, let's look at some of the choices we have when we navigate to **Configure->Intrusion Prevention** from the home page in the Cisco SDM, as indicated in Figure 8.10. Along the top of the Intrusion Prevention System (IPS) window are these choices, presented as tabs:

- ▶ **Create IPS.** Contains a single choice—the IPS Rule wizard (see the following note) used to automate the creation of a Cisco IOS IPS rule and all facets of configuring the IPS.

- ▶ **Edit IPS.** Enables you to manually edit Cisco IOS IPS rules and either associate or disassociate them from interfaces.

- ▶ **Security Dashboard.** Enables you to view Cisco's Top Threat table and deploy signatures to counter those threats.

- ▶ **IPS Migration.** This is used to migrate IOS IPS configurations, which were created in earlier versions of the Cisco IOS software. You must be running IOS Software Release 12.4(11)T or later to use this function.

There is also the **Launch IPS Rule Wizard** button that (although you really want to press it now!) we will look at shortly.

> **NOTE**
>
> Substitute the words "IPS signature configuration" for "IPS rule configuration" every time you see it in the SDM. In some of the dialogs, SDM calls signatures "rules." This is inconsistent use of the word "rule" because the Launch IPS Rule Wizard button (see Figure 8.10, as well as the previous paragraph) does not launch a wizard where you can change the signatures! The word "rule" in that context means policy. Ouch!
>
> While we're on the subject, sharp-eyed readers will notice that the SDM wizard is called the Intrusion Prevention System wizard, whereas we have been calling it the Intrusion Protection System up to now. This is just semantics, and you shouldn't read anything into the difference because they actually mean the same thing. Just when you thought you were figuring out the terminology!

The reference diagram for configuring Cisco IOS IPS is found in Figure 8.11. It is a slight modification to the reference diagram found in Figure 8.6 that we have been using in this chapter. The management VLAN is VLAN 3. The production VLAN is VLAN 1. This is where the wired workstations reside that belong to our internal knowledge workers. Similarly, there is a separate VLAN, VLAN 99, deployed for our wireless hotspot. Essentially, all three of these VLANs represent internal networks for the purpose of configuring the IOS IPS. FastEthernet 4 is the external, Internet-facing interface.

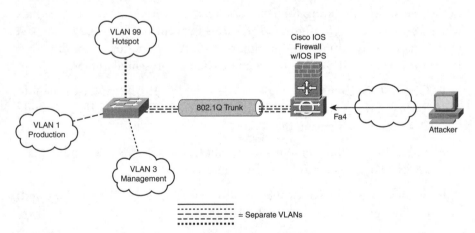

FIGURE 8.11 Reference diagram for configuring Cisco IOS IPS.

Because there is currently no IPS configured, we follow these steps to configure the Cisco IOS IPS:

1. Navigate to **Configure->Intrusion Prevention->Create IPS**. The screen that appears is illustrated in Figure 8.12.

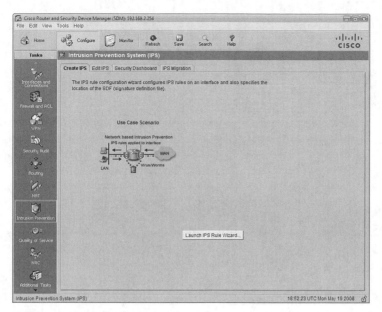

FIGURE 8.12 Cisco SDM Create IPS Wizard.

2. Push the **Launch IPS Rule Wizard** button.

3. If this is a first-time configuration, an information window appears, indicating that "SDM will open a subscription with the router to get the SDEE events." Press **OK**.

4. The Welcome to the IPS Policies Wizard screen appears. Click **Next**. The Select Interfaces screen opens and is illustrated in Figure 8.13.

5. Place a check mark beside each interface in the check box corresponding to the direction, **Inbound** and **Outbound**, that you want to inspect the packets for signs of intrusion. In this example, FastEthernet4 is the Internet-facing interface, and Vlan1, Vlan3, and Vlan99 are all inside the perimeter (refer to Figure 8.11) .

6. Click **Next**. The Signature File and Public Key window appears and is illustrated in Figure 8.14.

NOTE

Recall that there are no built-in signatures as of IOS Software Release 12.4(11)T. Some IOS routers ship from Cisco with .SDF (Signature Definition Files) already in flash memory. Also, when you download and install the SDM, there are SDF files included with the SDM archive for different amounts of RAM that can get you started without having to go to CCO. That said, the latest signature files are available on CCO to users with sufficient access.

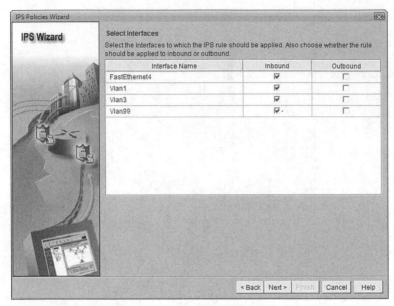

FIGURE 8.13 Select Interfaces screen of the IPS Policies Wizard.

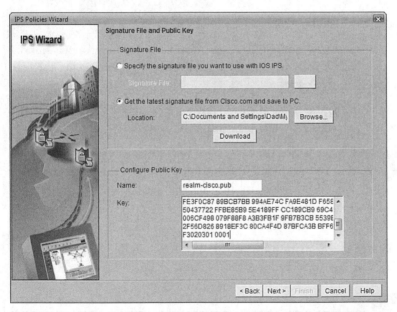

FIGURE 8.14 Signature File and Public Key screen of the IPS Policies Wizard.

In this window, you can push either of two radio buttons:

▶ **Specify the signature file you want to use with the IOS IPS.**

▶ **Get the latest signature file from Cisco.com and save to PC.**

If you choose the first choice, you will be led through a dialog that enables you to fetch the signature file from one of the following: router flash, the local PC, or the URL of an external source such as a web server.

> **NOTE**
>
> When fetching the file from your PC, the signature file will be of the form *sigv5-SDM-Sxxx.zip*, where xxx is the signature set's version number. If you choose to specify the router's flash, use the format *IOS-Sxxx-CLI.pkg*.

If you choose the second choice, you will be prompted for where you want to save the file; you then are prompted for your username and password on CCO and to save the SDF file (in .zip format) to your local PC's hard drive and subsequently install on the IPS. Incidentally, this will also download the update files in the form of a *.pkg* file, which you can push to the router (see the preceding note).

In both cases, you must enter the name and value of Cisco's public key before you proceed. This is because any changes you make to the signatures (so called "deltas") will need to be signed with this key for security reasons. You must visit this URL to look up both the name of the key to put in the Name field and the key's value to put in the Key field. The URL is http://www.cisco.com/pcgi-bin/tablebuild.pl/ios-v5sigup.

Enter the values in both fields as indicated; then proceed by clicking Next.

7. The Config Location and Category windows appear as illustrated in Figure 8.15.

   You are presented with these options:

   ▶ Config Location. Specify where the IPS configuration, .pkg files, and delta files are located. This may be in router flash or on an external server such as an HTTP server specified by URL. Follow the prompts.

   ▶ Signature Category.

   ▶ Basic. If the router has 128MB or less of flash, Cisco recommends using the Basic category to avoid memory allocation errors.

   ▶ Advanced. If the router has more than 256MB of flash, you may choose the Advanced category.

Press this ellipse to add a config location

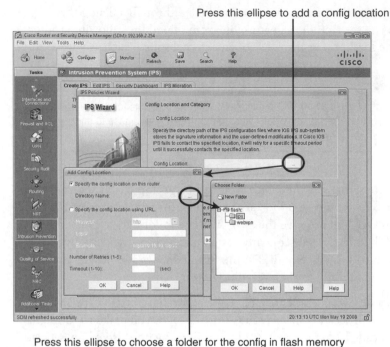

Press this ellipse to choose a folder for the config in flash memory

FIGURE 8.15   Config Location and Category screen of the IPS Policies Wizard.

NOTE

The Cisco IINS v1.0 courseware that was referenced for this Exam Cram specifies that Basic is recommended for 128MB or less of flash memory vs. RAM. This isn't correct (and doesn't make sense). This URL at Cisco indicates otherwise. Remember, though, that what's in the course is always the right wrong answer! (http://www.cisco.com/en/US/prod/collateral/iosswrel/ps6537/ps6586/ps6634/prod_white_paper0900aecd8066d265.html)

8. Click **Next** when you have filled out the information per the previous step. The Summary window of the IPS Policies Wizard appears. This is illustrated in Figure 8.16.

9. Review the information in the window; then click **Finish** to deliver the configuration to the router. Click **OK** on the Commands Delivery Status window when this has been completed. The IOS IPS Configuration Status window appears, indicating that the signatures are being configured on the router. This is illustrated in Figure 8.17.

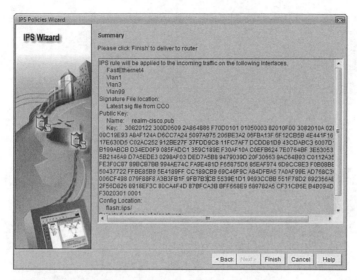

FIGURE 8.16 Summary screen of the IPS Policies Wizard.

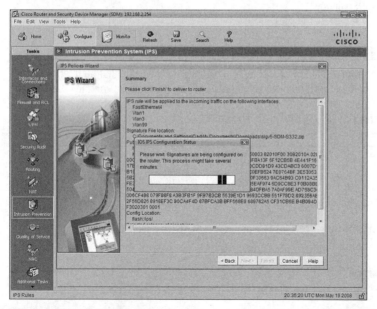

FIGURE 8.17 IOS IPS configuration status progress indicator.

10. After the IPS Configuration has been completed, the **Configure> Intrusion Prevention** window appears, this time with the **Edit IPS** tab selected, as illustrated in Figure 8.18. Review the information in this window:

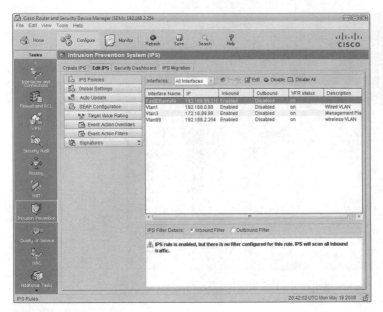

FIGURE 8.18 Edit IPS window.

NOTE

Looking at the bottom of the Edit IPS screen in Figure 8.18 indicates that no filters have been set for the traffic that will be inspected (inbound, in this example) on the interfaces. Thus when you select an interface, the warning "IPS rule is enabled, but there is no filter configured for this rule. IPS will scan all inbound traffic" appears. This can be fine-tuned separately if desired.

When you return to the Cisco SDM home page, the working IPS configuration can be seen as in Figure 8.19.

In the right-bottom quadrant of the screenshot in Figure 8.19, we learn the following:

▶ **Total Active Signatures: 373.** These are the number of signatures that are active out of the total possible signatures in the signature database.

▶ **No. of IPS-enabled Interfaces: 4.** This makes sense because we enabled IPS on VLANs 1, 3, and 99 and FastEthernet 4 (see Figures 8.11 and 8.13).

▶ **Signature Version: S332.0.** This is the version of the signature file that we downloaded and installed from Cisco.

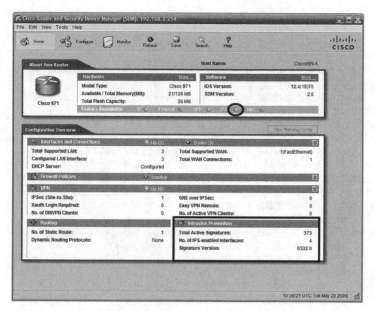

FIGURE 8.19 Cisco SDM home page showing IPS active.

If you were looking at syslog output (if configured) or you had a terminal window to the CLI open while the IPS was being configured, you might see some interesting output as the micro-engines are being compiled into RAM. First, let's examine what the %IPS-6-ENGINE message text means in the IPS messages that are displayed to the terminal:

- **ENGINE_BUILDS_STARTED.** Each micro-engine starts the compile process. Recall from the previous section that this part of the process consumes more RAM than is used once the build completes.

- **ENGINE_BUILDING.** The micro-engines is in the process of being compiled. Note that this is done consecutively until all the micro-engines that have enabled signatures are compiled into memory.

- **ENGINE_READY.** The compile process for the micro-engine is complete. The next engine starts.

Now here is an example of the screen output of an actual terminal session. Note that the **term monitor** command has been executed to ensure that the terminal windows that we are using will see output that would normally be directed to the default output device, *console 0*. We would not need to use this command if this output was taken from a terminal connected to console 0. The output represents the 13 signature micro engines (SMEs) compiling signatures and the number of signatures that are being compiled per SME.

```
CiscoISR-A#terminal monitor
CiscoISR-A#
May 19 20:36:32.906: %IPS-6-ENGINE_BUILDS_STARTED:  20:36:32 UTC May 19
2008
May 19 20:36:32.910: %IPS-6-ENGINE_BUILDING: multi-string - 8 signatures -
1 of 13 engines
May 19 20:36:33.070: %IPS-6-ENGINE_READY: multi-string - build time 160 ms
- packets for this engine will be scanned
May 19 20:36:33.086: %IPS-6-ENGINE_BUILDING: service-http - 627 signatures
- 2 of 13 engines
May 19 20:36:43.339: %IPS-6-ENGINE_READY: service-http - build time 10256
ms - packets for this engine will be scanned
May 19 20:36:43.363: %IPS-6-ENGINE_BUILDING: string-tcp - 1045 signatures
- 3 of 13 engines
May 19 20:36:49.258: %IPS-6-ENGINE_READY: string-tcp - build time 5896 ms
- packets for this engine will be scanned
May 19 20:36:49.266: %IPS-6-ENGINE_BUILDING: string-udp - 75 signatures -
4 of 13 engines
May 19 20:36:50.034: %IPS-6-ENGINE_READY: string-udp - build time 764 ms -
packets for this engine will be scanned
May 19 20:36:50.038: %IPS-6-ENGINE_BUILDING: state - 28 signatures - 5 of
13 engines
May 19 20:36:50.113: %IPS-6-ENGINE_READY: state - build time 76 ms - pack-
ets for this engine will be scanned
May 19 20:36:50.197: %IPS-6-ENGINE_BUILDING: atomic-ip - 287 signatures -
6 of 13 engines
May 19 20:36:52.333: %IPS-6-ENGINE_READY: atomic-ip - build time 2132 ms -
packets for this engine will be scanned
May 19 20:36:52.381: %IPS-6-ENGINE_BUILDING: string-icmp - 3 signatures -
7 of 13 engines
May 19 20:36:52.421: %IPS-6-ENGINE_READY: string-icmp - build time 36 ms -
packets for this engine will be scanned
May 19 20:36:52.421: %IPS-6-ENGINE_BUILDING: service-ftp - 3 signatures -
8 of 13 engines
May 19 20:36:52.441: %IPS-6-ENGINE_READY: service-ftp - build time 16 ms -
packets for this engine will be scanned
May 19 20:36:52.441: %IPS-6-ENGINE_BUILDING: service-rpc - 75 signatures -
9 of 13 engines
May 19 20:36:52.689: %IPS-6-ENGINE_READY: service-rpc - build time 244 ms
- packets for this engine will be scanned
May 19 20:36:52.693: %IPS-6-ENGINE_BUILDING: service-dns - 38 signatures -
10 of 13 engines
May 19 20:36:52.773: %IPS-6-ENGINE_READY: service-dns - build time 80 ms -
packets for this engine will be scanned
May 19 20:36:52.777: %IPS-6-ENGINE_BUILDING: normalizer - 9 signatures -
11 of 13 engines
May 19 20:36:52.785: %IPS-6-ENGINE_READY: normalizer - build time 4 ms -
packets for this engine will be scanned
May 19 20:36:52.785: %IPS-6-ENGINE_BUILDING: service-smb-advanced - 36
signatures - 12 of 13 engines
May 19 20:36:55.512: %IPS-6-ENGINE_READY: service-smb-advanced - build
time 2724 ms - packets for this engine will be scanned
May 19 20:36:55.536: %IPS-6-ENGINE_BUILDING: service-msrpc - 27 signatures
- 13 of 13 engines
```

```
May 19 20:36:55.712: %IPS-6-ENGINE_READY: service-msrpc - build time 164
ms - packets for this engine will be scanned
May 19 20:36:55.720: %IPS-6-ALL_ENGINE_BUILDS_COMPLETE: elapsed time 22820
ms
```

The highlights in the previous command output indicate the SME that was loaded as well as the number of signatures that have been compiled for each SME. Compare the output with the SME names in Table 8.7.

You can verify that the signatures are loaded by entering the **show ip ips signatures count** command. The Cisco SDF release version number, the names of the SMEs, and the total number of signatures is highlighted for reference.

```
CiscoISR-A#show ip ips signatures count

Cisco SDF release version S332.0
Trend SDF release version V0.0

Signature Micro-Engine: multi-string: Total Signatures 8
multi-string enabled signatures: 8
multi-string retired signatures: 3
multi-string compiled signatures: 5

Signature Micro-Engine: service-http: Total Signatures 627
service-http enabled signatures: 130
service-http retired signatures: 525
service-http compiled signatures: 102
service-http obsoleted signatures: 1

Signature Micro-Engine: string-tcp: Total Signatures 1045
string-tcp enabled signatures: 541
string-tcp retired signatures: 950
string-tcp compiled signatures: 95
string-tcpobsoleted signatures: 9

Signature Micro-Engine: string-udp: Total Signatures 75
string-udp enabled signatures: 2
string-udp retired signatures: 54
string-udp compiled signatures: 21
string-udpobsoleted signatures: 1

Signature Micro-Engine: state: Total Signatures 28
state enabled signatures: 15
state retired signatures: 25
state compiled signatures: 3

Signature Micro-Engine: atomic-ip: Total Signatures 287
atomic-ip enabled signatures: 88
atomic-ip retired signatures: 252
atomic-ip compiled signatures: 35
```

```
Signature Micro-Engine: string-icmp: Total Signatures 3
string-icmp enabled signatures: 0
string-icmp retired signatures: 1
string-icmp compiled signatures: 2

Signature Micro-Engine: service-ftp: Total Signatures 3
service-ftp enabled signatures: 1
service-ftp retired signatures: 2
service-ftp compiled signatures: 1

Signature Micro-Engine: service-rpc: Total Signatures 75
service-rpc enabled signatures: 44
service-rpc retired signatures: 43
service-rpc compiled signatures: 32

Signature Micro-Engine: service-dns: Total Signatures 38
service-dns enabled signatures: 30
service-dns retired signatures: 9
service-dns compiled signatures: 29

Signature Micro-Engine: normalizer: Total Signatures 9
normalizer enabled signatures: 8
normalizer retired signatures: 1
normalizer compiled signatures: 8

Signature Micro-Engine: service-smb-advanced: Total Signatures 36
service-smb-advanced enabled signatures: 36
service-smb-advanced retired signatures: 1
service-smb-advanced compiled signatures: 35

Signature Micro-Engine: service-msrpc: Total Signatures 27
service-msrpc enabled signatures: 27
service-msrpc retired signatures: 22
service-msrpc compiled signatures: 5

Total Signatures: 2261
    Total Enabled Signatures: 930
    Total Retired Signatures: 1888
    Total Compiled Signatures: 373
    Total Obsoleted Signatures: 11
```

NOTE

Note that the output of the **show ip ips signatures count** command shows the signatures organized by micro-engine and in the same order that they were compiled, as was seen in the syslog output.

Cisco IOS IPS CLI Configuration

Here are the basic commands used to configure the IOS IPS with the CLI. We'll start with an example that matches the worked example that we have just completed with the SDM and then look at the commands one by one and in the order shown (note: the configuration for interfaces Vlan99 and Vlan3 has been omitted):

```
ip ips config location flash:/ips/ retries 1
ip ips notify SDEE
ip ips name sdm_ips_rule
!
ip ips signature-category
  category all
    retired true
  category ios_ips basic
    retired false
!
interface Vlan1
 ip ips sdm_ips_rule in
 ip virtual-reassembly
!
interface FastEthernet4
ip ips sdm_ips_rule in
 ip virtual-reassembly
```

Here is an explanation of the commands (see the previous configuration for specific examples used in our reference network):

- **ip ips config location.** This global configuration command specifies the location of the IPS configuration. In this example, it is in the flash:/ips/ directory.

- **ip ips notify.** This global configuration command specifies the method of event notification. In this example, SDEE is being used.

- **ip ips name.** This global configuration command specifies the IPS rule (policy) name—*sdm_ips_rule* in this example.

- **ip ips signature-category.** This global configuration command configures the router to support the default basic or advanced signature set.

- **ip ips** *ips_rule_name*. This interface configuration command applies the named IPS rule (policy) on the selected interface.

- **ip virtual-reassembly.** This interface configuration command turns on Virtual Fragment Reassembly (VFR). Dynamic ACLs are created to protect the network against various fragmentation attacks.

Configuring IPS Signatures

This section examines the steps required to configure IPS signatures using the SDM.

Configuring IPS Signature Severity

You may recall earlier that one of Cisco's recommendations for IPS best practices is to set the alert level of any signature to the severity level of the signature itself. You can set the severity level of a signature, both the included ones as well as ones you create, by following these steps:

1. From the SDM, navigate to **Configure->Intrusion Prevention->Edit IPS->Signatures->All Categories**. The list of all signatures appears, as illustrated in Figure 8.20.

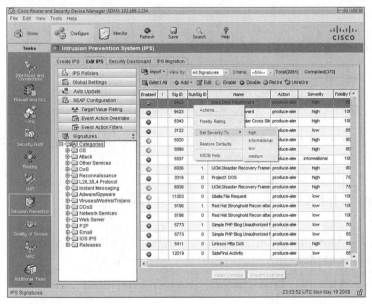

FIGURE 8.20   Edit IPS / Set Signature Severity dialog.

2. Select the signature whose severity level you want to change; then right-click to bring up the context menu. Select **Set Severity Level to** and select from: **high, informational, low,** or **medium**. This is illustrated in Figure 8.20

3. Click **Apply Changes** in the Edit IPS window when you are done.

Configuring Signature Actions

Recall that IPS signatures have default actions or "responses." (See the subsection "Signature Attack Responses" for a complete list of responses and their meaning.) The SDM enables you to change these actions. To change the action for a signature, follow these steps (using the Email signature category as an example):

1. From the SDM, navigate to **Configure->Intrusion Prevention->Edit IPS->Signatures->Email**.

2. Select the signature whose severity level you want to change; then right-click to bring up the context menu. Select **Assign Actions** from the context menu. A new Assign Actions window appears, as illustrated in Figure 8.21.

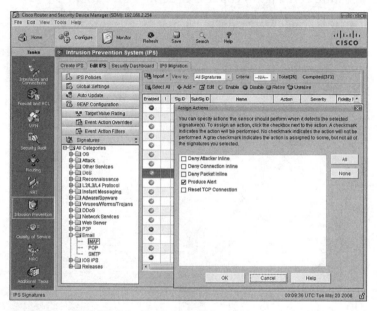

FIGURE 8.21 Edit IPS / Assign Actions dialog.

3. Place a check mark in the box beside the action(s) you want to take. The actions you can choose from are the following:

   ▶ **Deny Attacker Inline**

   ▶ **Deny Connection Inline**

   ▶ **Deny Packet Inline**

   ▶ **Produce Alert** (the default for this IMAP Email Signature)

   ▶ **Reset TCP Connection**

4. Click **OK**.

5. Click **Apply Changes** in the Edit IPS window when you are done.

Editing IPS Signatures Using Cisco SDM

You can edit a signature, both the included ones as well as ones you create, by following these steps. This example will choose a signature from the Reconnaissance category called TCP Ports Sweeps:

1. From the SDM, navigate to **Configure->Intrusion Prevention->Edit IPS->Signatures->Reconnaissance->TCP Ports Sweeps**.

2. Select the signature you want to edit and click the **Edit** button.

3. The Edit Signature window appears, as illustrated in Figure 8.22.

FIGURE 8.22 Edit IPS / Edit Signature dialog.

The parameters you see depend on the signature. Here's a list of what you may edit in this window, depending on the signature:

▶ **Signature ID.** Unique number assigned to each signature.

- ▶ **SubSignature ID.** Unique number assigned to the subsignature. Allows for more granularity of signature definitions.

- ▶ **Alert Severity.** Defines the severity of alert sent to the sensor when this signature triggers.

- ▶ **Sig Description.** This is a section where you can give the signature a name, put in user comments, alert notes, alert traits, and release number. Certain of these parameters are pre-defined (though editable) for Cisco signatures.

- ▶ **Engine.** Specifies information as to which micro-engine this signature uses.

- ▶ **Event Counter.** This is a section where you can define the event count, event count key, and whether a specific alert interval is to be specified (useful for rate-limiting to defend against DoS attacks against the IPS).

- ▶ **Alert Frequency.** Define frequency of the alert.

- ▶ **Status.** This section specifies whether the signature is enabled or disabled and whether or not it is retired.

4. Click **OK** when you are done with the changes.

5. Click **Apply Changes** in the Edit IPS window when you are done.

SDEE and Syslog Logging Protocol Support

The Cisco IOS IPS supports both the Security Device Event Exchange (SDEE) and syslog protocols to send alerts.

Recall that an alarm is generated when an enabled signature is triggered. The alarms are stored in a buffer on the sensor. One disadvantage of syslog is that the syslog server is *passive*, relying on the sensor to send alerts to it. This is indicated by the arrow in Figure 8.23 pointing to the syslog server from the Cisco IOS IPS. SDEE, on the other hand, is a subscription type of service where hosts can *pull* alarms from the sensor at any time. This is indicated by the two-headed arrow indicated in Figure 8.23. SDEE-format messages are much richer in their information content.

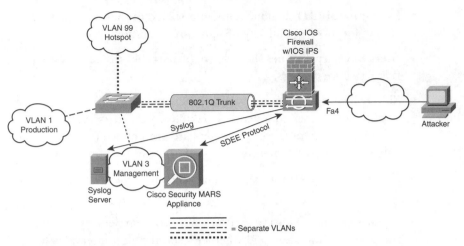

FIGURE 8.23 SDEE and Syslog support in Cisco IOS IPS.

Here are some other things you need to know about SDEE:

▶ 1,000 events can be stored in the SDEE buffer. 200 is the default. Disabling SDEE notification erases the buffer.

▶ Network management applications pull SDEE messages from the IOS IPS.

▶ SDEE is evolving as the standard format for security reporting network management.

▶ SDEE is vendor-independent.

▶ SDEE uses HTTP or HTTPS (more secure) for transport, thus must be enabled on the router.

▶ The IOS IPS still sends alerts via syslog.

Viewing the SDEE Message Log

Navigate to **Monitor->Logging->SDEE Message Log** to view the SDEE message log. This dialog is illustrated in Figure 8.24.

Here's an example of an SDEE message captured in the CLI. The IPS is sending an alert of a possible fragmentation attack since signature 1207 has been triggered:

```
May 20 12:37:24.723: %IPS-4-SIGNATURE: Sig:1207 Subsig:0 Sev:25 IP
Fragment Too Many Datagrams [192.168.2.119:0 -> 192.168.2.254:0]
RiskRating:25
```

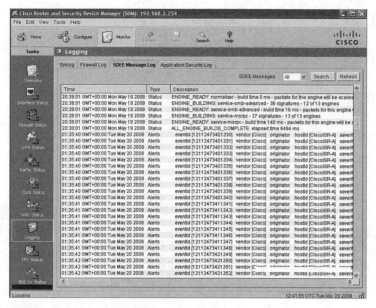

FIGURE 8.24 Viewing the SDEE message log.

Viewing the Syslog Message Log

Navigate to **Monitor->Logging->Syslog** to view the syslog message log. This dialog is illustrated in Figure 8.25.

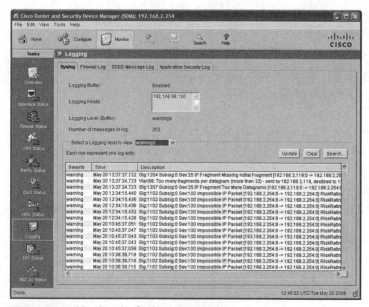

FIGURE 8.25 Viewing the Syslog message log.

Verifying IOS IPS Operation

This section outlines procedures to verify IOS IPS operation with both the SDM and the CLI.

Verifying IPS Policies (Rules)

Navigate to **Configure->Intrusion Prevention->Edit IPS** to verify that IPS has been enabled on interfaces and in which direction. This is illustrated in Figure 8.26.

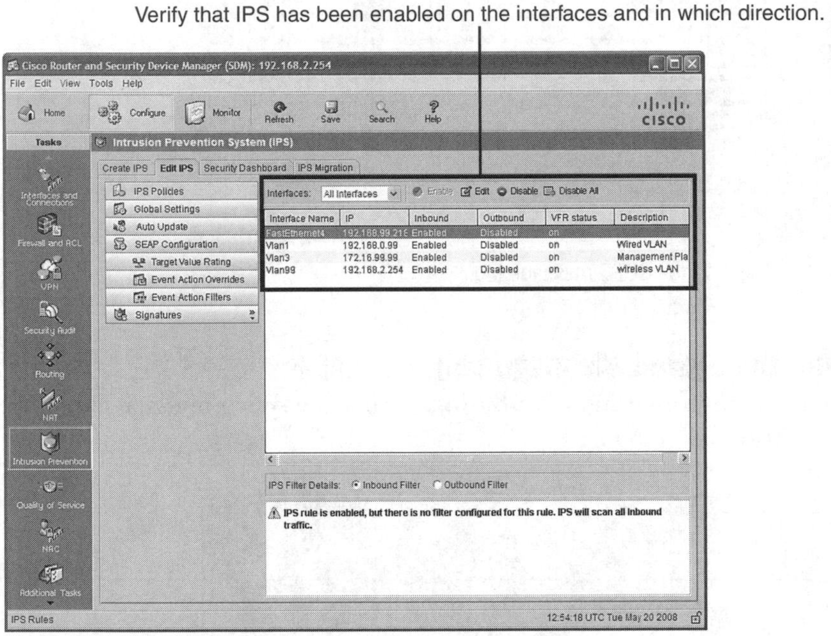

FIGURE 8.26   Verifying IOS IPS operation in the Cisco SDM.

Also note in Figure 8.26 that VFR (Virtual Fragment Reassembly) has been enabled on all of the interfaces. The IOS IPS cannot detect intrusions by examining fragments of IP packets. They must be coalesced so the entire packet can be checked.

Of course, the **Edit IPS** tab can be used to edit and not just verify the IPS!

Verifying the IPS Configuration

The command **show ip ips configuration** (reviewed previously) can be used to verify a summary of the IPS configuration, including the configured location of the files, name of policies (rules), and which interfaces they have been applied on and in which direction. These are highlighted in the following command output:

```
CiscoISR-A#show ip ips configuration

IPS Signature File Configuration Status
    Configured Config Locations: flash:/ips/
    Last signature default load time: 20:36:55 UTC May 19 2008
    Last signature delta load time: 20:38:01 UTC May 19 2008
    Last event action (SEAP) load time: -none-

    General SEAP Config:
    Global Deny Timeout: 3600 seconds
    Global Overrides Status: Enabled
    Global Filters Status: Enabled

IPS Auto Update is not currently configured

IPS Syslog and SDEE Notification Status
    Event notification through syslog is enabled
    Event notification through SDEE is enabled

IPS Signature Status
    Total Active Signatures: 373
    Total Inactive Signatures: 1888

IPS Packet Scanning and Interface Status
    IPS Rule Configuration
      IPS name sdm_ips_rule
    IPS fail closed is disabled
    IPS deny-action ips-interface is false
    Fastpath ips is enabled
    Quick run mode is enabled
    Interface Configuration
      Interface Vlan3
        Inbound IPS rule is sdm_ips_rule
        Outgoing IPS rule is not set
      Interface Vlan1
        Inbound IPS rule is sdm_ips_rule
        Outgoing IPS rule is not set
      Interface FastEthernet4
        Inbound IPS rule is sdm_ips_rule
        Outgoing IPS rule is not set
      Interface Vlan99
        Inbound IPS rule is sdm_ips_rule
        Outgoing IPS rule is not set

IPS Category CLI Configuration:
    Category all:
        Retire: True
    Category ios_ips basic:
        Retire: False

CiscoISR-A#
```

Verifying IPS Interfaces

If you simply want to see which interface(s) the policies (rules) have been applied on, you can use the **show ip ips interfaces** command. Here we see the SDM-generated IPS policy *sdm_ips_rule* applied inbound on Vlan1, Vlan3, Vlan99, and FastEthernet 4:

```
CiscoISR-A#show ip ips interfaces
    Interface Configuration
      Interface Vlan3
        Inbound IPS rule is sdm_ips_rule
        Outgoing IPS rule is not set
      Interface Vlan1
        Inbound IPS rule is sdm_ips_rule
        Outgoing IPS rule is not set
      Interface FastEthernet4
        Inbound IPS rule is sdm_ips_rule
        Outgoing IPS rule is not set
      Interface Vlan99
        Inbound IPS rule is sdm_ips_rule
        Outgoing IPS rule is not set
CiscoISR-A#
```

Verifying All Cisco IOS IPS Settings

To view all the Cisco IOS IPS settings, including information that is not displayed with the **show ip ips configuration** command, use the **show ip ips all** command. In the following output, we see that both syslog and SDEE logging has been enabled and that there are 373 active signatures and 1,888 inactive signatures:

```
(output omitted)
CiscoISR-A#showipips all

IPS Signature File Configuration Status
    Configured Config Locations: flash:/ips/
    Last signature default load time: 20:36:55 UTC May 19 2008
    Last signature delta load time: 20:38:01 UTC May 19 2008
    Last event action (SEAP) load time: -none-

    General SEAP Config:
    Global Deny Timeout: 3600 seconds
    Global Overrides Status: Enabled
    Global Filters Status: Enabled

IPS Auto Update is not currently configured

IPS Syslog and SDEE Notification Status
    Event notification through syslog is enabled
    Event notification through SDEE is enabled

IPS Signature Status
    Total Active Signatures: 373
    Total Inactive Signatures: 1888
```

Exam Prep Questions

1. True or false. An IDS is a passive technology that only reports when events trigger signatures, whereas an IPS not only reports but also blocks the intrusion.

2. Which in the following list are examples of where an IDS or IPS may be deployed? (Choose all that apply.)

   ○ **A.** Separate network device.

   ○ **B.** Option card in a router or security appliance.

   ○ **C.** Software on a router.

   ○ **D.** Add-on blade module on Cisco VPN 3000 Series Concentrator.

   ○ **E.** All of the above.

3. Match the list of IPS technologies below with the letter corresponding to the platform to which it belongs. Letters may be used more than once.

   1. AIP-SSM: _____

   2. IDSM-2: _____

   3. IPS AIM: _____

   4. IOS IPS: _____

   Choices:

   A. ASA 5500 Series Adaptive Security appliances

   B. Catalyst 6500 Series switches

   C. Cisco IOS router

4. Which of the following is part of Cisco's suite of IPS Management Software? (Choose one correct answer.)

   ○ **A.** Cisco IPS Device Manager (IDM)

   ○ **B.** Cisco IPS Event Viewer (IEV)

   ○ **C.** Cisco Security Monitoring, Analysis, and Response System (MARS)

   ○ **D.** Cisco Router Security Device Manager (SDM)

   ○ **E.** All of the above.

5. Fill in the blank. Cisco _____ Agent is Cisco's Host IPS (HIPS) software solution.

   ○ **A.** Integrity

   ○ **B.** Accountability

   ○ **C.** Information

   ○ **D.** Security

   ○ **E.** Trust

6. Which of the following is not considered an advantage of Network IPS? (Choose all that apply.)

   ○ **A.** New end system hosts and devices can be added without the need for new sensors.

   ○ **B.** A single sensor can monitor traffic from many hosts.

   ○ **C.** Network IPS can be deployed on every end system in the network.

   ○ **D.** Network IPS can see all traffic inside encrypted data streams.

   ○ **E.** None of the above.

7. Review the information in Figure 8.27. Which of the following statements is correct about the information it contains? (Choose all that apply.)

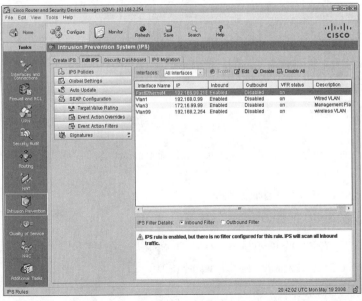

FIGURE 8.27   Configure->Intrusion Prevention System (IPS)->Edit IPS window.

   ○ **A.** Only inbound traffic from untrusted to trusted zones will be scanned for signs of intrusion since only the Inbound Filter radio button is pressed in the bottom pane.

○ **B.** VFR (Virtual Fragmentation Reassembly) is enabled on every interface.

○ **C.** Inbound inspection of packets for intrusive activity is enabled on every interface.

○ **D.** You cannot tell whether the IPS is active or not by looking at this screenshot.

○ **E.** None of the above.

8. Fill in the blanks in the following sentence with a choice from the list below. The IPS signature file that you download to your PC will end with a _____ file extension, whereas the file that you push to the IOS IPS will end with a _____ file extension. Both can be downloaded from Cisco.

○ **A.** .zip, .pkg

○ **B.** .cab, .zip

○ **C.** .tar, .zip

○ **D.** .pkg, .zip

○ **E.** .cab, .pkg

9. View the CLI output below of an incomplete IPS configuration. Which of the following statements best describes what is missing?

```
ip ips config location flash:/ips/ retries 1
ip ips notify SDEE
ip ips name sdm_ips_rule
!
ip ips signature-category
category all
retired true
category ios ips basic
retired false
!
```

○ **A.** The basic category of IPS signatures should not be used because it is unlikely to capture trigger packets.

○ **B.** The basic category of IPS signatures should not be used because it is known to cause memory allocation errors on IOS IPS routers with less than 128MB of DRAM.

○ **C.** Only retired signatures are being used.

○ **D.** The IPS is inactive because the configuration has not been applied to an interface.

○ **E.** The IPS is inactive because the configuration has not been applied globally to the device.

10. True or false. SDEE is a push-logging protocol that can optionally use encryption, whereas syslog uses a pull-logging protocol.

Answers to Exam Prep Questions

1. False. This is a bit of a trick question. What makes an IDS an intrusion *detection* system is that it might miss trigger packets from an attack because it is not inline to the traffic like an IPS. An IDS might be able to block attacks after they have started.

2. The correct answers are A, B, and C. There is no IPS or IDS add-on module for the concentrator.

3. The correct answers are: 1—A; 2—B; 3—C; 4—C.

4. The correct answer is E.

5. The correct answer is D.

6. The correct answers are C and D. C is correct because one of the advantages of a network IPS is that you don't have to deploy it on every end system in the network. D is also correct because one of the disadvantages of network IPS is that they are blind to encrypted data. Only a Host IPS (HIPS) can see the data in the encrypted data stream because they operate above the network and transport layers where encryption occurs. (Review Chapter 7, "Virtual Private Networks with IPsec," if you're not sure about this last point.)

7. The correct answers are B and C. Answer A is incorrect because the notice in the bottom pane of the Edit IPS screenshot just means what it says—all inbound traffic will be scanned by the IPS since no filter is set. The word "inbound" is with respect to the interface itself and has nothing to do with zones and zone pairs and levels of trust. Answer D is incorrect because this screen is used to verify that IPS is enabled on the interfaces. You can see that all the interfaces have an IPS policy enabled in the inbound direction.

8. The correct answer is A. When you elect to download the signature files from CCO in the course of configuring the IOS IPS, the Create IPS Wizard will ask you if you want to push the files to the router in addition to downloading them to your local PC. The file names that are pushed to the router are in the form of IOS-Sxxx-CLI.pkg, and the file names that are downloaded to your PC are in the form of sigv5-SDM-Sxxx.zip, where xxx is the version number of the signature set.

9. The correct answer is D. Answers A and B are incorrect because the basic signature category is for Cisco IOS IPS routers, which have less than 128MB of DRAM. This doesn't turn off the inline nature of the IPS either, so trigger packets (at least in the applied signatures) will not be missed. Answer C is incorrect because the word "retired" in the CLI output refers to whether retired signatures are used in a certain category. Answer E is incorrect because the IPS policy is only applied to interfaces and not globally to the entire device.

Here is an example of a complete configuration. Note that the IPS policy *sdm_ips_rule* has been applied in the inbound direction to interfaces Vlan1 and FastEthernet4:

```
ip ips config location flash:/ips/ retries 1
ip ips notify SDEE
ip ips name sdm_ips_rule
!
ip ips signature-category
category all
retired true
category ios_ips basic
retired false
!
interface Vlan1
ip ips sdm_ips_rule in
ip virtual-reassembly
!
interface FastEthernet4
ip ips sdm_ips_rule in
ip virtual-reassembly
```

10. False. One of SDEE's strengths is that it is a pull protocol that can optionally use HTTPS (vs. HTTP) for transport for encryption. Syslog is unencrypted, uses UDP port 514 for transport, and is a push protocol, meaning that a syslog server cannot query the IPS for alert message entries unlike SDEE.

PART IV

Security Inside the Perimeter

CHAPTER NINE

Introduction to Endpoint, SAN, and Voice Security

Terms You'll Need to Understand:

✓ Endpoint

✓ Worm

✓ Virus

✓ Trojan

✓ IronPort

✓ Network Admission Control (NAC) Framework

✓ Interceptors

✓ Storage Area Network (SAN)

✓ SCSI (Small Computer Systems Interface) over TCP/IP (iSCSI)

✓ Fiber Channel over IP (FCIP)

✓ Fiber Channel

✓ Logical Unit Number (LUN)

✓ Worldwide Number (WWN)

✓ Zoning

✓ Virtual Storage Area Network (VSAN)

✓ Voice over IP (VoIP)

✓ Vishing

✓ Voice VLAN (VVLAN)

Exam Topics Covered in This Chapter:

✓ Describe and list mitigation methods for common network attacks

✓ Describe and list mitigation methods for Worm, Virus, and Trojan Horse attacks

> **NOTE**
>
> These exam topics are from cisco.com. Check there periodically for the latest exam topics and info.

Now it's time to focus on the last element of implementation of a comprehensive network security policy: security *inside* the perimeter.

Inside the network perimeter is often where security is its most lax or, worse, nonexistent. Security practitioners are often guilty of spending so much time looking for the enemy outside the walls of the fortification that they become victims of attacks from within. Just ask the people of the ancient city of Troy what one well-placed Trojan horse can do to security! Many experienced security practitioners can relate to this last point.

This chapter examines the items that are often orphaned by a poorly implemented security policy, namely:

- ▶ Endpoints
- ▶ Storage Area Networks (SANs)
- ▶ Voice over IP (VoIP) Infrastructure

In examining these three areas, we will likely discover that there are many reasons to be somewhat insecure about their implementation. Security is often an afterthought (if it has been thought of at all!) in these technologies.

Introducing Endpoint Security

Perhaps a bit of history *is* in order…. When TCP/IP was but a baby, there were two different types of devices with IP addresses, as follows:

- ▶ **End Systems.** An end system is essentially to a network what an end user is to computing. An *end system* is a device that you connect to a network but does not comprise a network device. PC workstations, IP printers, network servers, VoIP phones, VoIP gateways, and so on are considered end systems.

- ▶ **Intermediate Systems.** Perhaps you recognize intermediate systems by their other name: routers. "Ahh!," you say. No surprise that one of the earliest scalable routing protocols was called IS-IS or Intermediate System–Intermediate System routing.

So, what is an endpoint, then? If you imagine a TCP connection as being a circuit between two devices, using a TCP/IP network for transport, the endpoints are the devices on each end of that circuit. According to Wikipedia:

> In computer science, in discussions of communications protocols, an endpoint is the name for the entity on one end of a transport layer connection. In service-oriented architecture, an endpoint is the entry point to a service, a process, or a queue or topic destination.

Cisco's Host Security Strategy

Securing endpoints in a Cisco Self-Defending Network falls within the category of Cisco Host Security Strategy. There are three prongs to this strategy:

- **Endpoint Protection (Cisco Security Agent).** Detecting and preventing viruses, worms, and trojans from implanting themselves in the network.

- **Cisco Network Admission Control (NAC).** Audits endpoint security posture and ensures that only endpoints that comply with the organization's security policy can access the network.

- **Network Infection Containment.** Mitigates the effect of infections by speeding up the process of identifying infections, isolating affected systems, and cleaning up traffic.

Securing Software

What constitutes secure software? In a word, it is its trustworthiness. In Chapter 6, "Introducing Cryptographic Services," we discovered that one of the important metrics for choosing the ciphers and other elements of a cryptosystem was the trustworthiness of each element. In Cisco's Host Security Strategy, there are two main software elements that must be secured in order that an endpoint proves its trustworthiness, as follows:

- Operating systems

- Applications that run in the environment provided by the operating system

Because software is often the sole entry point when interfacing with an endpoint, it naturally follows that software is often a primary vector for a variety of attacks that might be leveraged against an endpoint. According to Cisco, the two elements of software—operating systems and applications—have specific vulnerabilities, which if not secured, can lead to exploits. Table 9.1 provides an overview of these software elements, their vulnerabilities and exploits, as well as which Cisco product(s) could be implemented to secure the software system.

TABLE 9.1   Cisco Products Used to Secure Software Element Vulnerabilities

Element	Vulnerability	Exploit	Cisco Product
Operating System	Operating systems provide services to application, including: ▶ Trusted code and trusted path. ▶ Privileged context of execution (system resources' execution space). ▶ Process memory isolation and protection (so one crashed application does not affect others). ▶ Access control to system resources. Operating system may be required to provide support for legacy protocols.	An attacker can subvert all of these services.	Cisco Network Admission Control (NAC) and Cisco Security Agent (CSA) provide protection.
Applications	The more privileges the application has, the more damage that system, if compromised, can inflict on the entire host system. (See following note.)	Direct attack: An attacker tricks the system into performing a task within its privileges. Indirect attack (privilege escalation): An attacker first compromises one system and then leverages that system to attack. the application.	Cisco Security Agent prevents both types of exploits.

NOTE

Applications are very much like *users* of an operating system, and like users, the concept of least privileges should be followed. Applications should only have as much privilege given to them by the host operating system as they need to perform their functions.

Endpoint Attacks

Applications and operating systems are susceptible to DoS and access attacks in the same way that network devices are. Some specific attacks that endpoints may be susceptible to include the following:

- ▶ **Buffer Overflows.** The conduit through which entry is made to an unsecure system.

- ▶ **Worms, Viruses, and Trojan Horses.** The method or vector in which code is introduced to compromise the unsecure system.

Buffer Overflows

Buffer overflows usually result from a failure to properly validate input data. For example, a web server might be used to accept form data from an Internet user and then pass that data to a database server inside the organization's network. Even if the communication path between the web server and the database server is secured and inspected for signs of intrusion by systems such as an IPS, these types of attacks are hard to discover. There is frequently nothing untoward in the pattern of data within the packets, and signature-based systems will be ineffective. Thus, to ensure endpoint security, software needs to be deployed on the endpoint to scan for anomalous behavior of the application stack.

Characteristics of a buffer overflow attack include the following:

- ▶ Input data that contains untested parameters, such as:

  - ▶ Improperly formatted data.

  - ▶ Too much data.

  - ▶ Unexpected and improperly formatted control sequences.

  - ▶ Embedded executable code and scripts.

- ▶ Not easy to discover and exploit by the hacker community but....

- ▶ When exploit code is discovered or invented by the hacker community, it can be prepackaged for widespread use.

- ▶ They generally overwrite memory in an application stack by cramming too much data into an application's input.

The Cisco solution for preventing buffer overflows is Cisco Security Agent. This HIPS product was discussed in some detail in Chapter 8, "Network Security Using Cisco IOS IPS."

Figure 9.1 illustrates how Cisco Security Agent (CSA) protects the operating system kernel from attack. Referring to Figure 9.1, when an application (step 1) attempts to make a call to the operating system kernel, CSA intercepts this call (step 2). In effect, CSA acts as a firewall in establishing a perimeter between the application and the operating system kernel. Once CSA establishes the trustworthiness of the application, the call is allowed to progress (step 3) to the operating system kernel.

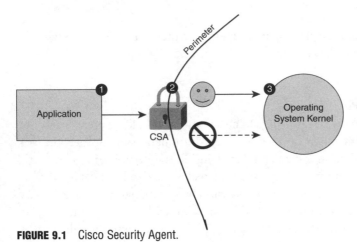

FIGURE 9.1   Cisco Security Agent.

There are two main types of buffer overflows:

▶ Remote exploits

▶ Local exploits

The most common methods of spreading buffer overflow attacks are the following:

▶ Worms

▶ Trojan horses

▶ Viruses

▶ Infected spam

EXAM ALERT

According to Cisco (and thus this book), the most common methods of spreading buffer overflows are worms, Trojan horses, viruses, and infected spam. In the real-world that we all live in, however, this is false. Buffer overflows are targeted attacks designed to exploit vulnerabilities in a particular application. Trojan horses and viruses have nothing to do with buffer overflows, but worms and (it's a stretch) infected spam can be used to inject code, which results in a buffer overflow. In the end, if you are asked on the exam what the most common methods of spreading buffer overflows are, you might have to choose the right wrong answer.

Other characteristics of buffer overflows include the following:

▶ Most common software vulnerability

▶ Mostly used to root a system or create a DoS attack

NOTE

Rooting a system means to hack a system to become the superuser or root user. This is a UNIX term for someone who possesses the highest level of system privilege.

DoS attacks are not designed to access information, but to make a system unusable. This was discussed in Chapter 1, "Network Insecurity."

Worms, Viruses, and Trojan Horses

The most common vector of attack for worms, viruses, and Trojan horses is buffer overflows. As previously stated, CSA is Cisco's product that prevents buffer overflows so logically. CSA is extremely effective in defeating these vectors of attack.

EXAM ALERT

Know the definitions of worms, viruses, and Trojan horses.

The terms worm, virus, and Trojan horse are often improperly used at best, and are sometimes used interchangeably at worst. Here are accurate, succinct, high-level definitions for these terms:

▶ **Worm.** Takes its name from burrowing organisms that live in the "soil" of an infected host. The worm replicates, often without any user interaction, into the memory of an infected host that, in turn, infects other computers. Worms have three different parts:

    ▶ The enabling vulnerability (used to worm into the host).

    ▶ A propagation mechanism (to replicate and choose additional targets).

    ▶ Payload (contains the exploit code; to root the system and gain privileged access, for example).

▶ **Virus.** Like microorganisms that invade a human host, viruses attach to other programs and files and execute unwanted functions on that host. Unlike worms, viruses require a careless user's interaction as their enabler (such as opening an infected email attachment), for their invasion to establish a beachhead on the endpoint.

▶ **Trojan horse.** Like the fabled Trojan horse that fooled the defenders of Troy, a Trojan horse is an application that is written to look like something innocuous, whereas it is actually an attack tool. Trojans are allowed past the defenses by unwitting (or witless!) defenders. Firewalls, for example, are rendered useless by this type of attack.

The Five Ps of a Worm Attack

Worms have five phases of operation, as follows:

1. **Probe.** The worm uses various methods such as ping sweeps, and OS and application fingerprinting, to identify vulnerable targets.

2. **Penetrate.** The exploit code in the worm's payload is transferred to the host.

3. **Persist.** The worm drops anchor and sets up shop in memory, installing new code that will survive even if the host is power-cycled.

4. **Propagate.** Not satisfied with penetrating one host, the worm searches for vulnerabilities on neighbor systems, exploiting the likelihood that these neighbor systems might trust the infected host in order to replicate itself to those other systems. Active TCP connections, file transfers, and file and print sharing are common vectors.

5. **Paralyze.** After the worm has used the host system to propagate to other systems to ensure its continuing survival, the worm can now paralyze the system that it first penetrated, erasing files, stealing data, and launching DDoS attacks.

Figure 9.2 illustrates these five phases.

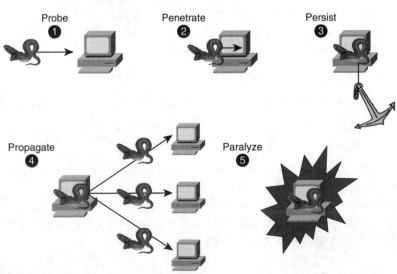

FIGURE 9.2 The five Ps of a worm attack.

Cisco Solutions to Secure Systems and Thwart Endpoint Attacks

As you have probably inferred from the preceding discussion, an Intrusion Protection System would not, by itself, be effective against viruses, worms, and Trojan horses. Many vendors, including Cisco, have products in their security portfolio that are especially effective against such network-borne contagions. We examine three solutions at a high level:

- ▶ IronPort
- ▶ NAC
- ▶ CSA

IronPort

IronPort is a recent acquisition by Cisco. IronPort comprises a line of security appliances, deployed at the network perimeter. There are three main series of IronPort security appliances:

- ▶ **C-Series.** Email security appliances. These use the same code base as on IronPortSenderBase, an email traffic-monitoring system used by 80% of the largest ISPs.

- ▶ **S-Series.** Web security appliances. These devices protect against web-borne malware using IronPort's Web Reputation technology and the Dynamic Vectoring and Streaming™ (DVS) engine.

- ▶ **M-Series.** Security management appliances.

NAC

Network Admission Control has two components, the rather confusingly named NAC Framework and the Cisco NAC Appliance. (Why is the "framework" a component of NAC? Isn't that backwards? Oh well....)

- ▶ **NAC Framework.** Software embedded inside NAC-enabled products, including some Cisco IOS routers. This software acts as an agent and allows the device to collect the bona fides (or "credentials") of a user or other entity and determine whether they have sufficient privileges to be granted access to the network. These network access devices do not themselves determine whether access privileges should be granted. They forward the credentials to the NAC Appliance. The NAC framework integrates Cisco and other vendors' NAC-enabled products.

▶ **Cisco NAC Appliance.** Rolls the four key NAC components into a single device. It is a good fit for enterprises that need a simple way to keep track of patch revisions of operating systems, as well as updates for antivirus software and vulnerabilities. Cisco's NAC Appliance works in a mixed vendor environment and does not need a Cisco network to operate. The four key NAC components are as follows:

   ○ **Cisco NAC Appliance Server (NAS).** A device deployed in-band or out-of-band to perform network access control. As users attempt network access, the user is redirected to the NAS, which checks the device's compliance. A Cisco IOS router with the right version of Cisco IOS software can perform this function. (See the following Exam Alert for more about using the acronym NAS.)

   ○ **Cisco NAC Appliance Manager (NAM).** A GUI-based central administrative interface for IT security personnel. Security policies and users are created and managed. The NAM manages the NAS, with the NAS remaining the device that actually enforces access.

   ○ **Cisco NAC Appliance Agent (NAA).** This is software that resides on a client endpoint. It is queried by NAM to determine an endpoint's compliance with the network security policy. The endpoint machine is deep-inspected for the following:

     Registry settings

     Services

     Files

     Required hot fixes for remediation can be determined, as well as the correct version of antivirus software and CSA. From a user's perspective, this is the interface that they see when they interact with the NAC appliance.

   ○ **Rule-Set Updates.** Quarantined hosts can obtain the latest patches, software revisions, hot fixes, and so on through automatic updates.

EXAM ALERT

Don't you just hate acronyms that are made up of other acronyms! Even worse are acronyms that are reused. We saw "NAS" before in Chapter 3, "Security at the Network Perimeter." In that context, NAS stood for Network Access Server. Even in the NAC context, a NAS (now a "NAC Appliance Server") still decides whether an entity is allowed access to the network. They both collect credentials to validate against another device, but unlike AAA where the credentials validate a user's identity, NAC credentials validate a user's security posture and determine whether they are sufficient to gain access to the network. No wonder, then, that Cisco prefers to call an AAA NAS an "AAA client." This terminology is becoming more prevalent.

In order to show how all of these components work in practice, Figure 9.3 represents a slight modification of our reference network design. A NAM and NAS have been added to the network in order to manage network admission control (NAC) to the Internet (or a company intranet) for a user.

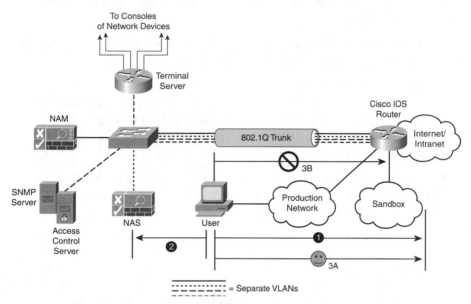

FIGURE 9.3 NAC in action.

Figure 9.3 illustrates these three basic steps:

1. A user attempts to access a site on the corporate intranet or on the Internet. The connection attempt is intercepted and blocked by a network device (IOS router in the diagram) until the next steps complete.

2. The user is redirected to a login page, where he is prompted for his login credentials by the NAS. While this occurs, the user's PC and the network are scanned to determine whether they are compliant to the organization's security policy.

3. If the device is compliant, it is allowed to connect to the original destination (indicated by the "3A" in Figure 9.3). If the device is noncompliant, the connection is redirected to a quarantine network or sandbox, where remedial action can be taken (indicated by the "3B" in Figure 9.3). The user might be presented with a web page where they download the latest version of the organization's anti-virus software or invited to reread the organization's security policy. This network is typically deployed in a separate VLAN.

CSA

CSA was covered at a high level in Chapter 8. Take a look at Figure 8.5 of that chapter. You may recall that CSA sits between an application (malicious or not) and the operating system kernel. The question is what type of intelligence is in CSA, which is represented by the padlock in that figure. CSA comprises four interceptors, as follows:

▶ **File System Interceptor.** All file read/write requests are intercepted and permitted or denied based on the security policy.

▶ **Network Interceptor.** All network read/write requests (network connections) through the NDIS (Network Driver Interface Specification) driver are filtered through the security policy. DoS attacks can be stymied by limiting the number of connections that can be made in a specified period.

▶ **Configuration Interceptor.** Read/write requests to the Windows system registry or (in Unix) the run control (rc) files are cleared by the security policy.

▶ **Execution Space Interceptor.** This interceptor ensures that each application plays by the rules by only allowing write access to memory that is owned by that application. It also blocks the injection of arbitrary code in Dynamic Link Libraries (DLLs) and buffer overflows and maintains the integrity of dynamic resources such as memory and network I/O.

> **EXAM ALERT**
>
> Memorize these four CSA interceptors.

You may have guessed that the interceptors perform functions similar to some of the functions of HIPS and firewalls. Very intuitive! In fact, CSA's interceptors perform many functions, some of them complimentary. Table 9.2 lists the interceptors and how they correspond to certain high-level security applications

TABLE 9.2   CSA Interceptors and Corresponding Security Applications

Security Application	Interceptor Network	File System	Configuration	Execution Space
Distributed Firewall	Yes	No	No	No
Host Intrusion Detection	Yes	No	No	Yes
Application Sandbox	No	Yes	Yes	Yes
Network Worm Prevention	Yes	No	No	Yes
File Integrity Monitor	No	Yes	Yes	No

Endpoint Best Practices

As always, there is the classic tradeoff between usability and security. That said, assume the worst and design for the worst. A reasonable level of paranoia in operating system and application design is not only healthy but strongly encouraged.

Specifically for applications, consider the following best practices:

- Make security part of the design and not an afterthought.
- Follow the principle of least privilege.
- Modularize.
- Employ practices of secure programming.
- Use cryptography where practical against both inside and outside attacks.
- Assume data from outside sources is untrustworthy.
- Assume that your application users are malicious.

The following are best practices for operating systems:

- Consider using trusted operating systems for critical systems.
- Hardening of the operating system remains critical for sensitive environments.
- NAC firewalls are recommended to limit hosts' exposure.
- Other security add-ons are indicated, including integrity checkers and HIPS and host-based firewalls.

Exploring SAN Security

A Storage Area Network (SAN) is a fast and reliable network that provides access to internal and external storage resources. Typically, the intra-SAN traffic does not cross any of the cables of the production network and is usually deployed in its own IP subnet and VLAN for security and performance reasons. Storage devices are shared as peer resources amongst all network servers and are not owned by any one server. A well-designed SAN exemplifies the principle of separation of services.

SAN Advantages

There are three main benefits of SANs:

- Reduced capital and operating expenses.

▶ Flexibility and scalability as the business grows and application requirements change.

▶ Greater reach for replication and backups when compared with storage devices collocated with network servers.

SAN Technologies

There are three main SAN interconnection technologies, all based on the Small Computer Systems Interface (SCSI) communications model:

▶ **Fiber Channel.** This is SCSI over a network infrastructure and has these features:

    ▶ Used for host-to-SAN connections.

    ▶ Is the primary transport technology for SANs.

▶ **iSCSI (SCSI over TCP/IP).** This is SCSI using TCP/IP for transport and has these features:

    ▶ Used for host-to-SAN connections.

    ▶ Typically used for implementing SAN connectivity in a LAN environment.

▶ **FCIP (Fiber Channel over IP).** Used to communicate fiber channel commands over IP and to interconnect SANs:

    ▶ SAN-to-SAN connections.

    ▶ Typically used in a Metropolitan Area Network (MAN) or WAN.

> **EXAM ALERT**
>
> Understand which SAN technology is used for host-to-SAN and SAN-to-SAN connectivity.

SAN Address Vulnerabilities

There are two types of logical addresses implemented within a SAN:

▶ **Logical Unit Number (LUN):** A 64-bit field that SCSI uses to identify a logically addressable unit of a *target* within a SCSI device. This address can be masked through a process called LUN masking to hide physical or logical volumes from misbehaving servers but is considered unsecure because these addresses can be spoofed.

> **NOTE**
>
> In a SAN, iSCSI volumes will definitely be "targets." Ugly pun, but you'll remember the terminology now, right?

▶ **World Wide Names (WWN).** A 64-bit field used by Fiber Channel to uniquely identify each element on that fiber channel network. Zoning of the fiber switch fabric (similar to VLANs) can use WWNs to assign security permissions, but this is considered unsecure because WWNs are user-configurable. This zoning capability is only possible in a fiber-switched infrastructure and not a simple fiber channel.

Virtual SANs (VSANs)

Given the relative ease of spoofing both LUNs and WWNs, existing SAN technology cannot be trusted to separate the different SANs' data planes. With virtual SANs (VSANs):

▶ SAN traffic is isolated by hardware.

▶ A single switch can be configured with ports in multiple VSANs.

▶ Only ports in the same VSAN can communicate with each other.

▶ In a similar fashion to VLANs, a VSAN can span several switches because all the inter-switch traffic is tagged with the VSAN membership info.

> **NOTE**
>
> Cisco invented VSANs, although VSANs have since been adopted as an ANSI standard.

SAN Security Strategies

There are six areas to target in securing a SAN, as follows:

▶ **SAN Management Access.** Secure management services access.

▶ **Fabric Access.** Secure access of devices to fiber fabric service.

▶ **Target Access.** Secure access to LUNs and targets. Can be secured with zoning (see the next section).

▶ **IP Storage Access.** iSCSI and FCIP use IP for transport. Secure the underlying IP network. Can be secured with these features in Cisco IOS routers:

  ▶ IPSec VPNs when transiting public carriers.

  ▶ Hardware-accelerated encryption.

  ▶ Firewall filters.

▶ **SAN Protocol.** Secure FCIP, the switch-to-switch communication protocol.

▶ **Data Integrity and Confidentiality (Secrecy).** Secure data that crosses the network, as well as stored on volumes.

> **NOTE**
>
> iSCSI has many similarities to security features that we have examined in previous chapters:
> ▶ Fiber Channel zones are similar to ACLs.
> ▶ Fiber Channel VSANs are similar to VLANs.
> ▶ Fiber Channel port security is similar to 802.1X port-based authentication.

Zoning

The main strategy for securing access to SAN targets is zoning. We saw zoning a bit earlier in the context of using user-configurable WWNs to place SAN devices in different zones. This is the same idea, but a different context. In fact, zoning to assure target access security is probably most analogous to zones in the Zone-Based Policy Firewall (ZPF) that we introduced in Chapter 5, "Using Cisco IOS Firewalls to Implement a Network Security Policy."

There are two basic steps, as follows:

1. Associate physical ports on the SAN Fiber switch with VSANs (again, much like a VLAN).

2. Logically divide the VSANs into zones. Zones can be either soft or hard:

  ▶ **Soft Zoning.** The visibility of device IDs is restricted, although a server can still connect to a known target using its address.

  ▶ **Hard Zoning.** More secure than soft zoning. Access to SAN resources is physically controlled across the switch fabric. This is most commonly used.

Zoning is illustrated in Figure 9.4. Two VSANs are created inside a single physical topology, with each VSAN containing more than one zone. Disks and hosts can exist across multiple zones in a single VSAN but can never span VSANs.

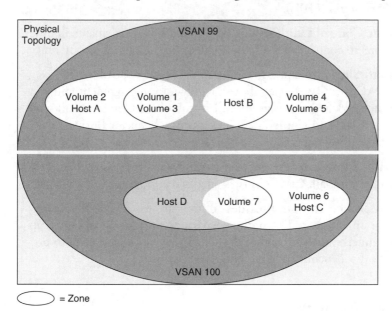

FIGURE 9.4 VSANs and zoning.

Exploring Voice Security

Given that VoIP is another application that uses an IP network, it is also fair to say that many of the best practices that we have discussed in previous chapters will be employed in securing a VoIP network. Before we look at methods of securing a VoIP network, we first look at some basic VoIP terminology. Only then can we examine specific vulnerabilities and the possible exploits that might be leveraged against those vulnerabilities.

VoIP Components

In order to understand VoIP security, you should first understand these basic VoIP components and concepts:

▶ **IP Phones.** Responsible for delivering voice over IP to the desktop.

▶ **Gatekeeper.** Like a traffic cop on a VoIP network. Provides Call Admission Control (CAC), bandwidth management and control, and network address translation.

▶ **Gateway.** Translates VoIP to PSTN and vice versa. A gateway also represents a physical connection point for an organization's local analog and digital voice devices (phones, fax machines, and so on) and Private Branch Exchanges (PBXs).

▶ **Multipoint Control Unit (MCU).** Allows multiple participants in different locations to connect to the same conference call or video conference.

▶ **Call Agent.** Similar to a proxy, acts as an agent for controlling IP phones, CAC (see Gatekeeper above), bandwidth management and control, and network address translation. Cisco Unified Communications Manager (UCM) and Unified Communications Manager Business Edition serve as call agents.

▶ **Application Servers.** These provide extra services such as unified messaging and voice mail. Cisco Unity is an application server.

▶ **Videoconference Station.** Provides an interface to videoconferencing services for an end user. The stations have a camera for video input capture and a microphone for audio, as well as screens and speakers to provide two-way videoconferencing with a remote user.

Common VoIP Protocols

Table 9.3 lists and defines some common VoIP protocols.

TABLE 9.3 Common VoIP Protocols

VoIP Protocol	Who Owns?	Where Used?
H.323	ITU	ITU standard, originally used for conferencing. Complex but flexible.
Media Gateway Control Protocol (MGCP)	IETF	Currently evolving standard that defines a method to control PSTN gateways or thin devices.
H.248 (Megaco)	IETF and ITU	Similar to MGCP but more flexibility over a wider range of vendor applications and gateways.
Session Initiation Protocol (SIP)	IETF	A complex protocol (but simpler than H.323), very similar to HTTP, which defines security, proxy, and transport services (TCP or UDP) for a VoIP call. Describes processes for setting up and tearing down calls. Works with: . Session Announcement Protocol (SAP) . Session Description Protocol (SDP)
Real-Time Transport Protocol (RTP)	IETF	Media-streaming protocol.

TABLE 9.3 Common VoIP Protocols *continued*

VoIP Protocol	Who Owns?	Where Used?
RTP Control Protocol (RTCP)	IETF	Provides flow control out-of-band for RTP.
Secure RTP (SRTP)	IETF	Provides for encryption of voice data as it leaves a voice device.
Skinny Client Control Protocol (SCCP)	Cisco	Proprietary. Used between Cisco UCM and Cisco IP phones.

EXAM ALERT

Memorize these terms, as they will likely be on the exam. Also, although all of these VoIP protocols have their own specific vulnerabilities, SIP has such a large (and growing) installed base that Cisco has chosen SIP alone as an example to analyze shortly in the subsection, "SIP Vulnerabilities."

Threats to VoIP Endpoints

Regardless of the VoIP protocol chosen, there are common threats to a VoIP network:

- ▶ **Reconnaissance.** Using commonly known reconnaissance techniques to discover the protocols that are being used for the VoIP implementation.

- ▶ **Spam over IP Telephony (SPIT).** Not a problem yet, but the fact that we are talking about it means that it might be a future threat. Traditional anti-spam measures (such as IronPort) will not be effective in dealing with this threat. That said, simple measures, such as implementing authentication and TLS (Transport Layer Security), would be effective tools to mitigate its threat.

- ▶ **DoS Attacks.** These fall into three general categories:

  - ▶ **Network resource overload.** Most commonly uses bandwidth overloading to make a network resource such as a VoIP phone or a call agent unavailable.

  - ▶ **Host resource starvation.** Using up host resources such that the host can no longer serve legitimate connection requests. A SYN flood is a good example.

  - ▶ **Out-of-bounds attacks.** The process of creating anomalous data packets with unexpected data that is outside the scope (or bounds) causing system crashes.

▶ **Eavesdropping.** The unauthorized interception of RTP media streams of VoIP packets for the purpose of accessing confidential information. Can be mitigated simply by using encryption.

▶ **Man-in-the-Middle Attacks.** Common man-in-the middle attacks such as those discussed in Chapter 1, "Network Insecurity," could prove to be effective.

Fraud

The two most common forms of fraud on VoIP networks are the following:

▶ **Vishing.** Phishing a VoIP network to attempt to compromise confidentiality.

▶ **Theft and Toll Fraud.** Fraudulently using VoIP services that do not belong to you.

These Cisco Unified Communications Manager (UCM) features can protect the VoIP network against fraud:

▶ **Partitioning.** Limit phone access to only certain parts of the dial plan.

▶ **Dial Plans.** Filter possibly exploitive phone numbers.

▶ **Forced Authorization Codes (FACs).** A feature in UCM that can track calls and prevent unauthorized calls in the first place.

SIP Vulnerabilities

As mentioned, all VoIP protocols have specific vulnerabilities. SIP is a good example of a protocol whose design did not include security, and as such is a poster child for examining securing VoIP protocols. SIP has very little integral security. It is a relatively immature protocol that is nevertheless seeing widespread adoption. There are three main vulnerabilities with the protocol, as follows:

▶ **Registration Hacking.** Hackers can intercept incoming calls and spoof the registration server, thus rerouting the calls through themselves. This is similar to an ICMP redirect (see Chapter 1).

▶ **Message Tampering.** Because the VoIP messages are carried in cleartext, it is relatively simple for a hacker to alter the VoIP packet contents traveling between SIP endpoints.

▶ **Session Tear-Down.** Allows a hacker to prematurely tear down an existing VoIP session. Similar to an RST attack employed in many IP DoS attacks.

These three main vulnerabilities can be mitigated using the techniques and technologies discussed in the next section, "Mitigating VoIP Hacking."

Mitigating VoIP Hacking

Although we have only (and briefly) examined specific SIP vulnerabilities, the following techniques can be used to secure any VoIP infrastructure regardless of the protocol employed and will be examined separately:

- ▶ Voice VLANs (VVLANs)
- ▶ Firewalls
- ▶ VPNs
- ▶ Correct VoIP Endpoint Configuration
- ▶ Correct VoIP Server Configuration

Voice VLANs (VVLANs)

Recall the concept of separating traffic into different planes. For example, the data plane should be kept separate from the management plane whenever possible. This same discussion holds true for VoIP too. If the VoIP traffic can be separated into a VLAN separate from the data VLAN, it would be much more difficult for a hacker to use a Man-in-the-Middle (MiM) attack or similar to eavesdrop, tamper with, or reconnoiter the VoIP traffic. Figure 9.5 illustrates using separate VLANs for voice and data. A VoIP phone is connected via an IEEE 802.1Q trunk to a Cisco Catalyst switch. A user's PC is connected to the VoIP phone via the supplied data jack. The switch port in which the VoIP phone is connected is set to trust the VoIP phone's tagging of its own Ethernet frames with the VLAN number of the Voice VLAN (VVLAN). Other frames, such as those from the PC connected to the VoIP phone, will be tagged for the data VLAN, keeping the data and voice planes separate. This has the further advantage of making Quality of Service (QoS) possible for the VoIP traffic because the VLAN tag makes it simple to identify and allows the QoS-aware switch to apply differentiated, possibly preferential, treatment to the VoIP traffic.

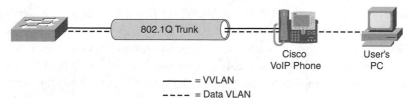

```
──── = VVLAN
- - - - = Data VLAN
```

FIGURE 9.5 Cisco VoIP phone trunked into switch.

Protect VoIP Networks with Firewalls

Firewalls such as the Cisco Adaptive Security Appliance (ASA) 5500 Series are an integral part in an overall VoIP security policy. Here are some of the features of Cisco firewalls that you can leverage on in order to increase the security of the VoIP implementation and mitigate some of the common threats that were previously outlined:

- ▶ **Standards Compliance.** Ensure that VoIP protocols are standard-compliant and that only SIP methods are sent to UCM.

- ▶ **Rate Limiting.** Rate limit SIP requests to prevent DoS attacks.

- ▶ **Enforce Call Policies.** Create an acceptable use policy of white lists, black lists, SIP URIs, and matching called/caller parties and enforce it.

- ▶ **Inspection.** Firewall dynamically opens TCP and UDP ports for Cisco applications by inspecting the VoIP sessions for this embedded information. Also enable the inspection of encrypted phone calls by the firewall.

- ▶ **Registration.** Permit only registered phones to make calls.

Protect VoIP Networks with VPNs

As we saw in Chapter 7, "Virtual Private Networks with IPsec," VPNs seem to be the magic bullet for many issues where network confidentiality, integrity, and authentication are required. For example, an IPsec VPN could be constructed for VoIP-only traffic between two IOS routers acting as gateways. To accomplish this, an ACL specifying which protocols, addresses, port numbers, and so on will be necessary to properly differentiate the VoIP traffic from other site-to-site flows. The use of ACLs and their application to an IPsec crypto map were discussed in Chapter 7. The ACLs that we used in Chapter 7 were not very granular, in that they specified site-to-site flows based solely on IP addresses. These were essentially layer 3-only filters. There are some drawbacks to using an IPsec VPN solution for VoIP, though. Cisco points out that the more specific filtering for which traffic should be transported inside an IPsec VPN (such as would be needed for VoIP flows) should only be used if necessary, because this more granular filtering is more CPU-intensive.

Another caveat in using IPsec VPNs with VoIP is in the area of quality of service (QoS). The VoIP endpoint or server will definitely map the bits in the ToS (Type of Service) byte of the IP header in attempt to express its requirement for QoS on the network. This process is called marking. The IPsec VPN solution must find a way to map these bits into the unencrypted IP packet header, such that QoS-aware devices that are intermediate to the VoIP devices can properly honor the QoS marking of VoIP systems, and thus preserve end-to-end QoS in the network, even over the VPN.

> **NOTE**
>
> Be careful when you implement VoIP inside a VPN across a large public network such as the Internet. QoS is impossible to maintain end-to-end over the Internet because we have no control over the routers that will be forwarding the packets. This makes VoIP over the Internet somewhat problematic since QoS is traditionally a big issue with VoIP in general. An optimum solution would be a VPN constructed over a service provider's network where the service provider is required to maintain a certain level of service as stipulated in a service level agreement (SLA).

Protect VoIP Networks with Correct Endpoint Configuration

Careful configuration of the VoIP telephone endpoints will go a long way to creating a secure VoIP network. Password protecting or disabling the ability to configure the device altogether by the user is a good first step. The following are other things you may consider:

- **Firmware.** Make sure that only firmware digitally signed by the manufacturer is installed on the devices. (Digital signatures and HMACs are covered in Chapter 6, "Introducing Cryptographic Services.")

- **Configuration files.** Use only signed configuration files.

- **Disable unnecessary features.** Disable the following features if they are not needed. (Remember the principle of least privileges.):

  - PC port
  - Setting button
  - Speakerphone
  - WWW access

Protect VoIP Networks with Correct Server Configuration

Using a Cisco solution that includes the Unified Communications Manager means that several security features will be built in, as follows:

- File system and OS applications are inaccessible.

- Only images digitally signed by Cisco are installable.

- The device follows best practices for hardening including:

  - Unused services are removed, and defaults such as usernames are disabled.
  - UCM is constantly improved over time as new threats are discovered.

- UCM logs security events.

- CSA is enabled on UCM by default.

Exam Prep Questions

1. Which is not one of the three prongs of the Cisco Host Security Strategy?

- ○ **A.** Endpoint protection
- ○ **B.** Cisco network admission control
- ○ **C.** Network infection containment
- ○ **D.** Comprehensive network security policy
- ○ **E.** Cisco routers

2. What are the two main software elements that must be secured in order that an endpoint proves its trustworthiness? (Choose one answer.)

- ○ **A.** Applications, operating system
- ○ **B.** Encrypted code, peer review
- ○ **C.** Cisco NAC, CSA
- ○ **D.** Anti-virus software, host firewall
- ○ **E.** None of the above.

3. Applications and operating systems are susceptible to DoS and access attacks in the same way that network devices are. What are some specific attacks that endpoints may be susceptible to?

- ○ **A.** Brute force attacks
- ○ **B.** Known cipher attacks
- ○ **C.** Buffer overflows
- ○ **D.** Worms, viruses, and Trojan horses
- ○ **E.** None of the above.

4. True or false. Worms are like microorganisms that invade a human host, attaching to other programs and executing unwanted functions on that host.

5. Put the five Ps of the phases of a worm attack in the correct order by putting the number indicating the correct order in the blank opposite the phase name.

Penetrate: ___

Propagate: ___

Persist: ___

Probe: ___

Paralyze: ___

6. Match the following descriptions of NAC components with the letter corresponding to its name from the list of choices.

   1. A device deployed in-band or out-of-band to perform network access control.

   2. Software that resides on a client endpoint and is queried to establish an endpoint's compliance with the network security policy.

   3. A GUI-based central administrative interface for IT security personnel.

   Choices:

   a. NAS

   b. NAM

   c. NAA

   d. NAD

   e. NAC

7. Cisco Security Agent (CSA) comprises four interceptors to intercept application calls to the operating system kernel. Fill in the blanks in the description of two of these interceptors with the choices from the list.

   The _____ interceptor ensures that each application plays by the rules by only allowing write access to memory that is owned by that application.

   The _____ interceptor intercepts read/write requests to the system registry or (in Unix) the run control (rc) files.

   Choices:

   a. Execution space

   b. Network

   c. File System

   d. Configuration

8. Which one of the following SAN interconnection technologies is used for SAN-to-SAN connectivity?

   ○ A. FCIP

   ○ B. iSCSI

   ○ C. Fiber Channel

   ○ D. None of the above.

9. Fiber Channel VSANs are most analogous to what security feature?

   ○ A. VLANs

   ○ B. ACLs

   ○ C. 802.1X

10. True or false. SPIT (SPAM over IP Telephony) is a very real and current threat for VoIP networks.

Answers to Exam Prep Questions

1. Answers D and E are the correct choices. Cisco's Host Security Strategy comprises endpoint protection using CSA, network admission control using NAC, and network infection containment.

2. The correct answer is A. Cisco has specific products to address application and operating system security. The other choices, while ostensibly software (and also good ideas!), do not represent the high-level answer that was being looked for.

3. The correct answers are C and D. Answers A and B are incorrect because these are attacks against cryptosystems and were explained in Chapter 6, "Introducing Cryptographic Services." They are deliberately misleading because the reader will recognize the terminology.

4. The correct answer is false. The definition provided is for a virus. Worms take their names from burrowing organisms that live in the "soil" of an infected host. The worm replicates into the memory of an infected host that, in turn, infects other computers.

5. The correct order is 1—Probe, 2—Penetrate, 3—Persist, 4—Propagate, and 5—Paralyze (a—2, b—4, c—3, d—1, e—5).

6. The correct answers are 1—a, 2—c, 3—b. Answers d and e do not match any of the descriptions. NAS stands for NAC Appliance Server. NAM stands for NAC Appliance Manager, and NAA stands for NAC Appliance Agent. A rule of thumb is that the GUI used to manage a single network device is called a "manager." For example, Cisco IPS appliances use the IPS Device Manager (IDM). Cisco IOS routers use the Cisco Security Device Manager (SDM). Thus, the GUI to manage a single NAC appliance is the NAC Appliance Manager (NAM).

7. The correct answers are a and d (in that order).

8. The correct answer is A. Fiber Channel over IP (FCIP) is used to interconnect SANs over an IP network. Choice B, iSCSI, is used for host-to-SAN connectivity over an IP network, whereas choice C, Fiber Channel, is a technology used in the fabric of a fiber SAN switch to connect hosts (such as application servers) to the SAN volumes.

9. The correct answer is A. Fiber channel zones are analogous to ACLs (answer B) and Fiber Channel port security is similar to 802.1X port-based authentication (answer C).

10. False. SPIT is an emerging threat, but not one that has been seen in the wild as yet. It serves most to underline that as the technology evolves, so do the attack methods.

CHAPTER TEN

Protecting Switch Infrastructure

Terms You'll Need to Understand:

✓ Virtual LAN (VLAN) hopping

✓ Rogue trunks

✓ Double-tagging

✓ Bridge Protocol Data Unit (BPDU)

✓ Root guard

✓ Port security

✓ Switched Port Analyzer (SPAN)

✓ Storm control

Exam Topic Covered in This Chapter:

✓ Describe how to prevent layer 2 attacks by configuring basic Catalyst switch security features

> **NOTE**
>
> These exam topics are from cisco.com. Check there periodically for the latest exam topics and info.

Why worry about layer 2 security? After all, if an attacker can access our Ethernet switch, the enemy is already among us, right? Besides being defeatist, this attitude almost certainly results in laxness of security in one of the most vulnerable parts of our network: inside the perimeter. The most obvious reason for switch security is the domino effect; or, risking another metaphor, a chain is only as strong as its weakest link. Security is that chain. If switch security is lax, it stands to reason that because layer 2 of the OSI model supports all the other layers where we have already deployed mitigation techniques, these efforts can be rendered useless by this weak link. This chapter examines some common layer 2 attacks and then looks at ways that they can be mitigated, if not eliminated.

VLAN Hopping Attacks

EXAM ALERT

Be sure to review basic virtual LAN (VLAN) and IEEE 802.1Q trunk configuration and operation from the prerequisite CCNA material.

VLAN hopping attacks occur when an attacker tricks a switch into allowing traffic to hop to a different VLAN than the VLAN assigned to the port to which they are connected. Normally, routers are required to route traffic between VLANs at layer 3.

NOTE

Recall "router-on-a-stick" and inter-VLAN routing from your CCNA studies. For traffic to move between VLANs, it needs to be routed either by a router integral to the switch, or by an external router attached to the switch by a trunk port. When diagramming the latter scenario, the router appears connected to the switch by a stick, hence the term "router-on-a-stick." VLAN hopping attacks break this rule, and trick the switch to allow traffic that arrives on a switch port to hop to a different VLAN without involving a router.

Allowing traffic to hop to a different VLAN is very dangerous; if an attacker can fool the switch into revealing traffic from another VLAN, sensitive information carried in cleartext, such as passwords, may be obtained. For example, an attacker might be able to hop into the management VLAN, a mission-critical traffic plane whose use we first examined in Figure 4-1, our reference network diagram in Chapter 4, "Implementing Secure Management and Hardening the Router."

This is ironic because, according to Cisco, the three main advantages of VLANS are as follows:

▶ Segmentation

▶ Flexibility

▶ Security

The first and third points are related. By segmenting a network into different virtual broadcast domains, security is achieved; under normal operations, a user connected to a switch port is able to see only the following traffic and only in their VLAN:

- **Unicast traffic:** These are frames destined to the user's PC.

- **Flooded traffic:** These are frames that are forwarded out all but the originating interface and consist of the following:

  - Unknown unicast frames

  - Majority of multicast frames

  - Broadcast frames

We examine two common VLAN hopping attacks, as follows:

- VLAN hopping by rogue trunk

- VLAN hopping by double tagging

VLAN Hopping by Rogue Trunk

VLAN hopping by rogue trunk is one of the simplest attacks to explain and also one of the simplest to mitigate. A rogue trunk (like a rogue access point) is where an attacker sets up an unauthorized trunk on the switch port to which they are connected. Trunks (either Cisco ISL or IEEE 802.1Q) carry traffic from all VLANs by default. Add to this the fact that Cisco switch ports will auto-negotiate trunking, and you have a problem. Here is how such an attack might be performed:

1. An attacker needs just to trick the switch into negotiating a trunk by using the signaling protocol for automatic trunk negotiation, Dynamic Trunking Protocol (DTP). The attacker connects a rogue switch to an unused switch port and spoofs DTP messages to automatically negotiate and thus turn on trunking between the rogue switch and the victim switch.

2. The attacker can now send traffic into the network tagged with the VLAN ID of a VLAN that has been learned from the trunk.

VLAN Hopping by Rogue Trunk Attack Mitigation

Attack mitigation is simple:

- Turn off trunking on ports unless they specifically need it:

```
Catalyst1(config-if)#switchport mode access
```

▶ Disable DTP on the remaining ports that require trunking and manually enable trunking on them:

```
Catalyst1(config-if)#switchport mode trunk
Catalyst1(config-if)#switchport nonegotiate
```

VLAN Hopping by Double-Tagging

This is sometimes also called a *double encapsulation attack*. This type of attack leverages how the switch hardware works. Figure 10.1 illustrates the attack. When most switches receive a frame with 802.1Q encapsulation (indicated by its Ethertype), they unencapsulate them only once, assuming (correctly) that normally 802.1Q frames have only one frame tag in them.

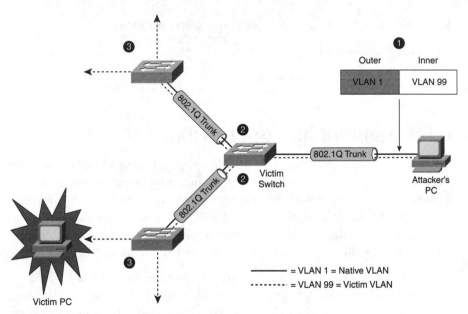

FIGURE 10.1 VLAN hopping by double-tagging.

The following is a detailed explanation of the numbered steps in Figure 10-1:

1. Knowing that the switch will only unencapsulate 802.1Q frames once, the attacker will send broadcast or unicast traffic into the switch, hiding a tagged 802.1Q frame inside another tagged 802.1Q frame. For example, VLAN 99 might be hidden inside VLAN 1. There is some guesswork involved in this attack; once the outer 802.1Q frame has been stripped of its tag, the inner frame will only travel in a trunk (to another switch) whose native VLAN is the same as the VLAN tag of the outer 802.1Q frame.

2. Because this native VLAN traffic is not tagged (per the 802.1Q protocol), the inner frame is transmitted in trunks to neighbor switches of the victim switch.

3. All the victim switch's neighbors see is an 802.1Q frame tagged with VLAN 99, and they do what switches do: They examine the VLAN tag, and if the frame is a broadcast, it is flooded to all ports and trunks in that VLAN. If the frame is a unicast, and the entry is in the switch's Content Addressable Memory (CAM) table, it is forwarded just to the port where the victim host is connected. (Figure 10-1 illustrates what happens when an unknown unicast is flooded.)

> **NOTE**
>
> Both types of VLAN hopping attacks are only possible when the switch's ports are misconfigured.

VLAN Hopping by Double-Tagging Attack Mitigation

A double-tagging VLAN hopping attack is unidirectional and works only if the attacker and the trunk port(s) are in the same native VLAN. The best way to prevent this type of attack is to make sure that the native VLAN of the trunked ports is different than any of the users' ports (VLAN 10, for example):

```
Catalyst1(config-if)switchport trunk native vlan 10
```

STP Manipulation Attack

> **EXAM ALERT**
>
> Stop! If you are unfamiliar with spanning tree protocol (STP) operation, now is the time for you to review the subject from the CCNA prerequisite material. Pay particular attention to the role of the root bridge in spanning tree, as well as the role that Bridge Protocol Data Units (BPDUs) play in electing the root bridge.

In an STP manipulation attack, an attacker connects to a switch port and either directly themselves, or through the use of a rogue switch, attempts to manipulate Spanning Tree Protocol (STP) parameters to become the root bridge. Because the root bridge is responsible for calculating the spanning tree from topology changes advertised by non-root bridges, attackers see a variety of frames that they would normally not see.

To perform this attack, the attacker needs only to inject BPDU frames with a Bridge ID (BID) that is lower than the current root bridge into the network. Recall that the BID is made up of a 16-bit Bridge Priority + 48-bit MAC address. If the attacker selects a bridge priority (range 0–65535) that is lower than the existing root bridge, they will become root. The default priority for a Cisco Catalyst switch is 32768. The attacker could simply guess this, or they could find out what the priority is for the STP root bridge by using a protocol analyzer on a switch port, recognizing that such multicast traffic is flooded by the switch.

> **NOTE**
>
> You might have heard about another spanning tree protocol called Per VLAN Spanning Tree Plus (PVST+). One of the features of PVST+ is its ability to elect a different root bridge per VLAN. Its use is very common in large switched networks with multiple VLANs.
>
> With PVST+, the first 16 bits of the bridge ID have been remapped to include the VLAN ID and other information. Thus, not all 16 bits are used to define the bridge priority. The attacker could learn what type of bridge ID is being used by using a protocol analyzer on a switch port and examining the BPDUs. Then, they need to only inject frames with the more attractive bridge ID per the protocol used in an attempt to become the root bridge.

There are three features that can be used together or separately to mitigate STP manipulation attacks. (They are most effective when used together.) These features are as follows:

1. The Portfast feature, which disables spanning tree on a port.

2. The BPDU guard feature, which guards against learning erroneous STP information on a port.

3. The Root guard feature, which explicitly disables root bridge election on a port.

STP Manipulation Attack Mitigation: Portfast

An important first step to mitigate this type of attack is to ensure that the attacker can only guess information about the network topology and can't directly read it. For example, any port that is not participating in the STP calculation can be put in *portfast* mode. This prevents the switch from putting that interface in blocking mode.

EXAM ALERT

Be very sure that this switch port is not part of a topological loop before you put it in portfast mode. Portfast means that you think you are smarter than STP, which unfortunately (for many of us) is not the case!

This command enables portfast globally on all non-trunking ports:

```
Catalyst1(config)#spanning-tree portfast default
```

If you want to turn on portfast selectively on an interface, use this command:

```
Catalyst1(config-if)#spanning-tree portfast
```

STP Manipulation Attack Mitigation: BPDU Guard

As a second step toward mitigating an STP attack, consider setting up BPDU guard on an interface. With BPDU guard enabled, an interface can be put into a blocking state when it receives a BPDU. This seems a bit severe, like cutting your nose off to spite your face, but remember that any security policy is a balance between usability and security. With BPDU guard enabled, an attacker will be unable to force root bridge election because the BPDU will be refused on the port that they are connected to. It is also used to enforce the boundaries of the spanning tree, recognizing that typically it is only in parts of a network where loop-causing redundancies might be deployed.

To enable BPDU guard globally on all ports where portfast is enabled, use the following command:

```
Catalyst1(config)#spanning-tree portfast bpduguard default
```

Intuitively, BPDU guard complements portfast and can only be enabled on ports where portfast has been enabled in any case. To verify BPDU guard, use the following command:

```
Catalyst1#show spanning-tree summary
Switch is in pvst mode
Root bridge for: VLAN0001-VLAN0002, VLAN0010
Extended system ID          is enabled
Portfast Default            is enabled
PortFast BPDU Guard Default is enabled
Portfast BPDU Filter Default is disabled
Loopguard Default           is disabled
EtherChannel misconfig guard is enabled
```

```
UplinkFast                   is disabled
BackboneFast                 is disabled
Configured Pathcost method used is short
```

Name	Blocking	Listening	Learning	Forwarding	STP Active
VLAN0001	0	0	0	8	8
VLAN0002	0	0	0	12	12
VLAN0010	0	0	0	10	10
3 vlans	0	0	0	30	30

The preceding command output indicates that portfast and BPDU guard are enabled on that switch.

STP Manipulation Attack Mitigation: Root Guard

The third step is to enable the root guard feature. The root guard feature is enabled on a per-interface basis. If enabled, the switch will examine any received BPDU on that interface and compare it with the current root bridge. If the BID is superior to that of the current root bridge, the port is moved to a root-inconsistent state (effectively a listening state) and ceases to pass traffic. This effectively mitigates an STP attack. When the superior BPDUs cease, the port transitions back to a normal mode. Here is the command to enable root guard on an interface:

```
Catalyst1(config-if)#spanning-tree guard root
```

CAM Table Overflow Attack

A switch's Content Addressable Memory (CAM) table contains MAC addresses that can be reached, organized by the port where they have been learned, as well as the associated VLAN ID. The CAM table can hold a finite number of entries depending on switch model. For example, many 2900 series Catalyst switches are designed to contain as many as 4,096 entries, whereas higher-end switches such as the 6500 series Catalyst switches can contain many tens of thousands of entries. Switches learn these MAC addresses by analyzing the source address of Ethernet frames that arrive on a particular port.

A CAM table overflow attack leverages this simple process by injecting thousands of frames with bogus source MAC addresses on a single port. An example of such a utility is *macof*. When the CAM table reaches capacity with these bogus MAC addresses, older, legitimate MAC addresses are pushed out of the CAM table.

Subsequent frames whose destination address is the MAC address of a legitimate host are flooded out all of the switch's ports as with any unknown unicast traffic. Attackers, listening on any port, will be able to capture a flood of traffic that they would not normally see. For example, frames encapsulating sensitive traffic that are destined to a network server might be visible by the attacker.

CAM Table Overflow Attack Mitigation: Port Security

This type of attack can be mitigated by configuring port security. Port security is explained in the "Configuring Port Security" section to follow.

> **NOTE**
>
> Arguably, you could configure port security to statically hard code the MAC addresses permitted on each switch port, but such a solution would be unmanageable and unscalable.

MAC Address Spoofing Attack

In a MAC address spoofing attack, an attacker injects frames into a switch port with the source address of a known host. Assuming that the spoofed host is not transmitting, this causes the switch to send frames that would normally be destined to the spoofed host's switch port to the attacker's switch port instead. Again, the attacker is leveraging the switch's learning process.

MAC Address Spoofing Attack Mitigation: Port Security

This attack also can be mitigated with port security. Port security is explained in the following "Configuring Port Security" section.

Configuring Port Security

Essentially, port security enables you to configure a switch port to allow specific statically-assigned MAC addresses or to set a maximum for the number of MAC addresses learned on that port. For example, setting a finite number of MAC addresses that can be learned on a port would effectively mitigate a MAC address spoofing attack. As another example, a CAM table overflow attack could be mitigated by using port security to define specific MAC addresses that can be reached by a specific port, thus limiting the scope of flooding of unknown uni-cast traffic. Furthermore, port security can be tuned as to what action will be performed when that maximum has been reached or when a MAC address does-n't match the statically assigned MAC address(es).

The switch could be configured to

▶ Send an alert to the console or a logging server.

▶ Simply not accept the violating frame.

▶ Shut down the port altogether.

▶ Perform a combination of these actions.

NOTE

Cisco recommends that a port be shut down when a violation occurs because it will prob-ably be eventually disabled anyway if an attack creates too much load.

Also, port security cannot be configured on trunk ports because it is only appropriate on access ports.

Port Security Basic Settings

Because port security is only applicable to access ports (and not trunks), you need to enable a port for access mode. Use this interface command:

```
Catalyst1(config-if)#switchport mode access
```

To enable port security on a port, use this command:

```
Catalyst1(config-if)#switchport port-security
```

Port Security Optional Settings

By default, when you enable port security on a Catalyst switch port, it will learn a maximum of 132 secure MAC addresses; the violation mode (that is, the action it will take if there is a violation) is to send an alert. The following optional set-tings tune the configuration.

EXAM ALERT

If you are asked in the exam what the port security defaults are for a Catalyst switch port, the right answer is that a maximum of 132 secure MAC addresses are learned on a switch port. In reality, the default for the maximum number of secure MAC addresses is dependent on the model of the switch. For example, a Catalyst 2960 defaults to a maximum of one secure MAC address when port security is enabled on a port.

To set a maximum number of MAC addresses that can be learned on a port, use the **switchport port-security maximum** command. For example, the following command allows a maximum of 32 addresses to be learned on a port:

```
Catalyst1(config-if)#switchport port-security maximum 32
```

To set the violation mode for the port, use this command:

```
switchport port-security violation {protect | restrict | shutdown |
shutdown vlan}
```

The following is a detailed explanation of the command's syntax:

> ▶ **protect:** When the maximum number of secure MAC addresses configured on a port is reached, subsequent frames are silently dropped (that is, no notification) until the number of MAC addresses learned falls back below the maximum.

> ▶ **restrict:** Same as protect, except a notification of the violation is sent. If you have Simple Network Management Protocol (SNMP) set up, a trap is sent to the SNMP Network Management Station (NMS). If syslog is set up, a syslog message is logged. The violation counter is also incremented.

> ▶ **shutdown:** This setting will shut down the port on which the violation occurred. The port is put in an error-disabled state and the port LED is extinguished. It also sends an SNMP trap and/or syslog message per the restrict option.

> ▶ **shutdown vlan:** Same as shutdown, but the switch port will only be put in an error-disabled state for the VLAN in which the violation occurred.

In this example, the switch's port will be error-disabled for frames for VLAN 5 if there has been a violation in that VLAN:

```
Catalyst1(config-if)#switchport port-security violation shutdown vlan 5
```

Port security can be configured to allow only specified MAC addresses to use a port. The **switchport port-security mac-address** command needs to be entered for every secure MAC address; for example:

```
Catalyst1(config-if)#switchport port-security mac-address 0013.b638.8567
```

Sticky learning means that designated MAC addresses learned on a switch port can be configured to age out more slowly than other dynamically learned entries. They are harder to get rid of; thus, they are sticky. To enable sticky learning of secure MAC addresses on a port, you can use this command:

```
Catalyst1(config-if)#switchport port-security mac-address sticky
```

In this manner, the secure MAC addresses are designated as sticky; thus, they remain in the running configuration on the switch.

You also can define how long the secure addresses that are learned on a switch port stay in the CAM table. The command to configure this is the **switchport port-security aging** command:

```
switchport port-security aging {static ¦ time time ¦ type {absolute ¦
inactivity}}
```

The command options are as follows:

- ▶ **static:** Enables aging for static secure MAC addresses on this port.

- ▶ **time:** Specifies the aging time for this port (0 to 1,440 minutes). If set to 0, aging is disabled.

- ▶ **type absolute:** Sets the aging type to absolute. After the time specified expires, all secure MAC addresses are removed from the secure address list.

- ▶ **type inactivity:** Sets the aging type to inactivity. After the time specified expires, all secure MAC addresses are removed from the secure address list.

For example, if you wanted secure MAC addresses to age out of the CAM table after 100 minutes of inactivity, you could type this command:

```
Catalyst1(config-if)#switchport port-security aging time 100
Catalyst1(config-if)#switchport port-security aging type inactivity
```

Port Security Verification

To verify port security, you can use the **show port-security** command or the **show port-security interface** *interface-id* command. Here are some examples of the output of these commands:

```
Catalyst1#show port-security
Secure Port  MaxSecureAddr  CurrentAddr  SecurityViolation  Security Action
             (Count)        (Count)      (Count)
   Gig0/1         32            29              0             Shutdown
------------------------------------------------------------------------
Total Addresses in System (excluding one mac per port)   : 0
Max Addresses limit in System (excluding one mac per port) : 6272

Catalyst1#show port-security interface gigabitEthernet 0/1
Port Security              : Enabled
Port Status                : Secure-down
Violation Mode             : Shutdown
Aging Time                 : 100 mins
Aging Type                 : Inactivity
SecureStatic Address Aging : Disabled
Maximum MAC Addresses      : 32
Total MAC Addresses        : 29
Configured MAC Addresses   : 0
Sticky MAC Addresses       : 0
Last Source Address:Vlan   : 0000.0000.0000:0
Security Violation Count   : 0
```

In the output of the **show port-security** command, port security is enabled on port Gig0/1 with a maximum MAC address count of 32. There have been 29 MAC addresses learned on the port, and there have been no violations. The aging time (we set this previously) is set to 100 minutes, and the aging type is inactivity.

The output of the **show port-security interface gigabitEthernet 0/1** command indicates that a policy violation has occurred because the port has been placed in a *secure-down* status.

EXAM ALERT

A port that is in an *err-disabled* state is one that has been disabled due to a port security violation. There are two ways to bring a port out of the *err-disabled* state, as follows:

► Enter the **errdisable recovery cause psecure-violation** command in global configuration.

► Alternatively, you can manually re-enable the specific port by toggling it with the **shutdown** and **no shutdown** interface configuration commands.

To view all the secure MAC addresses on all interfaces, you can use the **show port-security address** command. If you want to see the secure MAC addresses learned on one specific interface, you can use the **show port-security interface** *interface-id* **address** form of the command. Both forms of the command also show you the aging information for each address. Here's an example:

```
Catalyst1#show port-security address
          Secure Mac Address Table
-----------------------------------------------------------------------

Vlan    Mac Address     Type                Ports     Remaining Age
                                                         (mins)
----    -----------     ----                -----     -------------
 10     0000.e3fd.39ca  SecureConfigured    Gig0/1         99

-----------------------------------------------------------------------
Total Addresses in System (excluding one mac per port)     : 0
Max Addresses limit in System (excluding one mac per port) : 6272
```

In the example, port GigE0/1 is in VLAN 10 and has a secured MAC address of 0000.e3fd.39ca. The device with that MAC address can use port GigE0/1, and there is a remaining age of 99 minutes for that entry.

Miscellaneous Switch Security Features

Following is a high-level discussion of some additional switch security features that can be used by themselves or in conjunction with the mitigation techniques previously examined

Intrusion Notification

In some situations, you might want to configure the switch to send a notification to an SNMP NMS when MAC addresses are learned by the system or deleted from the CAM table. An example of where this might be used could be a switch that is deployed in a particularly restrictive security zone in the network, like an R&D lab or a DMZ, and where you want to determine if there is anomalous MAC address learning behavior in that part of the network. The following command enables this feature:

```
Catalyst1(config)#mac-address-table notification
```

Only dynamic and secure MAC addresses generate a MAC address notification. Traps are not sent for self, multicast, or other static addresses.

> **NOTE**
>
> Use the **mac-address-table notification** command with caution. It can generate a lot of traffic to the NMS. You might consider changing the interval at which alerts are sent to the NMS by using the following format of the command:
>
> ```
> Catalyst1(config)#mac-address-table notification interval 120
> ```
>
> In this example, the interval at which events are trapped to the NMS server has been set to 120 seconds.

Switched Port Analyzer (SPAN)

Chapter 8, "Network Security Using Cisco IOS IPS," discusses how an IDS should be deployed in the network in such a way that it will see all the traffic in a particular part of the network. If it doesn't see all the traffic, its effectiveness as an IDS is questionable at best. Referring to Figure 10.2, if an organization's perimeter router is connected to an ISP router via a switch, an IDS deployed on a single switch port would normally see only flooded traffic, namely unknown unicasts, broadcasts, and multicasts. It would not see the majority of ingress and egress traffic in and out of the organization's network, rendering it ineffective.

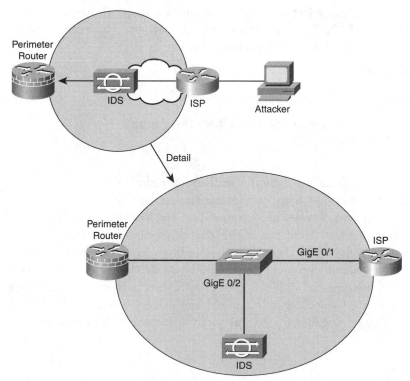

FIGURE 10.2 SPAN in action.

A way must be found to replicate the traffic that hits the GigE 0/1 interface to the GigE 0/2 interface where the IDS resides. This is the idea behind SPAN. The destination port (GigE 0/2, in our example) is dedicated to monitor the activity on another port or VLAN. SPAN can copy traffic sent or received. The port dedicated for SPAN use does not receive or forward any other traffic than that which is required for SPAN use. This type of port monitoring is often called port mirroring. SPAN does not affect switch operation.

The following are the commands to create a monitoring session, number 1, which mirrors traffic from gigabitEthernet 0/1 to gigabitEthernet 0/2. The **encapsulation replicate** part of the second command preserves the encapsulation method of the monitored port. For example, if the mirrored port is an IEEE 802.1Q trunk, the port that the frames are replicated to will see copies of tagged VLAN traffic and native VLAN traffic.

```
Catalyst1(config)# monitor session 1 source interface gigabitEthernet0/1
Catalyst1(config)# monitor session 1 destination interface
gigabitEthernet0/2 encapsulation replicate
```

Storm Control

Broadcast storms are not just a product of topological loops. If they were, then spanning tree would be the sole requirement for mitigating broadcast storms. Broadcast storms can also result from the following:

- ▶ DoS attacks

- ▶ Poorly-designed, chatty applications

- ▶ Protocols that rely heavily on broadcasts (for example, NetBIOS, AppleTalk, and Novell)

Storm control is essentially a method of traffic suppression. A threshold is set for the number of incoming broadcast, multicast, and unicast frames that are allowed on each port. Frames are counted in a one-second interval, and the switch blocks broadcasts that rise above that threshold within that interval. Control frames such as BPDUs are exempt, but other, necessary traffic, such as frames that carry routing protocol packets, may be discarded. It is good practice to understand the type and disposition of protocol traffic that may arrive on a specific switch interface before setting these thresholds; weighing the likelihood of attack on that port against the criticality of traffic that needs to flow for normal operation.

EXAM ALERT

Remember that storm control is configured on an interface and not globally.

In the end, storm control only treats the symptoms and not the cause of broadcasts if the problem is simply poor design. A network should be designed to limit the amount of broadcast and multicast traffic.

To enable storm control, use the following interface configuration command:

```
Catalyst1(config-if)#storm-control
```

You can then specify a traffic suppression level for the type of traffic in a variety of different ways:

▸ Percentage (up to two decimal places of accuracy) of total bandwidth on the port

▸ Rate in packets per second (pps)

▸ Rate in bits per second

To verify the storm control that has been configured on a particular interface, you might choose to use the following command:

```
Catalyst1(config-if)#do show running-config interface GigabitEthernet0/1
Building configuration...

Current configuration : 271 bytes
!
interface GigabitEthernet0/1
 storm-control broadcast level 62.50
 storm-control multicast level pps 3k 2k
 storm-control unicast level bps 50m 25m
 storm-control action shutdown
end
```

In the previous CLI example

▸ Broadcast traffic is limited to no more than 62.5% of total bandwidth on the port, and traffic exceeding this threshold is blocked until it falls back to 62.5% (see the following note).

▸ Multicast traffic is limited to no more than 3,000 packets per second on a rising threshold and continues to be blocked until the number of multicast packets per second drops to the falling threshold of 2,000.

▶ Unicast traffic is limited to no more than 50 Mbps on a rising threshold and continues to be blocked until the falling threshold of 25 Mbps is reached.

▶ The port is shut down if any of these thresholds is exceeded.

NOTE

If you define the threshold in pps or bps (as in this example of the **storm-control** command), you can use **k**, **m**, or **g** to specify thousand, millions, and billions of packets per second or bits per second respectively.

If a falling threshold is not specified (2k pps for multicasts and 25m bps for unicasts in this example), the traffic will be blocked until the traffic falls below the rising threshold.

For the action in the **storm-control** command, you can also specify the option **trap**, which sends an SNMP alert to the NMS when a storm occurs.

Switch Security Best Practices

Cisco makes the following recommendations for switch security best practices:

▶ **Secure management:** Think security for switch management. Use SSH, a dedicated management VLAN, OOB, and so on as much as possible.

▶ **Native VLAN:** Always use a dedicated VLAN ID for trunk ports and avoid using VLAN 1 at all.

▶ **User ports:** Non-trunking. (Cisco VoIP phones being the exception. See Chapter 9, "Introduction to Endpoint, SAN, and Voice Security.")

▶ **Port security:** Use for access ports whenever possible.

▶ **SNMP:** Limit to the management VLAN if possible and treat community strings like superuser passwords. (See Chapter 4, "Implementing Secure Management and Hardening the Router," for more information.)

▶ **STP attacks:** Use BPDU guard and root guard.

▶ **CDP:** Only use if necessary. CDP should be left on for switch ports connected to VoIP phones. An attacker can learn much from CDP advertisements.

▶ **Unused ports:** Disable and put them in an unused VLAN for extra security.

Exam Prep Questions

1. Examine the following partial switch configuration and choose all the statements that correctly describe what is being accomplished.

```
interface GigabitEthernet0/1
 storm-control broadcast level 62.50
 storm-control multicast level pps 3k 2k
 storm-control unicast level bps 50m 25m
 storm-control action shutdown
```

- ○ **A.** When the level of broadcasts has reached 62.5% of total traffic, the multicasts will be limited to 3,000 packets per second (pps) and unicast traffic will be limited to 50 Mbps.

- ○ **B.** Broadcast traffic will be allowed up to 62.5% of total bandwidth on the interface. When this is exceeded, frames will be discarded until the broadcast traffic falls back below that level.

- ○ **C.** Multicast traffic will be discarded above 3,000 packets per second (pps) on this port, and will only start being forwarded again after it has fallen below the 2,000 pps lower threshold.

- ○ **D.** Unicast traffic will be discarded above 50 Mbps on this port, and will only start being forwarded again after it has fallen below the 25 Mbps lower threshold.

- ○ **E.** A shutdown notification message will be sent to the SNMP NMS when all of the three configured thresholds (broadcast, multicast, and unicast) have been reached.

2. True or false. A CAM table overflow attack is an attack whereby the attacker injects frames into a switch port with the source address of a known station. This is done in an attempt to fool the switch into forwarding frames that are supposed to go to the known station to the attacker's switch port instead.

3. Which statements best describe the effect or application of the following interface configuration command? (Choose all that apply.)

```
Catalyst1(config-if)#spanning-tree portfast
```

- ○ **A.** BPDU guard is enabled, ensuring that the switch will refuse BPDUs on this port.

- ○ **B.** Root guard is enabled, ensuring that the switch will refuse root bridge BPDUs that have a superior Bridge ID (BID) to the current root bridge.

- ○ **C.** The port immediately transitions to a forwarding state when a link is established, bypassing spanning tree blocking mode.

    ○ **D.** The assumption is that there is no possibility of topological loops on this port as this command will prevent the root bridge from blocking on this port.

    ○ **E.** None of the above.

4. True or false. The **switchport port-security** interface configuration command cannot be used on a trunk port.

5. What are the two methods for bringing a port out of the *err-disabled* state?

    ○ **A.** Enter the **errdisable recovery cause psecure-violation** command in global configuration.

    ○ **B.** Enter the **recover-lockout enable** command in global configuration.

    ○ **C.** Enter the **shutdown** and **no shutdown** commands in order in interface configuration mode on the affected port.

    ○ **D.** Enter the **no port-shutdown sticky-learn** command in interface configuration mode on the affected port.

    ○ **E.** None of the above.

6. True or false. The switched port analyzer (SPAN) feature on Cisco Catalyst switches can be configured to copy all the traffic only from a specific VLAN to a dedicated monitoring port.

Answers to Exam Prep Questions

1. The correct answers are b, c, and d. Answer a is incorrect because the thresholds for multicast and unicast traffic are independent of one another. Answer e is incorrect because the **action shutdown** command will shut down the port if any of the configured thresholds have been reached.

2. False. The attack described is a MAC address spoofing attack. A CAM table overflow attack sends many frames into a switch port with various source MAC addresses in an attempt to overflow the CAM table and make the switch act like a hub for subsequent frames; this floods frames out all ports, including the one that the attacker is connected to.

3. Answers c and d are correct. A and b are incorrect because, though the descriptions are accurate, BPDU guard and root guard are enabled with different commands.

4. True. The **switchport port-security** command can only be used on an access port. Access ports are used for endpoint connectivity.

5. Answers a and c are correct. Answers b and d are non-existent commands.

6. False. SPAN can copy (replicate) traffic from specific ports as well as VLANs to a dedicated monitoring port. It is very useful when certain flows through the switch need to be monitored for signs of intrusion and other purposes.

PART V

Practice Exams and Answers

Practice Exam 1

Hints and Pointers

If you are preparing for the CCNA Security exam, you already have your CCNA certification, which means you are already an expert at Cisco exams, right? Possibly, but don't be over-confident. The CCNA Security is most definitely a big step, and although it leverages your basic network knowledge of the CCNA certification, it also introduces new ways of looking at topics that just may force you to go back and re-study large sections of the prerequisite CCNA material. That is why I have included tips throughout the book of CCNA areas that are particularly important to brush up on.

These practice exam questions have been created by the author and reviewed by Cisco technical experts. They are representative of (and possibly a little bit harder than) the questions that you will see in the real exam.

The following are general tips for using the two practice exams in this book:

▶ **Time yourself:** Each sample exam is 50 questions. Try to stay within a 60-minute time limit for each exam.

▶ **Find a quiet place:** You need a place free of distractions to attempt the sample exams. I find a public library is often the best place. Equip yourself with only a notepad and pen, just like the real exam. Oh, and turn off your personal communication device when you're taking the exam!

▶ **Practice data dumping:** The Cram Sheet at the beginning of this Exam Cram is meant to represent the kind of arcane but important information that is hard to retain. Practice dumping this information from your brain onto the aforementioned notepad just before you sit down to attempt the practice exam.

▶ **Don't get beached on a single question:** If you don't know the answer for a question, then choose an answer anyway, recognizing that you don't get marked down for a wrong answer and that you get no points at all for one that you do not attempt. Take note of the question that stumped you and be prepared to drill down on that topic area later.

▶ **Don't be overconfident:** If you take the practice exam and ace it, you're probably ready for the real thing. That said, although these practice exam questions are meant to represent the real exam to the best of this author's knowledge, you owe it to yourself to at least read every chapter in its entirety to obtain the complete context for every topic area. Use the exams to identify topics you struggle with consistently and brush up on them.

▶ **Practice, practice, practice:** Keep on taking the practice exams until you obtain a perfect score on both of them. Book your exam appointment. You're ready!

So in the end, I have these pieces of advice: Study hard and practice, practice, practice!

I wish you good luck, too. But remember, sometimes you have to be good to be lucky.

—Eric Stewart

Practice Exam #1

1. You are a decision maker in formulating your organization's comprehensive network security policy. You accept that some tradeoffs will be required when implementing the policy but you are also smart enough to make some assumptions that will aid your decisions as to which tradeoffs are acceptable and which are not. Which of the following assumptions are true?

   ○ **A.** Openness is often traded off against security.

   ○ **B.** Insider attacks are less damaging than external attacks.

   ○ **C.** Insider attacks often render technical security solutions ineffective.

   ○ **D.** Vendors' recommendations for hardening a system should be ignored because they are usually incorrect.

   ○ **E.** Insider attacks are particularly serious because they leverage on insiders' knowledge of the system.

2. Access control is considered an effective countermeasure in minimizing the possibility of confidentiality breaches. Access control limits access to (choose three):

   ○ **A.** Data

   ○ **B.** Files and objects

   ○ **C.** Network resources

   ○ **D.** Mobile computing platforms

   ○ **E.** Wireless access points

3. Match the terms "due diligence" and "due care" with their definitions below:

   Due Diligence:

   Due Care:

   Definitions:

   1. Concerns itself with the implementation of adequate security controls (administrative, technical, and physical) and establishing best practices for ongoing risk assessment and vulnerability testing.

   2. Ongoing operation and maintenance of implemented security controls.

   3. In the following figure, Internet users are able to access a public server to purchase books online. The server is on a dedicated switch port in the same internal network as the company's knowledge workers. Both the knowledge workers' computers and the book-selling server are protected by a Cisco IOS router firewall. Choose the sentences which best describe this scenario from the perspective of network security (choose one or more):

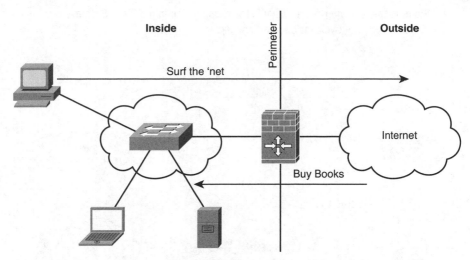

○ **A.** The public server is on a different switch port from the knowledge workers' computers, meaning that it is completely secure.

○ **B.** A compromise of the public server could be leveraged to attack the inside knowledge workers' computers.

○ **C.** Putting the public server on the same network as the inside knowledge workers' computers is insane.

○ **D.** There is no depth of defense in this network design.

○ **E.** The Cisco IOS firewall provides sufficient protection against all external threats.

5. Which of the following are considered best practices for technical controls? (Choose all that apply.)

○ **A.** Use hardware and software that can mitigate risk to an appropriate level.

○ **B.** Keep up-to-date with firmware, hardware, and software patches.

○ **C.** Ensure all stakeholders are aware of the dangers of social engineering.

○ **D.** Encrypt all sensitive data, especially if it passes over hostile networks.

○ **E.** Configure the network so that only necessary services are exposed.

6. Refer to the following figure. What is the missing step in the Cisco System Development Life Cycle for Secure Networks?

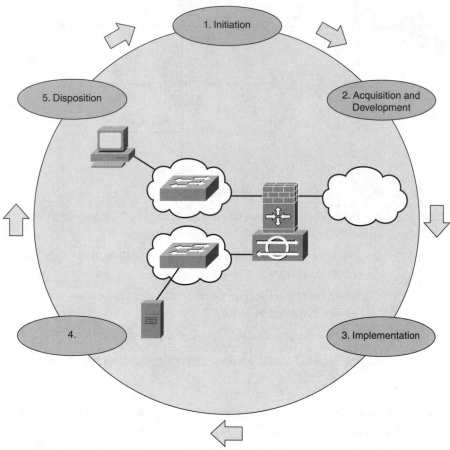

- ○ **A.** Examination
- ○ **B.** Operations and Management
- ○ **C.** Operations and Maintenance
- ○ **D.** Extrapolation
- ○ **E.** None of the above.

7. True or false. Scanners monitor (scan) a network for signs of probes and attacks, whereas sensors probe (sense) a network for vulnerabilities.

8. In the context of network security, there are policies, standards, guidelines, and procedures. True or false: Policies stipulate the details of day-to-day implementation.

9. Cisco specifies four systems that integrate, collaborate, and adapt to prevent attacks. Match the Cisco products below with the system that they provide:

Cisco Security MARS: ___

Cisco NAC Appliance: ___

Cisco IPS Sensor: ___

Cisco Security Management: ___

Choices:

> **A.** Policy management
>
> **B.** Threat management
>
> **C.** Endpoint security
>
> **D.** Network infrastructure

10. True or false. The concept of least privileges specifies that every network security element should have at least the minimum privileges necessary to perform a task.

11. Look at the following commands and pick the answers that best represent what is being accomplished:

```
CiscoISR(config)#line vty 0 4
CiscoISR(config-line)#login
CiscoISR(config-line)#password sanjose
```

- ○ **A.** In-band users on the 5 default vty line interfaces on a Cisco router will be required to enter the password sanjose before they can access user mode.

- ○ **B.** In-band users on the 5 default vty line interfaces on a Cisco router will be required to enter the password sanjose before they can access enable mode.

- ○ **C.** In-band users on the 5 default vty line interfaces on a Cisco router will be able to login to enable mode with the same password. The password is automatically encrypted.

- ○ **D.** In-band users on the 5 default vty line interfaces on a Cisco router will be unable to login to enable mode without a separate enable password or enable secret.

- ○ **E.** None of the above.

12. Examine the following commands, and then answer the question:

```
CiscoISR(config)#privilege exec level 3 configure
CiscoISR(config)#enable secret level 3 sanjose
```

True or false. When users attempt to access enable level 3 with the **enable 3** command, they will be prompted for the correct password (*sanjose*, in this case). They will be allowed to enter the global configuration mode.

13. Examine the following output of the **show flash** command.

True or false: This router has all the required files to run the Cisco Security Device Manager from flash.

```
ciscoISR#show flash
28672K bytes of processor board System flash (Intel Strataflash)

Directory of flash:/
   1 -rwx   18924888 Mar 15 2008 16:51:09 -05:00 c870-advipservicesk9-
mz.124-15.T4.bin
   2 -rwx       3179 Feb 14 2008 19:21:31 -05:00 sdmconfig-8xx.cfg
   3 -rwx       1038 Feb 14 2008 19:21:10 -05:00 home.shtml
   4 -rwx     112640 Feb 14 2008 19:21:46 -05:00 home.tar
   5 -rwx     931840 Feb 14 2008 19:23:48 -05:00 es.tar
   6 -rwx    1505280 Feb 14 2008 19:28:44 -05:00 common.tar
... output omitted …
27611136 bytes total (4065280 bytes free)
```

14. Which command do you use to clear all local AAA users who have been locked out?

   ○ **A.** clear aaa local user lockout

   ○ **B.** clear aaa local-user lockout

   ○ **C.** clear aaa local-db lockout

   ○ **D.** clear aaa local db lockout

   ○ **E.** None of the above.

15. Choose the statement that best describes what is being accomplished in the following figure.

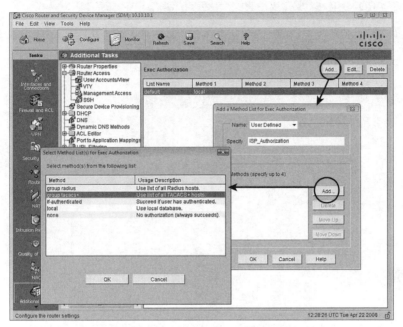

- ○ **A.** These steps create and apply the default authorization method list for exec (character mode) access.

- ○ **B.** These steps create and apply the default authentication method list for exec (character mode) access.

- ○ **C.** These steps create and apply the default accounting method list for exec (character mode) access.

- ○ **D.** These steps create and apply the global defaults for the TACACS+ protocol when used to authenticate unprivileged users.

- ○ **E.** None of the above.

16. When deploying a syslog server in a network, it is considered a good practice to install it [in-band | out-of-band] (choose one) with production data traffic.

17. True or false. You cannot configure SNMP versions 1 and 2 using the SDM.

18. Examine the figure and then answer the subsequent question.

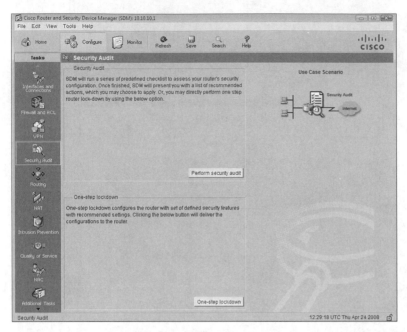

If you have only a rudimentary knowledge of security principles and wanted a quick method for locking down the router against the most common threats, which button would you press and why?

- ○ **A.** The **Security Audit** button, because it steps the user through recommended actions that they manually choose to apply or not.

- ○ **B.** The **One-step lockdown** button, because it immediately applies a defined set of security features with Cisco-recommended settings and doesn't require user interaction.

- ○ **C.** The **One-step lockdown** button, because it steps the user through recommended actions that they manually choose to apply or not.

- ○ **D.** The **Security Audit** button, because it immediately applies a defined set of security features with Cisco-recommended settings and doesn't require user interaction.

19. True or false. Once you have pressed the **Deliver** button on the One-step lockdown (as shown in the following figure) or the Security Audit feature, you cannot reverse the changes at a later time.

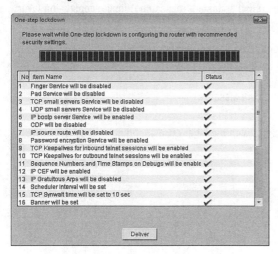

20. Cisco Discovery Protocol is globally _____ by default, and as a general rule should not be used once the network has been constructed and tested. Also, an unused _____ should be disabled to limit unauthorized access to both the router and the network. (Pick the answers that fill in the blanks in the correct order.)

   ○ **A.** Enabled

   ○ **B.** Router interface

   ○ **C.** Virtual terminal line

   ○ **D.** Console port

   ○ **E.** Auxiliary port

   ○ **F.** Disabled

21. Firewalls are one key component in a network security architecture. Besides the possibility of traffic bottlenecks, which of the following are known disadvantages of firewalls? (Choose all that apply.)

   ○ **A.** Firewall misconfiguration can cause single points of failure.

   ○ **B.** Many applications are not firewall-friendly and are therefore hard to securely pass.

   ○ **C.** End-users may try to find ways around an overly restrictive firewall.

   ○ **D.** Tunneled traffic (covert channels) is difficult to detect and protect against.

   ○ **E.** Firewalls cannot protect against the exploitation of protocol flaws.

22. Access Control Lists (ACLs) can mitigate what types of attacks? (Choose all that apply.)

- ○ **A.** DoS smurf attacks
- ○ **B.** Tunneled applications (such as instant messaging) inside application layer flows
- ○ **C.** Outbound and inbound IP address spoofing
- ○ **D.** MAC address table overflow attacks
- ○ **E.** Traceroute (used for reconnaissance)

23. Match the following ICMP messages with the letter corresponding to their description:

ICMP Message

echo-reply   __

packet-too-big __

unreachable   __

echo   __

redirect   __

Description

- **A.** Allows pinging to IP hosts
- **B.** Replies to pinging
- **C.** Reply indicating that a host cannot be reached
- **D.** Command to alter a routing table
- **E.** Required for Maximum Transmission Unit (MTU) path discovery

24. Which of the following are not one of the three main categories of actions that ZPF can take on traffic?

- ○ **A.** Permit
- ○ **B.** Inspect
- ○ **C.** Deny
- ○ **D.** Drop
- ○ **E.** Pass

25. Examine the figure and answer the subsequent question.

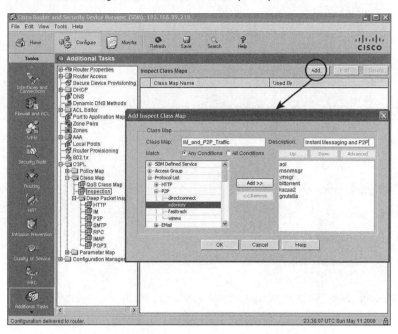

True or false. A class map is being created that will match on IM and P2P traffic tunneled inside HTTP.

26. IPsec VPNs encrypts data at the _____ layer of the OSI model and SSL VPNs encrypt data at the _____ layer of the OSI model. (Pick the answers that fill in the blanks in the correct order.)

○ **A.** Data link

○ **B.** Application

○ **C.** Session

○ **D.** Network

○ **E.** Transport

27. You are considering implementing a new cryptosystem, which uses PKI, but abandon the effort because you think that PKI will not provide the level of encryption you are looking for. What is the flaw in this last statement?

○ **A.** PKI VPNs use the strongest ciphers in the industry.

○ **B.** PKI encryption is considered unbreakable. Only the encryption keys are vulnerable.

○ **C.** PKI (Private Key Infrastructure) provides for a complete cryptosystem infrastructure.

○ **D.** PKI (Public Key Infrastructure) provides for a complete cryptosystem infrastructure.

○ **E.** PKI does not provide encryption.

28. Fill in the blank. HMACs are considered a crucial component of a cryptosystem because, unlike hashes alone, they provide for _____ as well as integrity. (Choose only one.)

○ **A.** Encryption

○ **B.** Encryption keys

○ **C.** Ciphers

○ **D.** Origin authentication

○ **E.** Guaranteed delivery

29. Match the following Public Key Cryptography Standards (PKCS) with their descriptions:

PKCS Standard

PKCS #10 __

PKCS #2 __

PKCS #7 __

PKCS #1 __

Descriptions

    A. RSA Cryptography

    B. DH Key Agreement

    C. Cryptographic Message Syntax

    D. Cryptographic Request Syntax

30. Examples of PKI architectures include:

○ **A.** Cross-certified CAs

○ **B.** Hierarchical CA

○ **C.** Central CA

○ **D.** Subordinate CA

○ **E.** Multi-redundant CA

31. Circle the correct choices. EasyVPN represents Cisco's [remote-access | site-to-site] VPN solution, which uses [IPsec | SSL] at the [transport | network] layer. WebVPN represents Cisco's [remote-access | site-to-site] VPN solution, which uses [IPsec | SSL] at the [transport | network] layer.

32. What are the three methods supported for peer authentication for IPsec VPNs?

- ○ **A.** RSA-encrypted HMACs

- ○ **B.** Dynamic Hashing Media Authentication Control (DHMAC)

- ○ **C.** Dynamic Hashing (DH) Groups 1, 2, and 5

- ○ **D.** Pre-shared keys (PSK)

- ○ **E.** RSA signatures

- ○ **F.** RSA encrypted nonces

33. Circle the correct choices. If an IPsec VPN requires confidentiality through encryption, [ESP | AH] must be chosen. This protocol is encapsulated in an IP packet as protocol [47 | 50].

34. Examine the following commands. CiscoISR-A is the local peer where these commands are executed:

```
CiscoISR-A(config)#crypto map multipurpose 999 ipsec-isakmp
CiscoISR-A(config-crypto-map)#set peer 172.16.32.1
CiscoISR-A(config-crypto-map)#set transform-set CantHackMe
CiscoISR-A(config-crypto-map)#match address 102
CiscoISR-A(config-crypto-map)#set security-association lifetime
seconds 86400
CiscoISR-A(config-crypto-map)#set security-association lifetime
kilobyte 4000000
```

Which statements are correct with respect to these commands? (Choose all that apply.)

- ○ **A.** The local peer will identify itself with its IP address 172.16.32.1 versus its domain name.

- ○ **B.** The remote peer must have an IKE Phase II transform set called CantHackMe for successful negotiations to occur.

- ○ **C.** ACL 102 defines the traffic (local to remote) that will be protected inside the VPN.

- ○ **D.** The remote peer's IP address is 172.16.32.1.

- ○ **E.** The IKE Phase II SA has a lifetime of 86,400 seconds or 4,000,000 kilobytes, whichever comes first.

35. True or false. When using the SDM's Site-to-Site VPN Wizard, if the VPN fails to connect immediately, you can troubleshoot it by having the SDM generate traffic, which should bring up the VPN.

   True. See the following figure and also Figure 7.19. You can have SDM generate VPN traffic or you can generate the VPN traffic from the source network yourself and ask SDM to wait a specific interval before it tests the status of the tunnel again.

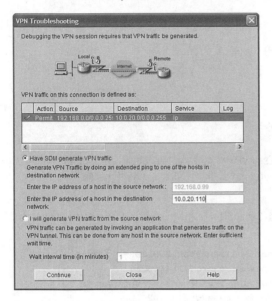

36. Which of the following are attributes of an IPS? (Choose all that apply.)

   ○ **A.** Monitors copies of the data flow.

   ○ **B.** Monitors traffic and content from layers 2 through 7 in real-time.

   ○ **C.** Allows some traffic deemed malicious to enter or leave the network.

   ○ **D.** Must be capable of handling all ingress and egress traffic where it is deployed.

   ○ **E.** Prevents traffic deemed malicious from entering or leaving the network.

37. True or false. The Cisco IOS IPS is an inline host-based IPS.

38. Examine the following figure and answer the subsequent question.

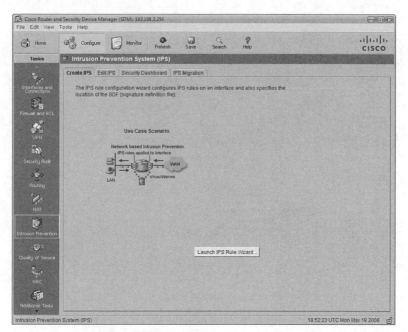

From this screen, what action do you next need to take in order to configure the IPS for the first time?

○ **A.** Push the Launch IPS Rule Wizard button.

○ **B.** Select the Edit IPS tab.

○ **C.** Select the Security Dashboard tab.

○ **D.** Select the IPS Migration tab.

○ **E.** None of the above.

39. Examine the following figure and answer the subsequent question.

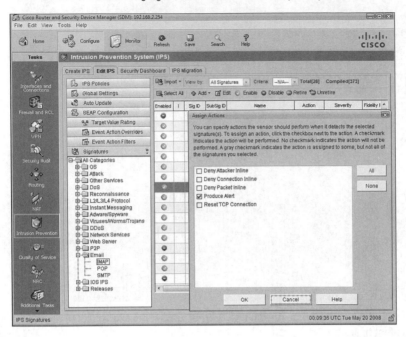

The action assigned to the selected signature is **Produce Alert**. What does this mean?

○ **A.** Sends an encoded dump (capture) of the offending packet in the alert.

○ **B.** Instructs the sensor to send an SNMP trap.

○ **C.** Sends an alert to the Event Store (internal log buffer).

○ **D.** Logs all packets with a victim's IP address.

○ **E.** None of the above.

40. Which of the following best describe advantages of SDEE versus syslog?

○ **A.** SDEE-format messages are much richer in information content.

○ **B.** Syslog is passive from the perspective of the logging server, relying on the sensor to send alerts to a syslog server, whereas SDEE is active, pulling alarms from the sensor on demand.

○ **C.** SDEE is a Cisco-proprietary protocol with much richer metrics than syslog.

○ **D.** SDEE is evolving as a standard format for security reporting and is vendor-neutral.

○ **E.** SDEE can use HTTPS for secure transport of log messages.

41. Fill in the blanks. (Choices can be used more than once.) In Cisco's Host Security Strategy, there are two main software elements, _____ and _____. The design of _____ should follow the concept of least privileges.

    ○ **A.** Firmware

    ○ **B.** Networks

    ○ **C.** Operating systems

    ○ **D.** Applications

    ○ **E.** Drivers

42. Match the following terms with their definitions:

    Terms:

    1. Worm

    2. Virus

    3. Trojan Horse

    Definitions:

    A. Replicates into the memory of an infected host and infects other computers in turn.

    B. An application written to look like something innocent, whereas it is actually an attack tool.

    C. Attaches to other programs and executes unwanted functions on the host.

43. Which of the following is the best definition of iSCSI interconnection technology employed in Storage Area Networks (SANs)? (Choose one.)

    ○ **A.** Used for SAN-to-SAN connections, typically within a MAN or WAN.

    ○ **B.** Used for host-to-SAN connections and is the primary transport technology for SANs.

    ○ **C.** Used for host-to-SAN connections, typically implemented in a LAN.

    ○ **D.** Used for RAID arrays within a discrete SAN endpoint.

    ○ **E.** None of the above.

44. Which VoIP protocol is proprietary to Cisco and used between Cisco Unified Communication Manager (UCM) and Cisco VoIP phones?

    ○ **A.** H.323

    ○ **B.** SIP

    ○ **C.** RTP

    ○ **D.** SCCP

    ○ **E.** RTCP

45. What VoIP phone features does Cisco recommend disabling if they are not needed? (Choose three.)

- ○ **A.** Setting button
- ○ **B.** 802.1Q VLAN trunking
- ○ **C.** WWW access
- ○ **D.** PC port
- ○ **E.** SIP

46. Cisco's recommends turning off DTP on switch ports, which require trunking to mitigate a VLAN hopping attack, which uses a rogue trunk. Which two interface configuration commands will perform this task?

- ○ **A.** Switchport mode access
- ○ **B.** Switchport mode trunk
- ○ **C.** Switchport nonegotiate
- ○ **D.** No switchport DTP
- ○ **E.** Switchport DTP disable

47. What are Cisco's recommendations for mitigating a Spanning Tree Protocol (STP) manipulation attack? (Choose all that apply.)

- ○ **A.** Portfast
- ○ **B.** BPDU guard
- ○ **C.** Root guard
- ○ **D.** CAM table guard
- ○ **E.** Per VLAN Rapid Spanning Tree Plus (PVST+)

48. True or false. Port security can be enabled on a trunk port.

49. Besides topological loops, what are some other things that can cause broadcast storms in a switched network? (Choose all that apply.)

- ○ **A.** Poor cabling plant design
- ○ **B.** Electromagnetic interference (EMI) sources and sinks
- ○ **C.** DoS attacks
- ○ **D.** Poorly-designed, chatty applications
- ○ **E.** Protocols that rely heavily on broadcasts for discovery

50. True or false. A port that is put in portfast mode is not part of STP calculations and cannot be put in blocking mode by the root bridge.

Answers to Practice Exam 1

1. A, C, and E

2. A, B, and C

3. Due Diligence—1, Due Care—2

4. B, C, and D

5. A, D, and E

6. C

7. False

8. False

9. Cisco Security MARS—B; Cisco NAC Appliance—C; Cisco IPS Sensor—D; Cisco Security Management—A

10. False

11. A and D

12. True

13. False

14. A

15. A

16. out-of-band

17. False

18. B

19. False

20. A and B

21. A, B, C, and D

22. A, C, and E

23. B, E, C, A, and D

24. A and C

25. False

26. D and E

27. E

28. D

29. D, B, C, and A

30. A, B, and C

31. remote-access, IPSec, network, remote-access, SSL, and transport

32. D, E, and F

33. ESP and 50

34. C, D, and E

35. True

36. B, D, and E

37. False

38. A

39. C

40. A, B, D, and E

41. C, D, and D

42. 1—A; 2—C; 3—B

43. C

44. D

45. A, C, and D

46. B and C

47. A, B, and C

48. False

49. C, D, and E

50. True

Question 1

Answers A, C, and E are correct. B is incorrect because data indicates that insider attacks are potentially more damaging than external attacks; for instance, insiders often have sufficient access to systems to inflict damage without password-cracking tools. D is incorrect because Cisco recommends exactly the opposite. When in doubt, read the manual!

Question 2

The correct answers are A, B, and C. Access control is considered a broad category of a network security policy and does not address specifics as to what types of devices it is applied to. This is why answers d and e are incorrect.

Question 3

Due Diligence—1, Due Care—2. Due diligence is more of a static, security preparation activity, whereas due care is a dynamic, ongoing process that involves day-to-day operations.

Question 4

Answers B, C, and D are correct. An axiom of network security is that production data traffic should never cross the cables of a hostile network. Putting a public server on an internal network segment shared by knowledge workers' computers is lunacy—if the public server is compromised, it becomes a hostile system. The enemy is amongst us. Answer A is incorrect because even though the server is on a different switch port, the resulting segmentation is not proof against various types of switch infrastructure attacks (see also Chapter 10, "Protecting Switch Infrastructure"). Answer E is incorrect because, at a minimum, the server should be in a separate security zone. The IOS firewall cannot protect against insider attacks, which result from a compromised server.

Question 5

Answers A, D, and E are correct. Answers B and C are incorrect because they are examples of administrative controls.

Question 6

The correct answer is C. Answers A and D are made up and do not appear elsewhere in any network security context in this course. Answer B is deliberately misleading because management sounds like maintenance.

Question 7

The correct answer is false. Scanners probe a network for vulnerabilities, whereas sensors monitor a network for signs of probes and attacks. IDSs and IPSs are sensors. (See also Chapter 8, "Network Security Using Cisco IOS IPS.")

Question 8

False. Policies specify overall statements of direction including management's position on security issues, but they don't stipulate details of day-to-day operations. Procedures do.

Question 9

Cisco Security MARS—B; Cisco NAC Appliance—C; Cisco IPS Sensor—D; Cisco Security Management—A.

Question 10

False. This is a trick question. The concept of least privileges specifies that network security elements should have **no more** than the minimum privileges necessary to perform a task.

Question 11

Answers A and D are correct. This password protects the user mode on the router only. Furthermore, a security feature on Cisco routers refuses Telnet or SSH connections to the vtys if an enable password or enable secret has not also (but separately) been set. Answer B is incorrect per the preceding explanation. Answer C is incorrect because the enable password is set separately, and there is no automatic encryption of these passwords by default.

Question 12

True. The IOS enables you to create interim privilege levels (1–14) between user mode and enable mode where you can customize what commands are allowed to be issued at that level.

Question 13

False. Not all the files required to run the SDM are present. The *sdm.tar* file is missing.

Question 14

The correct answer is A. The other answers don't exist, are wrong, and moreover are tricky for someone who hasn't studied the right command syntax.

Question 15

The correct answer is A. Answers b and c are incorrect because they specify authentication and accounting and not authorization. Answer D is just plain wrong.

Question 16

The correct answer is *out-of-band*. Care must be taken to ensure the integrity of the communication path between the syslog server and its clients; otherwise, data obtained might be legally inadmissible as evidence of a security breach.

Question 17

False. Although SNMP versions 1 and 2 are configurable by SDM, SNMP version 3 must be configured via CLI.

Question 18

The correct answer is B. A is incorrect because, even though the chosen fixes are automatically applied, the user has to decide which vulnerabilities have to be addressed in the first place, and this takes some knowledge. Answers C and D are incorrect because the definitions are incorrect.

Question 19

The answer is false. If you later want to undo some of the changes, you can run the Security Audit wizard again and select **Undo Security configurations**.

Question 20

The correct answers are A and B, respectively. Answers C, D, and e are incorrect because access to the virtual terminal lines, console port, and auxiliary ports have no effect on network access, only access to the router itself. Answer F is incorrect because CDP is enabled by default.

Question 21

Answers A, B, C, and D are correct. Answer E is incorrect because the opposite is true; firewalls can even sanitize protocols in some cases.

Question 22

The correct answers are A, C, and E. ACLs cannot be used to mitigate tunneled applications because ACLs do not operate above the Transport layer. MAC address table overflow attacks cannot be mitigated against with ACLs either. (See Chapter 10, "Protecting Switch Infrastructure," for details of how to mitigate this and other types of layer 2 attacks.)

Question 23

echo-reply	B
packet-too-big	E
unreachable	C
echo	A
redirect	D

Question 24

The correct choices are A and C. The three main categories of actions that ZPF can take on traffic are inspect, drop, and pass.

Question 25

False. The class map *IM_and_P2P_Traffic* pictured filters on native IM and P2P traffic. Filtering services tunneled inside HTTP is outside the scope of this Exam Cram.

Question 26

The correct answers are D and E, respectively. Encryption can occur at other layers of the OSI model as well.

Question 27

The correct answer is E. PKI defines a whole protocol for the secure issuance, exchange, revocation, destruction, storage, and backup of digital certificates and integral asymmetric keys used for device and individual authentication and encryption. Answers a through d are incorrect because PKI neither provides for encryption nor does it specify a specific cryptosystem. It simply makes the management of the credentials and keys used easier.

Question 28

Answer D is correct because Hashing Message Authentication Codes (HMACs) not only assure that the 1's and 0's haven't changed in transit between the transmitter and the receiver (integrity), but that they uniquely and only came from the transmitter (origin authentication). Answers A, B, and C are incorrect for this reason. Answer E is incorrect because there is no guaranteed delivery provided by HMACs.

Question 29

PKCS #10   D

PKCS #2   B

PKCS #7   C

PKCS #1   A

Question 30

Answers A, B, and C are correct. Answer D is incorrect because a subordinate CA exists within a hierarchical CA model. Answer E is incorrect because this terminology doesn't exist.

Question 31

Respectively, the answers are *remote-access*, *IPSec*, *network*, *remote-access*, *SSL*, and *transport*.

Question 32

The correct answers are D, E, and F. All three are supported on Cisco security appliances and PSKs, and RSA signatures only are supported on Cisco IOS routers. Answers A and B are incorrect because they use a mashup of existing terminology such as RSA and HMAC in an attempt to mislead. Answer C is incorrect because DH stands for Diffie-Hellman, and DH is not used for authentication in any case. It is used to create a shared encryption key in-band over a hostile network.

Question 33

The correct answers are *ESP* and *50*, respectively. Authentication Header (AH) is encapsulated in IP packets as protocol 51 traffic and does not provide encryption. Encapsulating Security Payload (ESP), on the other hand, provides for encryption of the payload and is encapsulated in IP packets as protocol 50.

> **NOTE**
>
> This might sound like trivia, but actually it is important to remember. Because ESP and AH don't use TCP or UDP for transport, a packet might be dropped by a router that performs Port Address Translation (PAT). No port number = no translation.

Question 34

The correct answers are C, D, and E. Answer A is incorrect because the IP address specified in the crypto map is that of the remote peer. Answer B is incorrect because the transform set name, CantHackMe, is of local significance only. The transform set's values and *not* its name are transmitted during quick mode.

Question 35

True. See the following figure and also Figure 7.19. You can have SDM generate VPN traffic or you can generate the VPN traffic from the source network yourself and ask SDM to wait a specific interval before it tests the status of the tunnel again.

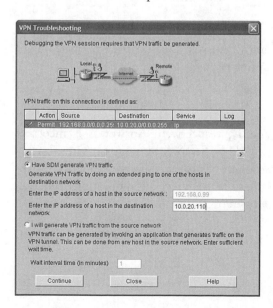

Question 36

The correct answers are B, D, and E. Answer A is incorrect because an IPS is deployed inline with traffic and does not simply monitor copies of the data flow in the way that an IDS does. Similarly, answer C is incorrect because an IPS sees all packets including the trigger packets in an attack.

Question 37

False. The Cisco IOS IPS is an inline *network* IPS.

Question 38

The correct answer is A. Curiously, this button does not launch a wizard where you can change the signatures. The word "rule" in this context means "policy." Your intuition probably tells you that answer B would be correct, but this is not the case. This is something to watch for on the exam.

Question 39

The correct answer is C. Answer A is incorrect because this is what the Produce Verbose Alert action does. Answer B is incorrect because this is what the Request SNMP Trap action does. Answer D is incorrect because this is what the Log Victim Packets action does. These actions are in the "IPS Attack Responses" section of Chapter 8 and should all be memorized for the exam.

Question 40

The correct answers are A, B, D, and E. Answer C is incorrect because one of SDEE's features is that it is not proprietary.

Question 41

The correct answers are C, D, and D, respectively. Answer A is incorrect because "host" in the context of Cisco's Host Security Strategy refers to an endpoint. Answer B is incorrect because a network isn't a software element. Answer E is incorrect because while drivers are software, they, like applications, function in the environment provided by the operating system.

Question 42

The correct answers are: 1—A; 2—C; 3—B.

Question 43

The correct answer is C. Answer A is incorrect as it describes FCIP (Fiber Channel over IP). Answer B is incorrect as it describes Fiber Channel. Answer D is incorrect because it is a made-up answer that sounds like it might be right!

Question 44

Answer D is correct. The other choices are standards-based protocols and thus incorrect.

Question 45

The correct answers are A, C, and D. Answer B is incorrect because 802.1Q trunking is required to separate the VVLAN from the data VLAN for QoS and security reasons. Answer E is incorrect because SIP stands for Session Initiation Protocol and Cisco makes no specific recommendation about it in this context.

Question 46

The correct answers are B and C. Answer B is correct because this command manually enables trunking. Answer C is correct because this command turns off autonegotiation of trunks. Answer A is incorrect because this command specifies that this port should be in access mode (wrong!), but doesn't turn off autonegotiation in any case (as with answer C). Answers D and E are incorrect because these commands don't exist.

Question 47

The correct answers are A, B, and C. Answer D is incorrect because this feature doesn't exist. Answer E is incorrect because PVST+ defines a protocol for rapid spanning tree convergence per VLAN and does not specifically mitigate an STP manipulation attack. It is a red herring and is found nowhere in this Exam Cram but is part of the CCNA curriculum.

Question 48

False. Port security is only appropriate on access ports because, unlike trunks between switches, shutting down these ports only results in loss of connection to a finite number of attached stations. If this logic fails to sway you, you should know that port security can't be configured on trunk ports because the IOS won't let you.

Question 49

The correct answers are C, D, and E. Answers A and B are incorrect because poor cabling and EMI issues are more likely to cause much more general failures and certainly not broadcast storms.

Question 50

True. This is why you must take great care in making sure that putting this switch port in portfast mode doesn't inadvertently create a topological loop.

Practice Exam 2

Hints and Pointers

If you are preparing for the CCNA Security exam, you already have your CCNA certification, which means you are already an expert at Cisco exams, right? Possibly, but don't be overconfident. The CCNA Security is most definitely a big step, and although it leverages your basic network knowledge of the CCNA certification, it also introduces new ways of looking at topics that just may force you to go back and re-study large sections of the prerequisite CCNA material. That is why I have included tips throughout the book of CCNA areas that are particularly important to brush up on.

These practice exam questions have been created by the author and reviewed by Cisco technical experts. They are representative of (and possibly a little bit harder than) the questions that you will see in the real exam.

The following are general tips for using the two practice exams in this book:

▶ **Time yourself:** Each sample exam is 50 questions. Try to stay within a 60-minute time limit for each exam.

▶ **Find a quiet place:** You need a place free of distractions to attempt the sample exams. I find a public library is often the best place. Equip yourself with only a notepad and pen, just like the real exam. Oh, and turn off your personal communication device when you're taking the exam!

▶ **Practice data dumping:** The Cram Sheet at the beginning of this Exam Cram is meant to represent the kind of arcane but important information that is hard to retain. Practice dumping this information from your brain onto the aforementioned notepad just before you sit down to attempt the practice exam.

▶ **Don't get beached on a single question:** If you don't know the answer for a question, then choose an answer anyway, recognizing that you don't get marked down for a wrong answer and that you get no points at all for one that you do not attempt. Take note of the question that stumped you and be prepared to drill down on that topic area later.

▶ **Don't be overconfident:** If you take the practice exam and ace it, you're probably ready for the real thing. That said, although these practice exam questions are meant to represent the real exam to the best of this author's knowledge, you owe it to yourself to at least read every chapter in its entirety to obtain the complete context for every topic area. Use the exams to identify topics you struggle with consistently and brush up on them.

▶ **Practice, practice, practice:** Keep on taking the practice exams until you obtain a perfect score on both of them. Book your exam appointment. You're ready!

So in the end, I have these pieces of advice: Study hard and practice, practice, practice!

I wish you good luck, too. But remember, sometimes you have to be good to be lucky.

—Eric Stewart

Practice Exam #2

1. Implementing network security is often described as a balancing act between three competing needs. Choose these needs from the following:

   ○ **A.** Evolving business requirements

   ○ **B.** Freedom of information initiatives

   ○ **C.** Personal safety

   ○ **D.** Physical plant security

   ○ **E.** Protection of data

2. Fill in the blank. A disturbing recent trend has been what Cisco calls _____ threats, which focus on the application layer of the OSI model.

   ○ **A.** External

   ○ **B.** Internal

   ○ **C.** Custom

   ○ **D.** Hacker

   ○ **E.** None of the above.

3. What are the three broad categories of security controls?

   ○ **A.** User education

   ○ **B.** Firewalls

   ○ **C.** Administrative

   ○ **D.** Physical

   ○ **E.** Technical

4. True or false. Hackers are known for thinking "inside the box" because their integral understanding of a system's inner workings make them uniquely able to exploit weaknesses in design.

5. Which of the following are not considered attacks against availability? (Choose all that apply.)

   ○ **A.** SYN floods

   ○ **B.** MAC flooding

   ○ **C.** Social engineering

   ○ **D.** Dumpster diving

   ○ **E.** DoS

6. Fill in the blanks in the quantitative risk analysis formula with the missing variables. (Choose two; the order makes no difference.)

ALE = (AV * EF) * ARO

- ○ **A.** Asset Value (AV)
- ○ **B.** Exposure Factor (EF)
- ○ **C.** Single Loss Expectancy (SLE)
- ○ **D.** Rate of Functional Loss (ROFL)
- ○ **E.** Return on Investment (ROI)

7. Network security testing is considered an important part of assessing a network's resilience against attacks and establishing the requirement for security controls (physical, administrative, and technical). Which of the following is *not* a goal of network security testing?

- ○ **A.** Create a baseline for corrective action.
- ○ **B.** Define ways to mitigate discovered vulnerabilities.
- ○ **C.** Create a baseline of an organization's current security measures.
- ○ **D.** Measure an organization's progress in fulfilling security policy.
- ○ **E.** Analyze the relative cost vs. benefit of security improvements.
- ○ **F.** None of the above.

8. Some of the items in the following list represent categories of disruption. Identify the three correct categories of disruption by putting them in order from least disruptive to most disruptive:

- ○ **A.** Catastrophe
- ○ **B.** Disaster
- ○ **C.** Nondisaster
- ○ **D.** Cataclysm
- ○ **E.** Armageddon

9. What are the three main groups of stakeholders in a security policy?

- ○ **A.** Senior management, security staff, end users
- ○ **B.** Senior management, law enforcement agencies, IT staff
- ○ **C.** Law enforcement agencies, customers, security staff
- ○ **D.** Senior management, security staff, the public
- ○ **E.** None of the above.

10. Which of the following Cisco products cannot be managed by the Cisco Security Manager?

- ○ **A.** ASA 5500 Series Adaptive Security Appliances
- ○ **B.** Catalyst 6500 Series switches
- ○ **C.** PIX 500 series Security Appliances
- ○ **D.** Cisco 4200 Series Sensors
- ○ **E.** None of the above.

11. In the following figure, what do scenarios 1, 2, and 3 represent, respectively?

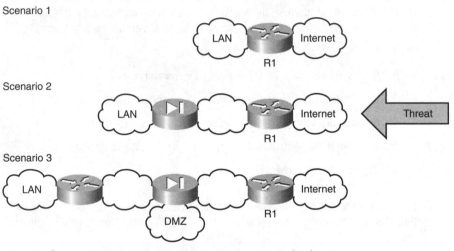

Scenario 1

Scenario 2

Scenario 3

- ○ **A.** Two perimeters, single perimeter, screened subnet
- ○ **B.** Screened subnet, single perimeter, two perimeters
- ○ **C.** Single perimeter, two perimeters, screened subnet
- ○ **D.** Single DMZ, double DMZ, triple DMZ
- ○ **E.** None of the above.

12. True or false. The **service password-encryption** command encrypts all the passwords on the device with the exception of the enable secret, which uses a hash.

13. Views are very useful in creating role-based rules as to which commands are authorized for execution. Examine the sequence of commands and choose all the correct statements from the list that follows them.

```
CiscoISR(config)#aaa new-model
CiscoISR#enable view
Password: enablesecretpassword
CiscoISR#config terminal
Enter configuration commands, one per line. End with CNTL/Z.
CiscoISR(config)#parser view ISP
CiscoISR(config-view)#secret 0 hardtoguess
CiscoISR(config-view)#commands exec include ping
CiscoISR(config-view)#commands exec include all configure
```

   - ○ **A.** The **aaa new-model** command is required before a view can be created.
   - ○ **B.** The user who accesses the ISP view will require the password *hardtoguess*.
   - ○ **C.** The user who accesses the ISP view will be authorized to use the **ping** command.
   - ○ **D.** The user who accesses the ISP view will not be authorized to use the **copy running-config startup-config** command.
   - ○ **E.** None of the above.

14. With respect to AAA, access to the router is called remote _____ access and access through the router is called remote _____ access. (Pick the answer that fills in the blanks in the correct order.)

   - ○ **A.** Network, administrative
   - ○ **B.** Vty, packet
   - ○ **C.** Administrative, network
   - ○ **D.** Proxy, cut-through
   - ○ **E.** None of the above.

15. What are the three *main* task areas for setting up external AAA? Choose from the following list:

   - ○ **A.** Set up users (server).
   - ○ **B.** Configure the AAA network (client and server).
   - ○ **C.** Install AAA 802.1X supplicant support in SDM (client).
   - ○ **D.** Identify traffic to which AAA will be applied (client).
   - ○ **E.** Choose digital certificates to authenticate the AAA server to the client (and vice versa).

16. With respect to secure management and reporting, traffic can flow either _____, meaning that it is separate from the production network, or _____, meaning that the traffic flows across the production network. (Pick the answer that fills in the blanks in the correct order.)

- ○ **A.** Extranet, intranet
- ○ **B.** Intranet, extranet
- ○ **C.** Internet, intranet
- ○ **D.** Out-of-band, in-band
- ○ **E.** In-band, out-of-band

17. For the following names of Cisco log severity levels, fill in their level:

Names:

Errors __

Informational__

Alerts __

Emergencies __

Debugging __

Warnings__

Notifications __

Critical __

18. Choose the statement that best describes what is being represented in the following figure.

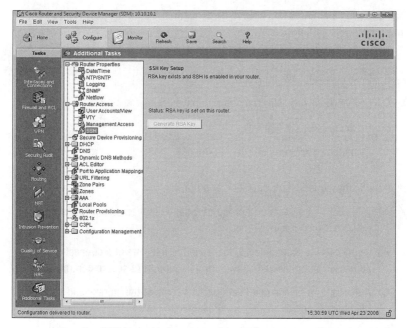

○ **A.** SSH is enabled system wide on the router, and a user should now be able to SSH to any interface.

○ **B.** SSH is enabled on the router, but has to be separately enabled on the vty lines.

○ **C.** SSH is not enabled on the router until the **Save** button is pressed.

○ **D.** SSH is not enabled on the router until the **Refresh** button is pressed.

○ **E.** SSH is enabled on the router, but has to be separately enabled on the physical interfaces (Ethernet, serial, and so on).

○ **F.** None of the above.

19. What are the Cisco AutoSecure features that SDM Security Audit does not implement? (Choose all that apply.)

○ **A.** Disabling NTP

○ **B.** Configuring AAA

○ **C.** Setting Selective Packet Discard (SPD) values

○ **D.** Enabling TCP intercepts

○ **E.** Configuring anti-spoofing ACLs on outside-facing interfaces

○ **F.** All of the above.

20. What are the two parameters that have to be configured before RSA keys can be generated to support SSH on the router?

   ○ **A.** Hostname, domain name

   ○ **B.** Enable secret, SSH transport on the vtys

   ○ **C.** Enable password, SSH transport on physical interfaces

   ○ **D.** Hostname, default gateway

   ○ **E.** Encryption key protocol, hashing method

21. Which of the following is Cisco's definition of a firewall?

   ○ **A.** A firewall is a system or a group of systems that enforce an access control policy between two networks.

   ○ **B.** A firewall is a stateful device that analyzes the state of a connection built across it and opens and closes ports in support of secure communication.

   ○ **C.** A firewall is a device that filters packets, both in the ingress and egress direction, based on static packet header content.

   ○ **D.** A firewall is software deployed on an end system to protect a specific application.

   ○ **E.** None of the above.

22. Match the following firewall types with the letter corresponding to the layers of the TCP/IP protocol stack at which they operate:

Firewall Types

   1. Static packet-filtering firewall   __

   2. Application layer gateway __

   3. Dynamic (or stateful) packet-filtering firewall   __

   4. Application inspection firewall   __

   5. Transparent firewall   __

TCP/IP Layers

   A. 1 to 4

   B. 1 to 5

   C. 1 to 2

23. True or false. Assuming that the IOS router is also the VPN endpoint, encrypted packets are tested on an inbound ACL twice.

24. Fill in the blanks. Interface ACLs are still relevant and can be used to complement Zone-Based Policy Firewall (ZPF) policies. Inbound ACLs are applied _____ ZPF policies and outbound ACLs are applied _____ ZPF policies.

25. Examine the figure and answer the subsequent question.

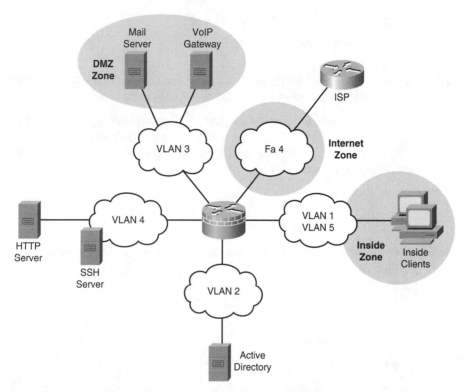

True or false. The traffic from Vlan 2 to FastEthernet4 (Fa 4) will be forwarded.

26. What is the area of the largest vulnerability in modern cryptosystems?

○ **A.** Ciphers

○ **B.** Hashes

○ **C.** VPN endpoints

○ **D.** Users

○ **E.** Encryption keys

27. Fill in the blank. You are asked to implement a new cryptosystem that uses ciphers to provide for confidentiality of data transmitted. Researching industry data, you decide to use 3DES and not AES because 3DES _____.

   ○ **A.** Is cryptographically stronger.

   ○ **B.** Uses longer keys.

   ○ **C.** Is more trusted.

   ○ **D.** Is less computationally intensive.

   ○ **E.** None of the above.

28. True or false. Modern SSL VPNs use Transmission Level Security (TLS) instead of Secure Sockets Layer (SSL) because it is a newer, standards-based replacement for SSL.

29. In a typical asymmetric key cryptosystem, node A will encrypt messages with the node B's _____ and will decrypt messages from node B using node A's own _____. Safeguarding the _____ is essential. (Pick the answers that fill in the blanks in the correct order; choices can be reused.)

   ○ **A.** Private key

   ○ **B.** Public key

30. Which of the following represent common Cisco applications of certificate-based authentication?

   ○ **A.** SSL VPN servers

   ○ **B.** TN3270 over SSL

   ○ **C.** 802.1X using EAP-TLS

   ○ **D.** IPsec VPNs

   ○ **E.** None of the above.

31. What are the two main categories of VPN?

   ○ **A.** Dynamic multipoint (DMVPN)

   ○ **B.** Client-Server

   ○ **C.** Site-to-site

   ○ **D.** Remote-access

   ○ **E.** Full mesh

32. True or false. In IPsec VPNs, Internet Key Exchange (IKE) Phase I carries data, and IKE Phase II exists only to negotiate and authenticate, but does not carry data.

33. Fill in the blanks in the following description of IKE Phase I negotiations.

    The separate elements of IKE Phase I negotiation are grouped in a _____. During IKE Phase I, either main mode or _____ may be chosen to perform negotiations. When this negotiation is complete, some vendors use their own proprietary negotiation protocol to negotiate additional parameters. Cisco's proprietary protocol for remote-access IPsec VPNs is called _____. After Phase I is complete, _____ negotiates the IKE Phase II parameters.

    Choices:

    ○ **A.** Policy set

    ○ **B.** Transform set

    ○ **C.** Aggressive mode

    ○ **D.** Mode configuration

    ○ **E.** Quick mode

    ○ **F.** Active mode

34. Examine the following commands:

    ```
    CiscoISR-A(config)#crypto isakmp policy 99
    CiscoISR-A(config-isakmp)#hash sha
    CiscoISR-A(config-isakmp)#authentication pre-share
    CiscoISR-A(config-isakmp)#group 5
    CiscoISR-A(config-isakmp)#lifetime 86400
    CiscoISR-A(config-isakmp)#encryption aes
    CiscoISR-A(config-isakmp)#
    ```

    Which statements are correct with respect to these commands? (Choose all that apply.)

    ○ **A.** A site-to-site tunnel group, number 5, is being created.

    ○ **B.** The VPN peers will authenticate using a pre-shared key (PSK).

    ○ **C.** The separate policy elements are being grouped as policy set 99.

    ○ **D.** The Advanced Enterprise Security (AES) encryption algorithm is specified.

    ○ **E.** 128-bit Advanced Encryption Standard (AES) encryption algorithm is specified.

35. Examine the figure. It is a screenshot showing the summary of a VPN created with the Cisco SDM Site-to-Site VPN Wizard.

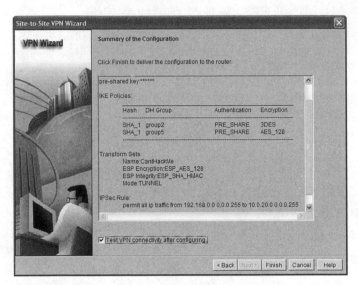

Which statements are correct with respect to the figure? (Choose all that apply.)

○ **A.** PSKs are used for authentication.

○ **B.** One IKE Phase I policy indicates SHA-HMAC with DH group 2, and 3DES for the cipher.

○ **C.** One IKE Phase II policy indicates SHA-HMAC with DH group 2, and 3DES for the cipher.

○ **D.** One IKE Phase I transform set indicates that ESP will be used with an AES 128-bit cipher and integrity uses SHA-HMAC.

○ **E.** All the traffic between 192.168.0.0/24 to 10.0.20.0/24 will be protected by the IPsec tunnel.

36. Which of the following are examples of Cisco IDS or IPS solutions? (Choose all that apply.)

○ **A.** AIP-SSM module for ASA 5500 Series security appliances

○ **B.** IOS IPS

○ **C.** HIPS

○ **D.** 4200 Series sensors

○ **E.** IPS AIM

37. Match the types of IPS alarms below with their descriptions:

IPS Alarms:

   1. False positive   __

   2. False negative   __

   3. True positive   __

   4. True negative   __

Descriptions:

   ○ **A.** Normal traffic or a non-malicious action causes the signature to fire.

   ○ **B.** An attack is properly detected by the IPS.

   ○ **C.** An attack is not detected by the IPS.

   ○ **D.** The signature doesn't fire on traffic that it's not supposed to.

38. What are the three main detection technologies that the Cisco IOS IPS employs?

   ○ **A.** Protocol analysis-based

   ○ **B.** Signature-based

   ○ **C.** Predictive algorithm protocol (PAP)-based

   ○ **D.** Stochastic interpolation statistical anomaly

   ○ **E.** Profile-based

39. True or false. Cisco recommends that the alert level of any signature should be set to the severity level of the signature, both for the included signature as well as for created signatures.

40. Which CLI command verifies all Cisco IOS IPS settings?

   ○ **A. show ip ips configuration all**

   ○ **B. show ip ips all**

   ○ **C. show ips all**

   ○ **D. show ips configuration all**

   ○ **E.** None of the above.

41. What are the three prongs of Cisco's Host Security Strategy?

   ○ **A.** Perimeter security

   ○ **B.** End-user security

   ○ **C.** Endpoint protection

   ○ **D.** Cisco Network Admission Control (NAC)

   ○ **E.** Network infection containment

42. What is Cisco's solution for preventing a buffer overflow attack?

   ○ **A.** Storm control

   ○ **B.** IOS IPS

   ○ **C.** Network Admission Control (NAC)

   ○ **D.** Cisco Security Agent (CSA)

   ○ **E.** Trend Micro attack signatures

43. Match the following interceptors that CSA employs with their definitions:

Terms:

   1. Network interceptor   __

   2. Execution space interceptor   __

   3. File system interceptor   __

   4. Configuration interceptor   __

Definitions:

   A. All file read/write requests are intercepted and permitted or denied based on the security policy.

   B. Stymies DoS attacks by limiting the number of connections that can be made in a specified period.

   C. Examines read/write requests to system configuration files.

   D. Ensures that each application is only allowed write access to memory that it owns.

44. What is the main strategy for securing access to SANs?

○ **A.** VLANs

○ **B.** VSANs

○ **C.** Zoning

○ **D.** ZPF

○ **E.** Physical security

45. Which of the following Cisco Unified Communications Manager (UCM) features can protect the VoIP network against fraud? (Choose all that apply.)

○ **A.** Partitioning

○ **B.** Dial Plans

○ **C.** Forced Authorization Codes (FACs)

○ **D.** VVLANs (Voice VLANs)

○ **E.** Anti-Vishing Agent (AVA)

46. What statement best describes a VLAN hopping attack in general terms?

○ **A.** An attacker tricks a switch into routing traffic to a different IP subnet than the subnet to which the VLAN 1 interface is assigned in the management domain.

○ **B.** An attacker tricks a switch into allowing traffic to hop to a different VLAN than the VLAN that is assigned to the port to which they are connected.

○ **C.** An attacker tricks the switch into allowing an attack to propagate to the Internet VLAN.

○ **D.** An attacker tricks the switch into dynamically assigning the attacker a VLAN ID to which they are not entitled via VTP (VLAN Trunking Protocol) and turns off trunking between all switches.

○ **E.** An attacker tricks the switch into turning off traffic to the Internet VLAN, thus creating a DoS for all users whose traffic is destined to the Internet.

47. True or false. The best way to prevent a double-tagging VLAN hopping attack is to make sure that the native VLAN of the trunked ports is different than any of the users' ports.

48. Examine the following commands and answer the subsequent question.

```
Catalyst1(config-if)#switchport mode access
Catalyst1(config-if)#switchport port-security
Catalyst1(config-if)#switchport port-security maximum 30
Catalyst1(config-if)#switchport port-security violation shutdown vlan 5
```

Which of the following statements about this series of commands is correct? (Choose all that apply.)

- ○ **A.** Port security will be performed for a maximum of 30 learned MAC addresses; thereafter, it will be disabled.

- ○ **B.** Port security will be enabled for a maximum of 30 seconds on any one MAC address.

- ○ **C.** Only the first 30 MAC addresses in VLAN 5 learned on this switch port will be able to use the port.

- ○ **D.** When the 31st MAC address in VLAN 5 tries to use this port, the switch port will be administratively disabled.

- ○ **E.** None of the above.

49. Which commands do you use to verify that port security is configured and operational on an interface? (Choose two.)

- ○ **A.** show interface port-security address

- ○ **B.** show port-security interface *interface-id* address

- ○ **C.** show port-security address

- ○ **D.** show interface

- ○ **E.** show mac-address-table interface *interface-id*

50. Which of the following interface configuration commands set the native VLAN of a trunk to 10?

- ○ **A.** switchport native vlan 10 trunkport

- ○ **B.** switchport trunk mode native vlan 10

- ○ **C.** switchport trunk native vlan 10

- ○ **D.** switchport-native trunk 10

- ○ **E.** switchport-trunk native 10

Answers to Practice Exam 2

1. A, B, and E
2. C
3. C, D, and E
4. False
5. C and D
6. A and B
7. F
8. C, B, and A
9. A
10. B
11. C
12. True
13. A, B, C, and D
14. C
15. A, B, and D
16. D
17. 3, 6, 1, 0, 7, 4, 5, 2
18. B
19. F
20. A
21. A
22. 1—A; 2—B; 3—A; 4—B; 5—C
23. True
24. Before and after
25. False
26. E
27. C
28. False
29. B, A, and A
30. A, B, C, and D
31. C and D
32. False
33. A, C, D, and E
34. B, C, and E
35. A, B, and E
36. A, B, C, D, and E
37. 1—A; 2—C; 3—B; 4—D
38. A, B, and E
39. True
40. B
41. C, D, and E
42. D
43. 1—B; 2—D; 3—A; 4—C
44. C
45. A, B, and C
46. B
47. True
48. C and D
49. B and C
50. C

Question 1

The correct answers are A, B, and E. Personal safety and physical plant security, while admirable goals, are not directly addressed when implementing network security.

Question 2

The correct answer is C. A and B are incorrect because they represent broad categories of attacks and not specific threats. Answer D is incorrect because a hacker is a type of attacker.

Question 3

Answers C, D, and E are correct. You might find these easier to remember with an acronym—PAT, as in with these in place, you can stand pat! Answer A is incorrect because user education is an example of administrative control. Answer B is incorrect because firewalls are an example of a technical control.

Question 4

False. It is precisely because hackers think outside the constraints of normal system behavior that we say they think "outside the box."

Question 5

The correct answers are C and D. Social engineering and dumpster diving are considered to be attacks against confidentiality. SYN floods, MAC flooding, and DoS attacks can interrupt the continuous services offered by a data network and are thus considered availability attacks.

Question 6

The correct answers are A and B. Answer C is incorrect because Single Loss Expectancy (SLE) is the product of AV * EF. Answer D is incorrect as it is an invented term. Answer E, Return on Investment (ROI), is not part of the quantitative risk analysis formula.

Question 7

Answer F is correct. Answers A to E all represent some of the goals of network security testing according to Cisco.

Question 8

The correct answers, and in the right order, are C, B, and A. Answers D and E are made up.

Question 9

The correct answer is A. The other stakeholders listed in answers B, C, and D, while perhaps interested in an organization's security, are not considered stakeholders because the policy is particular to the organization and not outsiders.

Question 10

The correct answer is B. This is a trick question because CSM can manage the Intrusion Detection System (IDS-2) module in the Catalyst 6500 series switch, but not the switch itself.

Question 11

The correct answer is C. Answers A and B have the right terms but not in the right order. Answer D is simply incorrect but tricky, because it uses the term DMZ in a misleading way.

Question 12

True.

Question 13

The correct answers are A, B, C, and D. Answer D is also correct because after logging into the view, only the commands specified will be authorized to be executed. You can see an example of this behavior below, where we see that a user cannot execute the **copy running-config startup-config** command because it is not in the list of authorized commands:

```
CiscoISR>enable view ISP
Password: hardtoguess
Apr 19 13:19:03.892: %PARSER-6-VIEW_SWITCH: successfully set to view 'ISP'
CiscoISR#configure terminal
Enter configuration commands, one per line. End with CNTL/Z.
CiscoISR(config)#exit
CiscoISR#ping www.ciscopress.com
Translating "www.ciscopress.com"...domain server (206.248.154.22) [OK]
Type escape sequence to abort.
```

```
Sending 5, 100-byte ICMP Echos to 209.202.161.68, timeout is 2 seconds:
!!!!!
Success rate is 100 percent (5/5), round-trip min/avg/max = 52/52/56 ms
CiscoISR#copy running-config startup-config
        ^
% Invalid input detected at '^' marker.
CiscoISR#
```

Question 14

The correct answer is C. Answer A is incorrect because the choices are in the wrong order. Answer B is incorrect, even though it is true that you use the virtual terminal lines (vtys) to access the router, plus "packet" is wrong anyway. Answer D is incorrect because the terms are deliberate red herrings for people who have studied AAA with Cisco security appliances.

Question 15

The correct answers are A, B, and D. Answers C is incorrect because it does not constitute a *main* AAA configuration task. Answer E is incorrect because AAA servers and clients authenticate using pre-shared keys and not digital certificates. (See Chapter 6, "Introducing Cryptographic Services," for an explanation of authentication with digital certificates, as well as the Public Key Infrastructure (PKI) that manages digital certificates.)

Question 16

The correct answer is D. The other answers use terminology that doesn't apply in this context.

Question 17

Errors	3
Informational	6
Alerts	1
Emergencies	0
Debugging	7
Warnings	4
Notifications	5
Critical	2

Question 18

The correct answer is B. The Cisco SDM and CLI are quite consistent; typically, you create a policy and then apply it somewhere or separately activate it. All that is accomplished in this screenshot is to activate the router's SSH server. You have to separately enable it on the vtys. That is why answers A and E are incorrect. Answers C and D are incorrect because as soon as you press the **Generate RSA Key** button, the keys are generated and applied in the running-config. You do not have to separately press the **Save** button, as this simply saves the configuration to NVRAM. Similarly, the **Refresh** button only parses the router's *running-config* in case changes have been made that are invisible to the SDM.

Question 19

The correct answer is F. The **auto secure [no-interact]** command, though roughly equivalent, has some more functionality than the Cisco SDM Security Audit feature. Use the **no-interact** option of the command to make **auto secure** work more like the One-step lockdown feature of the SDM.

Question 20

Answer A is correct. The device's hostname and domain name must be configured, as these provide material for the public/private RSA key pair (see also Chapter 6, "Introducing Cryptographic Services"), which is required for the Secure Sockets Layer (SSL) encryption that SSH uses.

Question 21

The correct answer is A. Curiously, Cisco's definition of a firewall is the vaguest of all of them. Essentially, anything that manages access by analyzing flows between two or more networks constitutes a firewall. Answer B is incorrect because it most closely resembles a definition for a stateful packet inspection (SPI) firewall and is too specific. Likewise, answer C is incorrect, as it defines a static packet filter like an IOS router with ACLs. Answer D is incorrect, again because it's too specific.

Question 22

The correct answers are 1—A; 2—B; 3—A; 4—B; 5—C. Although a static packet-filtering firewall can filter on static packet (and segment) content up to layer 4, it will never be as smart as a dynamic packet-filtering firewall. Similarly, application layer gateways and application inspection firewalls both operate at up to layer 5, but an application inspection firewall is considered more intelligent because it analyzes application layer flows for standards compliance and can look for other protocols tunneled inside the application session. Good firewalls are typically a hybrid of the preceding firewall types.

Question 23

True. If a packet is encrypted, it will first be tested on the inbound ACL to determine whether encrypted packets are allowed. If it is allowed, the packet is decrypted before it is again tested on the inbound ACL.

Question 24

The correct answers are *before* and *after*, respectively. If there is an inbound ACL on an interface that is also part of a zone, the packet is tested on the ACL first, and if permitted is then tested on the ZPF policy. Similarly, if there is an outbound ACL on an interface, the packet is first tested on the ZPF policy, and if it is permitted, it is then tested on the outbound interface ACL.

Question 25

False. If one interface is in a zone and the other one isn't, the traffic is dropped. This is an important feature of ZPF because an interface that isn't in a zone cannot inadvertently pass traffic to an interface that is in a zone. The active directory server in the figure will not be able to initiate a connection out to the Internet Zone by default.

Question 26

The correct answer is E. In modern cryptosystems, the main area of vulnerability is the storage, generation, safeguarding, and transmission of encryption keys. The encryption algorithms (ciphers) themselves are not considered vulnerable, nor are hashes.

Question 27

The correct answer is C because 3DES has been used far longer than AES and has proven itself as a trusted cipher. Answer A is incorrect because even 128-bit AES is cryptographically stronger than 168-bit 3DES. Answer B is incorrect for two reasons: first, for the same reason that answer A is incorrect; and second, because AES can be configured to use 192- and 256-bit keys. Answer D is incorrect because AES is actually less computationally intensive than 3DES.

Question 28

False. This is a trick question; although TLS is the replacement for SSL, it stands for Transport Layer Security and not Transmission Level Security.

Question 29

The answers are B, A, and A respectively. Public keys are called public keys because they can be freely transmitted without compromising the cryptosystem; only the holder of the corresponding private key can decrypt messages that have been encrypted with the public key. This is why safeguarding the private key is essential—a compromised private key compromises the trustworthiness of the whole cryptosystem.

Question 30

The correct answers are A, B, C, and D.

Question 31

Answers C and D are correct. Answer A is incorrect because it is not a category as much as it is an implementation technology for site-to-site VPNs; it is not covered in this book in any case. Answers B and E are incorrect because these terms do not describe categories of VPNs.

Question 32

False. IKE Phase I Security Associations (SAs) are created to perform all negotiation and authentication between IPsec VPN peers. IKE Phase II SAs carry data only, using transform sets negotiated during IKE Phase I that can encrypt, verify, and authenticate the data.

Question 33

The correct answers (in order) are A, C, D, and E. Answer B is incorrect because a transform set is used to group a cipher and HMAC during IKE Phase II. Answer F is incorrect because it is a made-up term.

Question 34

The correct answers are B, C, and E. Answer A is incorrect because the "5" in the configuration represents Diffie-Hellman Group 5. Answer D is incorrect because

AES stands for Advanced Encryption Standard. This is a bit of a trick question because if **aes** is chosen and not **aes 192** or **aes 256**, a 128-bit cipher is specified. (See Table 7-5.)

Question 35

Answers A, B, and E are correct. Answer C is incorrect because the specified policy is a Phase I policy (per answer B) and not a Phase II transform set (watch the terminology!). Answer D is incorrect for the same reason...this is an IKE Phase II transform set, not IKE Phase I.

Question 36

The correct answers are A, B, C, D, and E.

Question 37

The correct answers are 1—A; 2—C; 3—B; 4—D.

Question 38

The correct answers are A, B, and E. Answers C and D are not correct because they comprise made-up terminology.

Question 39

True. Cisco makes this recommendation, suggesting this is a baseline for later tuning of the signatures.

Question 40

The correct answer is B. The other commands do not exist.

Question 41

The correct answers are C, D, and E. Perimeter security, while important, is not considered part of this strategy; thus, answer A is incorrect. Answer B is incorrect because end-user security is not part of this strategy. This answer is deliberately misleading as it sounds similar to endpoint and will trip someone who hasn't studied the subject.

Question 42

The correct answer is D. Answer A is incorrect because storm control is a feature of switch security found in Chapter 10, "Protecting Switch Infrastructure." It is misleading because it both sounds familiar and sounds right in this context. Buffer overflows cannot be prevented by the IOS IPS; therefore, answer B is incorrect. Answer C is incorrect because NAC has nothing to do with buffer overflow protection. Answer E is incorrect because Trend Micro's attack signatures are used in network IPSs.

Question 43

The correct answers are 1—B; 2—D; 3—A; 4—C.

Question 44

The correct answer is C. Answer A is incorrect because employing VLANs is a strategy in LAN security. Answer B is incorrect because employing VSANs is part of zoning and thus not a main strategy. Answer D is incorrect because ZPF (Zone-Based Policy Firewall) is a network firewall security strategy described in Chapter 5, "Using Cisco IOS Firewalls to Implement a Network Security Policy." Answer E is a nice idea but incorrect in this context.

Question 45

The correct answers are A, B, and C. Answer D is incorrect because the use of VVLANs is not a feature specific to UCM. AVA does not exist; thus, answer E is also incorrect.

Question 46

Answer B is correct. Answers A, C, and E are incorrect because they are nonsensical. Answer D starts off making sense, and then quickly goes downhill as it doesn't explain the general principle of a VLAN hopping attack.

Question 47

True. This is because a double-tagging VLAN hopping attack is unidirectional and works only if the attacker and the trunk port(s) are in the same native VLAN

Question 48

The correct answers are C and D. Answers A and B are therefore incorrect in their interpretation of the commands.

Question 49

The correct answers are B and C. Answer B is a variation of the **show port-security address** command in answer C. Answer A is incorrect because the command doesn't exist. Answer D is incorrect because this command does not display the port security settings of an interface. Answer E is incorrect because it will show you only the MAC addresses learned by the switch on a port but not the port security settings.

Question 50

The correct answer is C. The other answers are incorrect because these commands do not exist.

PART VI

Appendixes

APPENDIX A

What's on the CD-ROM

The CD-ROM features an innovative practice test engine powered by MeasureUp, giving you yet another effective tool to assess your readiness for the exam.

Multiple Test Modes

MeasureUp practice tests can be used in Study, Certification, or Custom modes.

Study Mode

Tests administered in Study mode allow you to request the correct answer(s) and explanation to each question during the test. These tests are not timed. You can modify the testing environment during the test by selecting the Options button.

You can also specify the objectives or missed questions you want to include in your test, the timer length, and other test properties. You can also modify the testing environment during the test by selecting the Options button.

In Study mode, you receive automatic feedback on all correct and incorrect answers. The detailed answer explanations are a superb learning tool in their own right.

Certification Mode

Tests administered in Certification mode closely simulate the actual testing environment you will encounter when taking a licensure exam and are timed. These tests do not allow you to request the answer(s) and/or explanation to each question until after the exam.

Custom Mode

Custom mode allows you to specify your preferred testing environment. Use this mode to specify the categories you want to include in your test, the timer length, number of questions, and other test properties. You can modify the testing environment during the test by selecting the Options button.

Attention to Exam Objectives

MeasureUp practice tests are designed to appropriately balance the questions over each technical area covered by a specific exam. All concepts from the actual exam are covered thoroughly to ensure that you're prepared for the exam.

Installing the CD

System Requirements:

- ▶ Windows 95, 98, ME, NT4, 2000, Vista, or XP
- ▶ 7MB disk space for testing engine
- ▶ An average of 1MB disk space for each individual test
- ▶ Control Panel Regional Settings must be set to English (United States)
- ▶ PC only

To install the CD-ROM, follow these instructions:

1. Close all applications before beginning this installation.

2. Insert the CD into your CD-ROM drive. If the setup starts automatically, go to step 6. If the setup does not start automatically, continue with step 3.

3. From the Start menu, select Run.

4. Click Browse to locate the MeasureUp CD. In the Browse dialog box, from the Look In drop-down list, select the CD-ROM drive.

5. In the Browse dialog box, double-click `Setup.exe`. In the Run dialog box, click OK to begin the installation.

6. On the Welcome screen, click MeasureUp Practice Questions to begin installation.

7. Follow the Certification Preparation Wizard by clicking Next.

8. To agree to the Software License Agreement, click the I Agree radio button, and then click Yes.

9. On the Select Installation Folder screen, click Next to install the software to `C:\Program Files\Certification Preparation`. If you cannot locate MeasureUp Practice Tests on the Start menu, see the section titled "Creating a Shortcut to the MeasureUp Practice Tests," later in this appendix.

10. On the Confirm Installation screen, click Next to confirm the installation. The software will then install.

11. In the Select Program Folder screen, you can name the program folder where your tests will be located. To select the default, click Next and the installation continues.

12. After the installation is complete, verify that Yes, I Want to Restart My Computer Now is selected. If you select No, I Will Restart My Computer Later, you cannot use the program until you restart your computer.

13. Click Finish.

14. After restarting your computer, choose Start, Programs, Certification Preparation, Certification Preparation, MeasureUp Practice Tests.

15. On the MeasureUp Welcome Screen, click Create User Profile.

16. In the User Profile dialog box, complete the mandatory fields and click Create Profile.

17. Select the practice test you want to access and click Start Test.

Creating a Shortcut to the MeasureUp Practice Tests

To create a shortcut to the MeasureUp Practice Tests, follow these steps:

1. Right-click your desktop.

2. From the Shortcut menu, select New, Shortcut.

3. Browse to `C:\Program Files\MeasureUp Practice Tests` and select the `MeasureUpCertification.exe` or `Localware.exe` file.

4. Click OK.

5. Click Next.

6. Rename the shortcut MeasureUp.

7. Click Finish.

After you complete step 7, use the MeasureUp shortcut on your desktop to access the MeasureUp products you ordered.

Technical Support

If you encounter problems with the MeasureUp test engine on the CD-ROM, please contact MeasureUp at (800) 649-1687 or email support@measureup.com. Support hours of operation are 7:30 a.m. to 4:30 p.m. EST. In addition, you can find Frequently Asked Questions (FAQ) in the Support area at www.measureup. com. If you would like to purchase additional MeasureUp products, call (678) 356-5050 or (800) 649-1687 or visit www.measureup.com.

Need to Know More?

This appendix provides a list of references that should be useful either for CCNA Security exam preparation or for general network security knowledge.

Network Security Policies

Site Security Handbook, RFC 2196, B. Fraser, ed.

http://www.ietf.org/rfc/rfc2196.txt

RFC 2196 is the IETF's *Site Security Handbook*. Reading from the abstract:

"This handbook is a guide to developing security policies and procedures for sites that have systems on the Internet. The purpose of this handbook is to provide practical guidance to administrators trying to secure their information and services. The subjects covered include policy content and formation, a broad range of technical system and network security topics, and security incident response."

Although the handbook might be old, that doesn't mean it's dated. There is some good practical advice contained within its pages, and it makes a good read as well as a good template for an organization that has yet to develop their own comprehensive network security policy.

Introduction to Security Policies, Four-Part Series, Charl van der Walt, SecurityFocus

http://www.securityfocus.com/infocus/1193

An entertaining, somewhat irreverent but always accurate executive-level summary of the need for network security policies and selling the idea to stakeholders.

Network Security Practices

Internet Denial of Service, Attack and Defense Mechanisms,
ISBN 0-13-147573-8

This is an excellent everyman's guide to network attack and defense mechanisms, focusing on DoS attacks. It is written in plain English, is technically competent, and is a good survey of the network security industry.

Router Security Strategies, Securing IP Network Traffic Planes,
ISBN 978-1-58705-336-8

This is a technical read and not for the faint of heart. It is written by two authors who, both Cisco CCIEs, are acknowledged experts in the field of network security. The book is an in-depth survey of securing IOS routers and separating and securing the traffic planes that they service.

Hacking Exposed, 5th Edition, ISBN 978-0-07226-081-6

This book is considered by many to be the preeminent field guide for hackers, those who aspire to be hackers, and those who aspire to think like hackers. The book covers the breadth of essential hacker secrets and techniques, from explore to exploit.

Cisco Self-Defending Network

http://www.cisco.com/en/US/solutions/ns170/networking_solutions_products_
genericcontent0900aecd80511fa4.html

This is a study of Cisco's recommendations for best-of-breed technology solutions for designing a self-defending network using a systems approach. There is a downloadable PDF available at http://www.cisco.com/en/US/solutions/
collateral/ns340/ns394/ns171/net_brochure0900aecd800efd71.pdf, which explains Cisco's self-defending network philosophy.

Cisco Security Center

http://www.cisco.com/security/

Cisco's launch pad for all things network security. There are links for technical resources, Cisco-recommended and validated security designs, as well as what Cisco calls "Early-warning intelligence, threat and vulnerability analysis, and proven Cisco mitigation solutions to help protect networks."

Inside Internet Security, What Hackers Don't Want You to Know,
ISBN 0-201-67516-1

This is another good read that covers a large breadth of network security topics at a high-level, but somehow manages not to insult the reader's intelligence.

Cryptography

The Code Book: The Science of Secrecy from Ancient Egypt to Quantum Cryptography, ISBN 978-0-38549-532-5

This book is an entertaining and engaging read on a fascinating topic. It puts the subject of cryptography in both historical and present-day context, while refusing to become a boring technical tome.

Handbook of Applied Cryptography, ISBN 0-8493-8523-7

This is a technical book that is very rewarding for those who want to have an authoritative read about the mathematics that are behind popular symmetric-key, asymmetric key, and other ciphers.

FIPS 197, Advanced Encryption Standard (AES)

http://csrc.nist.gov/publications/fips/fips197/fips-197.pdf

The link is to a PDF that outlines the Rijndael encryption algorithm, which was approved by NIST (The National Institute of Standards and Technology) in November 2001.

The AES Homepage

http://csrc.nist.gov/archive/aes/index.html

This site includes a detailed explanation of the selection process and development effort for the Advanced Encryption Standard.

Understanding PKI: Concepts, Standards and Deployment Considerations, ISBN 978-0-67232-391-1

This book is a comprehensive introduction to PKI components, technology fundamentals, and ideas. It is an excellent, vendor-neutral explanation of the often-misunderstood field of scalable key management.

Index

EXAM CRAM

The Smart Way to Study™

IINS Exam **640-553**

CCNA® Security

Eric Stewart

CD Features Multiple Practice Exams

FREE Online Edition

Your purchase of **CCNA Security Exam Cram** includes access to a free online edition for 45 days through the Safari Books Online subscription service. Nearly every Exam Cram book is available online through Safari Books Online, along with over 5,000 other technical books and videos from publishers such as Addison-Wesley Professional, Cisco Press, IBM Press, O'Reilly, Prentice Hall, Que, and Sams.

SAFARI BOOKS ONLINE allows you to search for a specific answer, cut and paste code, download chapters, and stay current with emerging technologies.

Activate your FREE Online Edition at www.informit.com/safarifree

> **STEP 1:** Enter the coupon code: PAEPAAA.

> **STEP 2:** New Safari users, complete the brief registration form.
> Safari subscribers, just login.

If you have difficulty registering on Safari or accessing the online edition,
please e-mail customer-service@safaribooksonline.com

   Cisco Press   IBM Press Microsoft Press New Riders

O'REILLY   PRENTICE HALL Que SAMS SAS Publishing Sun WILEY